Language Technology Resources and Tools for Digital Humanities (LT4DH 2016)

Osaka, Japan
11 – 16 December 2016

ISBN: 978-1-5108-3320-3

Preface

Language resources are increasingly used not only in Language Technology (LT), but also in other subject fields, such as the digital humanities (DH) and in the field of education. Applying LT tools and data for such fields implies new perspectives on these resources regarding domain adaptation, interoperability, technical requirements, documentation, and usability of user interfaces. The workshop Language Technology Resources and Tools for the Digital Humanities focusses on the use of LT tools and data in DH, the discussion focussing on example applications and the type and range of research questions where LT tools can be beneficial.

LT applications are often trained and adjusted to individual text types or corpora published in specific formats. Using the tools in other contexts results in a difference in the data that is to be processed, e.g. historical data or different 'genres'. Though it may seem obvious that the quality of the results may not be as high, the results may still be valuable, for example because of the sheer size of data that can be investigated rather than by manual analysis. Hence tools and resources need to be adaptable to different text types. Applying tools for data from non-LT areas such as the humanities also increases the demands on acceptable data formats, as the data to be processed may contain additional annotations or a variety of annotations. Additionally, in some cases new data conversion needs appear and the tools need to be robust enough to handle also erroneous data, giving meaningful status messages to a non-LT user. It is often also required that tools are adapted to the text types that they are intended to be used for. For example, data mining tools trained for one type of texts need to be adapted for another type.

LT tools often need to be combined in processing chains and workflows whose exact order and configuration depends on the particular LT application. The same is true for DH workflows. However, since the DH applications often significantly differ from those in LT, new configurations of tools need to be entertained and additional requirements for the interoperability of tools may arise. This is particularly the case for interfacing annotation and querying tools as well as the incorporation of data exploration and data visualization techniques.

The technical requirements of some LT tools and the considerable learning curve for its use poses another obstacle for non-expert users in the DH. This means, inter alia, that downloads of tools and complex local installations should be avoided and tools should be made available as web-applications whenever possible. Moreover, usability studies of LT tools for DH applications may give important feedback for the adaptation of user interaction, adaptation of algorithms, and the need for additional functionality.

Organisers

- Erhard Hinrichs (University of Tübingen, Germany)
- Marie Hinrichs (University of Tübingen, Germany)
- Thorsten Trippel (University of Tübingen, Germany)

Programme Committee

- Andre Blessing (University of Stuttgart, Germany)
- Mirjam Bluemm (Universtity of Göttingen, Germany)
- António Branco (University of Lisbon, Portugal)
- Thierry Declerck (DFKI, Germany)
- Stefanie Dipper (Ruhr-University Bochum, Germany)
- Thomas Gloning (University of Gießen, Germany)
- Elena Gonzalez-Blanco (National Distance Education University, Spain)
- Hanna Hedeland (University of Hamburg, Germany)
- Erhard Hinrichs (University of Tübingen, Germany)
- Marie Hinrichs (University of Tübingen, Germany)
- Nancy Ide (Vassar College, USA)
- Wiltrud Kessler (University of Stuttgart, Germany)
- Sandra Kübler (Indiana University Bloomington, USA)
- Gunn Lyse (University of Bergen, Norway)
- Monica Monachini (Institute for Computational Linguistics «A. Zampolli», Italian National Research Council, Italy)
- Stefan Schmunk (University of Göttingen, Germany)
- Stephanie Strassel (LDC, Philadelphia, USA)
- Thorsten Trippel (University of Tübingen, Germany)
- Arjan van Hessen (University of Utrecht, Netherlands)

Table of Contents

Conference Program

Flexible and Reliable Text Analytics in the Digital Humanities -- Some Methodological Considerations

Jonas Kuhn

Institute for Natural Language Processing
University of Stuttgart
`jonas.kuhn@ims.uni-stuttgart.de`

Abstract

The availability of Language Technology Resources and Tools generates a considerable methodological potential in the Digital Humanities: aspects of research questions from the Humanities and Social Sciences can be addressed on text collections in ways that were unavailable to traditional approaches. I start this talk by sketching some sample scenarios of Digital Humanities projects which involve various Humanities and Social Science disciplines, noting that the potential for a meaningful contribution to higher-level questions is highest when the employed language technological models are carefully tailored both (a) to characteristics of the given target corpus, and (b) to relevant analytical subtasks feeding the discipline-specific research questions.

Keeping up a multidisciplinary perspective, I then point out a recurrent dilemma in Digital Humanities projects that follow the conventional set-up of collaboration: to build high-quality computational models for the data, fixed analytical targets should be specified as early as possible -- but to be able to respond to Humanities questions as they evolve over the course of analysis, the analytical machinery should be kept maximally flexible. To reach both, I argue for a novel collaborative culture that rests on a more interleaved, continuous dialogue. (Re-)Specification of analytical targets should be an ongoing process in which the Humanities Scholars and Social Scientists play a role that is as important as the Computational Scientists' role. A promising approach lies in the identification of re-occurring types of analytical subtasks, beyond linguistic standard tasks, which can form building blocks for text analysis across disciplines, and for which corpus-based characterizations (viz. annotations) can be collected, compared and revised. On such grounds, computational modeling is more directly tied to the evolving research questions, and hence the seemingly opposing needs of reliable target specifications vs. "malleable" frameworks of analysis can be reconciled. Experimental work following this approach is under way in the Center for Reflected Text Analytics (CRETA) in Stuttgart.

Proceedings of the Workshop on Language Technology Resources and Tools for Digital Humanities (LT4DH),
page 1, Osaka, Japan, December 11-17 2016.

Finding Rising and Falling Words

Erik Tjong Kim Sang
Meertens Institute Amsterdam
erik.tjong.kim.sang@meertens.knaw.nl

Abstract

We examine two different methods for finding rising words (among which neologisms) and falling words (among which archaisms) in decades of magazine texts (millions of words) and in years of tweets (billions of words): one based on correlation coefficients of relative frequencies and time, and one based on comparing initial and final word frequencies of time intervals. We find that smoothing frequency scores improves the precision scores of both methods and that the correlation coefficients perform better on magazine text but worse on tweets. Since the two ranking methods find different words they can be used in side-by-side to study the behavior of words over time.

1 Introduction

Languages are changing all the time, under the influence of contact with other languages, communication media or reasons of production effort (Trask, 1994; Campbell, 1998). One of the type of changes that can be observed is the birth of new words (neologisms). At the same time other words are falling out of favor (archaisms). We are interested in these two processes. Finding new words in a language is also useful for lexicographers that want to keep dictionaries up-to-date.

In this paper we examine two different methods for extracting words with rising and falling relative frequencies. We apply the methods to decades of Dutch magazine text and years of tweets, and evaluate the quality of the output of the two methods[1].

After this introduction, we discuss some related work in section two. In section three we describe our data and the two ranking methods. Section four presents an overview of the experiments we performed with the magazine data and their results. In section five, we conclude.

2 Related work

Discovery of new words (neologisms) is often a chance process best fueled by reading news stories. Formal definitions in literature on lexicography do not deal with the process of discovering neologisms but with the survival chances of new words, which are estimated by their frequency and the diversity of the sources in which they were found (Metcalf, 2002; Barnhart, 2007; Kershaw et al., 2016).

O'Donovan and O'Neill (2008) collect recent texts for discovering neologisms for lexicon expansion. Breen (2009) suggests to use lexical indicators to retrieve neologisms from Japanese texts, an approach earlier applied by Paryzek (2008) for English. Cook (2010) identifies different types of neologisms and different methods for identifying them. Megerdoomian and Hadjarian (2010) use information gain to retrieve neologisms related to various topics. Michel et al. (2011) was the first to report that the Google books corpus contained valuable information for lexicon builders. Lau et al. (2012) used mathematical models for finding novel topics (word sets) in social media texts (tweets). Eisenstein et al. (2012) interestingly linked neologisms found on social media to geographical locations. Chiru and Rebedea (2014) recognize neologisms and archaisms by comparing their frequency progressions with prototype

[1]Data and software related to this paper are available at http://ifarm.nl/erikt/papers/lt4dh2016.zip

Proceedings of the Workshop on Language Technology Resources and Tools for Digital Humanities (LT4DH),
pages 2–9, Osaka, Japan, December 11-17 2016.

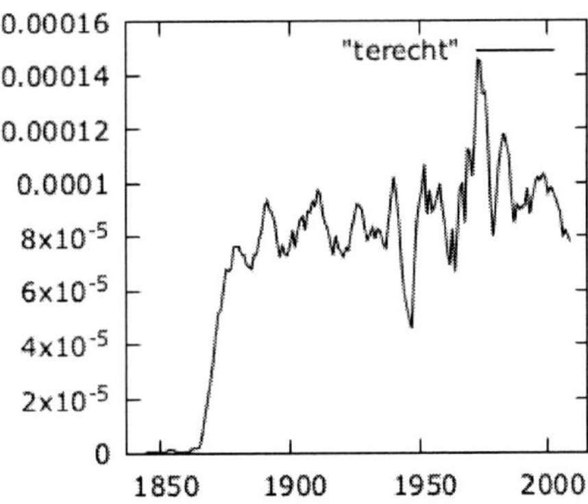

Figure 1: An example of the expected shape of the frequncy graph for new words: the modern spelling of *terecht* (right) is not used in the beginning of the nineteenth century and after a short steep rise (1866-1871) its frequency reaches a more or less stable value.

progressions. Kershaw et al. (2016) studied differences in new words from different regions of the United Kingdom with respect to frequency, form and meaning.

Recent work on language change goes one step further by not only studying vocabulary growth but also the change of word meanings over time. Kulkarni et al. (2015) use among other word co-occurrences to find shifts in word meaning. Wijaya and Yeniterzi (2011) apply cluster techniques on the Google books corpus to find the years in which the preferred meaning of ambiguous words changed.

3   Data and methods

We use two text corpora for our experiments. The first consists of the texts from the Dutch literary magazine De Gids[2], which are available from the Nederlab website[3] (Brugman et al., 2016). This a high-quality corpus spanning 173 years (1837-2009) and containing about 88 million tokens. We extracted counts for lower case versions of individual words (unigrams) for the 169 available years (editions 1945, 2003, 2004 and 2008 are unavailable). We have only used the words which occurred 100 times or more in the corpus. This data set contains 32,312 unique words.

The second text corpus consists of Dutch tweets as collected for the period January 2011-August 2016 (68 months) by the website twiqs.nl (Tjong Kim Sang and van den Bosch, 2013). This corpus contains 27 billion tokens of which the individual token counts are available per month. We only used the counts for the tokens consisting entirely of lower case characters with the additional restriction that each token needed to appear at least 10,000 times in the corpus. This data set consists of 38,230 unique tokens.

We are interested in words that become more popular or less popular in a certain time frame. In graphs showing relative word frequencies, such words can be identified by a period of a monotonically increasing or decreasing frequency. Note that the total number words per year or month can vary. Therefore we do not use absolute frequencies (like: occurs 10 times per year) but relative frequencies (like: 10 divided by the total number of words of that year).

An example of the expected frequency graph for a new word can be found in Figure 1. In 1837-1866 the preferred spelling of *terecht* (right) is different, so its frequency is close to zero. From 1866 the new spelling quickly gains popularity until 1871 when its relative frequency becomes more or less becomes stable. We define two mathematical methods for identifying such graphs.

The first method is a baseline which compares the final known relative frequency with the first known frequency. In principle we are looking for new words and obsolete words but we also want to find words

---

[2]The study on language usage in the magazine De Gids was funded by CLARIAH in the project CLARIAH-14-003 (*Use case Wie schreven er in De Gids en hoe vernieuwend is hun taalgebruik?*) led by René van Stipriaan and Nicoline van der Sijs.
[3]http://nederlab.nl

of which the frequency suddenly increased or decreased by a large margin. Therefore we do not require that the first frequency (new words) or the last frequency (obsolete words) is equal to zero. We will rank the words according the this function:

$$\delta = log_2 \frac{freq_{last} + \frac{0.5}{n}}{freq_{first} + \frac{0.5}{n}} \tag{1}$$

where $freq_{first}$ and $freq_{last}$ are the relative frequencies at the first and last time points, and n is the number of words. Since the first frequency could be equal to zero for rising words and we do not want to divide by zero, we add a small number to each relative frequency: $\frac{0.5}{n}$ (add 0.5 smoothing, a variant of add one smoothing (Jurafsky and Martin, 2000))[4]. We name this measure delta score. When the final frequency of a word is a lot higher than the first, the word is a good candidate for being a new word. When the reverse is true, the word has probably become obsolete. When we rank the words according from high to low delta score, the neologism candidates will appear on top of the list while the archaism candidates can be found at the bottom of the list.

The second method for finding new and obsolete words is based on correlation coefficients. We compute the correlation coefficients (r) of the relative frequencies of the words and time, and sort the words by this score:

$$freq_{avg} = \frac{1}{n} \sum_t freq_t \tag{2}$$

$$t_{avg} = \frac{1}{n} \sum_t t \tag{3}$$

$$freq_{sd}^2 = \frac{1}{n} \sum_t (freq_t - freq_{avg})^2 \tag{4}$$

$$t_{sd}^2 = \frac{1}{n} \sum_t (t - t_{avg})^2 \tag{5}$$

$$r = \frac{1}{n} \sum_t \frac{(freq_t - freq_{avg}) * (t - t_{avg})}{freq_{sd} * t_{sd}} \tag{6}$$

Here $freq_t$ is the relative frequency of a word at a certain time point (t) and n is the number of time points. Words with a rising graph will correspond to an r value close to plus one while words with a descending graph will be assigned an r value close to minus one. After sorting the words by r value, we expect to find new words on the top of the list, and the obsolete words at the bottom.

Delta scores and correlation coefficients are used to rank the words of the two corpora. In order to deal with noise in the data, we perform four different variants of each experiment. In the standard variant, the relative frequencies of words per years are used unchanged. In the two other variants, the frequencies in the computations are the average over five neighboring years, eleven neighboring years and twenty one neighboring years (smoothing factors 5, 11 and 21). Averaging frequencies will remove random noise from the data and could make it easier for the two methods to identify frequency trends.

The two methods will be used to select candidate neologisms and archaisms from corpus data, which be presented to expert language users for further evaluation. For this purpose, we would like to know which of the two methods is better in selecting candidate neologisms and archaisms. Evaluating the methods is difficult since the required gold standard data are scarcely available. Van der Sijs (2001) published a list of 18,540 Dutch words with their first year of appearance, of which 6,612 are from the publication period of the magazine. However, none of the words are from the period of the tweets and for archaisms we do not have any background information. Furthermore, we do not expect many of the 6,612 neologisms of the list to be found in the magazine texts since they cover a restricted topic (literature).

---

[4]Add one smoothing is not a particularly good smoothing method. In our future work we will instead use Good-Turing frequency estimation (Gale and Sampson, 1995).

| Smoothing factors | | | | | | | |
| | | | | | | | |

| | **Magazine text** | | | | **Tweets** | | |
Delta scores	1	5	11	21	1	5	11	21
Top 100	94%	88%	92%	96%	95%	96%	97%	97%
Bottom 100	92%	93%	93%	94%	97%	98%	99%	99%
Average	93%	91%	93%	95%	96%	97%	98%	98%
Correlation coefficients	1	5	11	21	1	5	11	21
Top 100	94%	94%	98%	94%	68%	81%	84%	86%
Bottom 100	93%	97%	100%	100%	90%	100%	100%	100%
Average	93%	96%	99%	97%	79%	91%	92%	93%

Table 1: Evaluation scores for the two ranking methods. The correlation coefficients perform best for magazine texts, with 99+% interesting words in the top-ranked 100 and bottom-ranked 100 for smoothing factor 11. Delta scores perform best for tweets, with a best average precision of 98% for smoothing factors 11 and 21.

Because of the lack of gold standard data, we have decided to evaluate the two methods by manually inspecting the frequency graphs of the top-ranked words and the bottom-ranked words based on the scores assigned by each method. In this evaluation procedure, we look for words with a frequency distribution over time that could be interesting for examination by linguists. Here we only consider the frequency progression and do not use external knowledge about the history of the words. We regard words as interesting when there was a significant rise (300%+) or drop (75%+) in the relative frequency and when the relevant levels were reached for ten years (magazine text) or ten months (tweets). Words which were only popular during a very short time, corresponding with a frequency spike, are not considered interesting (conform the endurance criterion of Metcalf (2002))[5].

Apart from this quantitative evaluation, we will also perform a small qualitative analysis by comparing candidate neologisms from the magazine texts with the the Chronological Dictionary (van der Sijs, 2001) and by inspecting some of the candidate neologisms and candidate archaisms from the tweets.

4   Experiments

We looked for neologisms and archaisms in 169 editions of word unigram data of the Dutch literary magazine *De Gids* (1837-2009; 4 missing editions) and in 68 months of word unigram data of Dutch tweets (January 2011-August 2016). We applied the two ranking methods described in the previous section in combination with four smoothing strategies for the word frequencies: no smoothing (smoothing factor 1) and processing data in sets of five, eleven and twenty one adjacent years (smoothing factors 5, 11 and 21). For each ranking variant, we evaluated the results by inspecting the graphs associated with the top-ranked 100 words and those corresponding with the bottom-ranked 100 words. The evaluation results can be found in Table 1.

For magazine texts, correlation coefficients outperformed delta scores, with a best average precision score of 99% for smoothing factor 11. For tweets, delta scores proved to be better than correlation scores, reaching 98% average precision for smoothing factors 11 and 21. We compared the two top 100 and bottom 100 magazine word lists suggested by the methods and found an overlap of only 24%. Since the two methods suggest different words, they can be used in parallel.

During the evaluation of the top and bottom lists of the ranking methods, we encountered the expected step function as shown in Figure 1. For all of the words with such a graph, the frequency progression was caused by a spelling reform. Figure 2 contains an example of this: the spelling of the word *zoo* (so, Figure 2A) was changed to *zo* (Figure 2B) in the spelling reform of 1947 (Neijt, 1991).

We expected that new words would need a few years to be accepted in the Dutch language and from then would have a stable frequency. However, to our surprise we found several examples of words in the

---

[5]It is possible to convert the evaluation method to a ranking method but that ranking method would not be perfect either: it would classify words with a periodic frequency, like *Olympics*, as neologisms and as archaisms.

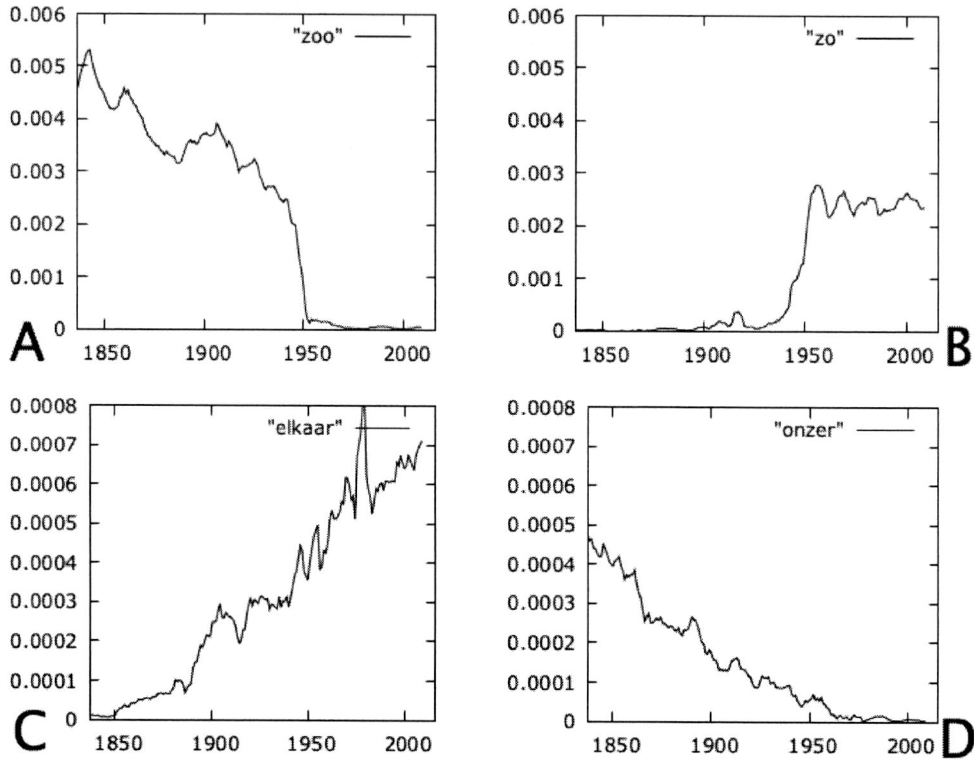

Figure 2: Examples of frequency graphs of neologisms and archaisms found in the magazine texts. A: the word *zoo* (so) was a common word in the magazine until its spelling was changed in 1947. B: the new spelling of the word: *zo*, frequent in the magazine texts since 1947. C: we found several words in the magazine texts of which the relative frequency had been rising for more than a hundred years: this is the graph for the word *elkaar* (each other). D: we also found words for which the relative frequency had been decreasing for more than a hundred years, this is the graph for *onzer* (ours). Graphs have been drawn using data with smoothing factor 5.

magazine texts of which the frequency was rising for more than a century while for others the frequency decreased for over a hundred years before reaching zero. Two examples can be found in Figure 2: the neologism *elkaar* (each other, Figure 2C) and the archaism *onzer* (ours, Figure 2D).

We did not expect to find perpetually rising and falling words but these are exactly the frequency progressions that the correlation coefficients prefer. This means that the words which rise and fall within smaller time frames, have a smaller chance of appearing in the top and in the bottom of the ranking lists. In order to find these words, we modified the correlation coefficient method to check only a limited window of adjacent years. We checked three different window sizes: 10 years, 20 years and 30 years. Since the rise or fall of a word could start in any year, we checked all possible overlapping windows for each word (sliding window approach) and kept the highest and lowest window correlation score for comparison with other words.

We manually checked the frequency graphs of the top 100 magazine words and the bottom 100 magazine words according to highest and lowest correlation coefficients obtained with smoothing factor 11. Table 2 contains an overview of the evaluation scores. We found that a window size of 10 years enabled the best average precision score (79%). This score was lower than the associated score for the complete time frame (99%). Apparently, finding words that quickly change frequency is more difficult than finding words of which the frequency slowly changes, or the words of the first category are more rare. The top

	Window size (yrs)		
Correlation coefficients	**10**	**20**	**30**
Top 100	75%	77%	73%
Bottom 100	83%	78%	73%
Average	79%	78%	73%

Table 2: Evaluation scores for the top 100 and bottom 100 words after ranking magazine words with correlation coefficients computed for sliding windows of 10, 20 and 30 years. The best performances were reached with a window size of 10 years.

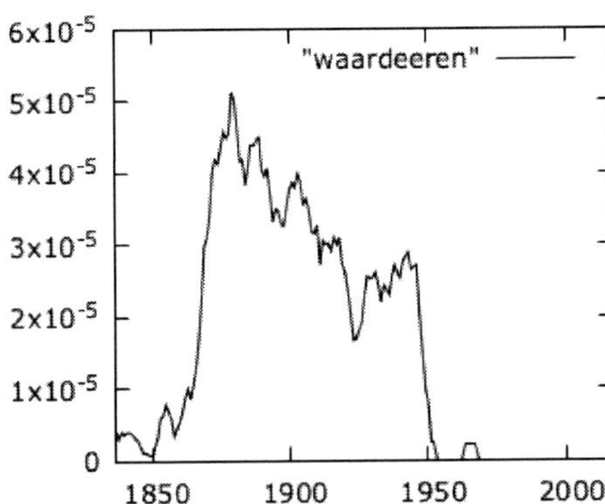

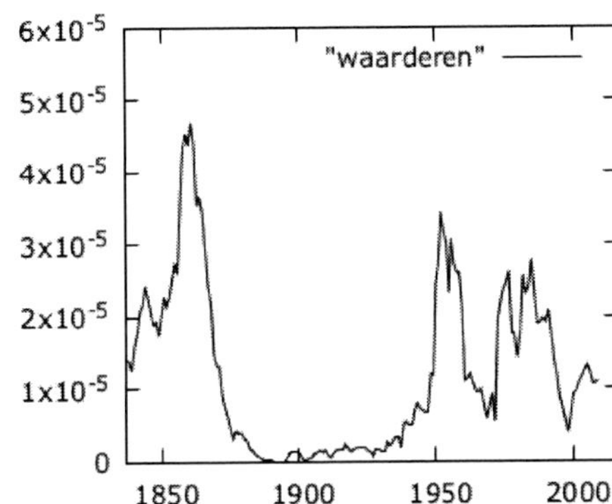

Figure 3: The sliding window approach found words which both rose and fell within the publication period of the magazine corpus: the use of *waarderen* (appreciate, right graph) was replaced by using *waardeeren* (left graph) after the spelling reform of 1863. This decision was turned around in the spelling reform of 1947.

100 lists of the two methods proved to be complementary: they had only four words in common. This means the window approach can be used in combination with the non-window approach to achieve a larger coverage.

With the window approach, we found two more interesting groups of words. First, it found words that rose in popularity and then fell within the publication lifetime of the magazine, like *waardeeren* (appreciate), which gained popularity around 1870 but disappeared after 1950 (see the left graph in Figure 3). Next, we found words that fell and came back after a few decades. An example of such a word is *waarderen* (appreciate, see Figure 3). It replaced the variant with three e's after the spelling reform of 1947 (Neijt, 1991). Its disappearance around 1870 was most likely caused by the spelling reform which was started in 1863.

In 2001, Nicoline van der Sijs published a list of 18,540 words together with the first year that each of the words were observed in the Dutch language (van der Sijs, 2001). The time span of the word list is about 1500 years. We compared the top 100 magazine words suggested by the delta scores with smoothing factor 21 with this list. Only two of the suggested neologisms appeared in the list (*poëzie* and *zowel*) but 25 more neologisms were inflections of words in the list. According the the years mentioned in the list, only three of the 27 words emerged during the life time of our magazine corpus. The word *culturele* was detected in the magazine nine years after its development in 1927. Interestingly enough *publiceerde* and *publiceert* appeared in the magazine corpus five decades before the year mentioned in the list for their root form (*publiceren*, 1902). Although the precision of the delta scores in his comparison is low, these examples show that they can provide useful information for lexicographers.

A large part of the top 100 list of magazine neologisms consisted of words which were missing in the Chronological Dictionary (van der Sijs, 2001). We cleaned this part of the list (removing proper names

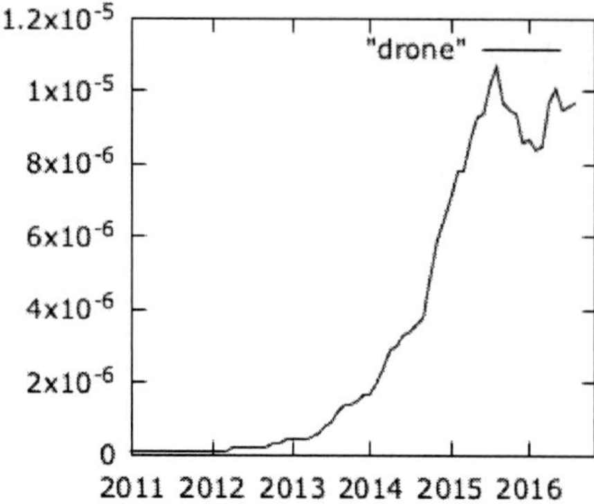

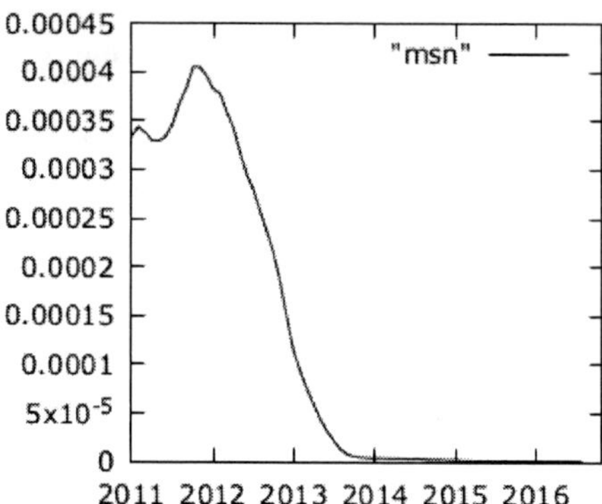

Figure 4: Examples of candidate neologisms and archaisms found in in tweets. *drone* (unmanned aircraft) was infrequently used in Dutch tweets but has gained popularity since 2012. Messenger program *MSN* was first renamed and then discontinued in 2012/2013.

and duplicate inflected forms) and presented 45 of the words to the author of the dictionary. We learned that the Chronological Dictionary was incomplete and that certain words like compounds had been left out on purpose. Many of the unseen words in the top 100 list turned out to be compounds, like for example *aflopen* (*to end*), *hoogleraar* (*professor*) and *vrijwel* (*almost*).

Inspection of top 100 tweet words suggested by the delta scores with smoothing factor 11 and window size 10, produced several interesting neologisms: *drone* (Figure 4, left), *emoji, jihadist, koningsdag* (King's Day), *matchfixing, onesie* (jumpsuit), *selfie, smartwatch* and *yolo*. Nearly all of these are loanwords from English. The list also included some names of new companies that could be of interest for lexicographers: *instagram, netflix, periscope snapchat, tinder, vine* and *wattpad*. Brand names could also be found at the bottom of the list: the obsolete *hyves* (Dutch social network), *msn* (Figure 4, right) and *xbox*. The time span of the tweet corpus is too small to find archaisms. Most words in the bottom 100 were slang words which went out of fashion after teenagers left Dutch Twitter in the summer of 2013.

5   Concluding remarks

We have presented two different methods for finding rising and falling words in texts with time stamps: one based on comparing the initial and the final relative frequencies (named: delta scores), and one based on correlation coefficients of relative frequencies and time. We have applied the two techniques to 173 years of Dutch magazine text and 68 months of Dutch tweets. Both methods performed well, returning 90+% interesting words in the top-ranked and bottom-ranked 100. Smoothing the frequency scores improved the precision scores of the two methods with a few percent.

We also tested a variant of the correlation coefficients which assigned word scores based on data of sliding time windows. Here the best performance was reached with a window size of 10 years. We found that the highest and lowest ranked words of this window approach had only a small overlap with the highest and lowest ranked words of the non-window approach. This means that the methods can be used together for generating rising and falling words from time-stamped text corpora.

We have more appropriate historic text material that we would like to apply these techniques to. A challenge is that most of these digital texts have been produced by optical character recognition which means that they contain many misspelled words. Future work will reveal how well the ranking methods can deal with this type of data noise.

References

David K. Barnhart. 2007. A Calculus for New Words. *Dictionaries: Journal of the Dictionary Society of North America*, 28:132–138.

James Breen. 2009. Identification of Neologisms in Japanese by Corpus Analysis. In *Proceedings of eLexicography in the 21st century*. Université catholique de Louvin.

Hennie Brugman, Martin Reynaert, Nicoline van der Sijs, René van Stipriaan, Erik Tjong Kim Sang, and Antal van den Bosch. 2016. Nederlab: Towards a Single Portal and Research Environment for Diachronic Dutch Text Corpora. In *Proceedings of LREC 2016*. ELRA, Portoroz, Slovenia.

Lyle Campbell. 1998. *Historical Linguistics: An Introduction*. Edinburgh University Press, United Kingdom.

Costin-Gabriel Chiru and Traian Eugen Rebedea. 2014. Archaisms and neologisms identification in texts. In *2014 RoEduNet Conference 13th Edition: Networking in Education and Research Joint Event RENAM 8th Conference*. IEEE.

C. Paul Cook. 2010. *Exploiting Linguistic Knowledge to Infer Properties of Neologisms*. PhD thesis, University of Toronto, Canada.

Jacob Eisenstein, Brendan O'Connor, Noah A. Smith, and Eric P. Xing. 2012. Mapping the geographical diffusion of new words. In *Proceedings of the NIPS Workshop on Social Network and Social Media Analysis: Methods, Models and Applications*. Lake Tahoe, Nevada.

William A. Gale and Geoffrey Sampson. 1995. Good-Turing frequency estimation without tears. *Journal of Quantitative Linguistics*, 3:217–237.

Daniel Jurafsky and James H. Martin. 2000. *Speech and Natural Language Processing*. Prentice Hall.

Daniel Kershaw, Matthew Rowe, and Patrick Stacey. 2016. Towards Modelling Language Innovation Acceptance in Online Social Networks. In *Proceedings of the Ninth ACM International Conference on Web Search and Data Mining (WSDM '16)*. ACM, San Francisco, CA, USA.

Vivek Kulkarni, Rami Al-Rfou, Bryan Perozzi, and Steven Skiena. 2015. Statistically Significant Detection of Linguistic Change. In *Proceedings of the 24th World Wide Web Conference*, pages 625–635. ACM, Florence, Italy.

JeyHan Lau, Nigel Collier, and Timothy Baldwin. 2012. On-line Trend Analysis with Topic Models: #twitter trends detection topic model online. In *Proceedings of Coling 2012*, pages 1519–1534. Mumbai, India.

Karine Megerdoomian and Ali Hadjarian. 2010. Mining and Classification of Neologisms in Persian Blogs. In *Proceedings of the NAACL HLT 2010 Second Workshop on Computational Approaches to Linguistic Creativity*. ACL, Los Angeles, CA.

Allan Metcalf. 2002. *Predicting New Words: The Secrets of Their Success*. Houghton Mifflin Company, Boston, USA.

Jean-Baptiste Michel, Yuan Kui Shen, Aviva Presser Aiden, Adrian Veres, Matthew K. Gray, The Google Books Team, Joseph P. Pickett, Dale Hoiberg, Dan Clancy, Peter Norvig, Jon Orwant, Steven Pinker, Martin A. Nowak, and Erez Lieberman Aiden. 2011. Quantitative analysis of culture using millions of digitized books. *Science*, 331:176–182.

Anneke Neijt. 1991. *Universele fonologie*. Floris Publications, Dordrecht. (In Dutch).

Rutch O'Donovan and Mary O'Neill. 2008. A Systematic Approach to the Selection of Neologisms for Inclusion in a Large Monlingual Dictionary. In *Proceedings of the XIII euralex International Congress*, pages 571–579. Institut Universitari de Lingüìstica Aplicada, Barcelona, Spain.

Piotr Paryzek. 2008. Comparison of selected methods for the retrieval of neologisms. In *Investigationes Linguisticae*, volume XVI. Poznan.

Erik Tjong Kim Sang and Antal van den Bosch. 2013. Dealing with Big Data: the Case of Twitter. *Computational Linguistics in the Netherlands Journal*, 3:121–134. ISSN: 2211-4009.

R.L. Trask. 1994. *Language Change*. Routledge, Oxon, United Kingdom.

Nicoline van der Sijs. 2001. *Chronologisch woordenboek: De ouderdom en herkomst van onze woorden en betekenissen*. Veen, Amsterdam/Antwerpen.

Derry Tanti Wijaya and Reyyan Yeniterzi. 2011. Understanding Semantic Change of Words Over Centuries. In *Proceedings of the International Workshop on DETecting and Exploiting Cultural diversity on the social web*, pages 35–40. ACM, Glasgow, Schotland.

A Dataset for Multimodal Question Answering in the Cultural Heritage Domain

Shurong Sheng
Department of Computer Science
KU Leuven
Shurong.Sheng@cs.kuleuven.be

Luc Van Gool
Department of Electrical Engineering
KU Leuven
luc.vangool@kuleuven.be

Marie-Francine Moens
Department of Computer Science
KU Leuven
Sien.Moens@cs.kuleuven.be

Abstract

Multimodal question answering in the cultural heritage domain allows visitors to museums, landmarks or other sites to ask questions in a more natural way. This in turn provides better user experiences. In this paper, we propose the construction of a golden standard dataset dedicated to aiding research into multimodal question answering in the cultural heritage domain. The dataset, soon to be released to the public, contains multimodal content about the fascinating old-Egyptian Amarna period, including images of typical artworks, documents about these artworks (containing images) and over 800 multimodal queries integrating visual and textual questions. The multimodal questions and related documents are all in English. The multimodal questions are linked to relevant paragraphs in the related documents that contain the answer to the multimodal query.

1 Introduction

Multimodal Question Answering (MQA) invokes answering a query that is formed using different modalities. This topic combines Computer Vision (CV), Natural Language Processing (NLP) and possibly Speech Recognition (SR). With the increasing use of mobile devices, taking pictures becomes an easy and natural way for people to interact with cultural objects. Therefore, we consider a question composed of a textual query combined with a picture of a cultural object or part thereof, where the picture and the natural language question can provide complementary information. Interest in MQA dramatically increased in recent years (Antol et al., 2015; Malinowski et al., 2015; Zhu et al., 2016).

Malinowski et al. (2015) show techniques for the joint processing of images and natural language sentences, Zhu et al. (2016) introduce object-level visual question answering research, which has some similarity with the visual question answering that we propose in this paper. Yet, no studies exist that regard MQA in the cultural heritage domain, with the objective of improving the user experience. Moreover, state-of-the-art research in the area of cultural heritage is uni-modal and either only demonstrates the recognition of images of a cultural object (Bay et al., 2005; Bay et al., 2006), or is only concerned with the processing of a vocal input (Santangelo et al., 2006; Ardito et al., 2009).

This paper reports on a new dataset constructed to facilitate MQA in the cultural domain. The dataset includes images of 16 fascinating artworks from the old-Egyptian Amarna period, documents with regard to this period, and 805 multimodal questions composed of both the full image and part-of-image level queries with regard to the artworks. A part-of-image level query is a question posed in natural language that regards part of the image of a cultural heritage object. In our dataset, the multimodal questions correspond to linked paragraphs in documents that are part of a larger document collection. Part-of-image level queries ask for more detailed information about an image than the identity of the object it shows. Their resolution requires the joint processing of the images and the natural language questions. All images and their related documents are collected from external web sources and the multimodal questions are collected from people of different ages and backgrounds, via a survey. The dataset is stored as a database using the unrelational database management system MongoDB.

Proceedings of the Workshop on Language Technology Resources and Tools for Digital Humanities (LT4DH),
pages 10–17, Osaka, Japan, December 11-17 2016.

The remainder of the paper is organized as follows: Section 2 discusses some advantages of using multimodal queries during cultural heritage visits. Section 3 describes how we have built the golden standard dataset and offers some analysis. Section 4 discusses a particular application of the dataset, Section 5 provides concluding remarks.

2   Why Multimodal Question Answering ?

MQA constitutes an innovative way of learning about cultural artefacts and offers a novel user experience as it provides a more natural way of interacting. Currently, cultural heritage information offered to the public is often still:
1) One way communication of predefined content;
2) A one-suits-all supply of information, not at all personalized;
3) Linear in that people are supposed to follow a pre-specified tour, with a fixed sequence in which predefined information is provided, or random, but therefore lacking of context and coherence;
4) Offered through dedicated hardware (e.g., as guided tours with audio devices), not belonging to the user and not providing a lasting souvenir of the visit.

MQA research in the cultural heritage domain intends to change this state of affairs:
1) The querying becomes personal, with users actively exploring parts and aspects of artworks or landmarks.
2) Consequently, the provided answers are personalized.
3) The visit does not have to follow a predefined tour. Instead, the user can influence the sequence through questions and queries, the answers to which may have to be found distributed in a variety of unstructured sources such as full texts and images described by text. Moreover, such system could be made to learn from earlier, multimodal interactions.
4) People can use their own mobile phones, tablets and other personal devices.
5) The MQA will have to bridge the fields of question processing, document content extraction and linking, and information search.

A visitor's multimodal query combined with her context helps turn general information about cultural heritage into a personalized guided tour. Such a framework is still rarely incorporated. A museum or landmark tour can be dynamically altered based on personal multimodal queries and artwork variance, resulting in an adaptive guidance system.

3   Dataset

In the context described so far, personalized and important questions of visitors are supposed to be expressed as a multimodal query. Such query is composed of a photo taken by the visitor of an artwork or of a detail of it, augmented by a question expressed in natural language, as Figure 1 shows.

3.1   Data Collection

The MQA dataset that is constructed consists of the following parts:
1) A selection of artworks of the old-Egyptian Amarna period;
2) A set of multimodal queries built by users, each composed of a natural language question and the photo of the cultural object or of part of it;
3) Textual documentation on the Amarna period;
4) The set of relevant paragraphs extracted from the documentation that answer a multimodal query.

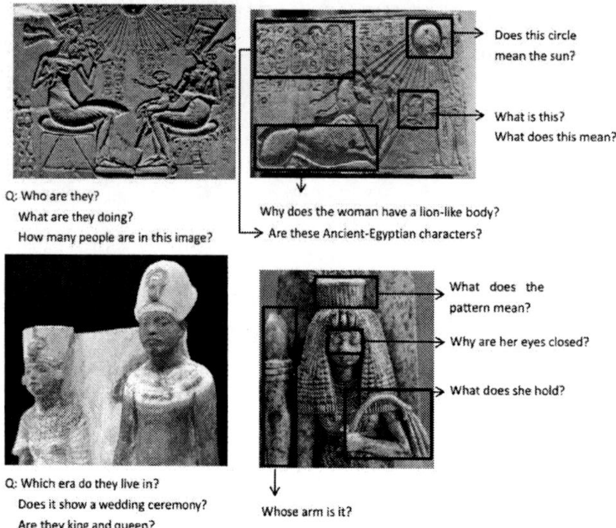

Figure 1. The images in the left column are two examples of full images with corresponding textual questions, and in the right column are two examples of visual queries specified by bounding boxes with corresponding textual questions.

We imagine a museum room where a set of artefacts have been collected for an exhibition. In our case the artefacts regard statutes, relief sculptures and paintings involving famous characters such as queen Nefertiti and pharaoh Akhenaten.

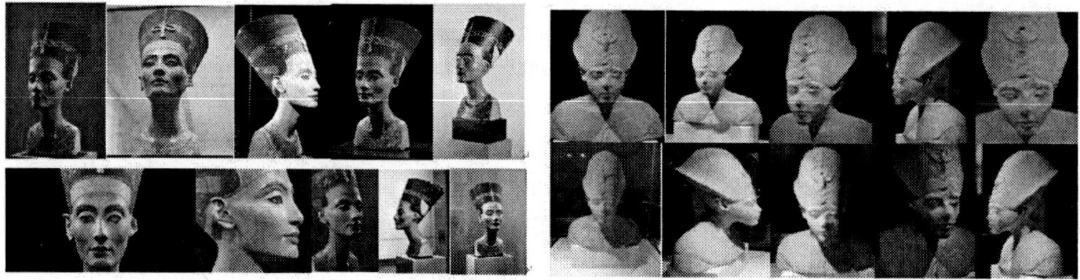

Figure 2. Example artwork images in our dataset, each shown from multiple viewpoints.

Images of Typical Artworks: The picture sets of the objects and their related documents were mainly collected from web sources such as Wikipedia, online collections of some museums, and Google Arts&Culture. Photos for 16 objects from the Amarna period were collected, with for each object up to 10 photos taken from different viewpoints. Example images are shown in Figure 2.

Multimodal Questions: To collect multimodal questions about the selected artworks, we have made a survey. This involved a document that contains photos of 16 artworks and a guideline document that were sent to all members of the department and all e-mail correspondents of the first author. The users were asked to give two kinds of questions for each artwork. The first was a textual question going with the full image and the second was a textual question along with a subpart of the image, marked by the user with a bounding box. Examples are shown in Figure 1. The guideline document explained the on-site scene of these artworks, the role of the users or respondents, and how they should draw a bounding box in the image. Also, the respondents were instructed to pose relevant and diverse questions about the artworks, with the help of some example questions. We finally received 42 responses from respondents with ages ranging from 20 to 60 and with varied backgrounds, and 1142 questions in total with regard to the artworks.

Documents on the Amarna period: We have downloaded multiple websites (we call this 'document collection on the Amarna period' further in this paper) relevant to the Amarna period from the highest ranked web pages by entering the keywords 'Amarna period','Nefertiti','Akhenaten','Tiye','Amarna style', respectively, using the Google search engine, and online collections of some museums and institutes including the Brooklyn Museum[1], Museum of Fine Arts, Boston[2], Egyptian Museum Berlin[3], Europeana[4] and Google Arts&Culture[5] with regard to the Amarna period. There are 204 documents in this collection. We have manually identified those documents that are related to the collected multimodal queries and have identified the paragraphs therein that are relevant to answer the queries.

3.2 Data Processing

The data collected from the Web and obtained from the users was noisy. Hence, several methods have been implemented for data cleaning.

Multimodal Questions: Different users may ask the same questions with regard to an artwork, so we first filtered the data by removing duplicate questions.

We wanted the questions to be of good quality, i.e. exhibiting a strong link between the images and the textual parts. For example, 'Who is the person in the picture?' is a good question, whereas 'Does not everyone like travelling?' clearly is not. To assure this we asked three annotators to check on the questions validity. We keep a question in our dataset when at least two annotators have labeled the query as 'valid', thus considering the textual question as relevant to the corresponding image.

These two steps reduced the number of queries from 1142 to 805. We noticed that quite a few questions were repeated by different users. So we assume that we have collected questions that are representative of what users would typically ask when interacting with the collected artworks in the simulated museum exhibition.

No.	Links	Number of related pictures
1	http://www.egyptian-museum-berlin.com/c53.php	5
2	https://en.wikipedia.org/wiki/Amarna_period	17
3	https://en.wikipedia.org/wiki/Amarna_art	20
4	http://www.heptune.com/art.html	15
5	http://www.touregypt.net/featurestories/amarnaperiod.htm	7
6	https://en.wikipedia.org/wiki/Nefertiti	19
7	http://www.crystalinks.com/nefertiti.html	9
8	http://www.ancient.eu/Nefertiti/	3
9	https://en.wikipedia.org/wiki/Tiye	4
10	http://quatr.us/egypt/art/amarna.htm	4

Table 1. List of example sources that form the related documents for the artworks.

Document Labeling: From the query collecting phase, we then get to the document collection. The documents in the collection are annotated as relevant to the collected artworks or not. As it is quite obvious whether a document is related to the collected artworks, a single annotator was asked to label them. With 204 documents about the Amarna period in the dataset, 101 documents (coined the 'related document collection') were labeled as related to at least one of the collected artworks. The remaining 103 unrelated documents were kept in the dataset and they will still be searched by the MQA system.

Question and Paragraph Linking: For our domain-specific question answering system, some of the questions are rather open-ended and the answers may be quite long. For example the answer to the question 'Why is the man's body so strange?' refers to the analysis of Akhenaten's body by several

---

[1] https://www.brooklynmuseum.org/opencollection/collections

[2] http://www.mfa.org/collections

[3] http://www.egyptian-museum-berlin.com/

[4] http://www.europeana.eu/portal/en

[5] https://www.google.com/culturalinstitute/beta/

experts and contains more than one paragraph from the same document. Therefore, within the related document collection, three annotators were asked to link paragraphs that are relevant for each question, with one of them acting as a judge if there is inconsistency between the other two annotators. Some of these paragraphs are part of the full text of a related document and some are obtained from the captions of pictures in the document (the latter are listed as related pictures in Table 1). Documents are uniquely defined by their URL and paragraphs (including image captions and titles) by their start and end word position in the HTML-document. The number of related paragraphs obtained from the related document collection ranges from 0 to 6 and a histogram of the number of related paragraphs forming an answer is shown in Figure 3(a). An example of a linked question with its sole related paragraph is given in Figure 3(b). In the task that we propose we have now only identified relevant paragraphs in which the answer to the multimodal question can be found and we have not yet identified relevant sentences or phrases that provide the answer. So far, the focus is on the difficult task of interpreting multimodal questions and not (yet) on extracting the answer from the document collection in its condensed form.

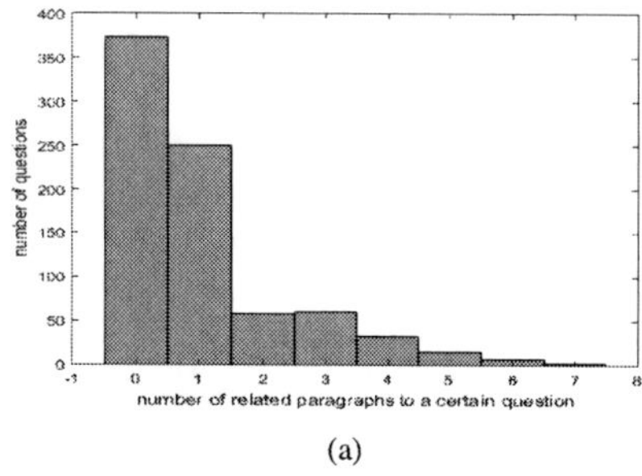

Image id	00801
Textual question	who is the person?
Related paragraph	Unfinished head of a statue of Queen Nefertiti.
Related document	https://www.flickr.com/photos/menesje/8507350000

(a)   (b)

Figure 3. (a) Histogram with the number of related paragraphs for each multimodal query; (b) Example of a textual question and related paragraph.

We show the whole processing procedure in Figure 4.

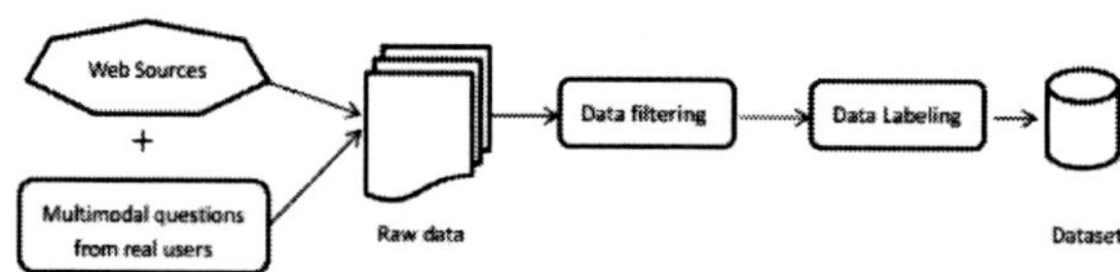

Figure 4. The diagram of the data processing procedure.

3.3   Dataset Analysis

Number of artworks	Number of questions	Number of documents	Document collection size	Number of related docs	Number of related paragraphs
16	805	204	261127	101	139

Table 2. Statistics of the dataset.

Table 2 shows some statistics for the dataset. 'Related paragraphs' denote the number of paragraphs linked to the multimodal questions, and the 'document collection size' describes the size of the document collection by the number of English words it contains. 55% of the questions in the dataset can be answered purely by the related document collection in the dataset. On the other hand, several questions such as 'How many colors does the image contain?' can be answered separately by low-level image analysis. Additionally, questions about cultural heritage objects are sometimes difficult to answer due to the lack of historical knowledge. Also, a lot of questions such as 'Why is the woman so ugly?' 'Do they really love each other?' are difficult to answer even for a human. We still keep these questions in our dataset as these questions are examples of what humans would ask.

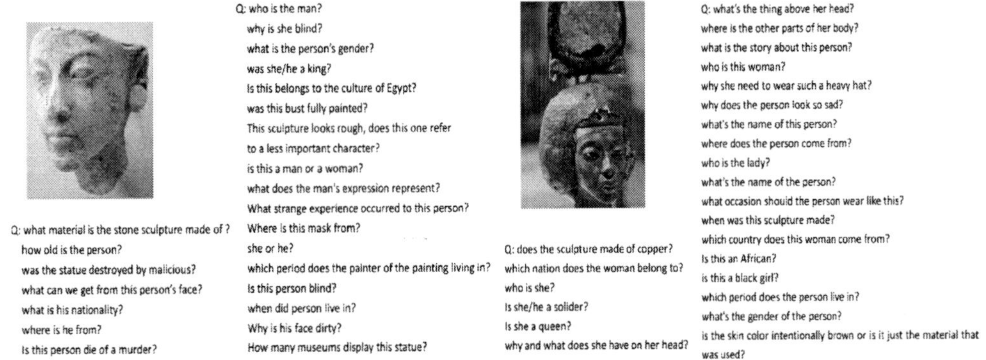

Figure 5. Sample textual questions with their corresponding images.

Some example questions are shown in Figure 5. The questions in this dataset are diverse and can be used for various artificial intelligence tasks, especially for natural language processing. They contain simple image understanding questions with regard to the object class (e.g., 'Is this a woman or man?') and the attributes of the objects (e.g., 'What material is the sculpture made of?'). Some questions are complex and need deep and common sense reasoning. For example, to answer the question 'Why do they give each other a hand?', we should know that this question is about the two persons who wear a similar crown in the image. Based on our common sense, the two persons wearing a similar crown and giving each other a hand should be a couple or more specifically king and queen, and a couple in this ancient culture like to give each other a hand to show their feelings and relationship.

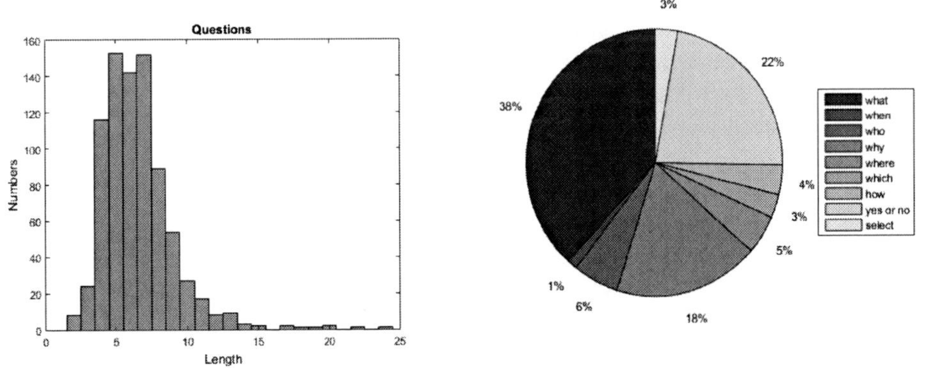

(a) Histogram of the length of the questions in words.   (b) Type distribution of the multimodal questions in the dataset.

Figure 6. Statistics related to the collected multimodal questions.

We categorize the questions based on the method of (Gao et al., 2015) into 9 types, the statistics of which are shown in Figure 6(b):
1) What: questions about the attributes and features of the object.
2) When: questions related to time with regard to the subject.
3) Who : questions about the identity of a person.
4) Why: questions about the reason of some phenomenon.
5) Where: questions about the location of the object.
6) Which: questions that need reasoning about the object.

7) How: questions about the methods related to the object.

8) Yes or No: questions that you can answer with Yes or No.

9) Select: Selective questions.

The questions' length in the dataset ranges from 2 to 24 English words and the average length of the questions is 6.56 words. A histogram of the questions' length in the dataset is shown in Figure 6(a).

Compared to other application areas of MQA such as in-door scenes and wild-life animals, MQA tasks in the cultural heritage domain are more difficult. Due to uniqueness of the artworks and historical reasons, it is hard to obtain a large amount of data for each artwork and thus few training data. As no MQA dataset in the cultural heritage domain has been released so far, our dataset, which will be made public soon, can be regarded as the first benchmark for MQA research in that field.

4 Dataset Application

This dataset is explicitly constructed for facilitating MQA. In this case, the answer estimation problem can be formulated as the probability of an answer a conditioned on a multimodal question q composed of an image q_i and its corresponding textual question q_t , as shown in the formula below.

$$P(a|q) = P(a|q_i, q_t, \theta)$$

In this formula, θ denotes a vector of all parameters to learn. q_i and q_t can be represented as real valued vectors: $q_i = [w_{1i}, w_{2i}, ...w_{pi}]$, $q_t = [w_{1t}, w_{2t}, ...w_{nt}]$ or other forms that the computers can directly use, q is a joint representation of q_i and q_t. With this formula, answers with the highest k probabilities will be retrieved as a ranked answer set A. Note that A can be an empty list if all probabilities are zero or are considered too low to yield a valuable answer.

Compared to other popular multimodal datasets composed of visual and language data (e.g., DAQUAR (Malinowski and Fritz, 2014), VQA Antol et al. (2015)), which provide only question-answer pairs that can be easily collected by online crowdsourcing platforms such as Amazon Mechanical Turk (AMT)[6], the dataset described in this paper, which contains a large set of documents and diverse multimodal questions, can give better perspectives for MQA research:

1) Natural language processing of the questions and textual documentation

   Query formation involves keywords selection from raw textual questions. To detect answer types in the dataset, named entity recognition and more specifically the recognition of person and location names and other types of entity information in the question and textual documents can be implemented. Also, the natural language questions and documents can be used to research coreference resolution.

2) Information retrieval models for searching documents and ranking paragraphs

   The dataset can also be used to study suitable information retrieval and answer ranking models for MQA, or to adapt existing retrieval models such as vector space and language models that allow to make inferences over textual and visual data.

3) Cross-modal semantic representation

   The multimodal questions in our dataset can be used to find suitable joint semantic representations of the multimodal data provided by the photo of the object or its part and the textual content of the question, cross-modal distributional semantics integrating text based representation of meaning with information coming from vision and from cross-modal coreference resolution.

4) Cross-modal coreference resolution

   The multimodal queries and documents can be used to research cross-modal coreference resolution by linking mentions of entities in the language and the visual data.

5) Additional image processing

   Several questions in our dataset can be used for variant image analysis tasks including image recognition (e.g., 'What does she hold in her hand?') and object detection (e.g., 'How many persons are in this picture?') and activity recognition (e.g., 'Is the man dancing?').

---

[6]https://www.mturk.com/mturk/welcome

5 Conclusion and Future Work

This paper describes the dataset manually built for multimodal question answering on a cultural heritage collection. The dataset concerns images of artworks from the ancient Egyptian Amarna period, a document collection relevant to the Amarna period and 805 multimodal questions composed of both natural language questions and images. The data is collected from web sources and processed in several steps including data cleaning, document labeling and question-paragraph linking. By analyzing and classifying the questions, we have proved that the multimodal questions in this paper are very diverse and this dataset can be used for research on many natural language processing tasks such as named entity recognition and coreference resolution, better information retrieval models, cross-modal semantic gap reduction and additional image processing tasks.

In the next stage of our research, we will design and develop real-time processing methods for analyzing the natural language questions and their corresponding pictures. We will also develop methods to instantly retrieve a relevant answer to a question. In the future we might expand the dataset with annotations of fine-grained answers in the form of text phrases or image segments that answer the multimodal queries, if they prove to be useful in our MQA research.

Acknowledgements

The authors would like to thank the respondents of the questionnaire for this dataset. This work is funded by the KU Leuven BOF/IF/RUN/2015, and is a part of the project "Mobile Augmented Reality and Vocal Explanations for Landmarks and visual arts (MARVEL)".

References

Stanislaw Antol, Aishwarya Agrawal, Jiasen Lu, Margaret Mitchell, Dhruv Batra, C. Lawrence Zitnick, and Devi Parikh. 2015. VQA: Visual question answering. In *Proceedings of International Conference on Computer Vision (ICCV)*.

Carmelo Ardito, Paolo Buono, Maria Francesca Costabile, Rosa Lanzilotti, and Antonio Piccinno. 2009. Enabling interactive exploration of cultural heritage: An experience of designing systems for mobile devices. *Knowledge, Technology & Policy*, 22(1):79–86.

Herbert Bay, Beat Fasel, and Luc Van Gool. 2005. Interactive museum guide: Accurate retrieval of object descriptions. In *Proceedings of the Seventh International Conference on Ubiquitous Computing UBICOMP, Workshop on Smart Environments and Their Applications to Cultural Heritage*.

Herbert Bay, Beat Fasel, and Luc Van Gool. 2006. Interactive museum guide: Fast and robust recognition of museum objects. In *Proceedings of the First International Workshop on Mobile Vision*.

Haoyuan Gao, Junhua Mao, Jie Zhou, Zhiheng Huang, Lei Wang, and Wei Xu. 2015. Are you talking to a machine? Dataset and methods for multilingual image question answering. In *Advances in Neural Information Processing Systems (pp. 2296-2304)*.

Mateusz Malinowski and Mario Fritz. 2014. A multi-world approach to question answering about real-world scenes based on uncertain input. In *Proceedings of the 27th International Conference on Neural Information Processing Systems*, NIPS'14, pages 1682–1690, Cambridge, MA, USA. MIT Press.

Mateusz Malinowski, Marcus Rohrbach, and Mario Fritz. 2015. Ask your neurons: A neural-based approach to answering questions about images. In *Proceedings of the IEEE International Conference on Computer Vision*, pages 1–9.

Antonella Santangelo, Agnese Augello, Antonio Gentile, Giovanni Pilato, and Salvatore Gaglio. 2006. A chat-bot based multimodal virtual guide for cultural heritage tours. In *Proceedings of the International Conference on Pervasive Systems and Computing*, pages 114–120.

Yuke Zhu, Oliver Groth, Michael Bernstein, and Li Fei-Fei. 2016. Visual7W: Grounded question answering in images. In *Proceedings of IEEE Conference on Computer Vision and Pattern Recognition*.

Extracting Social Networks from Literary Text with Word Embedding Tools

Gerhard Wohlgenannt
Vienna University of Economics
Inst. for Inf. Business
Vienna, Austria
wohlg@ai.wu.ac.at

Ekaterina Chernyak
National Research University
Higher School of Economics
Moscow, Russia
echernyak@hse.ru

Dmitry Ilvovsky
National Research University
Higher School of Economics
Moscow, Russia
dilvovsky@hse.ru

Abstract

In this paper a social network is extracted from a literary text. The social network shows, how frequent the characters interact and how similar their social behavior is. Two types of similarity measures are used: the first applies co-occurrence statistics, while the second exploits cosine similarity on different types of word embedding vectors. The results are evaluated by a paid micro-task crowdsourcing survey. The experiments suggest that specific types of word embeddings like word2vec are well-suited for the task at hand and the specific circumstances of literary fiction text.

1 Introduction

Word embeddings are language modeling techniques that transform the vocabulary of an input corpus into a continuous and low-dimensional vector representation. Word embeddings have shown state-of-the-art performance as language technology (LT) tools esp. for word similarity estimations, but also for more sophisticated operations like word analogies and as input component to various natural language processing (NLP) tasks (Mikolov et al., 2013; Ghannay et al., 2016). Word embeddings use artificial neural networks for generating the vector representations. Neural networks have become very popular and successful tools in NLP in the last couple of years, esp. with recent improvements in the deep learning field.

The performance of word embeddings in various task when using huge corpora of unstructured text has already been demonstrated in previous work. Here, we study the suitability of different types of word embeddings as a LT tool to extract social networks from literary fiction, ie. to a specific task and domain, and a comparably small corpus size. More precisely, we apply word embeddings to the text from the "A Song of Ice and Fire" book series by George R. R. Martin. The goal is to find book characters with the strongest relations to a given input character, and to compare the results from word embeddings to a very intuitive system, which uses term co-occurrence to determine the relatedness of characters. Furthermore, we evaluate the results from different word embedding tools and from a method based on co-occurrence statistics with human judgements generated with crowdsourcing. In this study, we did not focus on the detection and merging of character names, which is an interesting topic by itself, discussed for example in (Vala et al., 2015).

In this publication, we want to address the following research questions:

(i) How well does a traditional method based on co-occurrence statistics, such as the one presented in (Rodin et al., 2016), perform against state-of-the-art LT tools such as word embeddings for the task of social networks extraction in literary fiction?

(ii) Are there any differences between various types of word embeddings in the particular task of social networks extraction in literary fiction?

(iii) Furthermore, how well is paid micro-task crowdsourcing suited to evaluate facts in a domain with a lot of background necessary, such as a book series in the fantasy novel domain.

Proceedings of the Workshop on Language Technology Resources and Tools for Digital Humanities (LT4DH),
pages 18–25, Osaka, Japan, December 11-17 2016.

2   Related Work

A first step when extracting social networks from literary text, is the detection of characters. A state-of-the-art approach is presented by (Vala et al., 2015). Character detection often includes the usage of named entity recognition (NER) tools and methods for co-reference resolution. The authors present their own 8-step approach to character detection, and evaluate its usefulness.

An obvious next step is the actual extraction of social networks from novels. In the method by (Elson et al., 2010) the networks are derived from dialog interactions. Therefore their method includes finding instances of quoted speech, attributing each quote to a character, and identifying when certain characters are in conversation. They construct a weighted graph, where nodes correspond to actors, and the weights on the edges represents the frequency and amount of exchanges. In contrast to our work, (Elson et al., 2010) are solely focus on length and number of dialogues between persons to measure relatedness, whereas our approach looks at general co-occurrence or similarity as measured by LT tools which use word embeddings. Similarly, (Celikyilmaz et al., 2010) address a the problem related to the extraction of relations between characters. They attribute utterances in literary dialogues to actors, and apply the similarities in the language used to predict similarity and hidden relations between those actors. In contrast to our work, the approach also is restricted to dialogues between authors, and the evaluation of the method is of limited scope.

Another approach is presented by (Agarwal et al., 2013), who detect "social events" between persons (or groups of persons), where those persons interact. By using the connections from the social events, which help to form links between characters, the authors evaluate the extraction of social networks from literary text (*Alice in Wonderland*).

Our method of social network construction is more straightforward, and applies and evaluates existing word embedding tools. (Ghannay et al., 2016) did extensive evaluations to compare different kinds of word embeddings, such as word2vec CBOW and skip-gram, GloVe, CSLM and word2vec-f (see 3 for details on various algorithms). The different methods and tools perform very differently depending on the task. For NLP tasks, word2vec-f provided the best results, GloVe had the best performance in analogical reasoning, and CBOW/skip-gram were best at word similarity tasks. The authors also experiment with combinations of the methods in order to raise accuracy.

As already mentioned, we use crowdsourcing to evaluate the results produced by the various LT tools applied to the task of social network extraction. We selected paid micro-task crowdsourcing as scalable and in-expensive evaluation method, which has become popular in research only in recent years. There already exists a plethora of work on crowdsourcing in various fields, for example natural language processing (Bontcheva et al., 2014; Sabou et al., 2012), knowledge modeling (Wohlgenannt et al., 2016) or Bioinformatics (Mortensen et al., 2013). But, to our knowledge, it has not been applied in the digital humanities field on a similar task as social network extraction. In paid micro-task crowdsourcing the workload is usually split into small units, which are then presented to anonymous mass of crowd workers. A major issue is ensuring high quality results, typically measures in this direction are: (i) clear and extensive task description, (ii) careful worker selection, (iii) using test questions which workers need to pass before doing the real work, (iv) adequate worker remuneration, (v) assign work units to multiple workers and using aggregate results, etc.

3   Methods and Tools

In this section we briefly introduce and describe the methods used to find (the strongest) relations between the book characters. These include the co-occurrence based methods in Section 3.1 and the word embeddings tools in sections 3.2 to 3.4. Based on the results in (Ghannay et al., 2016) we picked three types of word embeddings to be applied: *word2vec, GloVe, and word2vec-f.* The configurations of the various methods used are found in Section 4.1 (Experiment Setup).

3.1   Co-occurrence based method

Our method is based on straightforward calculation of the so-called confidence coefficient. Given a text and two names, say A and B, we denote the frequency of name A by $F(A)$. The co-occurrence frequency of A and B is then $F(A \cap B)$. There are several ways how we detect the co-occurrence of A and B: first, we can check whether A and B occur in the same book chapter. Secondly, we can check whether A and B occur in the same paragraph, which can be problematic, if the book is ill-formatted and the paragraph splits are not present. Finally, we can check whether A and B occur in the same sentence. The resulting confidence formula is the following:

$$conf(A, B) = \frac{F(A \cap B)}{F(A)}.$$ (1)

This formula can be interpreted this way: given A, how probable it is that B occurs, so that the coefficient is normalized into an interval between 0 and 1.

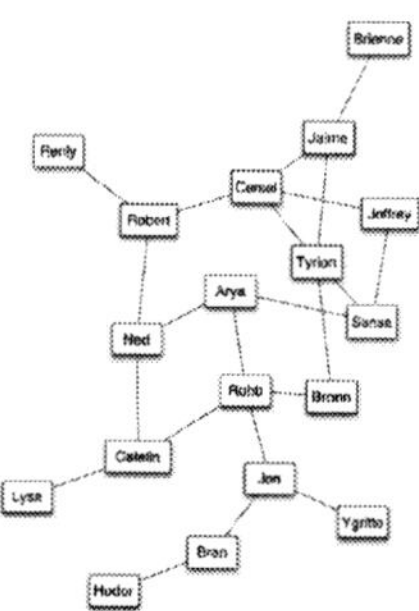

Figure 1: An example network, constructed using the co-occurrence-based method (on the paragraph level). Here, for the top 10 characters the top-3 connections are selected.

3.2 Word2vec

Word2vec (Mikolov et al., 2013) is a tool created by a team at Google led by Tomas Mikolov. Word2vec applies two-layer neural networks trained to reconstruct the linguistic contexts of words (or phrases). The input to word2vec is typically a large corpus (plain text), the output are word embeddings – which are continuous vector space representations of the words in the corpus. word2vec uses a dimensionality-reduced representation, usually with a vector length of 50 to 300. Proximity in vector space corresponds to similar contexts in which words appear. There are two model architectures to create the continuous vector representations: continuous bag-of-words (CBOW) or continuous skip-gram. With CBOW, the model predicts the current word by using a window of surrounding words. With skip-gram, the model predicts the surrounding window of context words by using the current word.

3.3 GloVe

Similar to word2vec, GloVe (Pennington et al., 2014) learns continuous vector representations of words. But it is not a predictive model, but rather a count-based model, using dimensionality-reduction on word-word co-occurrence statistics. The training objective of GloVe is to learn word vectors such that their dot product equals the logarithm of the words' probability of co-occurrence. We used the GloVe implementation from Stanford university[1].

3.4 Word2vec-f – Dependency-based Word Embeddings

Dependency-based word embeddings (Levy and Goldberg, 2014) are a modification of word2vec in order to generalize the skip-gram model with negative sampling to arbitrary contexts. Therefore, it is referred as the word2vec-f implementation[2]. In contrast to linear word contexts, dependency-based contexts are generated by a dependency-parser and produce markedly different embeddings. (Levy and Goldberg, 2014) expect "the syntactic contexts to yield more focused embeddings, capturing more functional and

---

[1] http://nlp.stanford.edu/projects/glove, GloVeversion1.2
[2] https://levyomer.wordpress.com/2014/04/25/dependency-based-word-embeddings

less topical similarity". In the evaluations by (Ghannay et al., 2016), word2vec-f was very effective in NLP tasks such as POS-tagging or Named Entity Recognition, but did not perform as well as word2vec on word similarity tasks.

4 Evaluation

In this section, we evaluate and compare the six methods to extract relations from text for a given set of input terms: (i) co-occurrence statistics on a chapter level, (ii) co-occurrence statistics on a paragraph level, (iii) co-occurrence statistics on a sentence level, (iv) word2vec, (v) GloVe, and (vi) word2vec-f – see Section 3 for details about the methods.

4.1 Evaluation Setup

Text corpus: For the evaluation we used the plain text versions of the first four books of the "A Song of Ice and Fire" (ASOIF) book series by George R. R. Martin. ASOIF is a series of fantasy novels. The action takes place in an fictional medieval-like universe. Although the number of character is immense, the are up to 40 main characters which communicate throughout the series. While narration is almost linear with minor flashbacks, the story is told in the first person. However there are different narrators telling the story from different viewpoints, i.e. different POVs. The raw books amounts to 6.9M of plain text, and contain 204 chapters with a mostly chronological storyline. There are 121098 sentences in total. Each chapter features a point of view character, which may live in any part of the ASOIF world. There are a few reasons behind our motivation to use ASOIF as the main source of data:

(i) it is popular nowadays, which gives the hope that the crowd will cope with the questions;

(ii) there is relatively large group of main characters, which interact intensively with each other in different circumstances, so that the social network might quite dense;

(iii) the book gives us more or less enough data to train selected word embedding models and conduct the powerful comparison.

Character detection: The problem of character detection was not a focus of our work, it has already been tackled for example by (Vala et al., 2015). We applied a very simple heuristic, which selects the 30 most frequent names of characters from the total list of characters – most frequent in the sense of counting the number of appearances per character in different chapters. If a character appears in various different chapters of the book series, this strongly hints at importance of the character to the story.

Relation selection: In order to make the results comparable for any of the three methods, we did the following: For any character in the list of 30 characters: get the *two strongest connections* to other characters on the list.

As described in Section 3, for method (i), (ii) and (iii) we selected the two characters with the strongest relation by co-occurrence between characters on a chapter, paragraph and sentence level, and for methods (iv)-(vi) we applied the different word embedding methods and tools.

For word embedding LT we used the gensim-word2vec toolkit. With Gensim, for any given character we compute the similarity to any other character – and then pick the two characters with the highest (cosine) similarity as strongest relations. Gensim[3] is a Python library (Řehůřek and Sojka, 2010), which provides tools for unsupervised semantic modeling from plain text, and also includes an implementation and extension of the original word2vec tool, which was written in C.

Method setup:

Co-occurrence: The computation of co-occurrence statistics $conf$ does not require any specific efforts. We introduced a threshold values: if B is among, say, top-3 candidates according to $conf$, we consider A and B similar and draw the corresponding vertex in the social network.

Word2vec: The corpus size of 6.9MB is a very small for word2vec standards, so it was interesting to see if word2vec will nevertheless produce good results. After a cleanup of the corpus (eg. removing

---

[3] http://radimrehurek.com/gensim

numbers and punctuation), we trained a CBOW model with 200 dimensions and a word-window size of 12. Those models are then used with gensim-word2vec, both for loading the pre-trained binary word2vec models, and for computing the similarity between terms (book characters).

GloVe: We applied the same basic settings as with word2vec – most importantly setting word vector length to 200 dimensions. For any other settings we kept the GloVe defaults. The resulting GloVe word embeddings were also used with Gensim, for this we adapted the following script[4].

Word2vec-f: Again, we trained vectors with 200 dimensions, but this time on the results of the Stanford Dependency Parser on the ASOIF books in CONLL-X format. After some tweaking, the trained model could be loaded with Gensim.

Crowdsourcing setup: The task of the user was the same as for the tool-based methods: Select the two characters with the strongest relation to the input ASOIF character. As options, we gave the users the whole set of candidates generated by the six methods to be evaluated, and also added a few random other characters to the list. Figure 2 shows a screenshot of a sample evaluation question posed to crowd

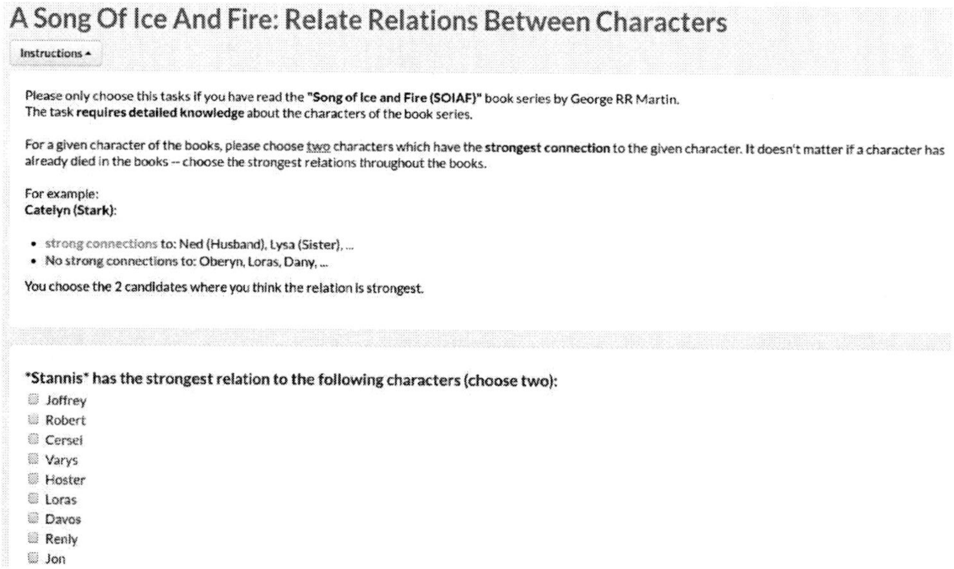

Figure 2: Screenshot of a CrowdFlower unit.

workers. We decided not to use all 30 available character options to be presented to the users, as this would be too many options to choose from, and be overwhelming and prohibitive for many users.

We used the following CrowdFlower settings: for all 30 units of work, we had 15 judgements each. We only allowed the highest quality workers (level 3), and we carefully designed test question to filter workers who lack knowledge about the ASOIF world. Workers had to answer at least 80% of test questions (gold units) correctly in order to be accepted to the job. The test questions were carefully created manually and test for general knowledge about the ASOIF universe.

4.2 Evaluation Results

We used the results of crowdsourcing as a gold standard, and compared them to the results for the automated methods (LT methods). We are aware that using results from crowd workers as gold standard is not without risk – so we also manually inspected the results retrieved to ensure high quality.

The crowdsourcing platform we used, CrowdFlower (CF), yields two types of results, the aggregated results, and the detailed results. In the aggregated results, CF gives exactly one ASOIF character which

---

[4]`https://github.com/manasRK/glove-gensim/blob/master/glove-gensim.py`

LT-Method	Top 1	Top 2
15 votes: Method i (Chapter Co-occ)	16.7%	50.0%
15 votes: Method ii (Paragraph Co-occ)	33.3%	63.3%
15 votes: Method iii (Sentence Co-occ)	33.3%	53.3%
15 votes: Method iv (word2vec)	36.7%	70.0%
15 votes: Method v (GloVe)	26.7%	53.3%
15 votes: Method vi (word2vec-f)	16.7%	20.0%

Table 1: Percentage where the suggested character of CF is also the No. 1 selection by the LT-method (Top 1), and where it is among the top 2 of automatically generated relations (Top 2).

has, according to the crowd workers, the strongest connection to the input character. And in the detailed results, CF gives all the single votes which where done by the individual crowd workers, which we then used to select the characters with the strongest connections. We used both aggregated and detailed results for evaluation, in Sections 4.2.1 and 4.2.2, respectively.

4.2.1 Aggregated CrowdFlower Results

As mentioned, in the aggregated results, the algorithms of CF select *one* character with the strongest connection to the input. As a first evaluation of the LT-generated relations we applied two scores:

1. The ratio of results where the character suggested by crowdsourcing is also the number one choice by the LT tool-based method (Top 1).

2. The ratio where the one character suggested by CF is among the top 2 of persons suggested by the LT method (Top 2).

Table 2 shows that paragraph-level and sentence-level co-occurrence, and also word2vec clearly outperform methods (i) chapter-level co-occurrence and (vi) word2vec-f. Agreement on the single most strongly related character (Top 1) is generally rather low, with values below 40%. But this is not unexpected, as it is a highly subjective choice if a book character has a stronger relation to his wife, his kids, or his best friend, for example. The *Top 2* score is much higher, up to 70%, which means that in 70% of cases the most related character selected by the crowd workers, is also in the top 2 picks of the LT methods. The best score here is provided by method (iv) word2vec, indicating that word embeddings can be very well suited for this task.

4.2.2 Detailed CrowdFlower Results

CF also provides all the individual votes of the crowd workers. As stated, we had 15 workers voting on each question. From the individual results, we selected the two characters that had the highest number of votes by the workers. Then we calculated the agreement between CF workers (the gold standard) and the tool-based methods with following formula:

$$score = Avg(\frac{A \cap B}{B}) \tag{2}$$

In this equation, A refers to the set of ASOIF characters suggested by the LT method, and B is the set of characters suggested by crowd workers. So, basically, we compute the average number of characters which are among the top two in the set of CF characters (our gold standard), and which are also in the top two characters suggested by the LT methods.

For example, if CF says that the set of (Renly, Davos) has the strongest connection to input character *Stannis*, and one of the LT tool-based methods suggests (Renly, Robert), then we have a 0.50 score on this single character. The final score then gives the average over all 30 input characters.

Similar to the results in Section 4.2.1, also with this score, methods (ii) to (v) are clearly more successful than chapter-based co-occurrence of characters and Word2vec-f. Again, word2vec had the highest score with a 58.3% match according to our metric. The GloVe word embeddings, and paragraph- and

LT-Method	Agreement
15 votes: Method i (Chapter Co-occ)	33.3%
15 votes: Method ii (Paragraph Co-occ)	53.3%
15 votes: Method iii (Sentence Co-occ)	51.3%
15 votes: Method iv (Word2vec)	58.3%
15 votes: Method v (GloVe)	53.3%
15 votes: Method vi (Word2vec-f)	26.7%

Table 2: Agreement between the sets of suggested character relations from CF workers and the LT methods, according to the score in Eq. 2.

sentence-level co-occurrence performed well, Word2vec-f and chapter-level co-occurrence are not suited for the job.

4.3 Discussion

The results are well in line with intuition and also with results from previous research. Confirming the results by (Ghannay et al., 2016), word2vec outperforms GloVe on word similarity tasks, while GloVe is superior on word analogy. For social network extraction, the word similarity feature is more important. Furthermore, as intuition suggests, chapter-level co-occurrence is not an optimal measure for relatedness between book characters.

Many interesting observations can be made about the method (vi) word2vec-f. As (Levy and Goldberg, 2014) argue, this method detects functional, not topical similarity, it gives words of same semantic type. For example for an input word like *go* it might suggest *run*, and *walk* as similar. In our task setup, this method is not well suited, as all input words are of same semantic type (book character) already. So word2vec returns words that associate with another, while word2vec-f suggests words that behave like one another. For extraction relations we seek primarily for associations between words.

Finally, with regards to research question (iii) and crowdsourcing itself, it is rather surprising how well crowdsourcing platforms like CrowdFlower seem to be suited even to address such specialized evaluation tasks such as relations between characters in the ASOIF book series. The high quality of results by crowdsourcing was confirmed by human inspection.

5 Conclusions

We considered the task of extracting a social network for literary texts and addressed a few main questions: do word embeddings outperform simple statistical similarity coefficients for our task? Which types of word embeddings are the most efficient? Is paid micro-task crowdsourcing suited to evaluate social networks extracted from literary texts? We came to the following results:

(i) To evaluate the quality of extracted social networks, we used the results of a crowdsourcing survey and the level of agreement between the crowd workers and the social networks extracted with language technology tools as the main quality measure. Although the social network of the highest quality is achieved by using the word2vec word embeddings toolkit, we can't say, that the co-occurrence statistics results are significantly worse, especially, when applied on paragraph level. Using GloVe embeddings we get a similar level of agreement, followed by the co-occurrence statistics applied to sentences. There are not drastic differences on the level of agreement, hence, we cannot say clearly, that one type of measures is significantly better than another;

(ii) There is a clear evidence, that word2vec-f embeddings are not suitable for the task.

(iii) Our results suggest that paid micro-task crowdsourcing is well suited to provide evaluation data even in such a specialized domain.

We have faced the following issues. First of all, there are some issues concerning the character names. Some character names have two or more forms (Dany and Daenerys, for example). Thus straightforward extraction of names will result in poor frequencies, and a tool for matching name forms should be applied. Some character names coincide (Jon Arryn and Jon Snow, for example). This fact can also spoil the frequencies for the co-occurrence coefficients and for word embedding similarity. In future work we will train the model based on improved entity extraction and character name disambiguation. Secondly, since there is no clear algorithm for setting up the thresholds for any type for similarity measure, we struggle with the problem of choosing the number of possible edges for the given node of the network.

Our main future direction is to introduce the time axis in our experiments. Since there is a clear timeline in the SOIAF books, we can extract a dynamic social network, which will show how intensive the characters interact during different time spans. This will require from us the improvement of word embeddings similarity measures to a dynamic case and also a more complex design of the crowdsourcing validation.

6 Aknowledgements

The article was prepared within the framework of the Basic Research Program at the National Research University Higher School of Economics (HSE) and supported within the framework of a subsidy by the Russian Academic Excellence Project '5-100'. This work was also supported by RFBR grants 16-01-00583 and 16-29-12982.

References

Apoorv Agarwal, Anup Kotalwar, and Owen Rambow. 2013. Automatic extraction of social networks from literary text: A case study on alice in wonderland. In *Sixth International Joint Conference on Natural Language Processing, IJCNLP 2013, Nagoya, Japan, October 14-18, 2013*, pages 1202–1208. Asian Federation of Natural Language Processing / ACL.

Kalina Bontcheva, Ian Roberts, Leon Derczynski, and Dominic P. Rout. 2014. The GATE crowdsourcing plugin: Crowdsourcing annotated corpora made easy. In *Proceedings of the 14th Conference of the European Chapter of the Association for Computational Linguistics, EACL 2014, April 26-30, 2014, Gothenburg, Sweden*, pages 97–100. The Association for Computer Linguistics.

Asli Celikyilmaz, Dilek Hakkani-Tur, Hua He, Greg Kondrak, and Denilson Barbosa. 2010. The actor-topic model for extracting social networks in literary narrative. In *Proc. of NIPS 2010 – Machine Learning for Social Computing*, page 7pp.

David K. Elson, Nicholas Dames, and Kathleen R. McKeown. 2010. Extracting social networks from literary fiction. In *Proceedings of the 48th Annual Meeting of the Association for Computational Linguistics*, ACL '10, pages 138–147, Stroudsburg, PA, USA. Association for Computational Linguistics.

Sahar Ghannay, Benoit Favre, Yannick Estve, and Nathalie Camelin. 2016. Word embedding evaluation and combination. In Nicoletta Calzolari et al., editor, *Proc. of the Tenth International Conference on Language Resources and Evaluation (LREC 2016)*, Paris, France, may. European Language Resources Association (ELRA).

Omer Levy and Yoav Goldberg. 2014. Dependency-based word embeddings. In *Proceedings of the 52nd Annual Meeting of the Association for Computational Linguistics (Volume 2: Short Papers)*, pages 302–308, Baltimore, Maryland, June. Association for Computational Linguistics.

Tomas Mikolov, Kai Chen, Greg Corrado, and Jeffrey Dean. 2013. Efficient estimation of word representations in vector space. *arXiv preprint arXiv:1301.3781*.

Jonathan Mortensen, Mark A Musen, and Natasha F Noy. 2013. Crowdsourcing the verification of relationships in biomedical ontologies. In *AMIA*.

Jeffrey Pennington, Richard Socher, and Christopher D. Manning. 2014. Glove: Global vectors for word representation. In *Empirical Methods in Natural Language Processing (EMNLP)*, pages 1532–1543.

Radim Řehůřek and Petr Sojka. 2010. Software Framework for Topic Modelling with Large Corpora. In *Proceedings of the LREC 2010 Workshop on New Challenges for NLP Frameworks*, pages 45–50, Valletta, Malta, May. ELRA. `http://is.muni.cz/publication/884893/en`.

Ivan Rodin, Ekaterina Chernyak, Mikhail Dubov, and Boris Mirkin. 2016. Visualization of dynamic reference graphs. In *Proceedings of the 10th Workshop on Graph-Based Methods for Natural Language Processing*, NAACL'16, pages 34–38.

Marta. Sabou, Kalina. Bontcheva, and Arno. Scharl. 2012. Crowdsourcing Research Opportunities: Lessons from Natural Language Processing. In *Proceedings of i-KNOW '12*, pages 1–8. ACM.

Hardik Vala, David Jurgens, Andrew Piper, and Derek Ruths. 2015. Mr. bennet, his coachman, and the archbishop walk into a bar but only one of them gets recognized: On the difficulty of detecting characters in literary texts. In Llus et al. Mrquez, editor, *EMNLP*, pages 769–774. The Association for Computational Linguistics.

Gerhard Wohlgenannt, Marta Sabou, and Florian Hanika. 2016. Crowd-based ontology engineering with the ucomp protege plugin. *Semantic Web Journal (SWJ)*, 7(4):379–398.

Exploration of register-dependent lexical semantics using word embeddings

Andrey Kutuzov
University of Oslo
Norway
andreku@ifi.uio.no

Elizaveta Kuzmenko
National Research University
Higher School of Economics
lizaku77@gmail.com

Anna Marakasova
National Research University
Higher School of Economics
anya.tiva@gmail.com

Abstract

We present an approach to detect differences in lexical semantics across English language registers, using word embedding models from distributional semantics paradigm. Models trained on register-specific subcorpora of the BNC corpus are employed to compare lists of nearest associates for particular words and draw conclusions about their semantic shifts depending on register in which they are used. The models are evaluated on the task of register classification with the help of the deep inverse regression approach.

Additionally, we present a demo web service featuring most of the described models and allowing to explore word meanings in different English registers and to detect register affiliation for arbitrary texts. The code for the service can be easily adapted to any set of underlying models.

1 Introduction

The phenomenon of language registers has long attracted the attention of linguists as well as specialists in other humanities areas. It is closely related to the issues of how humans produce and interpret texts. This paper and the accompanying demo web service intend to make exploration of these questions more accurate and data-driven.

We present an approach to track how words change their dominant meaning depending on the particular text register in which they are used. A typical example is the English word '*cup*' denoting mostly mugs in the fiction texts, but switching its primary meaning to the championship prize in the news texts. To find this (often rather slight) meaning shifts we use prediction-based distributional semantics models. In particular, we employ the *Continuous Bag of Words* model (Mikolov et al., 2013), trained on the register-separated subcorpora of the British National Corpus (BNC).

We evaluate this approach and show how it can be used to detect semantic shifts that cannot be discovered with traditional frequency-based corpus analysis methods. In addition, a similar algorithm is used to efficiently detect the most probable register of arbitrary text. We also present a convenient web service demonstrating the aforementioned techniques for English language material.

The paper is organized as follows. In Section 2 we discuss the related work, describe the notions of language registers and genres in more details, and put our work in the academic context. Section 3 presents our data and methods and provides examples of register-dependent semantic shifts. Section 4 is devoted to the algorithm of extracting register affiliation for texts based on the models we used in the previous section. It also evaluates the models. In Section 5 we conclude and draw main directions for the future work.

2 Related work

The notion of *language register* is often used as synonymous to *genre* or *style*. In any of these manifestations, it is a set of loosely defined categories of texts depending on both form and content (Chandler, 1997). It is very important that registers are not topics, which are defined on solely **internal** criteria (in

Proceedings of the Workshop on Language Technology Resources and Tools for Digital Humanities (LT4DH),
pages 26–34, Osaka, Japan, December 11-17 2016.

other words, they describe what the text is about). Meanwhile, registers are defined on the basis of **external** criteria (namely, they depend on who produces the text, for whom and under what circumstances).

Any system that classifies texts into 'registers' or 'genres' is unavoidably subjective: the distinction between registers is more of a convention than of some objective properties of texts. Notwithstanding this fact, this separation can be a useful tool in humanities as it is inherently relative to typical communicative situations and human behaviour within them, as well as the issues of the influence of language on the society. On the other hand, one can try to extract some objective linguistic phenomena associated with this or that register (cf., for example, (Biber, 1995)). Our work described in this paper also aims to facilitate the process of linguistic description of differences between registers and (to a lesser extent) genres.

It is important to note that we do not try to redefine existing register or genre classifications. Instead, we take them as is (see the thorough discussion in Section 3). We presuppose that the register separation introduced during compiling large and well-established corpora, like the BNC, makes at least some sense and represents linguistic reality to at least some extent. However, the same experiments can be performed with any other register classification scheme.

Our main source of data is the British National Corpus. The foundations of text classification in the BNC are described in (Lee, 2001). It states, *inter alia*, that there is no such thing as the 'general English language'. Instead, there exist several 'Englishes' (sublanguages), depending on the communicative situations. They can be called *registers*, whereas *genres* in this approach are their subdivisions: for example, sport column is a genre within news register.

(Lee, 2001) emphasizes that linguistic specificity is associated with registers, not genres; this is confirmed in NLP research, see, for example, (Dell'Orletta et al., 2013). We use this hypothesis in our work, as we are interested in differences of word meanings, which are manifested on the register level. This is the reason for us to compare macro-registers in the BNC (like *news*, *academic* and *fiction*) instead of comparing particular genres (like *humanities academic* texts and *fiction drama* texts). Of course, another reason is that the BNC is not a very large corpus and subcorpora consisting of texts belonging only to particular genres would be too small to train reasonable distributional models.

The size of the subcorpora is important, as we share the idea expressed in the seminal work of (Kilgarriff, 1997): the sets of word senses are absolutely dependent on the corpora we use to study them (and the purposes of the study). It essentially means that word meanings are abstractions over clusters of word usages. The word usage in corpus linguistics is traditionally defined through the frequencies of the word co-occurrences with other words (typical contexts). This is where distributional models come into play.

In natural language processing, distributional models, based on the foundational idea of 'meaning as context', are now one of the primary tools for semantic-related tasks. They stem from the so called *distributional hypothesis*, which states that co-occurrence statistics (word co-occurrence distributions) extracted from large enough natural language corpus can in some way represent the 'meaning' of words as perceived by humans (Firth, 1957). More formally, with a given *training corpus*, each word is represented as a vector of frequencies for this word occurring together with other linguistic entities (its contexts). These vectors are located in a *semantic space* with all possible contexts or semantic features as dimensions. Vector models of distributional semantics or vector space models (VSMs) are well established in the field of computational linguistics and have been studied for decades; see the review in (Turney et al., 2010), among others.

Recently, a particular type of these models has become very popular, namely, the *prediction models* that utilize artificial neural networks, introduced in (Bengio et al., 2003) and (Mikolov et al., 2013) and employed in a wide-spread *word2vec* software. Prediction models directly learn dense vectors (*embeddings*) which maximize the similarity between contextual neighbours found in the data, while minimizing the similarity for unseen contexts.

Initial vectors are generated randomly (the target vector size is set at the beginning of the training process, typically hundreds of components) and then gradually converge to optimal values, as we move through the training corpus with a sliding window. To this end, predictive models employ machine learning and consider each training instance as a prediction problem: one wants to predict the current word with the help of its contexts or vice versa. The outcome of the prediction for the given training example (context window) determines whether we change the current word vector (embedding) and in what direction.

To sum it up, prediction models learn meaningful vector representations of words in the training corpus by stochastically trying to predict a focus word from its context neighbours, and slightly adjusting vectors in case of mistake. These models are simple, fast and efficient in various NLP tasks; for evaluation, see (Baroni et al., 2014), among others.

Interestingly, this approach is absolutely compatible with (Lee, 2001) idea that registers exist independently of text-level structures. Thus, one can extract linguistic features of different registers without paying attention to particular texts, treating all of them as one large register-marked corpus. This is exactly what we do with the register-separated subcorpora of the BNC. The details of this are described in the next section.

There have been several studies dedicated to the task of automatic text register (or genre) identification; most of them were inspired by (Kessler et al., 1997). To the best of our knowledge, none of the studies made use of distributional semantics. The algorithms were mainly based on simple word and text statistics; see, for example, (Lee and Myaeng, 2002), (Amasyal and Diri, 2006). In some of the works ((Stamatatos et al., 2000), (zu Eissen and Stein, 2004)), apart from statistical features (word count, sentence count, character per word count, punctuation marks count), more complex linguistic features were employed: morpho-syntactic (passive count, nominalization count, relative clauses count and other frequencies of different syntactic categories) and lexical (type-token ratio).

More resent research, for example, (Biber and Egbert, 2015), also demonstrates the advantages of incorporating lexico-grammatical characteristics into text types prediction. We attempt to move it even further and use state-of-the art word embedding models in order to explore linguistic specificity of language registers.

3 Distributional approach to meaning across registers

(Lee, 2001) states that a text belonging to a particular register is '*the instantiation of a conventionalised, functional configuration of language tied to certain broad societal situations, that is, variety according to use*'. In a sense, we also follow the (Chandler, 1997) concept of 'ideal reader' for each register. Ideal reader shares semantic structures with the text producer. This is reflected in the meaning of the words used in producing register-specific texts. These meanings can be different from the so-called *core meaning* of the word. Note that the concept of 'core meaning' is disputable itself, but with a certain degree of confidence we can say that this is the meaning stored in the dictionaries *or* the one given by distributional models trained on a full balanced and representative corpus (for example, the whole BNC).

As stated above, distributional models compute meaning by analysing word co-occurrences. The trained model can represent semantics of a given word as a sequence of its 'nearest associates': words closest to the key word by the cosine similarity of their vectors (embeddings). Our work is based on the presupposition that in the models trained on register-specific subcorpora, the register-specific words would feature meaningfully different sets of nearest associates.

3.1 Data preparation

The data used for our experiments was compiled from the British National Corpus: it is freely accessible, comparatively large, well-balanced, and, therefore, supposed to be representative for the respective language. What is even more important is that the BNC features well-developed register and genre annotation. Since our aim is to discover semantic shifts associated with the switching from one register to another, we train several distributional semantic models on the texts of particular registers.

The BNC provides eight 'text type' categories: *academic writing, published fiction, published non-fiction, news and journalism, other published writing, unpublished writing, conversation, other spoken*. Although it might be an apparent way to split the BNC into subcorpora representing different registers, that is not something we were looking for. The share of each text type is highly disproportionate ('*news and journals*' contains 9.56% of all the corpus tokens, while '*published non-fiction*' – 24.58%; '*other published writing'* appears to be quite a large category (18.26%) that contains text of different registers). This disproportion would, for certain, affect the quality of distributional models.

Therefore, we have developed our own split into language registers based on the BNC genre classification[1] (Lee, 2001). The classification provides us not only with token and sentence counts for each genre, but also with "macro-genres" categories. For instance, the following genres of academic writings – 'humanities arts', 'medicine', 'nature science', 'politics law education', 'social science', 'technical engineering' – are encoded as *'W ac:humanities arts'*, *'W ac:medicine'*, *'W ac:nat science'*, *'W ac:polit law edu'*, *'W ac:soc science'*, *'W ac:tech engin'* respectively. This encoding let us form an 'academic' register out of the texts of the mentioned genres. Thus, we have obtained the split which is more balanced in terms of token counts and which, we hope, is more reliable. The registers are listed below:

1. academic texts (15 632 085 tokens);

2. fiction texts (15 950 682 tokens);

3. newspaper articles (14 214 484 tokens);

4. non-fiction and non-academic texts (18 307 605 tokens);

5. spoken texts (17 451 494 tokens).

The *'academic texts'* register comprises research papers and articles from the various fields of study: social and political science, law, education, natural science, medicine, humanities, arts and computer science. The same topics are covered in *'non-academic'* texts, the difference is that their intended audience is non-professional. *'Fiction'* texts include mainly prose, but also a small amount of drama and poetry. As for the *'news'* register, it consists of the following text types: report (the prevalent one), commerce, social, sport, science, arts. The remaining texts are of various genres (religion, parliamentary, email, advertisement, administrative etc.) and fall into miscellaneous category. As they do not represent any particular register, we exclude them from consideration.

These subcorpora were pre-processed, replacing each token with its lemma and PoS tag (*loved* $\rightarrow$ *love_VERB*). Data on lemmas and PoS affiliation was extracted from the BNC mark-up. We also removed all functional words and one-word sentences.

3.2 Training distributional models

Then, CBOW models (Mikolov et al., 2013) were trained on each of the subcorpora and on the whole BNC corpus. We used the standard set of hyperparameters for training, excluding the selection of prediction material: hierarchical softmax was employed, instead of more widely used negative sampling, as this makes it easier to implement text classification via deep inverse regression (see Section 4 for more details). Another important decision to make was the size of sliding window (how many words to the right and to the left of the focus word to consider). It is known from previous work that larger windows tend to generate more 'associative' models (*'cup'* is semantically close to *'coffee'*), while narrower windows favour more 'functional' models (*'cup'* is semantically close to *'mug'*). It is not immediately clear what mode is better for our task. That's why we trained two sets of models, with window sizes 3 and 10. The evaluation process is described in Section 4.

The resulting models indeed demonstrate semantic specificity of different registers. It can be observed through comparing the lists of nearest associates for a given word in different models. The Table 1 gives one example of such specificity.

One can clearly see the difference in the meaning of the word *'bank'* when it is used in the fiction register. While the dominant meaning in general English (and in academic and news registers) is related to financial institutions, fiction texts use the word in an absolutely different sense related to river shores. It is possible to quantify these differences using any of set comparing methods. At the moment we implemented Jaccard distance (Jaccard, 1901) which estimates the number of intersecting elements in

---

[1] http://www.natcorp.ox.ac.uk/docs/URG/codes.html#classcodes

Table 1: First 5 associates for '*bank*'

Model	Whole BNC	Academic	News	Fiction
1	banker	mortgage	banker	**spate**
2	banking	wales	banking	**slope**
3	loan	overdraft	deposit	**gully**
4	deposit	money	lender	**shore**
5	overdraft	loan	branch	**hill**
Jaccard distance to the whole BNC	0	0.75	0.57	**1**
Kendall's τ distance to the whole BNC	0	0.66	0	**0.85**

Table 2: First 5 associates for '*star*'

Model	Whole BNC	Academic	News	Fiction
1	hollywood	sun	superstar	moon
2	superstar	earth	singer	galaxy
3	movie	jupiter	legend	light
4	galaxy	galaxy	heart-throb	cloud
5	entertainer	stripe	guitarist	sky
Jaccard distance to the whole BNC	0	0.9	0.9	0.9
Kendall's τ distance to the whole BNC	0	0.56	0.26	0.4

two sets and normalized Kendall's τ (Knight, 1966) which calculates the differences between rankings. However, we also plan to test other metrics, for example, as described in (Kutuzov and Kuzmenko, 2016). Larger distance between the 'general' model and a particular register means that the key word is semantically shifted in this register.

The word '*bank*' is an example of homonymy, where different senses are totally unrelated. However, our approach also captures subtler cases of polysemy, in which senses are still connected to each other, like with the noun '*star*' described in the Table 2.

In this case, all the register-specific models seem to be on approximately the same distance from the general model (which comprises several meanings at once). However, it is easy to see that the academic and fiction registers are closer to each other, featuring the astronomical sense of '*star*'. At the same time, they share no associates with news register, which primarily employs the word in the sense of '*celebrity*'. The Table 3 shows the matrix of mutual distances between different registers for the word '*star*'.

RegisterExplorer, our demo web service at `http://ltr.uio.no/embeddings/registers`, based on *Gensim* framework (Řehůřek and Sojka, 2010), provides easy access to such comparative tables for the models trained on the BNC register subcorpora. It also features visualizations of the interaction between nearest associates within one register and between registers as well. The models are available to download, and the source code for the service is released as free software, making it easy to adapt the system to any set of models, depending on a researcher' aims. Among other applications, one can use

Table 3: Mutual Kendall's τ distances between registers for the word '*star*'

Register	Spoken	Academic	News	Fiction	Non-fiction
Spoken	0	**0.69**	0.50	**0.69**	**0.69**
Academic	**0.69**	0	**0.69**	0.40	0.49
News	0.50	**0.69**	0	**0.69**	**0.69**
Fiction	**0.69**	0.40	**0.69**	0	0.51
Non-fiction	**0.69**	0.49	**0.69**	0.51	0

the system to explore particular *genres*, not only large-scale registers, as in this work. For this, one needs only a large genre-annotated corpus to train genre-specific models (the BNC size is not enough for that).

The distributional approach allows to reveal register-specific senses, which cannot be discovered by traditional frequency-based analysis. Frequency distributions across registers are meaningful only for words which possess one dominant meaning. For instance, let us consider a word '*room*' (noun). Based on the 'Words and Phrases' web resource[2], compiled using the Corpus of Contemporary American English (COCA), we can only conclude that this word is much more frequent in the fiction register (frequency of 87 748, while the respective counts for the spoken, magazine, newspaper and academic registers are 19 948, 36 225, 31 908, 10 113). However, no conclusions about meaning differences across registers can be made.

The distributional approach (implemented in *RegisterExplorer*) supports the observation that in the fiction register the word 'room' is more frequent. However, it additionally allows us to see that the spoken register – unlike other registers and general English – is strongly associated with the sense 'the amount of space' (apart from much more common sense 'a part of a building with a floor, walls, and a ceiling').

Senses and registers are not always in one-to-one association. A register may feature two or more specific senses, while two or more registers may be similar in terms of the senses they share. Considering the verb 'mean', we can clearly see that the senses 'to be of a specified degree of importance to (someone)' and 'to intend something, often bad or wrong' are associated with the fiction register, while the academic and news registers share the sense 'to have as a consequence or result'.

4 Detecting registers with word embeddings

Any word embedding model can be turned into a text classifier via Bayes rule. The idea (dubbed 'deep inverse regression') was first introduced in (Taddy, 2015) and essentially allows to calculate the likelihood of an arbitrary sequence of words in the context of any trained distributional model.

Recall that we have a set of models trained on register-specific texts. It means that we can find out the extent to which a particular sentence or a text is prototypical for a given register or registers.

For, example intuitively it is obvious that the sequence '*star divorced yesterday*' is quite likely in the news texts, very unlikely in the academic texts, and in the spoken texts its likelihood should be somewhere in between. If we apply deep inverse regression to our models with window size 10 and the aforementioned sequence (lemmatized and PoS-tagged), it produces the following likelihood values (more negative values mean less likelihood):

- News: -27.53

- Spoken: -42.39

- Academic: -43.25

- Fiction: -48.42

The news register indeed turns out the most likely to produce such a sentence, with spoken register a bit less likely, and academic and fiction most unlikely.

RegisterExplorer allows users to analyse an arbitrary text and receive lists of registers ranked by their likelihood to produce such a text. This can be used to quickly explore 'linguistic profiles' of texts and to find out how different registers are manifested in language, helping to study their interactions.

To evaluate the applicability of this approach to unseen data we randomly sampled 1 000 sentences from each of our register-specific subcorpora (for the purposes of evaluation, these sentences were not used in the subsequent model training). For these sentences, we calculated the most likely register according to the deep inverse regression method and evaluated it against the real sentence affiliations. The results are summarized in the Table 4.

---

[2]`http://www.wordandphrase.info/`

Table 4: Models' performance scores

Register	Text classification, F1		Simlex999, Spearman correlation	
	Window size 3	Window size 10	Window size 3	Window size 10
Academic	0.52	0.50	0.05	0.05
Fiction	0.48	0.46	0.17	0.15
News	0.49	0.50	0.03	0.04
NonAcademic	0.39	0.39	0.03	0.11
Spoken	0.48	0.48	0.03	0.04
Average	**0.47**	0.46	0.06	**0.08**

The models with the smaller window size performed a bit better in text prediction, which supposedly implies that they are better in capturing linguistic specificity of language registers in the BNC. We hypothesize that the reason for this is that the smaller windows work as filters against too much influence of topics and content of the sentences. As a result, models are more 'concentrated' on lexical semantics *per se*. However we acknowledge that the difference is negligible and more experiments are needed to find out the best models' hyperparameters for our task.

For reference, we additionally evaluated the resulting subcorpora models against the well-known *SimLex999* semantic similarity dataset (Hill et al., 2016), as a measure of general 'quality' of the models. Relatively low values did not come as a surprise, considering rather small size of the subcorpora (as compared to billion-word corpora used in contemporary state-of-the-art models). There is no consistent advantage of one window size over another (unlike with text classification), the results vary depending on a register.

One can notice unusual behaviour of the *nonAcademic* model: with the increase of the window size, it becomes much better in *Simlex999* task, unlike models trained on other subcorpora. In our opinion, the reason for this is comparatively high average sentence length in the texts belonging this register (about 12 words), favouring settings with large window sizes. Another register with long sentences is *academic* (12.4 words), but it does not demonstrate such a behaviour, supposedly because of denser information load (less 'irrelevant' words), which allows to grab the meaning even with a narrow window. Of course, another reason for this can be a simple fluctuation caused by stochastic nature of word embedding models and small corpus size. It is also interesting that the *fiction* register model seems to represent semantic structure of language as a whole much better than others. However, we leave studying these phenomena for the future research.

Unfortunately, there is no clear way to directly evaluate how good the models are in capturing particular words' semantic differences across registers (as described in the previous section). That's why we use the values in the Table 4 as proxy measure of this, and subsequently, *RegisterExplorer* features the models with window size 3.

5 Conclusion

Thus, we presented an approach to detect differences in word semantics dependent on the language registers. It is believed that register variation can be found at different language levels. Our contribution is related to exploring this variation on the semantic tier of language. Our approach is very straightforward in implementation and based on distributional semantic models yielding state-of-the-art results in many NLP tasks.

We gave examples of semantic shifts detected by our approach and showed how it can be easily extended to detect the most likely register of an arbitrary text. As a proof of concept, we presented *RegisterExplorer* (`http://ltr.uio.no/embeddings/registers`), a web service to study difference in lexical semantics across several language registers extracted from the BNC corpus. The service comes with freely available source code[3] to enable researchers to quickly set up their own experimental design,

---

[3] `https://github.com/ElizavetaKuzmenko/dsm_genres`

with their own models and text types.

Among others, this framework can be used to study differences in word usage between different fiction genres or even between particular writers, or one and the same writer at certain time periods. It is also possible to analyse how dominant word meanings change depending on types of communicative situations, etc. Once the necessary corpora are available, distributional models can be trained using many available off-the-shelf tools and then easily loaded in to our framework.

In the future we plan to extend the web service with additional models trained on larger corpora (to allow exploration of finer genres), as well as improve its visualization abilities. We are also interested in defining what measures of similarity between lists of nearest associates in different models yield better performance and how to evaluate it. Furthermore, we hope that this service will enable us to investigate cross-linguistic register variation by examining comparable registers in different languages, for example, English and Russian.

References

M. Fatih Amasyal and Banu Diri, 2006. *Automatic Turkish Text Categorization in Terms of Author, Genre and Gender*, chapter Natural Language Processing and Information Systems, pages 221–226. Springer Berlin Heidelberg.

Marco Baroni, Georgiana Dinu, and Germán Kruszewski. 2014. Don't count, predict! A systematic comparison of context-counting vs. context-predicting semantic vectors. In *Proceedings of the 52nd Annual Meeting of the Association for Computational Linguistics*, volume 1, pages 238–247, Baltimore, USA.

Yoshua Bengio, Rejean Ducharme, and Pascal Vincent. 2003. A neural probabilistic language model. *Journal of Machine Learning Research*, 3:1137–1155.

Douglas Biber and Jesse Egbert. 2015. Using grammatical features for automatic register identification in an unrestricted corpus of documents from the open web. *Research Design and Statistics in Linguistics and Communication Science*, 2(1):3–36.

Douglas Biber. 1995. *Dimensions of register variation: A cross-linguistic comparison*. Cambridge University Press.

Daniel Chandler. 1997. An introduction to genre theory. *The Media and Communications Studies Site*.

Felice Dell'Orletta, Simonetta Montemagni, and Giulia Venturi. 2013. Linguistic profiling of texts across textual genres and readability levels. An exploratory study on Italian fictional prose. In *Proceedings of the International Conference Recent Advances in Natural Language Processing RANLP 2013*, pages 189–197. INCOMA Ltd. Shoumen, BULGARIA.

John Firth. 1957. *A synopsis of linguistic theory, 1930-1955*. Blackwell.

Felix Hill, Roi Reichart, and Anna Korhonen. 2016. Simlex-999: Evaluating semantic models with (genuine) similarity estimation. *Computational Linguistics*.

Paul Jaccard. 1901. *Distribution de la Flore Alpine: dans le Bassin des dranses et dans quelques régions voisines*. Rouge.

Brett Kessler, Geoffrey Nunberg, and Hinrich Schutze. 1997. Automatic detection of text genre. In *Proceedings of the 35th Annual Meeting of the Association for Computational Linguistics (ACL/EACL97)*, pages 32–38.

Adam Kilgarriff. 1997. "I don't believe in word senses". *Computers and the Humanities*, 31(2):91–113.

William R Knight. 1966. A computer method for calculating Kendall's tau with ungrouped data. *Journal of the American Statistical Association*, 61(314):436–439.

Andrey Kutuzov and Elizaveta Kuzmenko. 2016. Cross-lingual trends detection for named entities in news texts with dynamic neural embedding models. In *CEUR Workshop Proceedings*, volume 1568, pages 27–32.

Yong-Bae Lee and Sung Hyon Myaeng. 2002. Text genre classification with genre-revealing and subject-revealing features. In *Proceedings of the 25th annual international ACM SIGIR conference on Research and development in information retrieval*, pages 145–150.

David Lee. 2001. Genres, registers, text types, domains and styles: clarifying the concepts and navigating a path through the BNC jungle. *Language Learning & Technology*, 5(3):37–72.

Tomas Mikolov, Ilya Sutskever, Kai Chen, Greg S Corrado, and Jeff Dean. 2013. Distributed representations of words and phrases and their compositionality. In *Advances in Neural Information Processing Systems*, pages 3111–3119.

Radim Řehůřek and Petr Sojka. 2010. Software Framework for Topic Modelling with Large Corpora. In *Proceedings of the LREC 2010 Workshop on New Challenges for NLP Frameworks*, pages 45–50, Valletta, Malta, May. ELRA. `http://is.muni.cz/publication/884893/en`.

Efstathios Stamatatos, Nikos Fakotakis, and George Kokkinakis. 2000. Automatic text categorization in terms of genre and author. *Computational Linguistics*, 26(4):471–495.

Matt Taddy. 2015. Document classification by inversion of distributed language representations. In *Proceedings of the 53rd Annual Meeting of the Association for Computational Linguistics and the 7th International Joint Conference on Natural Language Processing (Volume 2: Short Papers)*, pages 45–49. Association for Computational Linguistics.

Peter Turney, Patrick Pantel, et al. 2010. From frequency to meaning: Vector space models of semantics. *Journal of artificial intelligence research*, 37(1):141–188.

Sven Meyer zu Eissen and Benno Stein. 2004. Genre classification of web pages. *Advances in Artificial Intelligence*, pages 256–269.

Original–Transcribed Text Alignment for Man'yōsyū Written by Old Japanese Language

Teruaki Oka[†]   **Tomoaki Kono**[†]

† National Institute for Japanese Language and Linguistics

`oka {at} ninjal.ac.jp`   `tkouno {at} ninjal.ac.jp`

Abstract

We are constructing an annotated diachronic corpora of the Japanese language. In part of this work, we construct a corpus of Man'yōsyū, which is an old Japanese poetry anthology. In this paper, we describe how to align the transcribed text and its original text semiautomatically to be able to cross-reference them in our Man'yōsyū corpus. Although we align the original characters to the transcribed words manually, we preliminarily align the transcribed and original characters by using an unsupervised automatic alignment technique of statistical machine translation to alleviate the work. We found that automatic alignment achieves an F1-measure of 0.83; thus, each poem has 1–2 alignment errors. However, finding these errors and modifying them are less work-intensive and more efficient than fully manual annotation. The alignment probabilities can be utilized in this modification. Moreover, we found that we can locate the uncertain transcriptions in our corpus and compare them to other transcriptions, by using the alignment probabilities.

1 Introduction

National Institute for Japanese Language and Linguistics (NINJAL) is constructing an annotated diachronic corpora of the Japanese language.[1] As part of this work, we are constructing a corpus of **Man'yōsyū** (萬葉集, "Collection of myriad leaves"), which is an old Japanese poetry anthology complied about 8th–9th century AD. Since it is a worldwide very rare example of literature written more than 1,000 years ago, Man'yōsyū is an major source for those who study old Japanese language (**OJ**). This anthology is composed of 20 volumes and contains more than 4,500 poems.[2] Our corpus is based on the transcribed version of the text from original text (see Figure 1), and a large amount of information is annotated semiautomatically by utilizing NLP tools. For example, word boundaries, part-of-speech (POS) tags, pronunciations, cross-references to original characters, and so on are included in this information. Table 1 shows the statistics of our Man'yōsyū corpus.

In this paper, we describe how to align the transcribed text and its original text semiautomatically to be able to cross-reference them in our Man'yōsyū corpus. This is because researchers of OJ frequently reference and consult the original texts. Eventually, we align the original characters to the transcribed words manually. However, to alleviate this work, we preliminarily align the transcribed and original characters by using an unsupervised automatic alignment technique of statistical machine translation and then modify the mistakes manually with less work.

2 Transcription

Most OJ researchers use some type of transcribed version of old Japanese texts. Therefore, we also employed the transcribed version of Man'yōsyū (Kojima et al., 1994) as the base text of our corpus. This

---

[1] `http://pj.ninjal.ac.jp/corpus_center/chj/overview-en.html`

[2] Although Man'yōsyū consists of several volumes (books), we deem the anthology to be one text and treat it as singular for clarification in this paper.

35

Proceedings of the Workshop on Language Technology Resources and Tools for Digital Humanities (LT4DH),
pages 35–44, Osaka, Japan, December 11-17 2016.

Table 1: The statistics of our Man'yōsyū corpus.

Number of poems	4,516
Number of syllabic units	29,489
Total number of words (total)	101,313
Total number of transcribed characters	148,352
Total number of original characters	128,063

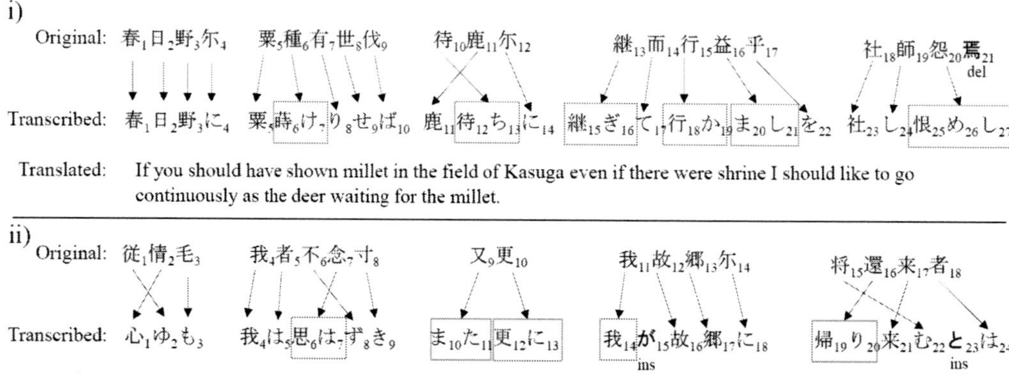

Figure 1: Examples of transcribed poems from Man'yōsyū (Kojima et al., 1994). For clarification, each character was indexed with subscript Arabic numerals. A bold character in an original poem that was deleted in the transcribed poem is indicated by "del," and bold characters in the transcribed poem that were inserted are indicated by "ins." The translated poems were cited from (Pierson, 1929–1963).

text was provided by Syogakukan, a major Japanese publishing company. The provided text is marked up using XML to digitally replicate the paper books and was already annotated with some information (e.g., page number; poem number; ruby, which is explained further in Section 4.1; and original text). This text is a transcription of a reading of the original text into a mixture of *kanji* and *kana* characters used in the writing of the modern Japanese language. The original Man'yōsyū text is written in OJ with only kanji characters, which are used in two different ways: logographically and phonographically (the latter use is known as *man'yōgana*).

In transcription works, the phonographic characters are replaced with kana characters,[3] and some logographical ones are also replaced with more suitable kanji characters or kana characters. Since several kanji characters have been used in the modern Japanese language, they are sometimes not replaced. In addition, since the original poems were sometimes written in the writing style of the Chinese language, the transcribed texts contain character-order replacements, deletions, and insertions with respect to the original poems, as in Chinese–Japanese translation (see Figure 1).

3 Related work

Techniques for automatic alignment between electronic parallel texts are mainly used in the field of statistical machine translation, and many NLP tools are available. The most popular alignment tool is GIZA++ (Och and Ney, 2003), which can align one source token (e.g., a word) to some number of target tokens (1-to-n alignment) in each type of unit (e.g., a sentence) in a parallel corpus by using IBM models (Brown et al., 2003) and HMM model (Brown et al., 2001). GIZA++ allows token-order replacements, deletions, and insertions among a source/target unit pair.

These techniques are used not only in the fields of machine translation, but also digital humanities. For example, (Moon and Baldridge, 2007) used them to induce POS taggers for Middle English text.

---

[3] If the kana character(s) can be additionally replaced with more easy-to-read logographic kanji character(s), the kana character(s) are replaced with the kanji characters (e.g., "波 奈" are replaced with "は な", and additionally replaced with "花.").

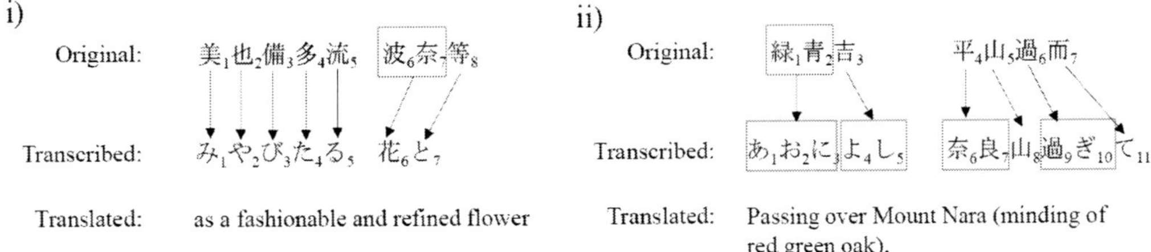

Figure 2: Examples of many-to-1 and many-to-many transcription (alignment) in Man'yōsyū(Kojima et al., 1994). The translated texts were cited from (Pierson, 1929–1963).

They aligned Modern English and Middle English bibles and then projected the POS tags from words in the Modern English bible to words in the Middle English bible for use as a training corpus for Middle English bigram POS taggers. This projection approach was proposed in (Yarowsky and Ngai, 2001) and has been used to create POS taggers or parsers for low-resource languages or domains, and so on (Drábek and Yarowsky, 2005; Ozdowska, 2006).

We also use GIZA++ because there are character-order replacements, insertions, and deletions between the transcribed and original text. Since (Moon and Baldridge, 2007) mainly intended to create POS taggers, they did not evaluate their autoalignment performance. However, our objective is annotating alignments themselves; thus, we need to evaluate and attempt to improve our automatic alignment performance. In addition, (Moon and Baldridge, 2007) treated texts written in English, which is a word-segmented language, and employed a word as an alignment token. In contrast, Japanese language does not use a space between words; moreover, in our Man'yōsyū corpus, although the transcribed text is already word-segmented because of our policy for creating the corpus, the original text is not segmented because it is merely additional information. Therefore, we employ a character as an alignment token; thus, our automatic alignment is characters-to-characters.

4   Original–transcribed character alignment

We start with the computerized parallel texts of Man'yōsyū (Kojima et al., 1994), in which each transcribed poem is associated with its original poem. In addition, both forms are spaced by caesura space marks. Therefore, we employ each syllabic unit[4], spaced by caesura space marks, as our alignment unit and each character as our alignment token. Since the number of (transcribed) words in the Man'yōsyū corpus is not very large, we can avoid the data sparseness problem as an advantage of employing characters-to-characters alignment. Although (Moon and Baldridge, 2007) employed 1-to-n alignment, our transcriptions have n-to-1 and m-to-n alignment pairs (see Figure 2). However, these are rare cases. Most alignment pairs are 1-to-n, as in Figure 1; thus, we also employ the 1-to-n (one original character to several transcribed characters) alignment of GIZA++[5] and utilize post-processing to cope with the n-to-1 and m-to-n alignments via rules. In addition, our task only has a character sequence-to-a character sequence alignments as a restriction.[6] This is because, most minimum m-to-n alignment pairs between the original and transcribed texts follow this restriction in the transcription works, as in Figures 1 and 2, and eventually, we want to align one original character sequence to one transcribed word (see Table 2).

4.1   Additional data

To improve alignment performance, we use original-transcribed (**or-tr**) unit pairs and other parallel units. First, we use ruby tags. A "ruby" is a small kana character (or characters) attached to the (mainly kanji) character (or characters) in the body text, generally to represent the pronunciation of the body character(s). Man'yōsyū (Kojima et al., 1994) also has ruby characters in both the transcribed and original

---

[4]Syllabic unit is the equivalent of a "line" in an English poem.
[5]We used *mkcls* for using IBM-Model 4 and HMM Model.
[6]We allow that this "sequence" consists of only one character.

Table 2: Examples of alignment one original character sequence to one transcribed word our Man'yōsyū corpus cross references. Upper example is the case of Figure 1 ii) and under example is the case of Figure 2 ii).

Word	POS tag	Original caharcters
心$_1$	noun	情$_2$
ゆ$_2$	particle	従$_1$
も$_3$	particle	毛$_3$
我$_4$	pronoun	我$_4$
は$_5$	particle	者$_5$
思$_6$は$_7$	verb	念$_7$
ず$_8$	auxiliary verb	不$_6$
き$_9$	auxiliary verb	寸$_8$
ま$_{10}$た$_{11}$	adverb	又$_9$
更$_{12}$に$_{13}$	adverb	更$_{10}$
我$_{14}$	pronoun	我$_{11}$
が$_{15}$	particle	NULL
故$_{16}$郷$_{17}$	noun	故$_{12}$郷$_{13}$
に$_{18}$	particle	尓$_{14}$
帰$_{19}$り$_{20}$	verb	還$_{16}$
来$_{21}$	verb	来$_{17}$
む$_{22}$	auxiliary verb	将$_{15}$
と$_{23}$	particle	NULL
は$_{24}$	particle	者$_{18}$
あ$_1$を$_2$に$_3$よ$_4$し$_5$	noun	緑$_1$青$_2$吉$_3$
奈$_6$良$_7$	noun	平$_4$
山$_8$	noun	山$_5$
過$_9$ぎ$_{10}$	verb	過$_6$
て$_{11}$	particle	而$_7$

texts and were computerized with ruby tags (see Figure 3). We use rt tags (body text) as transcribed units and rb tags (ruby text) as original units accessorily, because these tag annotations (computerizations) are not trusted and not every kanji character has a ruby. We call units from the ruby tags in the transcribed text **tr-ruby** and those in the original text **or-ruby**. To avoid data sparseness, only in *mono-ruby*[7] cases, we replace the kanji characters in the rt tags with the kana characters in the rb tags in the transcription text at or-tr as a preprocessing step.[8] These are replaced with rt characters after GIZA++ alignment step. These steps create m-to-1 alignments from 1-to-n alignments of GIZA++ outputs (see Figure 4).

Second, original units include characters that have been used in the modern Japanese language since the OJ, and these characters are sometimes not replaced in transcription work. Therefore, to successfully align these characters, we also use pairs consisting of a character and itself (e.g., "粟–粟", "種–種"), called **character-self**. Table 3 shows some examples of simplified input data for GIZA++, and Table 4 shows the numbers of units, source characters, and target characters.

4.2 Post-processing rules

For post-processing the GIZA++ output, we apply the following rules in order (see Figure 5 a)-g)). We note that since the transcribed text has already been word-segmented and POS-tagged, we can refer to the POS tags of all subscribed characters.

a) **Rule 1. Interpolating for alignments 1:** If a character in the transcribed unit is NULL-aligned and the POS tag of the character is not a particle, we assign it with the same character alignment of its leftmost character that is not NULL-aligned in the same unit.

b) **Rule 2. Interpolating for alignments 2:** If a lead character(s) in the transcribed unit is NULL-aligned, we assign it (them) with the same character alignment of its (their) rightmost character that is not NULL-aligned in the same unit.

---

[7]This is a particular ruby that is attached to only one character in the body text.

[8]Actually, we also replace all *odoriji* characters (ヾ) that represent iteration of the previous character(s), to the corresponding previous character(s) when we use GIZA++.

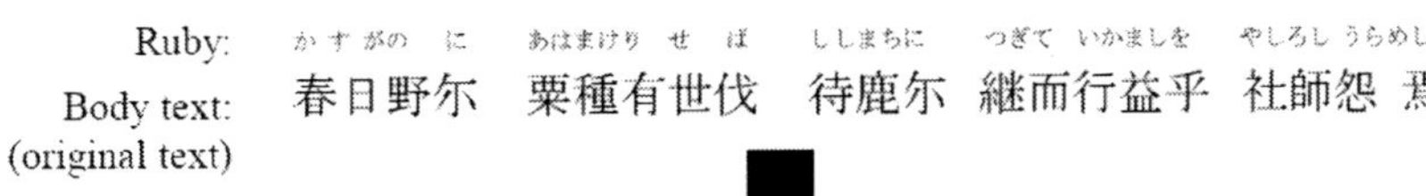

<ruby><rb>春日</rb><rt>かすが</rt></ruby><ruby><rb>野尓</rb><rt>のに</rt></ruby>
<ruby><rb>粟種有世伐</rb><rt>あはまけりせば</rt></ruby>
<ruby><rb>待鹿</rb><rt>ししまち</rt></ruby><ruby><rb>尓</rb><rt>に</rt></ruby>
<ruby><rb>継而行益乎</rb><rt>つぎていかましを</rt></ruby>
<ruby><rb>社</rb><rt>やしろ</rt></ruby><ruby><rb>師</rb><rt>し</rt></ruby><ruby><rb>怨</rb><rt>うらめ</rt></ruby><ruby><rb>焉</rb><rt>し</rt></ruby>

Figure 3: An example of ruby computerization for the original body text.

Table 3: Examples of simplified input data for GIZA++.

	Source: Original unit	Target: Transcribed unit
or-tr	粟種有世伐	粟蒔けりせば
tr-ruby	社師怨焉	やしろしうらめし
	社	やしろ
	師	し
	怨	うらめ
or-ruby	粟種有世伐	あはまけりせば
	社	やしろ
	恨	うら
	焉	し
character-self	粟	粟
	種	種

c) **Rule 3. Interpolating for alignments 3:** If a character is NULL-aligned and not in { 而, 於, 乎, 于, 矣 , 焉, 也, 兮 }[9] in the original units, we assign it with the same alignment of its rightmost caharcter that is not NULL-aligned in the same unit. If such a character is absent, we assign it same character alignment of the leftmost character that is not NULL-aligned in the same unit.

d) **Rule 4. Remove intersections:** If an m-to-n alignment is either not one original character sequence or one transcribed character sequence (or both), we remove all alignments for those characters without alignment between the leftmost sequences.

e) **Rule 5. Remove initial or final particles alignments:** If a transcribed character sequence start or end with a particle character (or characters) on an m-to-n alignment, we remove the connections to these characters from the original characters, unless the transcribed sequence consists only particle character(s).

f) **Rule 6. Remove "が" alignments:** If an original character is aligned with "我が" in the transcribed unit, we remove the connections from the original character to "が" and its right side characters. Although this "我が" is pos-tagged with noun, strictly speaking the "が" means a case particle.

g) **Rule 7. Remove "み" alignments:** If an original character is not only aligned with "み" whose POS tag is "suffix-substantive-general" in the transcribed unit, we remove the connections from the original character to"み" and its right side characters.

Rules a–c assign some non-NULL connection(s) to NULL-aligned characters (see examples of Figure 5 a–c). Furthermore, rule c makes m-to-1 or m-to-n alignments from 1-to-1 or 1-to-n align-

---

[9]These original characters are sometimes NULL-aligned, as in Figure 1, and called "置字 (Okiji)."

Table 4: The number of units, source characters, and target characters.

	Number of units	Number of original characters	Number of transcribed characters
or-tr	29,489	128,063	161,561
tr-ruby	25,187	35,543	56,901
or-ruby	44,778	126,646	181,597
character-self	2,196	2,196	2,196

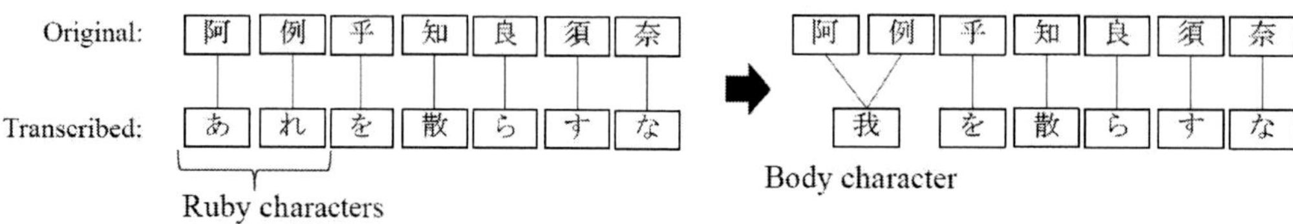

Figure 4: An Example of a created many-to-1 alignment, after mono-ruby characters were restored to a body character.

ments (see examples of Figure 5 c). Eventually, since we want to align one original character sequence to one transcribed word (see Table 2), we remove the intersections between several m-to-n alignments using Rule d. On the other hand, an original character sequence that is not a particle or suffix does not include the meaning of a particle or suffix. Therefore, we remove such alignments using Rules e–g. Such transcribed particle or suffix characters are called "読み添え (Yomisoe)."

5 Evaluation of automatic alignment performance

In our experiment, we compared the precision, recall and F1-measure of our approach across eight datasets. To evaluate alignment performance, we use 79 randomly selected poems from our Man'yōsyū corpus. Two professional researchers of Man'yōsyū probatively annotated the correct alignments for the poems. Table 5 presents the results of the evaluation.

The addition of tr-ruby or character-self to the dataset improves the performance of our alignment in comparison with the or-tr only or the addition of or-ruby. However, the or-tr+or-ruby+character-self dataset results in the best performance. This is because the data are noisy, even though the number of or-ruby units is the largest in our dataset, as can be seen when comparing Figure 3 to Figure 1. We believe that the addition of character-self reined in this noise as a restriction during unsupervised learning. In addition, the proportion of poems that have identical alignments as the correct alignments is 1/79 at most. Since the F1-measures are about 0.83, each poem has 1–2 alignment errors. However, finding these errors and modifying them are less work-intensive and more efficient than fully manual annotation.

Since GIZA++ uses probabilistic models, we can calculate the probability of each m-to-n alignment pair from the output. We normalized the probabilities and use them as the score of the m-to-n alignment pair. We set a threshold value for the score to predict the correct/wrong of the alignment pair, and then investigated a correlation with actual correct/wrong. Consequently, we found that we can distinguish the correctness of an m-to-n alignment pair with high coefficient of correlation (0.925) when the threshold value is 0.15035 (using the or-tr+tr-ruby+or-ruby+character-self). That is, we can modify the errors more efficiently if we begin our modification by checking the alignment pairs with scores below the threshold. We have already started this modification based on the results of our automatic alignment approach (using the or-tr+tr-ruby+or-ruby+character-self) and two workers have completed 1,023/4,516 poems during a period of five months.

6 Extra tries

We can calculate the alignment probability of each pair of unit. We normalized and sorted these probabilities (using the or-tr+tr-ruby+or-ruby+character-self). Table 6 shows the 10 best and Table 7 shows the 10 worst unit-pairs. The characters in the original units are all phonographic (1-to-1 alignment) in Table 6.

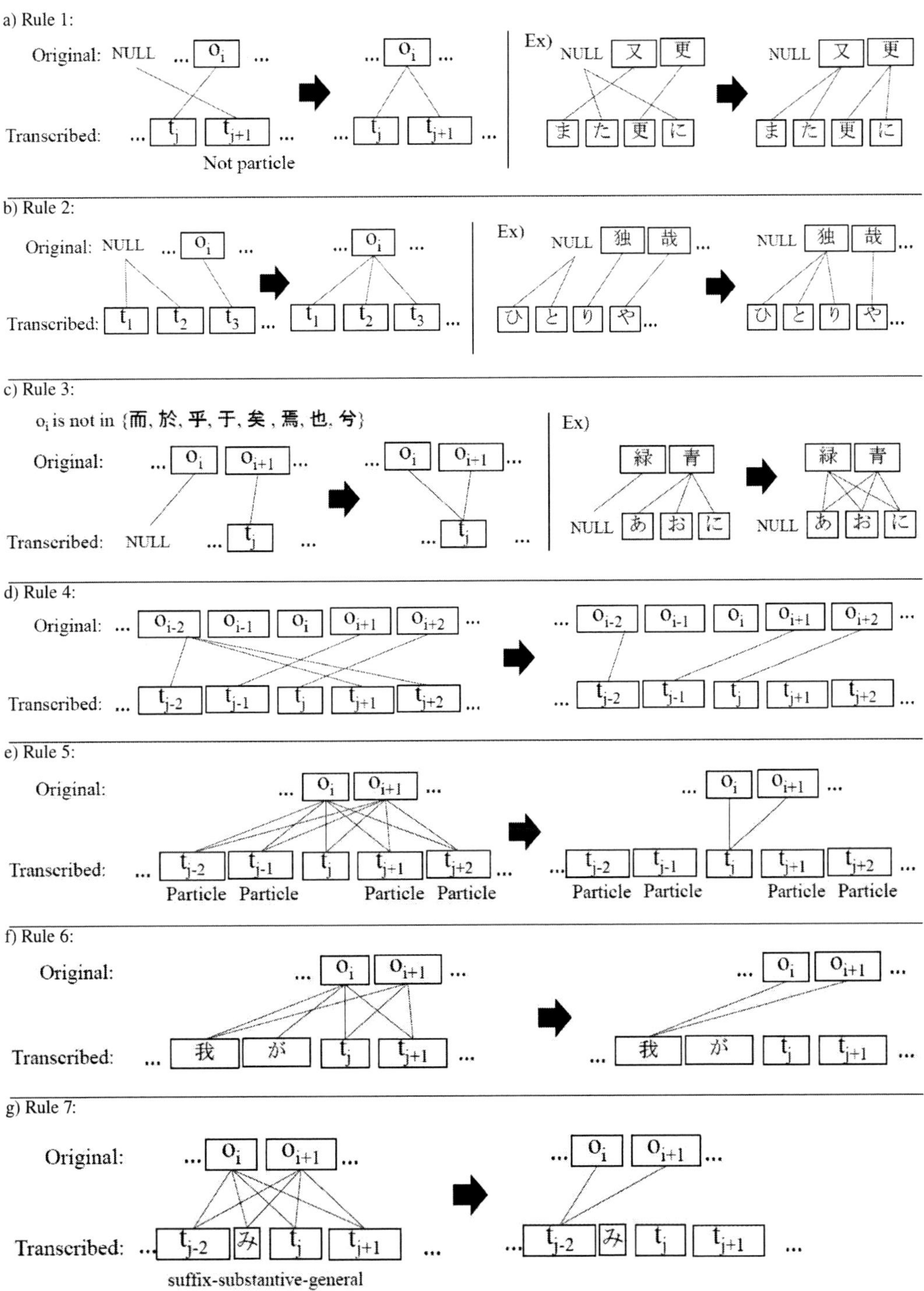

Figure 5: Post-processing rules. The above rules are applied to the GIZA++ output according to the order. The squares represent each character (token), and edges (connections) represent each character alignment between an original character and a transcribed character.

Table 5: Automatic alignment performances for each dataset.

			Perc.	Rec.	F1
(1)	or-tr		0.827	0.826	0.826
(2)	or-tr	+ tr-ruby	0.830	0.826	0.829
(3)	or-tr	+ or-ruby	0.827	0.822	0.825
(4)	or-tr	+ character-self	0.829	0.827	0.828
(5)	or-tr	+ tr-ruby + or-ruby	0.832	0.827	0.830
(6)	or-tr	+ tr-ruby + character-self	0.832	0.827	0.829
(7)	or-tr	+ or-ruby + character-self	**0.834**	**0.828**	**0.831**
(8)	or-tr	+ tr-ruby + or-ruby + character-self	**0.834**	0.827	0.830

Table 6: The 10 unit-pairs with the highest (normalized) alignment probabilities. The Correct/Wrong column shows whether the unit-pair alignments are completely correct. [] shows the mono-ruby (rt) or iterated characters.

Source: Original unit	Target: Transcribed unit	Probability	Correct/Wrong
毛 武 尓 礼 乎	も む に れ を	0.995	Correct
伊 牟 礼 氐 乎 礼 婆	い 群 [む] れ て 居 [を] れ ば	0.993	Correct
乎 氐 母 許 乃 毛 尓	を て も こ の も に	0.991	Correct
乎 呂 能 波 都 乎 尓	尾 [を] ろ の は つ を に	0.991	Correct
都 芸 奈 牟 毛 能 乎	継 [つ] ぎ な む も の を	0.991	Correct
保 杼 呂 ヽ [保] ヽ [杼] ヽ [呂] 尓	ほ ど ろ ほ ど ろ に	0.991	Correct
伊 乎 祢 受 乎 礼 婆	眠 [い] を 寝 [ね] ず 居 [を] れ ば	0.990	Correct
乎 良 牟 等 須 礼 杼	居 [を] ら む と す れ ど	0.990	Correct
乎 弓 毛 許 乃 母 尓	を て も こ の も に	0.990	Correct
乎 弓 毛 許 能 母 尓	を て も こ の も に	0.989	Correct

Conversely, in Table 7, most characters in the original units are difficult to read (logographical), which matches our intuition. Despite that both the original and transcribed units consist of only one character and are the same, the numeric characters in Table 7 —六 (six), 二 (two), 四 (four)— are scored poorly. This is because these characters in the original Man'yōsyū are mostly used as phonographic characters, such as "四具礼 (drizzling rain)," rather than for their numerical meanings. These all numeric characters in Table 7 are units for note, and they are exceptional uses. "紫–紫 の" also has similar result. However, most uses of "紫" in original units consist of several characters, such as "筑 紫 奈 留"; thus, the case that the original unit consists of only "紫" has low probability. Additionally, "雖 小–小 [ち ひ] さ け ど" has character-order replacement.

Many OJ researchers have transcribed Man'yōsyū using their own policies. Therefore, many syllable units in the original Man'yōsyū have several transcriptions. We compared the (normalized) probabilities of varied transcriptions that are listed in (Tsuru and Moriyama, 1977) and show this result in Table 8. In this table, we can find transcriptions with higher probabilities than ours. However, these probabilities are calculated from only our transcription; thus, they tell us only, "Which transcription is most likely in our corpus?" At least, from this results, we may as well think that we employ other transcriptions about these transcriptions in our corpus. In these ways, we can find units in our transcription that are difficult to read or uncertain, and then select more likely transcriptions using this comparison.

7 Conclusion

In this paper, we described how to semiautomatically align the transcribed and original characters to be able to cross-reference them in our Man'yōsyū corpus. Our approach uses GIZA++, which is used in the field of machine translation, and post-processing rules. We also utilized ruby tags as additional training data, and achieved an F1-measure of about 0.83, meaning that is each poem has only 1–2 alignment errors. However, finding and modifying these errors are cheaper and more efficient than using

Table 7: The 10 unit-pairs with the lowest (normalized) alignment probabilities. The Correct/Wrong column shows whether the unit-pair alignments are completely correct. [] shows the mono-ruby characters (rt).

Source: Original unit	Target: Transcribed unit	Probability	Correct/Wrong
石 穂 菅	巌 菅	0.094	Correct
向 南 山	北 山 に	0.092	Correct
紫	紫 の	0.090	Correct
雛 小	小 ［ち ひ］ さ け ど	0.087	Wrong
六	六	0.081	Correct
恵 得	愛 ［う る は］ し と	0.078	Wrong
二	二	0.061	Correct
従 来	昔 よ り	0.047	Wrong
四	四	0.039	Correct
美	愛 ［う る は］ し み	0.008	Correct

Table 8: Comparing of the normalized alignment probabilities of various transcriptions.

Original unit	Our transcribed unit	Other transcription	Alignment probability
恋 等 尓	こ ひ し ら に		0.270
		こ ほ し ら に	0.134
		こ ふ ら く に	0.196
		こ ふ と に し	**0.368**
		こ ふ ら む に	0.172
結 手 懈 毛	ゆ ふ 手 た ゆ き も		0.068
		ゆ ふ て た ゆ き も	0.084
		む す ぶ て う き も	**0.158**
		ゆ ふ 手 た ゆ し も	0.105
		ゆ ふ て た ゆ し も	0.141
		ゆ ふ て ゆ る ぶ も	0.043

completely manual annotation. Since the coefficient of correlation between the alignment score and alignment correctness is 0.925, the score can be utilized for increasing error-correction efficiency. We have already begun making modifications based on the result of our automatic alignment approach. In addition, we confirmed that we can find the uncertain transcriptions in our corpus and compare them with other transcriptions by using alignment probabilities. We plan to use this approach to investigate the various transcriptions from a statistical perspective as future work. We hope this research will ease and encourage further study of historical works.

Acknowledgements

The work reported in this paper was supported by the NINJAL collaborative research project, "The Construction of Diachronic Corpora and New Developments in Research on the History of Japanese."

References

Peter F. Brown, Jennifer C. Lai, and Robert L. Mercer. 1991. *Aligning Sentences in Parallel Corpora.* In proceedings of *the 29th Annual Meeting of the Association for national Linguistics (ACL-91)*, 169–176.

Peter F. Brown, Vincent J. Della. Pietra, Stephen A. Della. Pietra and Robert L. Mercer. 1993. *The Mathematics of Statistical Machine Translation: Parameter Estimation. Computational Linguistics*, 19(2):263–311.

Elliott F. Drábek and David Yarowsky. 2005. *Induction of Fine-grained Part-of-speech Taggers via Classifier Combination and Crosslingual Projection.* In proceedings of *the ACL Workshop on Building and Using Parallel Texts (ParaText '05)*, 49–56.

Noriyuki Kajima, Masatoshi Kinoshita and Haruyuki Touno. 1994. *Shinpen Nihon Koten Bungaku Zensyu*, volume 6–9. Syougakukan, JP.

Taesun Moon and Jason Baldridge. 2007. *Part-of-speech Tagging for Middle English through Alignment and Projection of Parallel Diachronic Texts.* In proceedings of *the 2007 Joint Conference on Empirical Methods in Natural Language Processing and Computational Natural Language Learning (EMNLP-CoNLL)*, 390–399.

Franz J. Och and Hermann Ney. 2003. *A Systematic Comparison of Various Statistical Alignment Models. Computational Linguistics*, 29(1):19–51.

Sylwia Ozdowska. 2006. *Projecting POS Tags and Syntactic Dependencies from English and French to Polish in Aligned Corpora.* In proceedings of *the International Workshop on Cross-Language Knowledge Induction* (In *EACL 2006*), 53–60.

Jan L. Pierson. 1929–1963. *The Manyôśû : Translated and Aannotated*, Book 1–20. Brill, Leiden, NED.

Hisashi Tsuru and Takashi Moriyama. 1977. *Man'yōsyū*, expanded edition. Ohfu, Japan.

David Yarowsky and Grace Ngai. 2001. *Inducing Multilingual POS Taggers and NP Bracketers via Robust Projection Across Aligned Corpora.* In proceedings of *the Second Meeting of the North American Chapter of the Association for Computational Linguistics* (*NAACL '01*), 1–8.

Shamela: A Large-Scale Historical Arabic Corpus

Yonatan Belinkov[1], Alexander Magidow[2], Maxim Romanov[3], Avi Shmidman[46], Moshe Koppel[56]

[1]MIT Computer Science and Artificial Intelligence Laboratory, Cambridge, MA, USA
[2]Department of Languages and Literatures, University of Rhode Island, USA
[3]The Humboldt Chair of Digital Humanities, Leipzig University, Leipzig, Germany
[4]Department of Hebrew Literature, Bar-Ilan University, Israel
[5]Department of Computer Science, Bar-Ilan University, Israel
[6]Dicta: The Israel Center for Text Analysis

`belinkov@mit.edu, amagidow@uri.edu, maxim.romanov@uni-leipzig.de`
`shmidman@gmail.com, moishk@gmail.com`

Abstract

Arabic is a widely-spoken language with a rich and long history spanning more than fourteen centuries. Yet existing Arabic corpora largely focus on the modern period or lack sufficient diachronic information. We develop a large-scale, historical corpus of Arabic of about 1 billion words from diverse periods of time. We clean this corpus, process it with a morphological analyzer, and enhance it by detecting parallel passages and automatically dating undated texts. We demonstrate its utility with selected case-studies in which we show its application to the digital humanities.

1 Introduction

Arabic has been used as a written language for more than fourteen centuries. While Arabic attracts significant interest from the natural language processing (NLP) community, leading to large corpora and other valuable resources, mostly in Modern Standard Arabic (MSA), we still lack a *large-scale, historical* corpus of Arabic that covers this entire time period. This lacuna affects three research communities: it hinders linguists from making corpus-driven historical analyses of the Arabic language; it prevents digital humanities (DH) scholars from investigating the history and culture of the Arabic-speaking people; and it makes it difficult for NLP researchers to develop applications for texts from specific historical periods.

We aim to close this gap by developing a large-scale historical Arabic corpus. Our corpus is drawn from the Al-Maktaba Al-Shamela website,[1] a website of Arabic texts from the early stages of the language (7th century) to the modern era. We have cleaned these texts and organized useful metadata information about them in a semi-automatic process. We have also lemmatized the entire corpus to facilitate semantic analysis. This step is especially important given the rich morphology of the Arabic language. The result is a corpus of over 6,000 texts, totaling around 1 billion words, of which 800 million words are from dated texts. We describe these procedures in some detail to facilitate future similar work. We present several case-studies showing how this corpus can be used for digital humanities research. The corpus itself will be made available to the research community.[2]

Finally, we improve and enhance our corpus in two different ways. First, we detect approximately-matching parallel passages in the entire corpus. This turns out to be a computationally challenging task, but yields a very large number of parallel passages. After excluding 18.6 million words of frequently recurring passages within the corpus, we proceeded to compare each of the texts against the entirety of the corpus. Our initial run compared one third of the corpus (over 308 million words) with the rest of the corpus and yielded more than 5 million pairwise matches of passages over 20 words in length. We shed some light on the nature of parallel passages with our analysis. Second, we develop a simple text dating

[1]`http://shamela.ws`
[2]An initial version is available in the RAWrabica collection: `https://github.com/OpenArabic/RAWrabica`.

Proceedings of the Workshop on Language Technology Resources and Tools for Digital Humanities (LT4DH),
pages 45–53, Osaka, Japan, December 11-17 2016.

algorithm based on language modeling in order to date the large portion of undated texts in the corpus (1,200 texts). We validate the text dating quality both quantitatively and qualitatively.

The remainder of this paper is organized as follows. In the next section we review related work on Arabic corpora. We then describe the initial corpus preparation (Section 3) and our enhancements (Section 4). We demonstrate the application of this corpus with several case-studies in Section 5 before concluding with ideas for future work.

2   Related Work

Though there has been increasing interest in compiling Arabic corpora in the past decade, very little work has been done on compiling historical corpora reflecting the long history of the Arabic language. Most of the existing corpora focus on modern written Arabic texts, particularly online print media, though there are a growing number of corpora which feature written and to a lesser degree spoken material from Arabic dialects. We mention here several relevant corpora and refer to other surveys for more details (Al-Sulaiti, 2004; Zaghouani, 2014; Shoufan and Alameri, 2015; Al-Thubaity, 2015).

To date, there is only a small number of diachronically oriented corpora of Arabic. The King Saud University Corpus of Classical Arabic (KSUCCA) (Alrabiah et al., 2013)[3] consists of approximately 50.6 million words from the first 4 Islamic centuries. It has been morphologically analyzed with the MADA tool (Habash and Rambow, 2005; Habash et al., 2009). Almost all of the texts are derived from the Shamela corpus. Text metadata is by century, so more granular buckets are not possible in the current state of this corpus. Other Classical Arabic corpora that are worth mentioning include a 5 million word corpus by Elewa (2004), which doesn't seem to be publicly available, a 2.5 million word corpus by Rashwan et al. (2011),[4] and Tashkeela, a 76 million word corpus of texts from Al-Maktaba Al-Shamela website.[5] All these corpora are rather small and lack temporal metadata.

Finally, a few large corpora are available only via online search interfaces: KACST Arabic Corpus (Al-Thubaity, 2015) has more than 700 million words, including around 16 million words from the beginning of the Islamic era. The Leeds Arabic Internet Corpus[6] and the International Corpus of Arabic[7] contain 300 and 100 million words, respectively, but they include mostly modern texts. The well-known Arabi-Corpus[8] has more than 170 million words from diverse periods of time, and arTenTen (Arts et al., 2014) is a 5.8 billion word web corpus, with a sub-corpus of 115 million words available through Sketch Engine (Kilgarriff et al., 2004). Milika and Zemnek (2014) mention CLAUDia , also based on Shamela, but with added genre metadata; however, only a subset appears to be accessible via a web interface.[9] While these corpora are very large and may contain texts from different periods, they are not directly accessible and also lack sufficient diachronic information.

In contrast to previous resources, our corpus has fairly fine-grained time information, it covers most of the history of the written Arabic language, and it is available for developing NLP applications or supporting digital humanities projects.

3   Initial Corpus Preparation

3.1   Metadata/data wrangling

Al-Maktaba Al-Shamela ("The Complete Library") is a website which collects and stores digitized copies of important texts from throughout the history of the Arabic language. Sponsored by a religious charity, the texts are largely religious in nature, though there was not a strong division between religious and secular texts in the pre-modern era, and so many of the pre-modern texts are simply part of the Islamicate intellectual and literary tradition. The project itself is primarily designed to be a resource for reading

---

[3]http://ksucorpus.ksu.edu.sa
[4]http://www.RDI-eg.com/RDI/TrainingData
[5]https://sourceforge.net/projects/tashkeela
[6]http://corpus.leeds.ac.uk/internet.html
[7]http://www.bibalex.org/ica/en/About.aspx
[8]http://arabicorpus.byu.edu
[9]http://arabiccorpus.com/index.htm

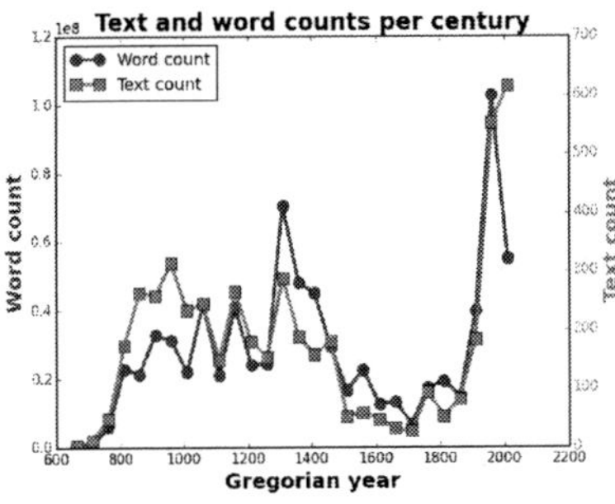
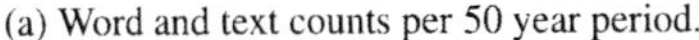

(a) Word and text counts per 50 year period.

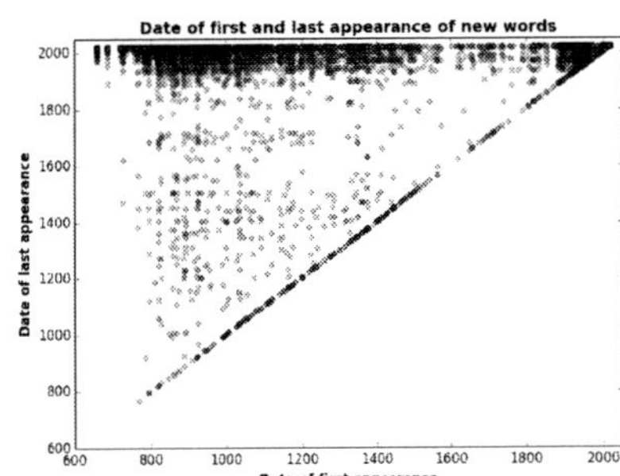

(b) The Arabic word life span, showing first and last usage date for every word lemma.

Figure 1: Word and text counts (left) and word lifespans (right) in the corpus.

individual texts — it is not designed as a corpus per se. Most of the texts available on the website have been digitized, largely by manual double-keying, though some have been automatically digitized and are marked as such within the website's metadata. Texts are digitized from specific print editions, which, in most cases, allows for accurate citation in scholarly works. Texts can be accessed directly through the website, but there is also a Windows-based proprietary application which allows for off-line access.

The EPUB versions of the documents were downloaded from Shamela website and converted into specially designed markup format which allows for rapid manual editing as well as automated processing.[10] One of the major challenges was inconsistent metadata, which was cleaned through automatic grouping of author names, book titles, and document distance using a custom script[11] to suggest matches which were then manually resolved. With most duplicates identified, records with more complete metadata were used to fill in the gaps in records where metadata was missing. We used Python scripts to further reconcile the metadata file with the Access databases included with the desktop application. Numeric author codes from the database were integrated into the metadata file where possible, as it can be important to try to investigate a feature on an author-by-author basis rather than on a text-by-text basis. Word counts were obtained and integrated as well.

3.2 Lemmatization

The raw corpus with accompanied metadata is already a useful resource for historical analysis. However, the orthography and morphology of the Arabic language pose several challenges for such research. First, the rich morphology leads to multiple surface forms for each common lemma, or dictionary entry. Second, orthographic norms in writing Arabic, such as the usual omission of diacritics, introduce a high degree of ambiguity. These phenomena hinder the ability to exploit Arabic corpora for lexical and semantic studies. To mitigate these problems, we automatically analyzed the entire corpus with MADAMIRA (Pasha et al., 2014), a state-of-the-art morphological analyzer and disambiguator. Given an Arabic sentence, it performs orthographic normalization (e.g. of many variant forms of the letter Alif), morphological analysis, and context-aware disambiguation. The result is a full analysis per word, including tokenization, lemmatization, part-of-speech-tagging, and various morphological features.

After lemmatization, we observe that the word vocabulary size in the corpus is about 16.8 million words, whereas the lemma vocabulary size is only 95 thousand lemmas. The lemmatized corpus will be made available to the research community, with future versions including other morphological features.

3.3 Corpus statistics and characteristics

The dataset contains more than 6,100 texts, of which a significant portion (about 1,200) are undated. In the next section we consider automatic dating for these texts. Excluding undated texts, the corpus

---

[10]https://github.com/maximromanov/mARkdown
[11]https://github.com/maximromanov/DuplAway

contains roughly 4,900 texts totaling 800 million words.

The texts are almost exclusively in formal Arabic, due to the religious focus, with a small number of contemporary texts showing colloquial elements. They are dated based on the author's date of death (DOD), with the earliest text dated to 41/661 Hijri/CE.[12] Figure 1a shows the distribution of word and text counts per century in the corpus, and

Genre	Date (H/CE)	Texts
Hadith Collections	335/946	179
Biographies	735/1334	377
Jurisprudence (*Fiqh*)	891/1486	157
Popular religious writing	1419/1998	298

Table 1: Average date and total number of texts for example genres.

Table 1 provides some statistics for the most common genres in the dataset. These genres are exemplary of the changes in dominant topics of discussion throughout the history of the Islamic world, with the collection of *hadith*, sayings of the prophet Muhammad, a major concern in early centuries as the living links to hadith reciters were still present, while biographical works are developed more during an age of encyclopedism in the Middle Ages (Muhanna, 2014). As literacy has become more widespread, popular religious writing has become a major genre. Thus there is an interaction of date and genre, though overall the genres of the corpus are relatively similar in their religious focus — i.e. there are few of the modern secular texts that one finds in corpora based on media.

The nature of writing in religious texts such as the ones in our corpus presents several challenges. First, authors tend to quote or paraphrase earlier texts, occasionally copying large chunks of texts. Second, many classical texts include contemporary introductions that are written in MSA. We touch upon the first issue in the next section, but leave a more systematic treatment of such problems for future work.

4 Corpus Enhancements

4.1 Text reuse and duplication

A major desideratum in approaching this corpus is being able to detect, and potentially eliminate duplicate and reused text segments. Quotation of extensive sections of material is common in the Islamicate literary tradition, but unlike modern quotation it is not distinguished from the text at large. Identification of reused text is valuable for computational linguistic work, and for DH projects.

Previous work on text reuse addressed the problem in the context of domains such as law bills or newspaper texts (Smith et al., 2014; Wilkerson et al., 2015). Much of the previous work relies on n-grams to align similar chunks of texts; we refer to Smith et al. (2014); Li (2016) for more details.[13] An especially interesting study is Zemánek and Milička (2014), which detected quotations in the CLAUDia corpus (Section 2) and built a network of documents based on metadata and quoted texts. However, their method focuses on long, verbatim quotations, whereas we are interested in approximately-matching parallel passages with possible variations. A standard approach to approximate-matching tasks is the use of edit-distance measures such as Levenshtein Distance; however, such an approach is unfeasible given a corpus of this size. Instead, we follow a recent approach introduced by Shmidman et al. (2016) for finding parallel passages in a Hebrew/Aramaic corpus. This method is appealing to use in our case for two reasons: the similarity between Arabic and Hebrew and the very efficient algorithm that can handle such a large corpus. We briefly review their approach and then describe our adaptation of the method.

In Shmidman et al. (2016), every word in the corpus is represented by a two-letter hash, containing the two least common-letters from within the word. Then, for every position in the text, the subsequent 5 words are represented by four separate skip-grams, each one omitting a different word. These hashes and skip-grams allow efficient hash-based identification of matching passages while allowing for variants in orthography, differing prefixes and suffixes, and interpolated or omitted words. However, in order to apply this algorithm to the Shamela corpus, we first needed to remove the many "boiler plate" sentences and paragraphs which recur dozens, hundreds, or thousands of times within the corpus. These numerous repetitions would otherwise cause the sets of matching skip-grams to expand to unwieldy sizes.

We ran a preprocessing procedure to identify and mark all such phrases over the entire corpus (815

---

[12]The texts are dated by the Islamic calendar ('H', for *hijriyy*), which we convert to Gregorian dates ('CE'). We coded texts by living authors with the date 1440 H/2018 CE to distinguish them from authors with a 1434-1435/2013 CE DOD.

[13]A notable system is `passim`, available at: `https://github.com/dasmiq/passim`. For a pilot application to Arabic, see `http://kitab-project.org/kitab/index.jsp`.

million words). It took two hours on a 32-CPU machine, marking 18,661,633 words (about 2 percent of the corpus) as part of frequently-recurring passages. After excluding those passages, we ran the full skip-gram algorithm. As of this writing, the skip-gram algorithm completed over one third of the corpus, running for about a week on a 128-CPU machine and outputting more than 5 million pairwise matches of passages over 20 words in length, with an average length of 40 words.

A manual inspection of the results shows that the text reuse algorithm is extremely promising. The preprocessing step largely identifies formulaic prayers and Quranic verses. Occasionally, it captures lengthy sayings of the prophet (*hadith*) when they are repeated frequently enough in the corpus. The results of the main run still included many sayings of the prophet, since they are an extremely important topic in Islamic thought, but almost no simply formulaic utterances. Furthermore, the repeated segments from the main run are more indicative of quotation. As one example among many, we are able to track the quotation of a single paragraph-length biography of a rather disreputable sheikh from its earliest quotation in 1359 CE, to another text in 1437 CE, to another in 1505 and finally to a modern text.

4.2 Text dating

While most of the texts in our corpus are dated by the author's date of death (Section 3), a large portion has no associated date. In most cases, the date metadata was simply never entered, but can usually be verified by manual inspection of the metadata records (author information is often in prose form and includes dates) or the text itself. Here we consider how to automatically date undated texts in our corpus.

There is a fairly large body of work on text dating, especially using clues like time expressions, but also various other features (Dalli and Wilks, 2006; Chambers, 2012; Niculae et al., 2014; Popescu and Strapparava, 2015). Previous research operated at different granularity levels and algorithmic methods, including pairwise learning-to-rank and multi-class SVMs (Niculae et al., 2014; Popescu and Strapparava, 2015). Here we choose a simple approach to text dating, based on language models, which were also used by de Jong et al. (2005), although in a different way.

We formulate our dating problem as a ranking task. Given an undated text, we would like to generate a ranked list of candidate dates. This formulation can facilitate subsequent manual inspection of the texts. It can also be useful for language technology applications that require an approximate date.

We randomly split the dated texts in our corpus into train and test sets, containing 80% and 20% of the texts, respectively. This resulted in about 4500 texts for training and 900 for testing. We excluded dictionary documents from this experiment, as they tend to contain word items from various periods in time and can obscure the results. In practice, we bin the range of dates into buckets of 100 years to avoid sparsity.[14] Then, for every 100 years range in our training corpus, we build a 5-gram language model with Knesser-Nay smoothing, using the SRILM toolkit (Stolcke, 2002; Stolcke et al., 2011). Finally, for each text in our test corpus, we evaluate all trained language models, record their perplexity scores, and rank the predicted date ranges based on increasing perplexity values.

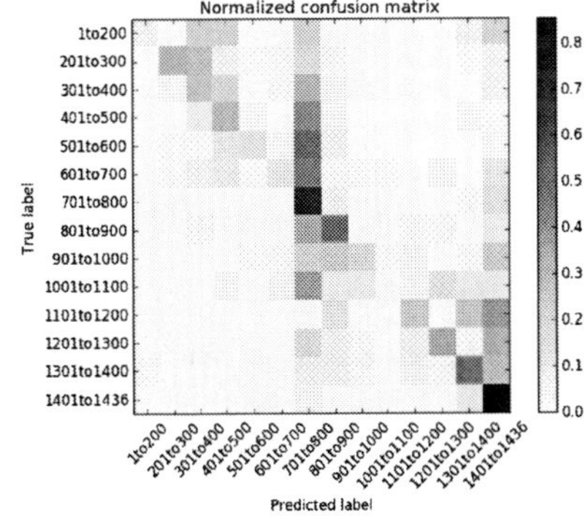

Figure 2: Text dating confusion matrix.

Table 2 shows the results of our text dating experiment, measured in accuracy at the top-k predicted dates. The standard accuracy (at top-1) of the algorithm is 42.95, far above a random baseline of 7.14 and a majority baseline of 20.29. The correct result is found at the top-3 predictions over 70% of the time, which we find encouraging for facilitating future dating of the undated portion of the corpus.

Figure 2 shows the confusion matrix of the text dating algorithm. Most of the confusion occurs between subsequent date ranges, with two exceptions: the vertical bands at 701to800 and 1401to1436,

---

[14]Our Hijri-dated bins are: 1-200, 201-300, 301-400, ..., 1301-1400, 1401-1436, where we merge the 1-100 bin with 101-200 because it only contains 3 texts; the last bin runs from 1401 to the latest year in our corpus.

k	1	2	3	4	5	6	7	8	9	10	11	12	13	14
Acc	42.95	60.09	71.14	78.24	83.65	88.39	92.00	94.70	96.05	96.96	98.08	98.99	99.66	100.00

Table 2: Accuracy@k of the text dating algorithm.

indicating that texts from other periods are often wrongly predicted as belonging to these two periods. It may be that texts from these periods use more diverse language, which is reasonable at least for the modern period (1401to1436 Hijri, turn of the 20th century) given the revival of the Arabic language in modern times. However, it is more likely an artifact of a larger number of texts from these periods (Figure 1a), leading to better language models. Controlling for the size of the texts in each period is an interesting direction that we leave for future work.

Having confirmed the validity of this approach, we trained similar language models of 100-year bins from the entire dated corpus (training+testing). Then, we used these models to date all the undated texts. We manually examined around 10% of the automatically dated texts, chosen randomly, and the results reflect those shown in Figure 2. In general, when a text is single-authored, the highest ranked candidate date is typically correct; if the two candidate dates are adjacent, it is almost definitely from within that period. However, many undated texts are compilations of one kind or another, and therefore it is difficult to assign an exact date of authorship that would align with the language used in the text. For example, one text having the 9th century as the first and the 15th century as the second candidate date is actually a reorganization of a 9th century text with a 15th century commentary. The interwoven nature of these texts suggests that the most productive annotation procedure will be to use the confusion index as a tool to prioritize manual tagging, a sort of tagging triage. Since the corpus has more than adequate coverage of modern texts, we are primarily interested in increasing pre-modern text coverage and so the automatic dating algorithm can be used to prioritize manual tagging of texts that are more likely to be pre-modern.

5   Corpus applications

In this section we give examples of how this corpus can be utilized for digital humanities applications.

5.1   Digital Humanities

The Shamela corpus, distributed privately, has been used in a number of projects in the digital Islamic humanities, though not all of these projects have reached publication stage.[15] Material from Shamela and similar text collections have been combined with computational methods to explore which eras biographical chroniclers were interested in, the importance of geographical locations across the history of the Islamicate empires, and even to develop pedagogical materials using frequency to determine the ease of foreign language readings.[16]

5.2   Linguistics

The Shamela corpus also represents an important resource for exploring the history of Standard written Arabic. Two brief case studies show the quantitative and qualitative analysis made possible by this corpus. Traditionally, questions about the history of Arabic are studied through impressionistic textual analysis, typically with no quantitative data. In this section we illustrate how our corpus can be used to provide a more objective, data-driven answer for these kinds of questions.

The lifespan of Arabic words   Standard written Arabic (SA) is the language of writing across the Arabic world and was standardized very early in the Islamic period. Qualitatively, there appears to be very little variation between modern written Arabic and pre-modern written Arabic from any era. Indeed, native speakers of Arabic do not regularly distinguish between SA in different eras, referring to both as "eloquent Arabic." To a certain degree, a highly educated native speaker of Arabic should be able to approach texts from throughout the history of Arabic writing with significantly greater ease than an

---

[15]Many of the presentations and workshops at Brown University's recurring Islamic Digital Humanities Workshops have made use of the Shamela corpus: `https://islamichumanities.org`

[16]See `http://maximromanov.github.io` and Romanov (2013)

English speaker approaching pre-modern texts. We can use the Shamela corpus to check the intuition that there is a quantitative difference in the development of Arabic writing and the development of English.

To do this, we track the "life" of an Arabic word: for every word in the corpus, we find its first and last chronological usages.[17] As Figure 1b shows, Arabic words tend to have a very long life span — words from all eras are still current. We can compare this to the Corpus of Historical American English (COHA) (Davies, 2010). In the Shamela corpus the average Arabic word lifespan is 1124 years (SD: 338 years, median: 1222), about 83% of the time span of the entire corpus. In COHA, the average English word lifespan is 68 years (SD: 58, median: 60), about 36% of the overall time span of the corpus.

First Attestations A frequent task in historical lexicography is to investigate first attestations of words, or of particular uses of words. The techniques mentioned above have been used to find absolute first uses, but it is necessary to look at word contexts to investigate how words change. We consider a common linguistic hygiene genre that takes the form of 'say/don't say' statements, usually implying that a modern usage of a word is inauthentic and not attested in earlier texts. Texts in this genre often circulate as memes, though there are also published works. Since it basically catalogs lexical innovations, this genre can be very helpful for finding words which have changed in meaning over time. To illustrate the application of qualitative research within the corpus, we report our findings for one claim of change found in a widespread online 'meme' which features several supposed common errors.[18] The meme argues that the word *ḥawālay* 'around, approximately' is incorrectly used for approximation of number, though the source offers no guidance on how that word should be used.

To determine what the 'original' meaning of *ḥawālay* was and when it changed into its innovative meaning, we ran a concordancing algorithm across the entire corpus. The concordance was sorted by date, and visually inspected to determine the original usage of the word, and to determine when and how it changes. We found that in early attestations *ḥawālay* is used for physical approximation, referring to objects which physically surround or which are placed around or near a central location. Only later does it develop a numerical approximation function. However, the change in meaning happened quite early, and is not a modern innovation over Classical Arabic, as implied by the 'say/don't say' meme. The first instance of use as a numerical approximation occurs in a text whose author died in 1201 CE, i.e. well before the modern era (Ibn al Jawzi, 1992, vol. 17: 285). The Shamela corpus thus allows us to rapidly investigate the histories of individual words using the traditional tools of linguistic investigation.

6   Conclusion and Future Work

In this work we described our efforts to develop a large-scale, historical Arabic corpus, comprising 1 billion words from a 14-century time span. We also improved the quality of this corpus by automatic text dating and reuse detection, and demonstrated its utility for digital humanities and historical research.

In future work, we aim to delve deeper into the history of the Arabic language and its possible periodization. We would also like to investigate mutual sources of influence between different scholars by analyzing automatically extracted parallel passages. Finally, we hope this corpus will serve the NLP/DH communities in promoting better understanding of the Arabic language and the culture of its speakers.

References

Latifa Al-Sulaiti. 2004. Designing and Developing a Corpus of Contemporary Arabic. Master's thesis, The University of Leeds, Leeds, UK.

Abdulmohsen O. Al-Thubaity. 2015. A 700M+ Arabic Corpus: KACST Arabic Corpus Design and Construction. *Lang. Resour. Eval.*, 49(3):721–751.

Maha Alrabiah, A Al-Salman, and ES Atwell. 2013. The design and construction of the 50 million words KSUCCA. In *Proceedings of WACL2 Second Workshop on Arabic Corpus Linguistics*, pages 5–8.

---

[17]In order to focus on word meaning, rather than morphological variation, we work with word lemmas from our lemmatized version of the corpus throughout this section.

[18]The meme is extremely widespread. An example instance can be found here: `http://www.inciraq.com/pages/view_paper.php?id=200914073` (accessed 28.4.2016)

Tressy Arts, Yonatan Belinkov, Nizar Habash, Adam Kilgarriff, and Vit Suchomel. 2014. arTenTen: Arabic Corpus and Word Sketches. *Journal of King Saud University - Computer and Information Sciences*, 26(4):357 – 371. Special Issue on Arabic NLP.

Nathanael Chambers. 2012. Labeling Documents with Timestamps: Learning from their Time Expressions. In *Proceedings of the 50th Annual Meeting of the Association for Computational Linguistics (Volume 1: Long Papers)*, pages 98–106, Jeju Island, Korea.

Angelo Dalli and Yorick Wilks. 2006. Automatic Dating of Documents and Temporal Text Classification. In *Proceedings of the Workshop on Annotating and Reasoning about Time and Events*, pages 17–22, Sydney, Australia.

Mark Davies. 2010. The Corpus of Historical American English: 400 million words, 1810-2009. `http://corpus.byu.edu/coha`.

FMG de Jong, Henning Rode, and Djoerd Hiemstra. 2005. Temporal language models for the disclosure of historical text. Royal Netherlands Academy of Arts and Sciences.

Abdel-Hamid Elewa. 2004. *Collocation and Synonymy in Classical Arabic: A Corpus-based Approach*. Ph.D. thesis, The University of Manchester, Manchester, UK.

Nizar Habash and Owen Rambow. 2005. Arabic Tokenization, Part-of-Speech Tagging and Morphological Disambiguation in One Fell Swoop. In *Proceedings of ACL*.

Nizar Habash, Owen Rambow, and Ryan Roth. 2009. MADA+TOKAN: A Toolkit for Arabic Tokenization, Diacritization, Morphological Disambiguation, POS Tagging, Stemming and Lemmatization. In *Proceedings of the Second International Conference on Arabic Language Resources and Tools*.

Jamāl al-Dīn Abū al-Faraj Ibn al Jawzi. 1992. *al-Muntaam fī tārīḫ al-mulūk wa-l-ummam*. Dār al-Kutub al-ᶜIlmiyya, Beirut. d. 597H/1201CE.

Adam Kilgarriff, Pavel Rychly, Pavel Smrz, and David Tugwell. 2004. The Sketch Engine. In *Proceedings of EURALEX*.

William P. Li. 2016. *Language Technologies for Understanding Law, Politics, and Public Policy*. Ph.D. thesis, Massachusetts Institute of Technology, Cambridge, MA, USA.

Ji Milika and Petr Zemnek. 2014. Ranking Search Results for Arabic Diachronic Corpora. Google-like search engine for (non)linguists. In *Proceedings of CITALA 2014 (5th International Conference on Arabic Language Processing)*. Association for Computational Linguistics.

Elias Muhanna. 2014. Why Was the 14th Century a Century of Arabic Encyclopaedism? In Jason Knig and Greg Woolf, editors, *Encyclopaedism from Antiquity to the Renaissance*, chapter 16, pages 343–356. Cambridge University Press, Cambridge.

Vlad Niculae, Marcos Zampieri, Liviu Dinu, and Alina Maria Ciobanu. 2014. Temporal Text Ranking and Automatic Dating of Texts. In *Proceedings of the 14th Conference of the European Chapter of the Association for Computational Linguistics, volume 2: Short Papers*, pages 17–21, Gothenburg, Sweden.

Arfath Pasha, Mohamed Al-Badrashiny, Mona Diab, Ahmed El Kholy, Ramy Eskander, Nizar Habash, Manoj Pooleery, Owen Rambow, and Ryan Roth. 2014. MADAMIRA: A Fast, Comprehensive Tool for Morphological Analysis and Disambiguation of Arabic. In *Proceedings of the Ninth International Conference on Language Resources and Evaluation (LREC'14)*, pages 1094–1101, Reykjavik, Iceland.

Octavian Popescu and Carlo Strapparava. 2015. SemEval 2015, Task 7: Diachronic Text Evaluation. In *Proceedings of the 9th International Workshop on Semantic Evaluation (SemEval 2015)*, pages 870–878, Denver, Colorado.

M. A.A. Rashwan, M. A.S.A.A. Al-Badrashiny, M. Attia, S. M. Abdou, and A. Rafea. 2011. A Stochastic Arabic Diacritizer Based on a Hybrid of Factorized and Unfactorized Textual Features. *Trans. Audio, Speech and Lang. Proc.*, 19(1):166–175.

Maxim G. Romanov. 2013. *Computational Reading of Arabic Biographical Collections with Special Reference to Preaching in the Sunni World (661–1300 CE)*. Ph.D. thesis, University of Michigan, Ann Arbor, MI, USA.

Avi Shmidman, Moshe Koppel, and Ely Porat. 2016. Identification of Parallel Passages Across a Large Hebrew/Aramaic Corpus. *arXiv preprint arXiv:1602.08715*.

Abdulhadi Shoufan and Sumaya Alameri. 2015. Natural Language Processing for Dialectical Arabic: A Survey. In *Proceedings of the Second Workshop on Arabic Natural Language Processing*, pages 36–48, Beijing, China.

David A. Smith, Ryan Cordell, Elizabeth Maddock Dillon, Nick Stramp, and John Wilkerson. 2014. Detecting and Modeling Local Text Reuse. In *Proceedings of the 14th ACM/IEEE-CS Joint Conference on Digital Libraries*, JCDL '14, pages 183–192, London, United Kingdom.

Andreas Stolcke, Jing Zheng, Wen Wang, and Victor Abrash. 2011. SRILM at sixteen: Update and Outlook. In *Proceedings of IEEE Automatic Speech Recognition and Understanding Workshop*, volume 5.

Andreas Stolcke. 2002. SRILM - An Extensible Language Modeling Toolkit. In *Proceedings of the International Conference on Spoken Language Processing*, volume 2, pages 901–904.

John Wilkerson, David Smith, and Nicholas Stramp. 2015. Tracing the Flow of Policy Ideas in Legislatures: A Text Reuse Approach. *American Journal of Political Science*, 59(4):943–956.

Wajdi Zaghouani. 2014. Critical Survey of the Freely Available Arabic Corpora. In *Proceedings of the Workshop on Free/Open-Source Arabic Corpora and Corpora Processing Tools*.

Petr Zemánek and Jiří Milička. 2014. Quotations, Relevance and Time Depth: Medieval Arabic Literature in Grids and Networks. In *Proceedings of the 3rd Workshop on Computational Linguistics for Literature (CLFL)*, pages 17–24, Gothenburg, Sweden.

Feelings from the Past—
Adapting Affective Lexicons for Historical Emotion Analysis

Sven Buechel[1]   **Johannes Hellrich**[2]   **Udo Hahn**[1]

[1]Jena University Language & Information Engineering (JULIE) Lab
`http://www.julielab.de`

[2]Graduate School 'The Romantic Model'
`http://www.modellromantik.uni-jena.de`

Friedrich-Schiller-Universität Jena, Jena, Germany

Abstract

We describe a novel method for measuring affective language in historical texts by expanding an affective lexicon and jointly adapting it to prior language stages. We automatically construct a lexicon for word-emotion association of 18th and 19th century German which is then validated against expert ratings. Subsequently, this resource is used to identify distinct emotional patterns and trace long-term emotional trends in different genres of writing spanning several centuries.

1 Introduction

For more than a decade, computational linguists have endeavored to decode affective information[1] from textual documents, such as personal value judgments or emotional tone (Turney and Littman, 2003; Alm et al., 2005). Despite the achievements made so far, the majority of work in this area is limited in at least two ways. First, employing simple positive-negative polarity schemes fails to account for the diversity of affective reactions (Sander and Scherer, 2009) and, second, in contrast to the humanities where numerous contributions focus on emotion expression and elicitation (Corngold, 1998), very little work has been conducted by computational linguists to unravel affective information in historical sources.

Arguably the main problem here relates to the availability of language resources for detecting affect. Algorithms for measuring semantic polarity (positive vs. negative) or emotion typically rely on either annotated corpora, lexical resources (storing the affective meaning of individual words) or a combination of both (Liu, 2015). To ensure proper affect prediction, these resources must accurately represent the target domain but speakers of historical language stages (19th century and earlier) can no longer be recruited for data annotation. Prior work aiming to detect affect in historical text ignored this problem and relied on contemporary language resources instead (Acerbi et al., 2013; Bentley et al., 2014).

Using word embeddings, we tackle this problem by jointly adapting a contemporary affective lexicon to historical language and expanding it in size. Collecting ratings from historical language experts, we successfully validate our method against human judgment. In contrast to previous work based on the categorical notion of polarity (Cook and Stevenson, 2010), we employ the more expressive dimensional Valence-Arousal-Dominance (VAD; Bradley and Lang (1994)) model of affect, instead. As a proof of concept, we apply this method to a collection of historical German texts, the main corpus of the 'Deutsches Textarchiv' (DTA) [*German Text Archive*], in order to demonstrate the adequacy of our approach. Our data indicate that, at least for historical texts, academic writing and belles lettres, as well as respective subgenres, strongly differ in their use of affective language. Furthermore, we find statistically significant affect change patterns between 1740 and 1900 for these genres.

2 Related Work

Prior computational studies analyzing affect in non-contemporary text are very rare. To the best of our knowledge, the work by Acerbi et al. (2013) and Bentley et al. (2014) constitute the first of this kind. They construct a *literary* misery index by comparing frequency of joy-indicating *vs.* sadness-indicating words

---

[1]We here use *affect* as an umbrella term for both *semantic polarity* and *emotion*.

Proceedings of the Workshop on Language Technology Resources and Tools for Digital Humanities (LT4DH),
pages 54–61, Osaka, Japan, December 11-17 2016.

in the *Google Books Ngram* corpus (see below) and find correlations with major socio-political events (such as WWII), as well as the annual U.S. *economic* misery index in the 20th century.

As stated above, most prior work focused on the bi-polar notion of semantic polarity, a rather simplified representation scheme given the richness of human affective states (a deficit increasingly recognized in sentiment analysis (Strapparava, 2016)). In contrast to this representationally restricted format, the VAD model of emotion (Bradley and Lang, 1994), which we employ here, is a well-established approach in psychology (Sander and Scherer, 2009) which also increasingly attracts interest in the NLP community (see among others Köper and Schulte im Walde (2016), Yu et al. (2016), and Wang et al. (2016)). It assumes that affective states can be characterized relative to three affective dimensions: *Valence* (corresponding to the concept of polarity), *Arousal* (the degree of calmness or excitement) and *Dominance* (the degree to which one feels in control of a social situation). Formally, the VAD dimensions span a three-dimensional real-valued space which is illustrated in Figure 1, the prediction of such values being a multi-way regression problem (Buechel and Hahn, 2016).

Thanks to the popularity of the VAD scheme in psychology, plenty of resources have already been developed for different languages. For English, the *Affective Norms of English Words* (ANEW; Bradley and Lang (1999)) incorporate 1,034 words paired with experimentally determined affective ratings using a 9-point scale for Valence, Arousal and Dominance, respectively (see Table 1 for an illustration of the structure of such a lexicon). Warriner et al. (2013) provided an extended version of this resource (14k entries) employing crowdsourcing. As far as German-language emotion lexicons are concerned, ANGST (Schmidtke et al., 2014) is arguably the most important one for NLP purposes—it was only recently constructed (comprising 1,003 lexical entries) and replicates ANEW's methodology very closely (see Köper and Schulte im Walde (2016) for a more complete overview of German VAD resources).

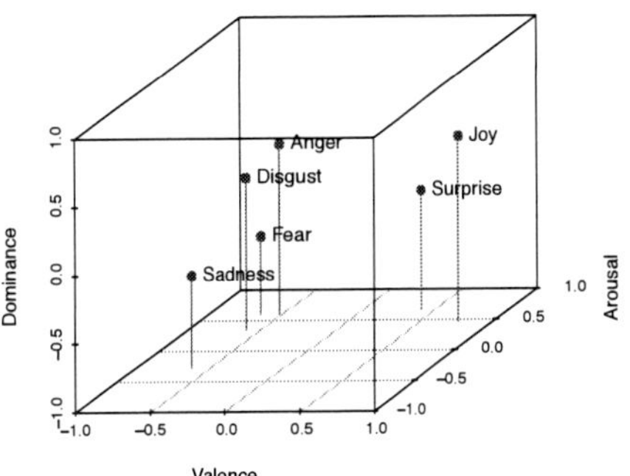

Figure 1: The three-dimensional space spanned by the VAD dimensions. For a more intuitive explanation, we display the position of six *basic emotions* (Ekman, 1992; Russell and Mehrabian, 1977).

As the manual creation of affective lexicons (polarity or VAD) is expensive, their automatic extension is an active field of research since many years (Turney and Littman, 2003; Rosenthal et al., 2015). Typically, unlabeled words are attributed affective values given a set of seed words with known affect association, as well as similarity scores between seed and unlabeled words. Concerning emotions in VAD representation, Bestgen (2008) presented an algorithm based upon a k-Nearest-Neighbor methodology which expands the original lexicon by a factor of 17 (Bestgen and Vincze, 2012). Cook and Stevenson (2010) were the first to induce a polarity lexicon for non-contemporary language from historical corpora by employing a pointwise mutual information (PMI) metric to determine word similarity and the much received algorithm by Turney and Littman (2003) for polarity induction. PMI is, like latent semantic analysis (LSA; Deerwester et al. (1990)), an early form of distributional semantics which, in the meantime, has been replaced by singular value decomposition with positive pointwise mutual information (SVD$_{PPMI}$; Levy et al. (2015)) and skip-gram negative sampling (SGNS; Mikolov et al. (2013)). Quite recently, evidence is available that the latter behaves more robust than the former (Hamilton et al., 2016).

Most prior studies covering long time spans (e.g., Acerbi et al. (2013)) rely on the *Google Books Ngram* corpus (GBN; Michel et al. (2011), Lin et al. (2012)). However, this corpus might be problematic for Digital Humanities research because of digitization artifacts and its opaque and unbalanced sampling (Pechenick et al., 2015; Koplenig, 2016). For German, we use the DTA[2] (Geyken, 2013; Jurish, 2013), which consists of books transcribed with double-keying and selected for their representativeness. The DTA aims for genre balance and provides a range of metadata for each document, e.g., authors, year, classification (like belles lettres and academic texts) and sub-classification (e.g., poem, biology, medicine).

---

[2]TCF version from May 11, 2016, available via www.deutschestextarchiv.de/download

3 Methods

Our methodology consists of two main parts. First, we adapt a contemporary VAD emotion lexicon to historical language and expand it jointly in size, and, second, we use this expanded lexicon to analyze emotions in historical language stages.

3.1 Inducing Historical VAD Lexicons

One of the most commonly used algorithms for affect lexicon induction was proposed a decade ago by Turney and Littman (2003) and put into practice for historical language by Cook and Stevenson (2010). Unfortunately, this procedure expects seed words of discrete polarity classes, a format we consider less informative for affective language analysis. For VAD vectors, we here employ the induction algorithm introduced by Bestgen (2008) instead. Bestgen's algorithm computes the affective score of the word w, $\bar{e}(w)$, given the set of the k nearest neighboring words to w from a seed lexicon, NEAREST(k, w), as

$$\bar{e}(w) := \frac{1}{k} \sum_{v \in \text{NEAREST}(k,w)} e(v) \tag{1}$$

where $e(v)$ is the emotion value of the word v, a three-dimensional VAD vector (see Table 1 and Figure 1 for illustration). We modify Bestgen's method by replacing LSA with SGNS for determining word similarity. In order to account for word-emotion association as present in historical language stages, we use word embeddings derived directly from the target language stage instead of contemporary ones. Seed values for the induction are taken from the contemporary ANGST lexicon (Schmidtke et al., 2014). This method results in a *hybrid* lexicon whose seed VAD values are empirically determined by contemporary speakers, whereas the similarity of words (and therefore the set of words taken into account when computing emotion values for words not in the seed lexicon) is determined from historical corpora. Although the emotion values computed in this way might be somewhat biased towards the contemporary language stage, such a hybrid lexicon should be more suitable for a historical analysis than lexicons with contemporary information only.

3.2 Measuring Textual Emotion

Building on an adapted lexicon, it is possible to (more) accurately determine the emotion values of historical texts. For this task, we use the Jena Emotion Analysis System[3] (JEMAS; Buechel and Hahn (2016)) since it has been (as one of the first tools for VAD prediction) thoroughly evaluated and is, to the best of our knowledge, currently the only tool for this purpose freely available. The lexicon-based approach it employs yields reasonable performance (Staiano and Guerini, 2014; Buechel and Hahn, 2016) and is easily adaptable to other domains by replacing the lexicon—a feature most valuable for historical applications as well. Basically,[4] it calculates the emotion value of a document d (a bag of words), $\bar{e}(d)$, as the weighted average of the emotion values of the words in d, $\bar{e}(w)$, as computed by Equation 1:

$$\bar{e}(d) := \frac{\sum_{w \in d} \lambda(w, d) \times \bar{e}(w)}{\sum_{w \in d} \lambda(w, d)} \tag{2}$$

where $\bar{e}(w)$ is defined as the vector representing a neutral emotion, if w is not covered by the lexicon, and λ denotes some term weighting function. Here, we use absolute term frequency as the resulting performance is among the best for automatically expanded lexicons (Buechel and Hahn, 2016).

4 Experiments

4.1 Gold Standard

One considerable difficulty concerning lexicons for historical language stages relates to their proper validation, since we lack native speakers for data annotation. Hence, to assess the quality of our results

---

[3] https://github.com/JULIELab/JEmAS
[4] For brevity, we only give a loose formal specification. See Buechel and Hahn (2016) for a more elaborated definition.

we constructed a small gold standard of 20 words annotated by seven doctoral students from various humanities fields. Their areas of expertise strongly overlap with the time periods covered by the slice of the DTA we are investigating. The instructions and rating scales follow the design of Warriner et al. (2013), yet with one crucial exception—subjects were requested to put themselves in the position of a person living between 1741 and 1900. We used such a wide temporal range since we expected different raters to ground their rating decisions on different time spans, varying with their historic expertise and acquaintance with a specific period. When averaging the different ratings, these biases should level off resulting in valid ratings relative to the entire time span. Our 20 stimulus words were randomly selected from words present within both the ANGST seed lexicon and the subset of the 1741–1900 DTA corpus, thus avoiding any "noisy" words such as annual figures. Table 1 provides some sample entries.

For comparison with existing resources, we measure inter-annotator agreement (IAA) by calculating the standard deviation between all given ratings for each word and dimension and then averaging these values for every VAD dimension (Average Standard Deviation; ASD). Our raters achieved an ASD of 1.61, 1.85, and 1.83 for Valence, Arousal, and Dominance, respectively. These IAA ratings are better than the ASDs reported by Warriner et al. (2013)—1.68, 2.30, and 2.16—suggesting that our experts are able to consistently rate non-contemporary word emotions.

4.2 Lexicon Expansion and Historical Adaptation

As mentioned before, we operate on the 1741–1900 part of the DTA. One text from this period written in Latin was excluded, leaving us with 1,022 texts. To ensure matches between this corpus and our VAD seed lexicon, we preprocessed ANGST (Schmidtke et al., 2014) with the CAB[5] lemmatization system used by the DTA (Jurish, 2013), without further filtering or modification of these entries. We then trained 200 dimensional SGNS embeddings[6] on this corpus.

Lemma	Valence	Arousal	Dominance
"Mutter" *(mother)*	2.00	-1.14	-1.29
"Erholung" *(recovery)*	0.86	-2.29	0.57
"giftig" *(poisonous)*	-2.29	1.86	-0.71
"Krise" *(crisis)*	-2.00	2.00	-0.86

Table 1: Sample entries from the historical gold standard relative to their empirically determined Valence-Arousal-Dominance (VAD) values.

We ran the modified version of Bestgen's expansion algorithm (see above) on these word embeddings using ANGST as seed lexicon. The k-parameter was determined by running the process for each integer $k \in [1, 50]$ measuring Pearson's r between original and induced values at each step. The correlation was highest for $k = 16$ ($r = 0.681$; average correlation over all three dimensions) which was thus employed to induce the final lexicon.

Our expanded and historically adapted lexicon comprises 143,677 word-emotion pairs. The correlation between these induced values and our historical gold standard amounts to $r = 0.75, 0.64$ and 0.56 for Valence, Arousal, and Dominance, respectively (the differences between the dimensions are consistent with prior work (Bestgen and Vincze, 2012)). Hence, our performance on historical data is even higher than the performance Bestgen and Vincze (2012) reported when using Bestgen's original algorithm to predict *contemporary* word emotions. We take this as a hint that our modifications (e.g., using SGNS instead of LSA) more than compensate for the additional difficulty of inducing *historical* word emotions.

4.3 Application to the DTA Historical Corpus

In order to demonstrate the potential of our approach for the Digital Humanities, we now examine the distribution of emotions in the DTA corpus relative to different categories of metadata. First, we take into account the genres of a document considering the whole study period. Second, we look at changes in emotions over time (also taking genre differences into account). Furthermore, of the three main genres distinguished within the DTA— belles lettres, academic texts and functional texts—we focus on the first

---

[5] Available via www.deutschestextarchiv.de/demo/cab/

[6] We used the PYTHON-based GENSIM implementation (accessible from https://radimrehurek.com/gensim/), with the following parameters: context window of up to 10 neighboring words, minimum word frequency of 10, negative sampling with 5 noise words and downsampling for words with a frequency of 10^{-3} or higher. We trained for 5 epochs, decreasing the learning rate from initial 0.025 down to 0.0001 in each of them.

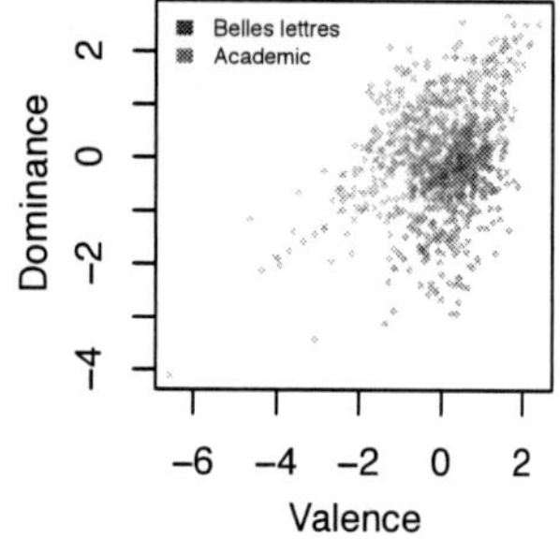
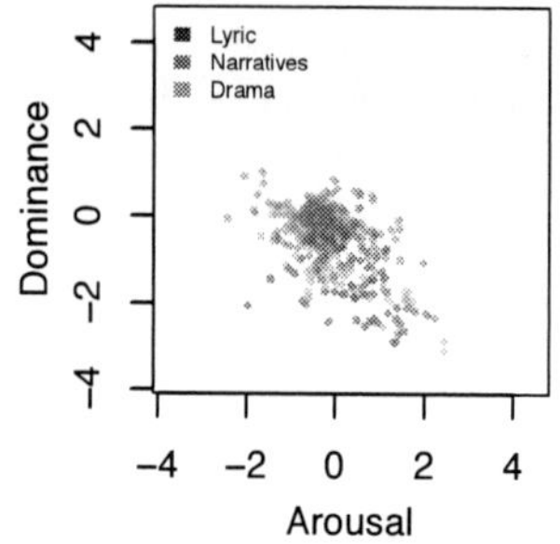
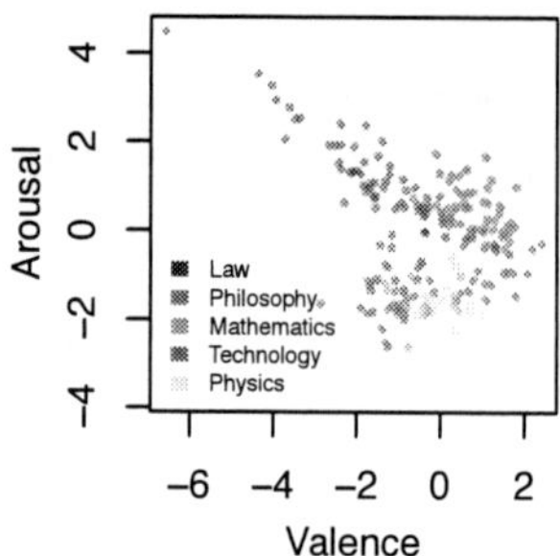

Figure 2: Distribution of two of the main document classes relative to Valence and Dominance.

Figure 3: Distribution of subclasses of belles lettres relative to Arousal and Dominance.

Figure 4: Distribution of five subclasses of academic texts relative to Arousal and Valence.

two because, upon inspection of the texts present in each category, they tend to be much more distinctively defined than the latter which, in our view, remains quite opaque.

For the following experiments, we processed the documents of the study period via JEMAS (see Section 3.2) employing the newly constructed historically adapted emotion lexicon. The VAD output of this system was standardized so that mean $M = 0$ and standard deviation $SD = 1$ for each dimension. Subsequently, we visualize our data with 2-D scatterplots each displaying two of the three VAD dimensions (Figures 2–4). Of the three possible plots (one for each pair of VAD dimensions) we here include the most illustrative ones for each comparison.

4.3.1 Distinction of Text Genres and Domains

Comparing belles lettres to academic texts, Figure 2 depicts their distribution relative to Valence and Dominance so that each data point relates to one document. The two genres are clearly separated[7] and their clusters show only little overlap. These observations suggest that the VAD values our system generates reflect the membership of a text for a certain genre. It may also indicate that our method is valid insofar as it catches some relevant intrinsic characteristics of the processed documents. To further illustrate the usefulness of our work for, e.g, literary studies or history of mind, we statistically tested whether these classes differ relative to the three emotional dimensions (using non-parametric tests; the data are, in general, not normally distributed) and give median (Md) values. In this setting, belles lettres display significantly higher Valence (Md = 0.39) and lower Dominance (Md = −0.40) than academic texts (Md = −0.22 and 0.42, respectively; $p < .05$ using a Mann-Whitney U test). This may reflect the technical nature of academic writing, e.g., explaining certain methodologies, and therefore expressing more control (which is closely related to Dominance).[8] Differences in Arousal were not significant.

Concerning the subgenres of belles lettres, we compared the predefined classes *lyric* and *drama*, and also *narratives*, a subclass we defined for this experiment subsuming different fine-grained distinctions between German terms for novels, novellas and tales. Again, a visual examination (see the Dominance-Arousal plot in Figure 3) reveals good separability. Dramas show lower Valence (Md = 0.00) than lyric and narratives (Md = 0.43 and 0.45, respectively), whereas lyric excels with high Arousal (Md = 0.43) contrary to narratives (Md = −0.22) and drama (Md = −0.13). Furthermore, narratives have a markedly higher Dominance (Md = −0.19) in contrast to lyric (Md = −1.44) and drama (Md = −1.23). The differences between the groups are significant relative to each dimension ($p < .05$; using the Kruskal-Wallis test, since we compare more than two groups).

Another striking distribution is depicted in Figure 4 which displays the relative positioning of five subclasses of academic texts, namely law, philosophy, mathematics, technology, and physics. Apparently, we come up with a clear (almost linear) separation between philosophy and law, on the one hand, and

---

[7]The notion of separability can be quantified as the performance of a classifier predicting the genre of a document given its VAD values. We ran these experiments in a pilot study finding good separability (almost 90% accuracy in this case) but exclude the details for brevity.

[8]The interpretations we offer in this section are meant as an illustration of how our quantitative data could be utilized within the (Digital) Humanities. We currently do not claim that these results can be taken for granted given our experimental data.

mathematics, physics and technology, on the other hand (thus empirically substantiating intuitions of different academic cultures dividing the sciences from the humanities (Kagan, 2009) in emotional terms). Also, the plot reveals more fine-grained features in line with common-sense intuitions about these study fields, e.g., parts of the philosophical texts are indistinguishable from law texts, while others show pronounced overlap with physics (possibly reflecting the impact of different subdisciplines, such as philosophy of law and philosophy of science). Also, physics and technology are fairly well set apart from each other, while mathematics seems to be equally similar to both. The qualitative fields display higher Valence and Arousal (Md = 0.26 and 0.54, respectively) than the quantitative ones (Md = -0.70 and -1.47). However, the sciences show higher Dominance than law and philosophy (Md = 1.12 as opposed to 0.53; all differences significant: $p < .05$ using a Mann-Whitney U test). Extending our interpretation concerning Figure 2, this may reflect the more technical nature of writings in the quantitative fields as opposed to the language-centered disciplines.

4.3.2 Shifts in Emotion over Time

We now turn to the question whether shifts in emotion can be traced in the texts of the DTA corpus over time. Again, we considered, first, all texts of the corpus, second, texts of the major academic class and, third, texts of the major class belles lettres. Due to data sparsity we did not take into account subclasses. We found clear evidence for long-duration shifts in emotion values considering the different groups. Performing linear regression, our data (quantified as the β-coefficient of linear regression models, i.e., the steepness of the regression line) suggest a specifically strong increase in Dominance concerning academic texts (possibly reflecting the establishment of a more technical style in scientific writing) and in the corpus as a whole, as well as a decrease of Arousal in belles lettres (possibly reflecting the shift from highly emotional sentimentalism via romanticism to rather descriptive realism (Watanabe-O'Kelly, 1997)). We summarize our findings concerning long-duration shifts in Table 2. These figures might seem rather small; recall, however, that the VAD values are normalized (given in SD) and that the documents we consider span 160 years so that, e.g., Arousal in belles lettres decreased by almost one SD (-0.96).

Lemma	Valence	Arousal	Dominance
Academic	-0.002*	0.000	0.003***
Belles lettres	0.001	-0.006***	0.001
All	-0.002*	-0.003***	0.004***

Table 2: β-coefficients of linear models predicting Valence, Arousal and Dominance (VAD), respectively, given a year. Levels of significance: * $p < .05$; ** $p < .01$; ***$p < .001$.

5   Conclusion

In this paper, we introduced a novel methodology for measuring emotion in non-contemporary texts by linking neural word embeddings derived from historical corpora, an adapted expansion algorithm for affective lexicons, and a lexicon-based method for emotion analysis. To demonstrate the potential of our approach for the Digital Humanities, we then conducted a study on emotional patterns within the DTA, a high-quality collection of historical German texts, using the multidimensional VAD model of emotion. This is the first application study of this kind, since prior studies on affect in historical texts were conducted with lexicons that were both non-specific for historical texts and less informative in terms of their affect representation scheme (Acerbi et al., 2013; Bentley et al., 2014).

We found evidence that different genres and subgenres of belles lettres and academic texts in the DTA show contrasting patterns in their emotional characteristics. Moreover, we identified pronounced long-term trends in textual emotions between 1741 and 1900. Both these observations can, though cautiously, be linked to explanatory patterns as discussed in the humanities (thus granting face validity to our findings).

We are interested in transferring these results to other languages, as well as conducting more fine grained temporal modeling, i.e., using multiple, temporally more specific lexicons for tracking emotional change. Future methodological work will focus on broadening the coverage of our gold standard as well as on the quality of induction algorithms for affective lexicons of historical language. Our induced historical word emotion lexicon in a format compatible with JEMAS and the gold standard are publicly available[9].

---

[9] https://github.com/JULIELab/HistEmo

Acknowledgements

This research was partly conducted within the Graduate School 'The Romantic Model' which is funded by grant GRK 2041/1 from the *Deutsche Forschungsgemeinschaft (DFG)*.

References

Alberto Acerbi, Vasileios Lampos, Philip Garnett, and R. Alexander Bentley. 2013. The expression of emotions in 20th century books. *PLoS ONE*, 8(3):e59030.

Cecilia Ovesdotter Alm, Dan Roth, and Richard Sproat. 2005. Emotions from text: Machine learning for text-based emotion prediction. In *HLT-EMNLP 2005 — Proceedings of the Human Language Technology Conference & 2005 Conference on Empirical Methods in Natural Language Processing. Vancouver, British Columbia, Canada, 6-8 October 2005*, pages 579—586.

R. Alexander Bentley, Alberto Acerbi, Paul Ormerod, and Vasileios Lampos. 2014. Books average previous decade of economic misery. *PLoS ONE*, 9(1):e83147.

Yves Bestgen and Nadja Vincze. 2012. Checking and bootstrapping lexical norms by means of word similarity indexes. *Behavior Research Methods*, 44(4):998–1006.

Yves Bestgen. 2008. Building affective lexicons from specific corpora for automatic sentiment analysis. In *LREC 2008 — Proceedings of the 6th International Conference on Language Resources and Evaluation. Marrakech, Morocco, 26 May - June 1, 2008*, pages 496–500.

Margaret M. Bradley and Peter J. Lang. 1994. Measuring emotion: The self-assessment manikin and the semantic differential. *Journal of Behavior Therapy and Experimental Psychiatry*, 25(1):49–59.

Margaret M. Bradley and Peter J. Lang. 1999. Affective norms for English words (ANEW): Stimuli, instruction manual and affective ratings. Technical Report C-1, University of Florida, Gainesville, FL.

Sven Buechel and Udo Hahn. 2016. Emotion analysis as a regression problem: Dimensional models and their implications on emotion representation and metrical evaluation. In *ECAI 2016 — Proceedings of the 22nd European Conference on Artificial Intelligence. Vol. 2: Long Papers. The Hague, The Netherlands, August 29 - September 2, 2016*, number 285 in Frontiers in Artificial Intelligence and Applications, pages 1114–1122.

Paul Cook and Suzanne Stevenson. 2010. Automatically identifying changes in the semantic orientation of words. In *LREC 2010 — Proceedings of the 7th International Conference on Language Resources and Evaluation. La Valletta, Malta, May 17-23, 2010*, pages 28–34.

Stanley Corngold. 1998. *Complex Pleasure: Forms of Feeling in German Literature*. Stanford University Press.

Scott C. Deerwester, Susan T. Dumais, George W. Furnas, Thomas K. Landauer, and Richard A. Harshman. 1990. Indexing by latent semantic analysis. *Journal of the American Society for Information Science*, 41(6):391–407.

Paul Ekman. 1992. An argument for basic emotions. *Cognition & Emotion*, 6(3-4):169–200.

Alexander Geyken. 2013. Wege zu einem historischen Referenzkorpus des Deutschen: das Projekt Deutsches Textarchiv. In Ingelore Hafemann, editor, *Perspektiven einer corpusbasierten historischen Linguistik und Philologie. Internationale Tagung des Akademienvorhabens "Altägyptisches Wörterbuch" an der Berlin-Brandenburgischen Akademie der Wissenschaften. Berlin, Germany, December 12-13, 2011*, pages 221–234.

William L. Hamilton, Jure Leskovec, and Daniel Jurafsky. 2016. Diachronic word embeddings reveal statistical laws of semantic change. In *ACL 2016 — Proceedings of the 54th Annual Meeting of the Association for Computational Linguistics. Berlin, Germany, August 7-12, 2016*, volume 1: Long Papers, pages 1489–1501.

Bryan Jurish. 2013. Canonicalizing the Deutsches Textarchiv. In Ingelore Hafemann, editor, *Perspektiven einer corpusbasierten historischen Linguistik und Philologie. Internationale Tagung des Akademienvorhabens "Altägyptisches Wörterbuch" an der Berlin-Brandenburgischen Akademie der Wissenschaften. Berlin, Germany, December 12-13, 2011*, pages 235–244.

Jerome Kagan. 2009. *The Three Cultures: Natural Sciences, Social Sciences, and the Humanities in the 21st Century*. Cambridge University Press.

Maximilian Köper and Sabine Schulte im Walde. 2016. Automatically generated affective norms of abstractness, arousal, imageability and valence for 350,000 German lemmas. In *LREC 2016 — Proceedings of the 10th International Conference on Language Resources and Evaluation. Portorož, Slovenia, 23-28 May 2016*, pages 2595–2598.

Alexander Koplenig. 2016. The impact of lacking metadata for the measurement of cultural and linguistic change using the GOOGLE NGRAM data sets: Reconstructing the composition of the German corpus in times of WWII. *Digital Scholarship in the Humanities*, 32.

Omer Levy, Yoav Goldberg, and Ido Dagan. 2015. Improving distributional similarity with lessons learned from word embeddings. *Transactions of the Association for Computational Linguistics*, 3:211–225.

Yuri Lin, Jean-Baptiste Michel, Erez Lieberman Aiden, Jon Orwant, William Brockman, and Slav Petrov. 2012. Syntactic annotations for the GOOGLE BOOKS NGRAM corpus. In *ACL 2012 — Proceedings of the 50th Annual Meeting of the Association for Computational Linguistics. Jeju Island, Korea, July 10, 2012*, volume System Demonstrations, pages 169–174.

Bing Liu. 2015. *Sentiment Analysis: Mining Opinions, Sentiments, and Emotions*. Cambridge University Press.

Jean-Baptiste Michel, Yuan Kui Shen, Aviva Presser Aiden, Adrian Veres, Matthew K. Gray, The Google Books Team, Joseph P. Pickett, Dale Hoiberg, Dan Clancy, Peter Norvig, Jon Orwant, Steven Pinker, Martin A. Nowak, and Erez Lieberman Aiden. 2011. Quantitative analysis of culture using millions of digitized books. *Science*, 331(6014):176–182.

Tomas Mikolov, Kai Chen, Gregory S. Corrado, and Jeffrey Dean. 2013. Efficient estimation of word representations in vector space. In *ICLR 2013 — Workshop Proceedings of the International Conference on Learning Representations. Scottsdale, Arizona, USA, May 2-4, 2013*.

Eitan Adam Pechenick, Christopher M. Danforth, and Peter Sheridan Dodds. 2015. Characterizing the GOOGLE BOOKS corpus: Strong limits to inferences of socio-cultural and linguistic evolution. *PLoS One*, 10(10):e0137041.

Sara Rosenthal, Preslav I. Nakov, Svetlana Kiritchenko, Saif M. Mohammad, Alan Ritter, and Veselin Stoyanov. 2015. SEMEVAL-2015 Task 10: Sentiment analysis in Twitter. In *SemEval-2015 — Proceedings of the 9th Workshop on Semantic Evaluation @ NAACL-HLT 2015. Denver, Colorado, USA, June 4-5, 2015*, pages 451–463.

James A. Russell and Albert Mehrabian. 1977. Evidence for a three-factor theory of emotions. *Journal of Research in Personality*, 11(3):273–294.

David Sander and Klaus R. Scherer, editors. 2009. *The Oxford Companion to Emotion and the Affective Sciences*. Oxford University Press.

David S. Schmidtke, Tobias Schröder, Arthur M. Jacobs, and Markus Conrad. 2014. ANGST: Affective norms for German sentiment terms, derived from the affective norms for English words. *Behavior Research Methods*, 46(4):1108–1118.

Jacopo Staiano and Marco Guerini. 2014. DEPECHE MOOD: A lexicon for emotion analysis from crowd annotated news. In *ACL 2014 — Proceedings of the 52nd Annual Meeting of the Association for Computational Linguistics. Baltimore, Maryland, USA, June 22-27, 2014*, volume 2: Short Papers, pages 427–433.

Carlo Strapparava. 2016. Emotions and NLP: Future directions. In *WASSA 2016 — Proceedings of the 7th Workshop on Computational Approaches to Subjectivity, Sentiment and Social Media Analysis @ NAACL-HLT 2016. San Diego, California, USA, June 16, 2016*, page 180.

Peter D. Turney and Michael L. Littman. 2003. Measuring praise and criticism: Inference of semantic orientation from association. *ACM Transactions on Information Systems*, 21(4):315–346.

Jin Wang, Liang-Chih Yu, K. Robert Lai, and Xuejie Zhang. 2016. Dimensional sentiment analysis using a regional CNN-LSTM model. In *ACL 2016 — Proceedings of the 54th Annual Meeting of the Association for Computational Linguistics. Berlin, Germany, August 7-12, 2016*, volume 2: Short Papers, pages 225–230.

Amy Beth Warriner, Victor Kuperman, and Marc Brysbært. 2013. Norms of valence, arousal, and dominance for 13,915 English lemmas. *Behavior Research Methods*, 45(4):1191–1207.

Helen Watanabe-O'Kelly, editor. 1997. *The Cambridge History of German Literature*. Cambridge Univ. Press.

Liang-Chih Yu, Lung-Hao Lee, Shuai Hao, Jin Wang, Yunchao He, Jun Hu, K. Robert Lai, and Xuejie Zhang. 2016. Building Chinese affective resources in valence-arousal dimensions. In *NAACL-HLT 2016 — Proceedings of the 2016 Conference of the North American Chapter of the Association for Computational Linguistics: Human Language Technologies. San Diego, California, USA, June 12-17, 2016*, pages 540–545.

Automatic parsing as an efficient pre-annotation tool for historical texts

Hanne Eckhoff
UiT The Arctic University of Norway
hanne.m.eckhoff@uit.no

Aleksandrs Berdičevskis
UiT The Arctic University of Norway
aleksandrs.berdicevskis@uit.no

Abstract

Historical treebanks tend to be manually annotated, which is not surprising, since state-of-the-art parsers are not accurate enough to ensure high-quality annotation for historical texts. We test whether automatic parsing can be an efficient pre-annotation tool for Old East Slavic texts. We use the TOROT treebank from the PROIEL treebank family. We convert the PROIEL format to the CONLL format and use MaltParser to create syntactic pre-annotation. Using the most conservative evaluation method, which takes into account PROIEL-specific features, MaltParser by itself yields 0.845 unlabelled attachment score, 0.779 labelled attachment score and 0.741 secondary dependency accuracy (note, though, that the test set comes from a relatively simple genre and contains rather short sentences). Experiments with human annotators show that preparsing, if limited to sentences where no changes to word or sentence boundaries are required, increases their annotation rate. For experienced annotators, the speed gain varies from 5.80% to 16.57%, for inexperienced annotators from 14.61% to 32.17% (using conservative estimates). There are no strong reliable differences in the annotation accuracy, which means that there is no reason to suspect that using preparsing might lower the final annotation quality.

1 Introduction

Parsing historical texts is a complicated venture. One challenge is high variation on all levels both across and within texts, in particular the absence of standardised spelling. Another is the small number of texts available in digital form, and the even smaller amount of annotated resources which could facilitate the development of new tools (Pettersson et al., 2012). Moreover, the overall amount of existing texts can be small too, which means that the gain achieved by developing highly specialised tools can be limited. In the meantime, historical linguists usually expect their corpora to have high-quality annotation, and tend to be less tolerant towards errors than computational linguists on average, which is probably reasonable, given the relatively small sizes of the corpora. With this in mind, it is not surprising that historical treebanks tend to be manually annotated (Piotrowski, 2012). One way to make use of automatic annotation would be to develop parsers that can handle historical texts (Schneider, 2012). Another would be use off-the-shelf tools for pre-annotation and then correct their output manually. In this paper, we test whether the latter approach is efficient for Old East Slavic (also known as Old Russian) texts. The idea to combine pre-annotation with subsequent manual correction is, of course, not at all new. It has been used, for instance, in the development of the TIGER treebank of German (Brants et al., 2002), the SynTagRus treebank of Russian (Apresjan et al., 2006) and ICEPAHC, the diachronic treebank of Icelandic (Rögnvaldsson et al., 2012). We are not, however, aware of any systematic evaluation of whether this routine is more efficient than a fully manual annotation with respect to historical texts.

In section 2, we describe the treebank we use for this purpose. In section 3, we outline the format conversions we have to perform and the technical details of our parsing experiments. In section 4, we describe a parsing experiment in an idealised setting, where the test set has manually corrected morphological annotation and lemmatisation. In section 5, we move to realistic experiments, where the parser

Proceedings of the Workshop on Language Technology Resources and Tools for Digital Humanities (LT4DH),
pages 62–70, Osaka, Japan, December 11-17 2016.

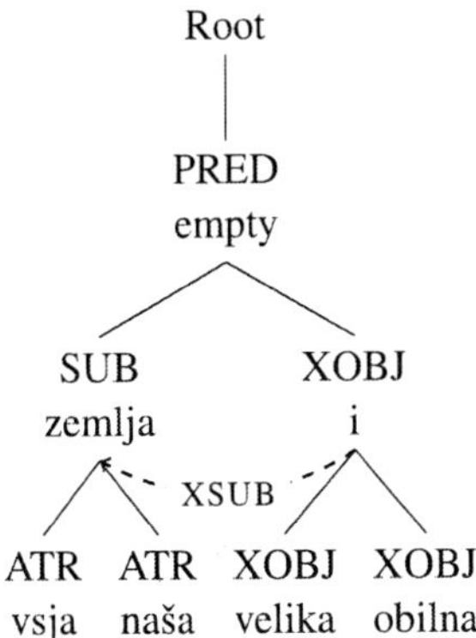

Figure 1: *vsja zemlja naša velika i obilna* 'all our land is great and bountiful' (Primary Chronicle 20.1–2, Codex Laurentianus)

has to deal with texts that have not been manually corrected. We present the results in section 6 and conclude in section 7.

2   The Tromsø Old Russian and OCS Treebank

The Tromsø Old Russian and OCS[1] Treebank (TOROT) is, to our knowledge, the only existing treebank of Old East Slavic and Middle Russian. It currently contains approximately 205,000 tokens equally divided between the two language stages.[2] The treebank belongs to a larger family of historical Indo-European treebanks originating in the project *Pragmatic Resources in Old Indo-European Languages* (PROIEL) at the University of Oslo, Norway, which built a parallel treebank consisting of the New Testament in its Greek original and translations into Latin, Gothic, Classical Armenian and Old Church Slavonic (OCS) (Haug et al., 2009). TOROT is an expansion of the OCS part of the PROIEL treebank.

All treebanks in the PROIEL family share an enriched dependency grammar scheme and a set of open-source online tools for annotation. The dependency scheme is inspired by Lexical-Functional Grammar, and is notable for allowing empty verb and conjunction nodes in ellipsis, gapping and asyndetic coordinations, and for the use of secondary dependencies to capture control and raising phenomena, shared arguments and predicate identity.[3] Figure 1 illustrates how empty tokens and secondary dependencies are used in a null copula construction.

The online annotation tool allows annotators to work online without any local installation of software. The tool guides the annotator through the annotation workflow: sentence division and tokenisation adjustment, lemmatisation and morphological annotation, and finally rule-guided manual dependency analysis. After the analysis, every sentence is reviewed, i.e. proofread by another project member.

The annotation tool allows import of texts with automatic pre-annotation. This is done as a matter of course for lemmatisation and morphological annotation in TOROT. In this paper we exploit the possibility to also import syntactic pre-annotation. It should be noted that the current annotation tool does not easily lend itself to merging sentences with syntactic pre-annotation. It is possible, but it requires a number of manual adjustments, which have been shown in pilot experiments to slow the annotators down to the extent that all speed gain is lost. In section 5, we therefore deal only with sentences that need no boundary adjustments.

---

[1] Old Church Slavonic

[2] TOROT can be browsed at `https://nestor.uit.no`, and versioned downloads may be obtained from `http://torottreebank.github.io/`. For a detailed description of the treebank, we refer the reader to Eckhoff and Berdičevskis (2015).

[3] See Haug et al. (2009). Full annotation guidelines and documentation are found at `http://folk.uio.no/daghaug/syntactic_guidelines.pdf`.

3   Parsing and format conversion

For the parsing experiments we used MaltParser (Nivre et al., 2007), version 1.9.0.[4] An earlier version
of MaltParser was shown to be able to parse modern Russian with decent accuracy (82.3% labelled
attachment score, Nivre et al. (2008)). For optimising the parser, we used MaltOptimizer (Ballesteros
and Nivre, 2012), version 1.0.3.[5] For evaluating parsing results in the CONLL format (this section), we
use MaltEval (Nilsson and Nivre, 2008), for evaluating full-fledged annotation in the PROIEL format we
use a specialised script (see below).

In order to do the parsing, we convert the PROIEL format annotation to CONLL-X format (Malt-
Parser 1.9.0 accepts the more convenient CONLL-U as input, but MaltOptimizer and MaltEval do not).[6]
After parsing is done, the output of MaltParser is converted back to PROIEL. In converting PROIEL
to CONLL, however, we lose information about empty nodes and secondary dependencies (see section
2). Technically, this information can be represented in the CONLL format (by adding empty tokens with
dummy form, lemma and features and by using columns 9 and 10 for secondary dependencies), but Malt-
Parser cannot reconstruct either empty tokens or secondary dependencies on its own, which means that
we have to sacrifice them. Shared dependencies are simply removed, while empty tokens are weeded
out from the trees according to a set of rules (designed to be simple and yet to facilitate subsequent
restoration of empty tokens).

In general, coordination is represented in PROIEL using a version of Prague-style coordination (according to the classification in Popel et al. (2013)): All conjuncts are attached under the coordinating
conjunction (empty conjunction if the coordination is asyndetic), the conjunction and the conjuncts have
the same incoming relation, as demonstrated in figure 1. When an empty conjunction is removed during
conversion to CONLL, the first conjunct is promoted into its place and gets a special temporary relation
"coord" (absent from the PROIEL inventory). During back-conversion to PROIEL, all nodes which have
the incoming relation "coord" are demoted, and empty conjunctions are restored, their original relations
restored from other conjuncts. Note that the removal of empty conjunctions leads to asyndetic coordination being represented in CONLL using what Popel et al. (2013) call Stanford style (the first conjunct
is the head and the remaining conjuncts and conjunctions are attached under it), the solution that is also
used in Universal Dependencies.[7] It means that syndetic and asyndetic coordination are represented differently in CONLL, which can arguably worsen the MaltParser's performance. It could potentially be
amended by converting the syndetic coordination to the same style, but at the cost of, first, additional
work, and second, potential loss of precision during back-conversion (in some cases it is not possible to
restore the original structure and labels).

For empty verbs, the conversion rules depend on whether the verb has a predicative complement
("xobj", see figure 1). If it does, the complement is promoted to the verb's place, and all other dependents
of the verb are attached under it. If it does not, all the dependents are placed directly under the node that
was the head of the empty verb. In all cases, all the dependents preserve their incoming relation labels,
i.e. we are losing information about the relation label that the empty verb had. When converting back
to PROIEL, a number of simple heuristics are used to reinsert empty verbs, to make sure that the nodes
placed directly under root conform to PROIEL requirements and to restore secondary dependencies
for control and raising ("xsub", see figure 1). No attempt is made to restore other types of secondary
dependencies, though that is technically possible (Berdičevskis and Eckhoff, 2015).

Obviously, some accuracy is lost during conversion and back-conversion processes. One particularly
important source of errors are structures where an empty token has another empty token as a head.
Before we move on to the parsing experiments, we want to evaluate how large the inevitable loss is.
Since the parsed output and the gold standard can potentially differ in the number of tokens (due to the
presence/absence of empty tokens), this makes applying standard attachment scores impossible. Various
evaluation methods that could be applied in such cases have been developed (Tsarfaty et al., 2011).

---

[4]http://www.maltparser.org/
[5]http://nil.fdi.ucm.es/maltoptimizer/install.html
[6]All data and scripts are found at http://dx.doi.org/10.18710/WIZHJN
[7]http://universaldependencies.org/

However, we use a simple script that was created specifically for PROIEL format and can handle both token misalignment and secondary dependencies.[8] Notably, this affects the LAS and UAS (labelled and unlabelled attachment score), since a missed or superfluous empty token counts as an attachment error.

The results of comparing the original manual annotation of the test set used in section 4 and the outcome of its conversion to CONLL and back to PROIEL are shown in table 1.

UAS	LAS	Empty token error	Secondary dependency accuracy
0.967	0.920	0.008	0.837

Table 1: Back-conversion accuracy, test set

The back-conversion is not perfect, but given that some loss of information is inevitable due to the richness of PROIEL format, we judge the final accuracy as acceptable. We use the same evaluation method for both parsing experiments, see sections 4 and 6. Note that the lossy conversion process contributes to making the PROIEL evaluator's UAS and LAS lower than those of MaltEval in section 4.

4 Parsing in an ideal world

Using the conversion process described in section 3, we first evaluate how well MaltParser can cope with Old East Slavic texts and PROIEL annotation in principle. We run the experiment in an idealised setting: For both training and test sets we use texts that have already been manually annotated and reviewed. That means that sentence division, tokenisation, lemmatisation and morphological annotation are as perfect as they can be, something which is never true for texts that have not been manually processed (see section 5). Obviously, the training sets also have high-quality syntactic annotation.

We use the 20160616 release of TOROT. As a test set, we take 20% of the sentences (randomly selected) from the Primary Chronicle, Laurentian Codex, one of the most important Old East Slavic manuscripts. The test set consists of 1453 sentences and 11105 tokens. We experiment with three training sets: LAV80, which consists of the remaining 80% of the Laurentian Codex (5816 sentences, 44174 tokens), KIEV, which comprises LAV80 and all other texts written at the same period (i.e. before 1400, during the so-called Kievan era; 8561 sentences, 76374 tokens), and ORV,[9] which comprises KIEV and all other Old East Slavic texts in the corpus (17661 sentences, 165104 tokens). We optimise the parser to each of the training sets. Following MaltOptimizer's recommendations, we use cross-validation for LAV80 and KIEV, but not ORV, since the ORV sample is large enough to make it unneccesary.

It can be expected that ORV will perform better than KIEV, while KIEV will perform better than LAV80 due to the differences in size. On the other hand, it is not impossible that genre will also matter. We expect LAV80 to be most similar to the test set, and ORV, which is most diverse as regards both genre and time of writing, to be least similar. The results show that size is the more important parameter, although the differences in performance are small. We estimate accuracy using both MaltEval on the CONLL format and the PROIEL evaluator on converted PROIEL xml, as shown in table 2. Note that the PROIEL evaluator yields considerably lower scores, both because it counts empty token errors as attachment errors, and because of the loss of accuracy in the conversion process (see section 3).

When preparsing texts for annotators to work on (see section 5), we use ORV as the training set.

5 Parsing in the real world

We are, however, interested in using parsing for practical purposes, i.e. for syntactic preprocessing to speed up the annotation process. Under these conditions, we are faced with a number of challenges.

---

[8]The script (found at `http://dx.doi.org/10.18710/WIZHJN`) compares gold and the compared analysis sentence by sentence, aligning the tokens of each. Since no retokenisations were allowed, all token number discrepancies were due to missed or superfluous empty tokens. In the PROIEL xml, empty tokens are always placed at the end, and are thus easy to align. If an empty token in either text had no match, it was aligned with nil. Such nil alignments are reported as "empty token errors". Note that since empty token errors also count as attachment errors, in this respect our UAS and LAS measures are stricter and more accurate than the ones obtained from MaltEval. "Secondary dependency accuracy" is the share of correctly attached secondary dependencies that are also correctly labelled and have the correct target, divided by the number of secondary dependencies in gold. LAS/UAS are calculated for primary dependencies only, not for secondary ones.

[9]orv is the ISO 639-2 code for Old Russian

Parse	Malt UAS	Malt LAS	UAS	LAS	Empty token error	Secondary dependency accuracy
LAV80	0.823	0.766	0.791	0.719	0.018	0.601
KIEV	0.831	0.775	0.797	0.727	0.018	0.622
ORV	0.839	0.786	0.804	0.734	0.018	0.627

Table 2: Parsing accuracy, test set

In order to preserve as much linguistic information as possible, we use manuscript-near text transcriptions with original mediaeval punctuation. Since we have a relatively large base of lemmatised and annotated forms, we are able to use a statistical tagger to provide morphological pre-annotation, as well as part-of-speech tags and lemma guesses. Old East Slavic displays particularly complex and linguistically interesting orthographic variation due to South Slavic influence, and it is not desirable to simply use a normalised text. The orthographic variation is, naturally, an impediment to statistical tagging. We solve the problem by normalising both the training data and the new text behind the scenes during the pre-annotation process, while the tokens stored in the treebank remain unnormalised (for a detailed description, see Berdičevskis et al. (2016)). However, the morphological and lemma/part-of-speech information we can provide is not good enough to use directly as linguistic data, and errors in the morphological preprocessing will necessarily cause problems in the parsing process as well. A single-feature morphological error, such as mistaking an accusative for a nominative, will typically produce label errors. A part-of-speech error, such as a verb misanalysed as a noun, can easily throw off the dependency structure of the whole sentence.

Sentence division is a larger problem. Texts are imported into TOROT with preliminary sentence division based on the original punctuation. Old East Slavic texts generally use syntactically motivated punctuation, but the punctuation usually indicates smaller syntactic units than the sentence. In the chronicle texts we are using in this paper, punctuation often separates subordinate clauses and participial constructions from the main clause, often quite neatly isolating a verb with its arguments. The conjuncts in a coordination are often also separated by punctuation, which is less convenient. A typical example is seen in (1), where the punctuation separates an adverbial participial construction from the main clause, and an adverbial PP from the participial construction. Within the main clause we see that the two coordinated complements of the preposition *s* 'with' are also split by punctuation.

(1)   i poide s družinoju svoeju. i perejaslavci. vzem mltvu vъ stěm mixailě. u jepspa jeufimъja.
      'and he went with his retinue. and the Pereyaslavians. having received prayer in St. Michael.
      from Bishop Jevfimij.' (The Suzdal' Chronicle, 6654)

Since we do not wish to use texts with editorial punctuation, and in many cases do not even have access to such punctuation, the final sentence division must necessarily be manual.[10] However, if the sentence division is done manually before syntactic preprocessing, we would be doing double work and would be likely to lose any speed gain.[11] Our syntactic preprocessing should therefore be performed before manual sentence boundary adjustment. This presents another problem (see section 2): if the annotators change boundaries of pre-parsed sentences, the effort required to save the existing trees will cost more than annotating sentences from scratch, as demonstrated in pilot experiments.

For the purposes of our experiment, we therefore selected a straightforwardly narrative passage from the Suzdal' Chronicle (year entries 6654, 6655, 6656, ms. Codex Laurentianus). We imported the text with preliminary sentence division according to the original punctuation, and manually selected only the sentences that did not need sentence boundary adjustment. Note that this limitation is a realistic one for our setting: The current version of the annotation tool will delete any preparsing if the annotator uses the in-built token and sentence boundary adjustment tools. The selected subset thus reflects the set of

---

[10]Automatic sentence division is not straightforward, since adverbial elements freely occur both before and after the main verb, making it difficult to automatically assess whether they belong to a preceding or subsequent verb.

[11]Note, however, that the developers of the diachronic Icelandic treebank ICEPAHC opted for exactly this solution: manual detection of clause boundaries before processing (Rögnvaldsson et al., 2012, 1980).

sentences that would retain preparsing in a real annotation setting.

We divided the passage into two approximately equal portions, hereafter referred to as Batch 1 and Batch 2 (see Table 4). Recall that it is impractical to change boundaries of pre-parsed sentences and attempt to save the trees. Due to the workflow organisation in TOROT, it is equally impractical to check the sentence division manually first and pre-parse later. A realistic solution is to pre-parse texts as they are, but spend no effort on preserving the trees if sentence boundaries have to be changed. However, in order to evaluate a potential speed gain, we run our experiment in a slightly artificial setting, i.e. limit the test set to the sentences that do not need boundary adjustment (as checked manually by the authors).

It should be noted that this experimental design systematically excludes longer and more complex sentences, which are known to be more difficult for the parser. The difference in sentence length between selected and non-selected sentences is given in table 3.

Batch	Sentence status	Mean	Max	Min	Median
batch 1	selected	4.9	10	2	5
batch 1	non-selected, unadjusted	4.9	10	2	5
batch 1	non-selected, adjusted	4.6	10	2	4
batch 2	selected	5.8	10	3	5
batch 2	non-selected, unadjusted	4.9	10	2	5
batch 2	non-selected, adjusted	10	21	2	9.5

Table 3: Sentence length in selected and non-selected sentences

Batch	Entries	Selected sentences	Selected tokens	Lemma/POS	Morphology
batch 1	6654, 6656	57	327	0.873	0.873
batch 2	6655	60	345	0.871	0.871

Table 4: Overview of selected sentences, accuracy of lemmatisation and morphological preprocessing.

The text batches were imported into the annotation web tool in four versions. In all four versions, the selected sentences were provided with automatic lemmatisation and part-of-speech tags with an accuracy of approx. 87%, as seen in table 4.[12] In two of the versions, the selected sentences were also preparsed as described in section 3. The annotators were presented with the full text entries, but used the presence of pre-annotation as an indication as to whether a sentence was to be annotated or not. They were also presented with a list of the ids of the selected sentences.

We selected four annotators for the experiment. Two of them, Volodimer and Olga,[13] had several years of experience with PROIEL-style annotation, and had annotated and reviewed around 200,000 tokens each. The other two, Rogned' and Lybed', were relatively inexperienced. Both had only annotated for a time span of a few months, and both had annotated a little over 2500 tokens each. Lybed' had been inactive for several months, Rogned' for several years. Thus, Volodimer and Olga had a perfect grasp of all technical aspects of the annotation tool, and very detailed knowledge of the annotation scheme. Lybed' and Rogned', on the other hand, had a good working knowledge of the annotation tool, but a much less detailed grasp of the annotation scheme. We expected Lybed' and Rogned' to benefit considerably more from the syntactic preprocessing.

The experienced annotators Volodimer and Olga received the following instructions:

- not to look at each other's annotation solutions

- to keep an accurate record of the time spent

- to annotate at their usual pace, but not spend time on major consistency checks

---

[12] Although the number of morphology and lemmatisation errors happen to be the same in both batches, they do not always occur in the same tokens – there are tokens with correct morphology but wrong lemmatisation and vice versa in both batches.

[13] We refer to the annotators by nicknames taken from the Primary Chronicle.

- to annotate *only* sentences with preprocessing and to use the sentence id list to go faster

- not to split, merge or retokenise, to accept the authors' sentence division and tokenisation judgements, even if they disagreed

Volodimer did the preprocessed text before the non-preprocessed one, while Olga did the non-preprocessed text before the preprocessed one. Rogned' and Lybed' were given the same instructions, but, unlike Volodimer and Olga, were both instructed to do the non-preprocessed text before the preprocessed one, thus deviating from the Latin square design. We made this change because both Rogned' and Lybed' were relatively inexperienced and had been away from annotation for a good while. They might therefore learn a lot from the first batch, which could improve their performance on the second batch. For the consequences of this design choice and handling the potential bias created by it, see section 6.

After the annotators had finished their annotation, their analyses were downloaded and saved, and the analyses in the production version of the text[14] were reviewed by the first author. This corrected version was also downloaded and saved, and serves as the gold standard in all of the comparisons in this paper.

6   Results: speed and quality

In the Suzdal' experiment, we see that all four annotators gained speed from working with preparsed sentences (table 6). The most inexperienced annotator, Rogned', had the greatest speed gain. To control for the potential bias caused by the fact that Rogned' and Lybed' were asked to do the the unparsed portion first, we also calculated separate annotation speeds for the first and second halves of each batch.[15]

	Unparsed 1	Unparsed 2	Parsed 1	Parsed 2
Rogned'	1.96	3.73	5.93	4.43
Lybed'	1.78	2.67	2.63	3.73

Table 5: Annotation speed gain, inexperienced annotators, tokens per minute

As seen in table 5, both did indeed increase their speed considerably from the first to the second half of the unparsed batch. We see that the benefits of preparsing are not easy to separate from the benefits of gained experience. However, it should be noted that Rogned', the least experienced annotator, does not gain speed between the first and second half of the preparsed batch, which suggests that most of her speed gain is due to the preparsing. In table 6 we report the gain from the second half of the unparsed batch to the whole preparsed batch as "conservative gain".

	Unparsed	Preparsed	Gain	Conservative gain
Olga	5.19	6.05	16.57%	–
Volodimer	3.45	3.63	5.80%	–
Rogned'	2.51	4.93	96.41%	32.17%
Lybed'	2.21	3.06	38.46%	14.61%

Table 6: Annotation speed, tokens per minute

The quality of parsing is reported in tables 7 and 8. We see that the quality of the raw parse is actually better than the "ideal-world" parse in section 4 (0.804 UAS, 0.734 LAS, with the same training set), even though we used imperfect automatic morphology and part-of-speech assignment/lemmatisation. This is probably due to our selection of text and sentences: The choice of a straightforward narrative passage means that the syntax is considerably simpler than it would be in e.g. a religious passage. The fact that we narrowed our selection down to only full sentences naturally delimited by the mediaeval punctuation effectively excluded all long sentences, which are more difficult for the parser.

---

[14]The non-preparsed version of Batch 1 and Batch 2 as analysed by Olga and Volodimer.

[15]Batch 1 part 1: year entry 6654 (174 tokens), Batch 1, part 2: year entry 6656 (153 tokens), Batch 2, part 1: the first 190 tokens of year entry 6655, Batch 2, part 2: the last 155 tokens of year entry 6655.

Status	Annotator	UAS	LAS	Empty token error	Secondary dependency accuracy
Raw parse		0.843	0.783	0.121	0.714
No preparsing	Olga	0.954	0.945	0.030	0.952
No preparsing	Rogned'	0.948	0.792	0	0.666
Preparsed	Volodimer	0.988	0.970	0	0.952
Preparsed	Lybed'	0.945	0.878	0	0.762

Table 7: Parsing accuracy, Batch 1

Status	Annotator	UAS	LAS	Empty token error	Secondary dependency accuracy
Raw parse		0.848	0.776	0.574	0.769
No preparsing	Volodimer	0.991	0.983	0	0.962
No preparsing	Lybed'	0.925	0.884	0	0.808
Preparsed	Olga	0.980	0.954	0	0.962
Preparsed	Rogned'	0.945	0.827	0	0.692

Table 8: Parsing accuracy, Batch 2

As expected, there is a great performance gap between the experienced and inexperienced annotators. All human annotators have better UAS than the parser, but the inexperienced annotators do not have much better LAS than the parser, and they sometimes perform worse when it comes to secondary dependencies. For Volodimer and Olga, there is no discernable quality gain or drop under the preparsed condition. For the inexperienced annotators, there are some differences: Lybed' has a better UAS under the preparsed condition, and Rogned' has a better LAS under the preparsed condition (but note again that, unlike Volodimer and Olga, they have become noticeably more experienced after having dealt with the unparsed condition).

7 Conclusions

While it is not possible, given state of the art, to create high-quality historical corpora using automatic parsing only, it is not unlikely that parsing can be an efficient pre-annotation tool. We examined whether this is the case using Old East Slavic texts. Using the most conservative evaluation method, which takes into account PROIEL-specific features, such as empty tokens, MaltParser yields 0.804 UAS, 0.734 LAS, 0.627 secondary dependency accuracy on an "ideal" test set and 0.845 UAS, 0.779 LAS, 0.741 secondary dependency accuracy on a "real" test set. Note that while the real test set does not boast perfect morphological annotation and lemmatisation, it comes from a relatively simple genre (narrative) and was limited to contain few long sentences, which probably explains the high performance.

Experiments with human annotators show that preparsing, if limited to sentences where no changes to word or sentence boundaries are required, increases their annotation rate. For experienced annotators, the speed gain varies from 5.80% to 16.57%, for inexperienced annotators from 14.61% to 32.17% (using conservative estimates). Since the current version of the annotation tool only allows us to retain preparsing in sentences that meet the test set conditions, this is a gain which would not be lost if we were to introduce preparsing as a routine procedure. There are no strong reliable differences in the annotation accuracy, which means that there is no reason to suspect that using preparsing might lower the annotation quality (if any effect can be expected, it is that of higher consistency).

From that, we can conclude that even given that historical texts are difficult to parse and that the current annotation interface of the TOROT is not well-suited for syntactic pre-annotation, parsing can still be used as an efficient pre-annotation tool.

References

Juri Apresjan, Igor Boguslavsky, Boris Iomdin, Leonid Iomdin, Andrei Sannikov, and Victor Sizov. 2006. A syntactically and semantically tagged corpus of Russian: State of the art and prospects. In *Proceedings of the Fifth International Conference on Language Resources and Evaluation, LREC 2006, Genoa, Italy, May 22–28, 2006*, pages 1378–1381.

Miguel Ballesteros and Joakim Nivre. 2012. MaltOptimizer: A system for MaltParser optimization. In *Proceedings of the Eighth International Conference on Language Resources and Evaluation (LREC)*, Istanbul.

Aleksandrs Berdičevskis and Hanne Eckhoff. 2015. Automatic identification of shared arguments in verbal coordinations. In *Computational Linguistics and Intellectual Technologies: Proceedings of the International Conference Dialogue 2015*, pages 33–43, Moscow.

Aleksandrs Berdičevskis, Hanne Eckhoff, and Tatiana Gavrilova. 2016. The beginning of a beautiful friendship: Rule-based and statistical analysis of Middle Russian. In *Computational Linguistics and Intellectual Technologies: Proceedings of the International Conference Dialogue 2016*, pages 99–111, Moscow.

Sabine Brants, Stefanie Dipper, Silvia Hansen, Wolfgang Lezius, and George Smith. 2002. The TIGER treebank. In *Proceedings of the Workshop on Treebanks and Linguistic Theories*, Sozopol.

Hanne Martine Eckhoff and Aleksandrs Berdičevskis. 2015. Linguistics vs. digital editions: The Tromsø Old Russian and OCS Treebank. *Scripta & e-Scripta*, 14–15:9–25.

Dag Trygve Truslew Haug, Marius Jøhndal, Hanne Martine Eckhoff, Eirik Welo, Mari Johanne Bordal Hertzenberg, and Angelika Müth. 2009. Computational and linguistic issues in designing a syntactically annotated parallel corpus of Indo-European languages. *Traitement Automatique des Langues*, 50.

Jens Nilsson and Joakim Nivre. 2008. MaltEval: an evaluation and visualization tool for dependency parsing. In *Proceedings of the Sixth International Conference on Language Resources and Evaluation (LREC'08)*, Marrakech. http://www.lrec-conf.org/proceedings/lrec2008/.

Joakim Nivre, Johan Hall, Jens Nilsson, Atanas Chanev, Gülsen Eryigit, Sandra Kübler, Svetoslav Marinov, and Erwin Marsi. 2007. MaltParser: A language-independent system for data-driven dependency parsing. *Natural Language Engineering*, 13(2):95–135.

Joakim Nivre, Igor Boguslavsky, and Leonid L. Iomdin. 2008. Parsing the SynTagRus treebank of Russian. In Donia Scott and Hans Uszkoreit, editors, *Proceedings of the 22nd International Conference on Computational Linguistics (COLING)*, pages 641–648.

Eva Pettersson, Beáta Megyesi, and Joakim Nivre. 2012. Parsing the past – identification of verb constructions in historical text. Workshop on Language Technology for Cultural Heritage, Social Sciences, and Humanities, European Association for Computational Linguistics, Avignon.

Michael Piotrowski. 2012. *Natural Language Processing for Historical Texts*. Morgan & Claypool, San Rafael.

Martin Popel, David Mareček, Jan Stepánek, Daniel Zeman, and Zdenek Zabokrtský. 2013. Coordination structures in dependency treebanks. In *ACL (1)*, pages 517–527. The Association for Computer Linguistics.

Eiríkur Rögnvaldsson, Anton Karl Ingason, Einar Freyr Sigurðsson, and Joel Wallenberg. 2012. The Icelandic Parsed Historical Corpus (IcePaHC). In *Proceedings of the Eighth International Conference on Language Resources and Evaluation, LREC 2012, Istanbul, Turkey, May 23–25, 2012*, pages 1977–1984.

Gerold Schneider. 2012. Adapting a parser to historical English. *Studies in Variation, Contacts and Change in English*, 10.

Reut Tsarfaty, Joakim Nivre, and Evelina Andersson. 2011. Evaluating dependency parsing: Robust and heuristics-free cross-annotation evaluation. In *Proceedings of the 2011 Conference on Empirical Methods in Natural Language Processing, EMNLP 2011, 27-31 July 2011*, pages 385–396.

A Visual Representation of
Wittgenstein's *Tractatus Logico-Philosophicus*

Anca Bucur
Center of Excellence in Image Study,
Faculty of Letters,
Solomon Marcus Center
for Computational Linguistics,
University of Bucharest
anca.m.bucur@gmail.com

Sergiu Nisioi
Faculty of Mathematics and
Computer Science,
Solomon Marcus Center
for Computational Linguistics,
University of Bucharest
sergiu.nisioi@gmail.com

Abstract

In this paper we present a data visualization method together with its potential usefulness in digital humanities and philosophy of language. We compile a multilingual parallel corpus from different versions of Wittgenstein's *Tractatus Logico-Philosophicus*, including the original in German and translations into English, Spanish, French, and Russian. Using this corpus, we compute a similarity measure between propositions and render a visual network of relations for different languages.

1 Introduction

Data visualization techniques can be essential tools for researchers and scholars in the humanities. In our work, we propose one such method that renders concepts and phrases as a network of semantic relations. In particular, we focus on a corpus built from different translations of the *Logisch-Philosophische Abhandlung* (Wittgenstein, 1921) from German into English, French, Italian, Russian, and Spanish.

Wittgenstein in his later works states that *meaning is use* (Wittgenstein, 1953): *43. For a large class of cases –though not for all– in which we employ the word "meaning" it can be defined thus: the meaning of a word is its use in the language game. And the meaning of a name is sometimes explained by pointing to its bearer.*

This idea anticipated and influenced later research in semantics, including the *distributional hypothesis* (Harris, 1954; Firth, 1957) and more recently, work in computational linguistics (Lenci, 2008). Distributional semantics works on this very principle, by making use of data to build semantic structures from the contexts of the words. Word embeddings (Mikolov et al., 2013) are one such example of semantic representation in a vector space constructed based on the context in which words occur. In our case, we extract a dictionary of concepts by parsing the English sentences and we infer the semantic relations between the concepts based on the contexts in which the words appear, thus we construct a semantic network by drawing edges between concepts.

Furthermore, we generalize on this idea to create a visual network of relations between the phrases in which the concepts occur. We have used the multilingual parallel corpora available and created networks both for the original and the translated versions. We believe this can be helpful to investigate not only the translation from German into other languages, but also how translations into English influence translations into Russian, French or Spanish. For example, certain idioms and syntactic structures are clearly missing in the original German text, but are visible in both the English and Spanish versions.

2 Dataset

The general structure of the text has a tree-like shape, the root is divided into 7 propositions, and each proposition has its own subdivisions and so on and so forth, in total numbering 526 propositions. A *proposition* is the structuring unit from the text and not necessarily propositions in a strict linguistic sense. Our corpus contains the original German version of the text (Wittgenstein, 1921) together with translations into 5 different languages: English, Italian, French, Russian, and Spanish. For English, we

Proceedings of the Workshop on Language Technology Resources and Tools for Digital Humanities (LT4DH),
pages 71–75, Osaka, Japan, December 11-17 2016.

have two translations variants, one by Ogden and Ramsey (1922) revised by Wittgenstein himself and another one by Pears and McGuinness (1961).

Since the text has a fixed form structure, it is straight forward to align each translation at the proposition level. In addition, we also employ a word-alignment method to create a multilingual parallel word-aligned corpus and to be able to inspect how certain concepts are translated into different languages. The exact size of each version in the corpus[1] is detailed in Table 1. Our corpus contains a relatively small number (526) of aligned examples and alignment methods often fail to find the correct pairs between words. To create the word-alignment pairs, we have experimented with different alignment strategies including GIZA++ (Och and Ney, 2000), fast align (Dyer et al., 2013) and efmaral (Östling and Tiedemann, 2016), while the later proved to output the best results in terms of our manual evaluation.

Language	Translator	No. of tokens	No. of types
German	——	18,991	4,364
English	Ogden and Ramsey	20,766	3,625
English	Pears & McGuinness	21,392	3,825
French	G.G. Granger	22,689	4,178
Italian	G.C.M. Colombo	18,943	4,327
Russian	M.S. Kozlova	10,682	4,090
Spanish	E.T. Galvan	13,800	3,191

Table 1: The size of each corpus in the dataset

The two translations into English share a lot in common, however they are not equivalent, for example, the German concept *Sachverhaltes* is translated by Ogden and Ramsey (1922) as *atomic facts* and in Pears and McGuinness (1961)'s version the same concept is translated as *states of affairs*. As for the other languages, the Spanish and Russian translations resemble more the former English version, *Sachverhaltes* being translated as *hechos atomicos* and атомарного факта *(atomarnogo fakta)*, respectively. In French and Italian, the concept is translated as *états des choses* and *stati di cosi* following the Pears and McGuinness (1961) English translation.

3 Wittgenstein's Network

3.1 Tractatus Network

The *Tractatus Network*[2] is obtained from different versions of the text by computing a pair-wise similarity measure between propositions. Each proposition is tokenized and each token is stemmed or lemmatized. The lemmatizer is available only for English by querying WordNet (Fellbaum, 1998), for the remaining languages different Snowball stemmers are available in NLTK (Bird et al., 2009). Stop words from each proposition are removed before computing the following similarity score:

$$Similarity(p_1, p_2) = \frac{|p_1 \cap p_2|}{max(|p_1|, |p_2|)} \tag{1}$$

The similarity score computes the number of common tokens between two propositions normalized by the length of the longest proposition, to avoid bias for inputs of different lengths. Two propositions are connected by an edge if their similarity exceeds the 0.3f threshold. To render the network, we use a browser-based drawing library[3], the lengths of the edges are determined by the similarity value and the nodes representing propositions are colored based on the parent proposition (labeled from 1 to 7). Furthermore, we added a character n-grams search[4] capability for the network that highlights the node with the highest similarity to the search string.

---

[1]The dataset is available upon request from the authors.
[2]The *Tractatus Network* is accessible at `https://tractatus.gitlab.io`
[3]`http://visjs.org/`
[4]`http://fuse.js/`

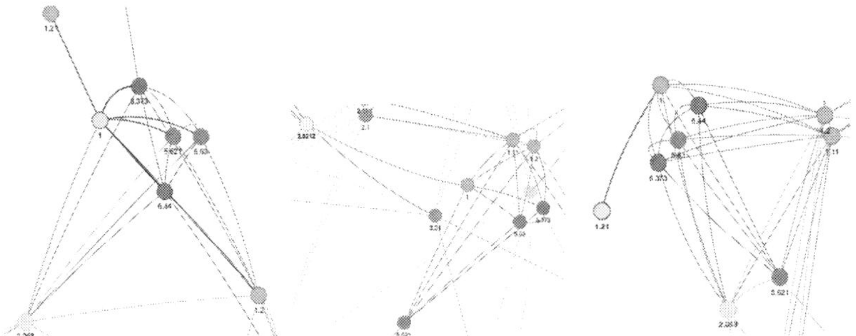

Figure 1: Two excerpts from the *Tractatus Network*. From left to right we have the German original, the translations into English by Pears and McGuinness (1961) in the center, and the Ogden and Ramsey (1922) translation on the right. Propositions from different groups may resemble each other more than the propositions within the same group.

By analyzing the resulted networks, we can observe that the seven main propositions in the text including the sub-divisions are not necessarily hierarchical, at leas not based on the topics addressed, rather the *Tractatus* has a rhizomatic structure in which the propositions are entangled and repeatedly make use of similar concepts. The excerpts rendered in Figure 1 and Figure 2 bring further evidence to this observation, as an example the proposition *die gesamte Wirklichkeit ist die Welt* meaning *the total reality is the world* appears in almost every version close to the propositions in group one in which *die Welt / the world* plays a central role. In Figure 1, the Pears and McGuinness (1961) English translation has a smaller number of relations between propositions, compared to the German counterpart on the left, and it also has an additional proposition from group two: *2.0212 In that case we could not sketch any picture of the world (true or false)*. However, in terms of topology, the Ogden and Ramsey (1922) translation resembles almost identically the German version.

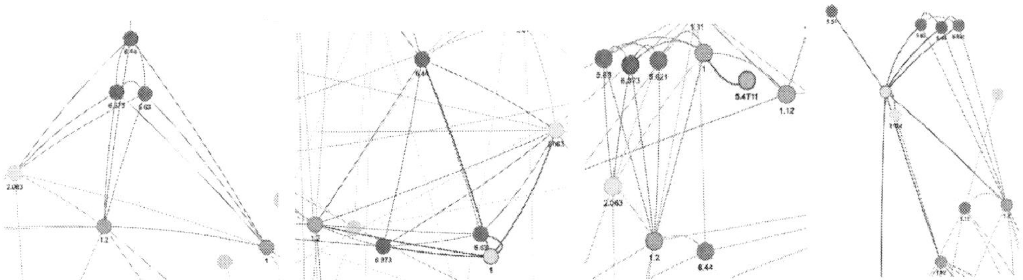

Figure 2: From left to right: Italian, Spanish, French, and Russian excerpts showing the neighbors of proposition 1. Italian and Spanish parts have identical nodes. The French and Russian topologies do not resemble the original or any other network.

On the one hand, looking at the remaining translations, we can observe the Italian and Spanish excerpts share the same nodes and comparable topologies with the original German version. On the other hand, by looking at the word aligned pairs and the translation of *Sachverhaltes* in particular, we may be able trace two separate influences for Spanish and Italian that stem from the different English versions of the *Tractatus*. Last but not least, the French and Russian parts reveal some particularities that cannot be traced to any other topology from the corpus.

It is well known that Wittgenstein did not write the propositions in the order they appear in the text and our results further evidence this fact by revealing specific clusters of similarity between propositions that do not belong to the same group. However, some groups of propositions do appear to be more compact than others, e.g. groups 4 and 2 usually have a more compact structure regardless of the language.

3.2 Concept Network

The *Concept Network*[5] is created from the main concepts/keywords extracted from each proposition in the corpus. For this part, we use only the Ogden and Ramsey (1922) translation into English, each proposition is split into sentences and the parse trees are extracted using the approach of Honnibal and Johnson (2015).

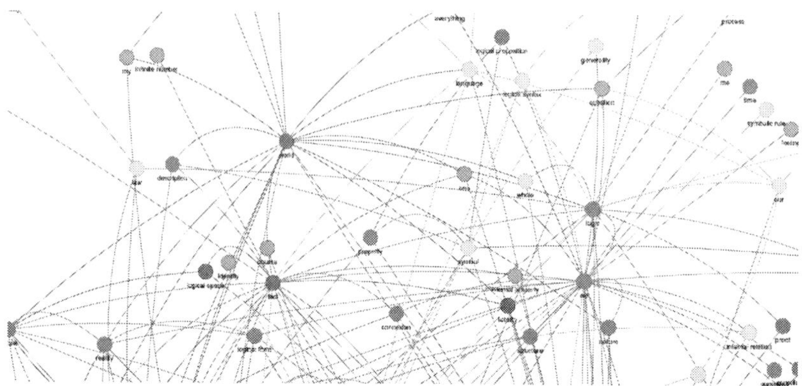

Figure 3: Excerpt from the concept network. The colors indicate the first group proposition in which the concepts appear (from 1 to 7).

The concept list consists of the noun-phrases extracted from the parse trees together with a few personal pronouns that appear in the corpus. We manually pruned the occurrences having low frequencies and the ones that have been wrongly annotated by the parser. The edges between the nodes (concepts) are created based on the number of times a concept appears in at least two propositions in the same context window, where the window varies depending on how many tokens a concept has. Multi word units are allowed to appear in windows of up to ten words, while single token concepts are limited to a maximum window of three words.

An excerpt from the network is rendered in (Figure 3). We noticed that concepts with a high number of edges usually occupy a central position in Wittgenstein's philosophy. Words such as: *elementary proposition*, *proposition*, *world*, *fact*, *form*, *we*, *logic*, *picture*, reveal relations that span across multiple propositions in the text.

4 Conclusions

We provide two resources which we believe to be important for scholars and researchers in digital humanities. The first resource is a compiled, word-aligned corpus extracted from the original and translated versions of Wittgenstein's *Tractatus Logico-Philosophicus*. This corpus may be used to study the original text or to extract meaningful comparisons from translations into other languages. The second resource is a web application that renders semantic networks of concepts and propositions from the *Tractatus*. These could be useful to visualize the semantic similarities between concepts and to examine the relations between different propositions, to clarify certain concepts and to search and explore the actual text, either in German or in translation. To summarize, therefore, we hope to provide another method of reading Wittgenstein's work.

Acknowledgements

This work was supported by a grant of the Romanian National Authority for Scientific Research and Innovation, CNCS/CCCDI – UEFISCDI, project number PN-III-P2-2.1-53BG/2016, within PNCDI III

---

[5]The *Concept Network* is accessible at `https://wittgenstein-network.gitlab.io`

References

Bird, S., Klein, E., and Loper, E. (2009). *Natural language processing with Python*. O'Reilly Media, Inc.

Dyer, C., Chahuneau, V., and Smith, N. A. (2013). A simple, fast, and effective reparameterization of ibm model 2. In *Proceedings of NAACL-HLT*, pages 644–648.

Fellbaum, C. (1998). *WordNet*. Wiley Online Library.

Firth, J. R. (1957). *A synopsis of linguistic theory, 1930–1955*. Blackwell.

Harris, Z. S. (1954). Distributional structure. *Word*, 10(2-3):146–162.

Honnibal, M. and Johnson, M. (2015). An improved non-monotonic transition system for dependency parsing. In *Proceedings of the 2015 Conference on Empirical Methods in Natural Language Processing*, pages 1373–1378, Lisbon, Portugal. Association for Computational Linguistics.

Lenci, A. (2008). Distributional semantics in linguistic and cognitive research. *Italian journal of linguistics*, 20(1):1–31.

Mikolov, T., Chen, K., Corrado, G., and Dean, J. (2013). Efficient estimation of word representations in vector space. *arXiv preprint arXiv:1301.3781*.

Och, F. J. and Ney, H. (2000). Giza++: Training of statistical translation models.

Ogden, C. and Ramsey, F. (1922). *Wittgenstein, L. - Tractatus Logico-Philosophicus*. Kegan Paul Ltd.

Östling, R. and Tiedemann, J. (2016). Efficient word alignment with Markov Chain Monte Carlo. *Prague Bulletin of Mathematical Linguistics*, 106. To appear.

Pears, D. and McGuinness, B. (1961). *Wittgenstein, L. - Tractatus Logico-Philosophicus*. Classics Series. Routledge.

Wittgenstein, L. (1921). *Logisch-Philosophische Abhandlung*. Annalen der Naturphilosophie, 14.

Wittgenstein, L. (1953). *Philosophical Investigations*. Basil Blackwell, Oxford.

A Web-based Tool for the
Integrated Annotation of Semantic and Syntactic Structures

Richard Eckart de Castilho[†◊] and **Éva Újdricza-Maydt**[*◊]
and **Seid Muhie Yimam**[‡] and **Silvana Hartmann**[†]
and **Iryna Gurevych**[†◊] and **Anette Frank**[*◊] and **Chris Biemann**[‡◊]

[†]**Ubiquitous Knowledge Processing Lab**
Department of Computer Science
Technische Universität Darmstadt

[‡]**FG Language Technology**
Department of Computer Science
Technische Universität Darmstadt

[*]**Department of
Computational Linguistics**
Heidelberg University

[◊]**Research Training Group AIPHES**
Heidelberg University and
Technische Universität Darmstadt

Abstract

We introduce the third major release of WebAnno, a generic web-based annotation tool for distributed teams. New features in this release focus on semantic annotation tasks (e.g. semantic role labelling or event annotation) and allow the tight integration of semantic annotations with syntactic annotations. In particular, we introduce the concept of *slot features*, a novel *constraint mechanism* that allows modelling the interaction between semantic and syntactic annotations, as well as a new annotation user interface. The new features were developed and used in an annotation project for semantic roles on German texts. The paper briefly introduces this project and reports on experiences performing annotations with the new tool. On a comparative evaluation, our tool reaches significant speedups over WebAnno 2 for a semantic annotation task.

1 Introduction

As natural language processing pushes towards natural language understanding, i.e. the ability for a machine to process the meaning of language rather than just its structure, there is a growing need for corpora analysed on the semantic level. Semantic structures pose different requirements for annotation tools than morphological or syntactic annotation. For example, the rich sets of semantic categories used in tasks such as semantic role labelling (SRL) or event annotation require special support to avoid the choice becoming a burden to the annotator. Also, due to the interaction of semantics with other levels of linguistic analysis, particularly syntax, it is desirable to work with generic annotation tools that simultaneously support multiple levels of annotation.

Generic web-based annotation tools do not sufficiently support the annotation of semantic structures with their rich tagsets. Also, specialised annotation tools, in particular for SRL, are not flexibly adaptable to other annotation schemes, and many of them are technologically outdated.

WebAnno 3[1] is the third major release of the web-based annotation tool WebAnno (Yimam et al., 2013; Yimam et al., 2014) introducing new functionalities enabling the annotation of semantic structures:

1. **Slot-features** allow the appropriate modelling of predicate-argument structures for SRL. We also support the following additional semantic annotation types: participants and circumstances for event annotation, *n*-ary relations for relation extraction, and slot-filling tasks for information extraction.

2. **Constraints** help annotators by performing a context-sensitive filtering of the rich semantic tagsets. For example, the sense of a semantic predicate determines available argument roles. Such a filtering is necessary to avoid loosing valuable time by having annotators search through a large number of tags or to manually type in tags. Constraint rules can be defined manually or they can be automatically

---

[1]https://webanno.github.io/webanno/

Proceedings of the Workshop on Language Technology Resources and Tools for Digital Humanities (LT4DH),
pages 76–84, Osaka, Japan, December 11-17 2016.

generated, e.g. from machine-readable lexical resources. To our knowledge, there is no other web-based annotation tool offering a comparable functionality.

3. **An improved annotation interface** for a streamlined annotation process using a permanently visible sidebar instead of a pop-up dialog for editing annotations and their features.

These new functionalities integrate well with the existing functionalities in WebAnno 2, in particular its support for the annotation of syntactic structures, thus enabling semantic annotation in coordination with syntactic annotation. To our knowledge, WebAnno 3 is presently the only web-based and team-oriented annotation tool to support both, the annotation of semantic as well as syntactic structures. This includes, but is not limited to the tools mentioned in Section 2.

WebAnno 3 was developed and implemented in close coordination with users in the context of an annotation project (cf. Mújdricza-Maydt et al. (2016)) for word sense disambiguation (WSD) and SRL on German texts and driven by its practical requirements. SRL is the task of identifying semantic predicates, their arguments, and assigning roles to these arguments. It is a difficult task usually performed by experts. Examples of well-known SRL schemes motivated by different linguistic theories are FrameNet (Baker et al., 1998), PropBank (Palmer et al., 2005), and VerbNet (Kipper Schuler, 2005). SRL annotation is typically based on syntactic structures obtained from treebanks, such as the constituent-based Penn Treebank (for PropBank annotation), or the German TIGER treebank for FrameNet-style annotation (Burchardt et al., 2009). An argument is typically identified by the span of its syntactic head or syntactic constituent. For some annotation schemes (e.g. FrameNet), the task also includes WSD. In this case, the sense label typically determines the available argument slots. The example below shows an annotation using FrameNet; the predicate *ask* receives the frame label *Questioning* (corresponding to its word sense) and its arguments are annotated as *Addressee*, *Speaker*, *Message*, and *Iterations*:

(1)   Fred$_{Role:Addressee}$ didn't answer.
       While I$_{Role:Speaker}$ had asked$_{Frame:Questioning}$ this question$_{Role:Message}$ twice$_{Role:Iterations}$ before.

Note that there are multiple interdependencies between annotations involved here. E.g. the available sense labels for the semantic predicate depend on its lemma. Also, the available argument roles depend on the sense label. We further describe the annotation project and the application of WebAnno 3 within the project in Section 4. While joint WSD and SRL annotations are conveniently supported and facilitated using constraints, they can also be performed separately and independently of one another.

2   Related Work

We briefly review presently available annotation tools that could be used for annotating semantic structures. Since we aim to support geographically distributed annotation teams, we consider recent generic web-based annotation tools. Additionally, we examine tools from earlier semantic annotation projects that are specialised for SRL but not web-based.

2.1   Web-based Annotation Tools

Anafora by Chen and Styler (2013) is a recent web-based annotation tool for event-like structures. Specifically, it supports the annotation of spans and n-ary relations. Spans are anchored on text while relations exist independently from the text and consist of slots that can be filled with spans. Annotations are visualised using a coloured text background. Selecting a relation highlights the participating spans by placing boxes around them. Anafora is not suited for annotation tasks that require an alignment of the semantic structures with syntactic structures such as constituent or dependency parse trees.

brat by Stenetorp et al. (2012) is another web-based annotation tool with a focus on collaborative annotation. The tool supports spans and n-ary relations (also called *events*). Annotations are visualised as boxes and arcs above the text. Multiple annotators can simultaneously work on the same annotations instead of being isolated from each other. However, this removes the ability to calculate inter-annotator agreement. All annotation actions are performed through a pop-up dialog, which necessitates many actions even for simple annotations. While in principle the support for semantic annotation in brat through the *n*-ary relations is good, there is no support for guiding the user through rich semantic tagsets, e.g. by showing only applicable tags based on the annotation's context.

WebAnno 2 (Yimam et al., 2014), for which we present an updated version here, is a generic and flexible annotation tool for distributed teams. To visualise the text and annotations, it uses the JavaScript-based annotation visualisation from brat.

The annotation of semantic structures can only be realised with great difficulty in WebAnno 2. It requires the creation of a custom span layer to represent semantic predicates and arguments. An additional custom relation layer is required to connect the arguments to the predicate. The distinction between predicates and arguments needs to be made through a feature on the span layer (e.g. *semanticType=pred|arg*), because the use of two distinct span layers for predicates and their arguments is not possible. The reason is that WebAnno 2 only allows relations to be created between annotations on the same layer. With such a setup, annotators have to take great care not to create invalid semantic structures, e.g. by linking predicates to other predicates or arguments to other arguments while the annotation guidelines only allow links between predicates and arguments. This complicates and slows down the annotation process and requires post-hoc consistency checks. Finally, WebAnno 2 offers no provisions to guide annotators through rich semantic tagsets. Due to the complex setup, annotating semantic structures also requires too many user interactions (*clicks*), making it also a very tedious task. This problem is aggravated by an annotation dialog popping up for each action.

2.2 Semantic Role Annotation Tools

SALTO by Burchardt et al. (2006) supports the annotation of constituency treebanks with FrameNet categories. Once a frame for a predicate has been selected, applicable roles from FrameNet can be assigned to nodes in the parse tree by drag-and-drop. SALTO supports discontinuous annotations, multi-token annotations, and cross-sentence annotations. It also offers basic team management functionalities including workload assignment and curation. However, annotators cannot correct mistakes in the underlying treebank because the parse tree is not editable. This is problematic for automatically preprocessed input. The final release of SALTO was in 2012.

Jubilee and Cornerstone by Choi et al. (2010) are tools for annotating PropBank. Jubilee supports the annotation of PropBank instances, while its sister tool Cornerstone allows editing the frameset XML files that provide the annotation scheme to Jubilee. The user interface (UI) of Jubilee displays a treebank view and allows annotating nodes in the parse tree with frameset senses and roles. Jubilee supports annotation and adjudication of annotations in small teams. It is a Java application that stores all data on the file system. Thus, the annotation team needs to be able to access a common file system, which does not meet our needs for a distributed team. Both tools appear to be no longer being developed since 2014.

2.3 Requirements of Semantic Annotation

The annotation of semantic structures imposes two main requirements on annotation tools: 1) the flexibility to support multiple layers of annotation including syntactic and semantic layers using freely configurable annotation schemes and 2) the ability to handle large, interdependent tagsets.

Flexible multi-layer annotation. While the usage-driven design of dedicated SRL annotation tools allows for a very efficient annotation, users face a serious lack of flexibility when trying to combine different annotation schemes (e.g. GermaNet senses (Hamp and Feldweg, 1997) and VerbNet roles), or when trying to use data preprocessed in different ways (e.g. for a crowdsourcing approach, automatically pre-annotating predicate and argument spans can be helpful, while experts may find pre-annotated dependency relations beneficial). This is not supported by current web-based annotation tools.

Handling rich annotation schemes. Tools need to specifically support rich semantic annotation schemes—like FrameNet—with interdependent labels (i.e. sense labels determine available argument roles). Manually typing sense and role labels is error-prone, and selecting them from a long list is cumbersome for the annotator. The tool must guide the annotator, e.g. by filtering or reordering possible sense labels based on the lemma and do the same for role labels based on the selected sense. E.g. SALTO only offers frames in the spectrum of the lemma under annotation.

3 Semantic Annotation using WebAnno 3

To meet the requirements described above, WebAnno 3 introduces support for arbitrary semantic role labelling schemes by geographically distributed teams. The great challenge in building WebAnno 3 was to identify a way of implementing support for semantic annotation not only without adversely affecting existing features of WebAnno 2, but also by capitalising on the existing features. The data model for annotations used by WebAnno is based on *feature structures*, i.e. typed key-value pairs. First, our tool adds a new type of features for use in these structures, namely *slot features*, that enable SRL and other slot-filling annotation tasks. Next, we introduce *constraint rules* to allow the modelling of tag interdependencies. Constraint rules can be used not only to provide context-sensitive assistance for semantic annotations, but in general for all kinds of annotations supported by WebAnno 3, including those inherited from WebAnno 2. Finally, an improved and streamlined user interface was introduced to enable annotation to be performed without disruptive pop-up dialogs.

3.1 Semantic Annotation using Slot Features

WebAnno provides a flexible configuration system for annotation layers supporting spans and relations. However, as outlined in Section 2.1, the provided features are insufficient for semantic annotation.

WebAnno 3 introduces a new feature type into the feature-structure-based system—the so-called *slot features*—to support semantic annotations like SRL. Slot features can be added to span layers and allow one span annotation (*slot owner*) to *link* to one or more other span annotations (*slot fillers*). Each link is qualified with a *role*, which may optionally be restricted by a tagset. Slot features can be configured to allow arbitrary slot fillers or only such pertaining to a specific layer. Figure 1 illustrates the annotation of word sense and semantic roles for *ask* as introduced in Example (1).

Declaration. We model the semantic predicate using a span layer *SemPred* with a slot feature called *arguments*. A second span layer—*SemArg*—represents the slot fillers.[2]

Interaction. To use the slot feature, the user first creates the slot-owning annotation, here a *SemPred* annotation. Then, the user selects a role to add a new slot to the feature *arguments*. Selecting a span then automatically creates the slot filler annotation (*SemArg*) and completes the link.

Visualisation. The links between slot owner and slot fillers are visualised as arcs in the colour of the slot owner. A special dashed style is used to distinguish them from other types of relations.

Agreement. With the introduction of slot features, we completely reimplemented the calculation of inter-annotator agreement. A single feature of a layer can be selected for agreement calculation (i.e. the word sense feature or the semantic argument feature). The first step in the calculation of agreement identifies which annotations actually need to be compared to each other. To address this, we first derive *coordinates* from the annotated data (Table 1). For regular span features, a coordinate is the tuple of <layer, feature, char offsets(begin-end)> and for relation features <layer, feature, char offsets(srcBegin-srcEnd, tgtBegin-tgtEnd)>. Then, agreement is calculated by comparing the labels assigned by each user for each coordinate.

We implemented two modes of calculating agreement for slot features. The first mode *role-as-label* calculates agreement based on the slot's *role*. Consider *asked* as the semantic predicate and *Fred* as a slot filler. Two annotators agree if they assigned the same role to *Fred*, e.g. *Addressee*. It is a disagreement if one annotator assigns the role *Speaker* to Fred and another assigns the role *Addressee* (cf. Table 1 d/e). In this mode, the slot filler is part of the annotation coordinates (cf. Table 1 column *extra*).

In the second mode, *target-as-label*, agreement is calculated based on the slot filler. Two annotators agree if they use the same slot filler for a slot with a given role. So consider again *asked* as the semantic predicate and *Addressee* as the role to be filled. In this case, there is an agreement if two annotators choose *Fred* as a slot filler and a disagreement if one annotator fills the slot with *Fred* and the other one with *I*. In this mode, the role label is part of the annotation coordinates (cf. Table 1 column *extra*).

Missing annotations are very common with slot features. For example, cases d) and e) in Table 1 differ in their coordinates, namely in the *extra* column which is used to discriminate between slots, but not in

---

[2]The layer names proposed here are meant as examples motivated by our use case. In WebAnno, the name of the layers and their features can in general be freely defined by the annotation project's creator.

Feature type	User	Coordinates				Label
		layer	feature	char offsets	extra	
a) string on span	A	Lemma	value	32-37 (*asked*)		ask
b) string on relation*	A	Dependency	DependencyType	26-27 (*I*), 32-37 (*asked*)		nsubj
c) slot (role-as-label)	A	SemPred	arguments	32-37 (*asked*)	0-4 (*Fred*)	Addressee
d) slot (target-as-label)	A	SemPred	arguments	32-37 (*asked*)	Addressee	0-4 (*Fred*)
e) slot (target-as-label)*	B	SemPred	arguments	32-37 (*asked*)	Speaker	0-4 (*Fred*)

Table 1: Examples of coordinates and labels for different layer and feature types in Figure 1 (except *).

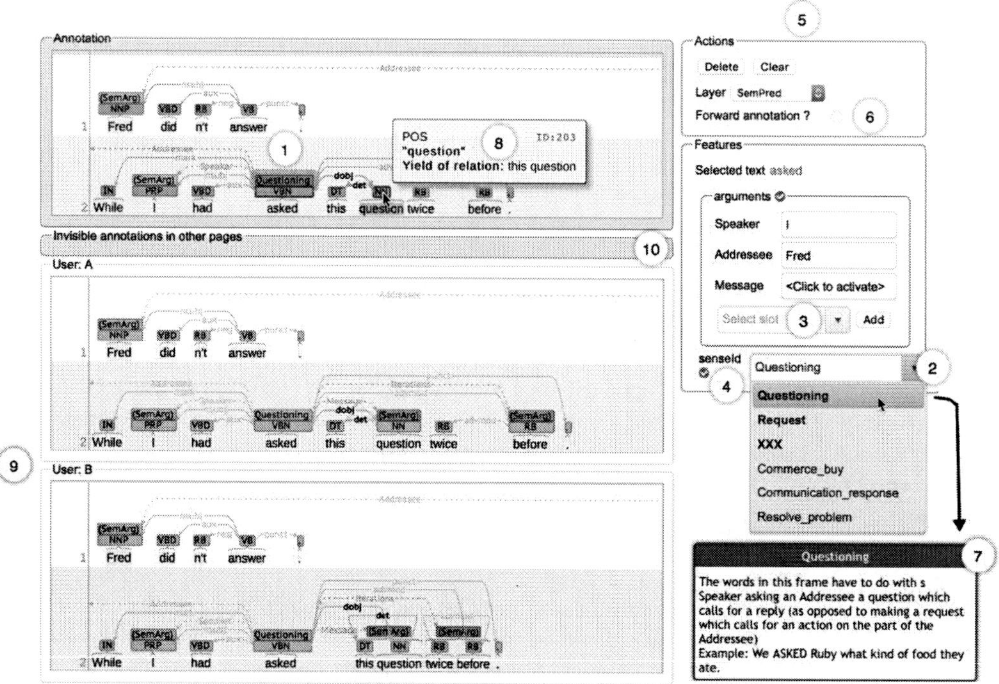

Figure 1: Cross-sentence annotation/curation with slot features and constraint rules.

their label. This makes them two entirely different annotations which the respective other user simply did not annotate rather than a case of disagreement. To cope with such missing annotations, Krippendorff's Alpha (Krippendorff, 1970) was added to the list of supported agreement measures. This measure is conceptually able to handle missing annotations.

The level of detail on agreement calculation provided by WebAnno 2 proved to be insufficient. It is often not clear how the agreement values related to the actual annotations. Thus, while reimplementing the agreement calculation to support for slot features into the agreement mechanism, we also greatly enhanced the level of detail in the UI to explain which data was (not) used for calculation and why it may not have been possible to calculate agreement. Finally, we added the ability to export raw agreement data as CSV files for detailed inspection and external agreement calculation.

3.2 Handling Rich Tagsets via Constraints

Semantic annotation tasks typically operate with a very large set of labels. While a typical part-of-speech tagset contains around 50 tags, FrameNet contains over 800 frame labels. We currently observe over 1,000 role labels and more than 8,000 frame-role combinations in the FrameNet lexicon. However, given a specific lemma, there is only a small set of applicable frame labels that it evokes (e.g. *ask* can evoke the frames *Questioning* and *Request*).

We introduce a generic mechanism that allows formalising such interdependencies as constraint rules.

Listing 1: Example FrameNet-style constraints

```
SemPred {
    // Rule 1
    @Lemma.value = "ask" -> senseId = "Questioning" | senseId = "Request" | senseId = "XXX";
    // .. other lemmata
    // Rule 2
    senseId = "Questioning" ->
        // core roles
        arguments.role = "Addressee" (!) | arguments.role = "Message" (!) | arguments.role = "Speaker" (!) |
        // non-core roles
        arguments.role = "Time" | arguments.role = "Iterations";
    // .. other senses
}

Dependency {
    governor.pos.value = "NN" & dependent.pos.value = "DET" -> dependencyType = "DET";
}
```

Listing 2: Grammar for constraint rules

```
// Basic structure ----------------------------------------    // Restrictions ---------------
<file>              ::= <import>* | <scope>*                   <actions>       ::= <action> |
<scope>             ::= <shortLayerName> "{" <ruleset> "}"                         <action> "|" <actions>
<ruleset>           ::= <rule>*                                <action>        ::= <actionPath> "=" <value>
<import>            ::= "import" <qualifiedLayerName>                              ( "(" <flags> ")" )
                        "as" <shortLayerName>                  <actionPath>    ::= <featureName> |
<rule>              ::= <conds> "->" <actions> ";"                                 <actionPath> "." <featureName>
// Conditions --------------------------------------------    <flags>         ::= "!" // core role
<conds>             ::= <cond> | <cond> "&" <conds>
<cond>              ::= <path> "=" <value>
<path>              ::= <featureName> | <step> "." <path>
<step>              ::= <featureName> | <layerSelector>
<layerSelector>     ::= <layerOperator>? <shortLayerName>
<layerOperator>     ::= "@" // select annotation in layer X
```

Rules are typically defined over annotations and their labels, but may also access the annotated text. A rule consists of a left-hand side expressing the conditions under which the rule applies and a right-hand side expressing the effect of the rule. A logical conjunction of multiple conditions can be specified. If multiple effects for a rule are specified, they are considered to be alternatives. The mechanism does not limit the annotator's choice. It only reorders the list of labels the users can choose from, showing first those labels covered by constraints in a bold font, then the rest of the labels. While constraint rules can be written manually, they can also be generated automatically from machine-readable schemes. We provide suitable conversions from FrameNet and GermaNet (cf. Section 4).

Listing 1 shows example constraint rules for a FrameNet-like annotation style. These apply to annotations on the layer *SemPred*. Rule 1 reorders the choice of sense IDs for the *SemPred* annotation: if a *Lemma* annotation with value *ask* exists at the same character offsets as the *SemPred* (Figure 1 ①), then the sense IDs *Questioning*, *Request*, and *XXX* (other/unknown) should be offered as top labels in the sense ID dropdown selection (Figure 1 ②). Similar rules for other lemmata would normally follow.

Rule 2 in Listing 1 illustrates constraints on the roles of slot features. If the *senseId Questioning* is chosen, *Addressee*, *Message*, *Speaker*, *Time*, and *Iterations* are offered as top labels in the argument role dropdown box (Figure 1 ③). Slots for core roles (marked with "*!*") are added automatically while slots for other roles need to be added manually.

The constraint mechanism is generic. It uses a path-like notation to navigate along features pointing to other annotations (e.g. *governor.pos.value*), as illustrated in the dependency rule. Within conditions, a path component may also be *@shortLayerName*, meaning *"select all annotations of the specified layer at the same offsets as the current annotation"*. We use this in Listing 1 to access information from the *Lemma* layer. Listing 2 shows the full constraint rule grammar in a BNF-like notation.

An indicator (Figure 1 ④) next to a feature in the editor panel shows the status of constraints. The indicator is *green* if there are matching rules (e.g. there is a *Lemma* annotation with the value *ask* and there is a rule with a condition *@Lemma.value="ask"*). It is *orange* if there are rules that affect the feature but none matches (e.g. there is at least one rule with a condition on the value of a *Lemma* but none that matches on the specific given value for the present annotation). Finally, it is *red* if there are rules, but the feature is not restricted by a tagset. In the latter case, the rules have no effect since without a tagset, there are no labels to be reordered.

3.3 Redesigned Annotation User Interface

The annotation user interfaces of WebAnno 2 and brat use a pop-up dialog whenever an annotation is created or modified. This was perceived as a major impediment to efficient annotation by our annotation team, not only because the dialog obscures the underlying annotation interface, but mainly because the dialog needs to be closed by an explicit user action. Hence, we implemented a dialog-less annotation user interface, similar to the one in the Anafora tool. Along with the new interface, additional user-expressed needs for semantic annotation were addressed. These include better support for keyboard-based annotation, the ability to create zero-length annotations to represent slot fillers not realised in the text, the display of descriptive tooltips explaining semantic tags, the indication of tokens transitively covered by dependency relations, and the ability for the curation of cross-sentence annotations.

Dialog-less annotation. The UI elements used for editing the annotation feature values have been moved from a dialog (cf. brat) to a permanently visible detail panel on the side of the screen (Figure 1 ⑤). Selecting a span of text or drawing an arc now immediately creates an annotation on the active layer and loads its features in the detail panel. Changes to the feature values are immediately reflected in the annotation view. For tasks that require repeatedly annotating the same feature values (e.g. annotating persons in a named entity task), the option *save feature* can be enabled for each feature individually. New annotations are then created with the same feature values as the previously selected annotation.

Keyboard-based annotation. Keyboard-based annotation can significantly speed up the annotation process. For annotation layers with a single tagset-controlled feature (e.g. part-of-speech), we introduce a new keyboard-based *forward annotation* mode (Figure 1 ⑥). In this mode, pressing a key selects the first tag starting with the respective character and pressing it again selects the next. As annotators memorise the number of key presses for the tags, we expect their efficiency to improve. Once a tag is chosen, pressing *space* automatically selects the next token for annotation.

Zero-width annotations. Zero-width span annotations can now be created (at arbitrary positions in the text), e.g. to instantiate semantic predicates or arguments that are not realised in the text.

Tooltips. Tag descriptions are now displayed as tooltips (Figure 1 ⑦) during annotation. In particular for rich semantic tagsets, this is an important improvement. The tag descriptions are part of the tagset definitions which can be edited via the user interface in the project settings. Alternatively, they can be externally generated and imported as JSON files. For the purpose of our annotation project, we automatically derived tagset files from VerbNet and GermaNet.

Relation yield highlighting. Moving the mouse cursor over a span with outgoing relations now displays a tooltip showing the *yield* of the relation (Figure 1 ⑧). E.g. for dependency relations, the yield represents all the tokens subsumed by the respective dependency node. This feature facilitates the coordination of syntactic and semantic annotations when using syntactic heads as slot fillers. In the annotation project, it was determined that dependency-based annotation, enhanced with highlighting of the dependency relation yield proved superior to span-based annotation, which is more error prone.

Cross-sentence curation. We extended the curation component of WebAnno to support the adjudication of multiple annotations for individual sentences. This was necessary in order to curate cross-sentence semantic relations, e.g. to use parts of a previous sentence as slot fillers. An example of such a case is provided in Figure 1 ⑨. Curators can now define the number of sentences to visualise and curate at a time. Additionally, an indicator is displayed for any relation annotations that are not rendered because one of their endpoints is realised outside of the window of currently displayed sentences (Figure 1 ⑩).

4 Experiences and Evaluation

4.1 Annotation Study

Our new tool was tested in a large-scale semantic annotation study on German standard as well as non-standard texts (cf. Mújdricza-Maydt et al. (2016)). An annotation team performed a combination of word sense and semantic role annotation based on GermaNet senses and VerbNet-style role labels. As basis for the annotation, the new slot features were used to model predicate-argument structures. Compared to

Doc	a) WebAnno 2	b) WebAnno 3 no constraints	c) WebAnno 3 constraints
1	14:58	10:07	08:57
2	12:21	10:29	08:16
3	05:19	04:16	03:47
4	10:40	08:22	07:22
All	43:18	33:14	28:22

Table 2: Annotation times in minutes:seconds for WebAnno 2 and 3 with and without constraints.

earlier experiences with predicate-argument annotation using relation layers in WebAnno 2, the annotation team reported improved comfort and efficiency with the new interface. Having the annotation detail panel visible all the time and no longer being forced to constantly switch between annotation dialog and annotation view was perceived as an important factor for this improvement. This study also made extensive use of constraint rules and relied heavily on the new tooltips explaining senses and roles to the annotators. In a pilot study for the project, different strategies of selecting slot fillers were examined. The strategy that was eventually selected relied on pre-annotated dependency relations and required the annotator to select the syntactic head of a phrase to be used as a slot filler (e.g. *house* instead of *the house*). The new ability to display the *yield* of the dependency relations proved to be instrumental in this task to locate the correct head words.

To facilitate SRL annotation projects for others, we provide in addition to the tool itself 1) the setup for our annotation study as a demo project; 2) configuration files for different predicate sense and semantic role labeling frameworks (VerbNet, FrameNet, and PropBank), including their respective tagsets and constraint rules.

4.2 Comparative Evaluation

After the development has been finalised, we conducted a comparative evaluation study in order to measure whether our efforts in tool engineering translate into annotation time speedups, which directly influences annotation cost. For this, we chose the following setup: an annotator was presented with a static display of gold standard predicate-argument annotations like the ones shown in Figure 1. In this way, we minimise fluctuations caused by cognitive load for choosing the right labels, simulating a maximally trained annotator. The annotator had ample experience with both the annotation tools, but not with the specific settings. Thus, for each setting, the annotator became familiar with the setup on a small training document. We conducted this annotation in three different settings: a) using WebAnno 2 (version 2.3.1), modelling the annotation task as outlined in Section 2.1, b) using WebAnno 3 without constraints and c) using WebAnno 3 with constraints for rules that re-order semantic predicates according to the lemma value, as exemplified in (Figure 1 ④). To avoid interpersonal differences in annotation speed, the same annotator worked on all three settings. The data set on which time was measured included four documents with a total of 64 semantic predicates, filling a total of 115 slots with overall 94 semantic arguments (*SemArg* in Figure 1). Note that the same semantic argument can fill slots of different predicates.

Table 2 shows the times in minutes and seconds measured for the four documents. The improvements of the user interface in setting b) already results in a speedup of about 23% less time compared to WebAnno 2. In combination with constraints, a speedup of over 34% is reached in setting c), meaning that the same annotator can produce 50% more annotations in the same time. The annotator reported that she needed to perform considerably fewer interactions in setting c).

5   Conclusion

We have introduced WebAnno 3,[3] the third major release of WebAnno. The new version introduces major improvements that significantly go beyond the state-of-the-art: they enable the annotation of semantic structure and the handling of rich semantic tagsets. The new version was developed in close coordination with an associated annotation project performing combined WSD and SRL annotation on German texts. Moreover, the tool can be used for many non-linguistic annotation tasks in various domains,

---

[3] https://webanno.github.io/webanno/

e.g. the annotation of metaphors and ambiguities (Digital Humanities), skills and qualifications (Human Resources), sentiment in product reviews (Advertisement/Marketing), etc. A comparative evaluation showed considerable speedups over previous tools and validates both, our adaptation to the user interface and the incorporation of the constraint language to facilitate the annotation of large, interdependent tagsets.

Acknowledgments

The work presented in this paper was funded by a German BMBF grant to the CLARIN-D project, by the German Research Foundation as part of the Research Training Group Adaptive Preparation of Information from Heterogeneous Sources (AIPHES) under grant No. GRK 1994/1, and by the Volkswagen Foundation as part of the Lichtenberg-Professorship Program under grant No. I/82806. We also thank Aakash Sharma and Sarah Holschneider for their active support in the development of WebAnno, the documentation of the tool, and for conducting the comparative evaluation study.

References

Collin F. Baker, Charles J. Fillmore, and John B. Lowe. 1998. The Berkeley FrameNet project. In *Proc. of COLING-ACL 1998*, pages 86–90, Montreal, Canada.

Aljoscha Burchardt, Katrin Erk, Anette Frank, Andreas Kowalski, and Sebastian Padó. 2006. SALTO – A Versatile Multi-Level Annotation Tool. In *Proc. of LREC 2006*, pages 517–520, Genoa, Italy.

Aljoscha Burchardt, Katrin Erk, Anette Frank, Andrea Kowalski, Sebastian Padó, and Manfred Pinkal. 2009. Using FrameNet for the Semantic Analysis of German: Annotation, Representation and Automation. In Hans C. Boas, editor, *Multilingual FrameNets – Practice and Applications*, pages 209–244. Mouton de Gruyter, Berlin, Germany.

Wei-Te Chen and Will Styler. 2013. Anafora: A web-based general purpose annotation tool. In *Proc. of the NAACL HLT 2013 Demonstration Session*, pages 14–19, Atlanta, GA, USA.

Jinho Choi, Claire Bonial, and Martha Palmer. 2010. Multilingual PropBank annotation tools: Cornerstone and Jubilee. In *Proc. of the NAACL HLT 2010 Demonstration Session*, pages 13–16, Los Angeles, CA, USA.

Birgit Hamp and Helmut Feldweg. 1997. GermaNet - a lexical-semantic net for German. In *Automatic Information Extraction and Building of Lexical Semantic Resources for NLP Applications*, pages 9–15, Madrid, Spain.

Karin Kipper Schuler. 2005. *VerbNet: A Broad-coverage, Comprehensive Verb Lexicon*. Ph.D. thesis, University of Pennsylvania, Philadelphia, PA, USA.

Klaus Krippendorff. 1970. Estimating the reliability, systematic error and random error of interval data. *Educational. and Psych. Measurement*, 30(1):61–70.

Éva Mújdricza-Maydt, Silvana Hartmann, Iryna Gurevych, and Anette Frank. 2016. Combining Semantic Annotation of Word Sense & Semantic Roles: A Novel Annotation Scheme for VerbNet Roles on German Language Data. In *Proc. of LREC 2016*, pages 3031–3038.

Martha Palmer, Daniel Gildea, and Paul Kingsbury. 2005. The Proposition Bank: An annotated corpus of semantic roles. *Computational Linguistics*, 31(1):71–105.

Pontus Stenetorp, Sampo Pyysalo, Goran Topić, Tomoko Ohta, Sophia Ananiadou, and Jun'ichi Tsujii. 2012. brat: a web-based tool for NLP-assisted text annotation. In *Proc. of EACL 2012*, pages 102–107, Avignon, France.

Seid Muhie Yimam, Iryna Gurevych, Richard Eckart de Castilho, and Chris Biemann. 2013. WebAnno: A flexible, web-based and visually supported system for distributed annotations. In *Proc. of ACL 2013: System Demonstrations*, pages 1–6, Sofia, Bulgaria.

Seid Muhie Yimam, Richard Eckart de Castilho, Iryna Gurevych, and Chris Biemann. 2014. Automatic annotation suggestions and custom annotation layers in WebAnno. In *Proc. of ACL 2014: System Demonstrations*, pages 91–96, Baltimore, MD, USA.

Challenges and Solutions for Latin Named Entity Recognition

Alexander Erdmann
The Ohio State University
Columbus, OH, USA
erdmann.6@osu.edu

Christopher Brown
The Ohio State University
Columbus, OH, USA
brown.2583@osu.edu

Brian Joseph
The Ohio State University
Columbus, OH, USA
joseph.1@osu.edu

Mark Janse
Ghent University
Ghent, Belgium
mark.janse@ugent.be

Petra Ajaka
The Ohio State University
Columbus, OH, USA
ajaka.3@osu.edu

Micha Elsner
The Ohio State University
Columbus, OH, USA
elsner.14@osu.edu

Marie-Catherine de Marneffe
The Ohio State University
Columbus, OH, USA
demarneffe.1@osu.edu

Abstract

Although spanning thousands of years and genres as diverse as liturgy, historiography, lyric and other forms of prose and poetry, the body of Latin texts is still relatively sparse compared to English. Data sparsity in Latin presents a number of challenges for traditional Named Entity Recognition techniques. Solving such challenges and enabling reliable Named Entity Recognition in Latin texts can facilitate many down-stream applications, from machine translation to digital historiography, enabling Classicists, historians, and archaeologists for instance, to track the relationships of historical persons, places, and groups on a large scale. This paper presents the first annotated corpus for evaluating Named Entity Recognition in Latin, as well as a fully supervised model that achieves over 90% F-score on a held-out test set, significantly outperforming a competitive baseline. We also present a novel active learning strategy that predicts how many and which sentences need to be annotated for named entities in order to attain a specified degree of accuracy when recognizing named entities automatically in a given text. This maximizes the productivity of annotators while simultaneously controlling quality.

1 Introduction: An Overview

We present here the first evaluated Named Entity Recognition (NER) system for Latin along with the annotated data on which it was trained and tested. Our practical NER solution both caters to the unique challenges of Latin and facilitates large scale digital historiography, enabling scholars to mine the relationships of historical persons, places, and groups from a variety of primary sources. The study of historical groups specifically is a desideratum of the Herodotos project, which aims to produce a definitive catalogue of group designations in historical works (u.osu.edu/herodotos) and provided the funding for the work reported here. Using a data set drawn from the Perseus corpus (Smith et al., 2000), we develop annotation guidelines and demonstrate high inter-annotator agreement (99.3% Fleiss' Kappa). Next, we build a fully supervised NER model and evaluate it across test sets from different domains, demonstrating that it consistently outperforms baseline models regardless of how the style or register of the test set compares to the training set. Then we further address the issue of domain adaptation with an active learning solution that selects sentences to be annotated which cover gaps in the model's knowledge due to linguistic idiosyncrasies of the target domain. In addition to rapidly increasing accuracy by minimizing the amount of annotation required, a detailed error analysis demonstrates that we can reliably predict how many (and which) sentences must be annotated in a given target domain to ensure that named entities (NE) can be recognized in the remaining text with a pre-determined degree of accuracy. This provides an element of quality control for Classicists who might otherwise be wary of

Proceedings of the Workshop on Language Technology Resources and Tools for Digital Humanities (LT4DH),
pages 85–93, Osaka, Japan, December 11-17 2016.

relying on large-scale data mining to address nuanced topics in the humanities. Finally, we discuss how the challenging qualities of Latin, being a low resource, morphologically complex language with free word order, affect our ongoing work in incorporating elements of self-training into an active learning pipeline.

2   Latin Data

The Latin language presents many challenges for NER. Being a non-standard language in terms of Natural Language Processing research, it is limited in the pre-existing training resources we can utilize. There is no annotated corpus available that makes fine-grained distinctions among NE's, and Perseus' digital gazetteers, mark-ups of Smith (1854; 1870; 1890), cover just individual persons (PRS) and geographical place names (GEO), not group names (GRP), which we want also to be able to recognize.[1] Additionally, the reliability of part-of-speech taggers (e.g. Schmid (1999) trained by Gabriele Brandolini (http://www.cis.uni-muenchen.de/~schmid/tools/TreeTagger/data/latin-par-linux-3.2.bin.gz) and Johnson et al. (2014)), dependency parsers (Bamman and Crane, 2009), and semantic models (Johnson et al., 2014) is very low due to data-sparsity. Ponti and Passarotti (2016) actually demonstrate reliable syntactic dependency parsing on Medieval Latin using the *Index Thomisticus* Treebank (McGillivray et al., 2009), but find that more work is needed to successfully adapt their model to handle other varieties of Latin. In broad terms, generalizing from linguistic patterns recognized in one Latin text when processing another is difficult because "a series of particular historical, geographical and cultural circumstances [led] to an inhomogeneous linguistic system where elements from different areas and registers met and were only partially transmitted by the sources" (McGillivray, 2014). In this section, we discuss the impact of the nature of the Latin language on our selection of the Perseus corpus and our annotation of portions of it.

2.1   Digital Latin Corpora

While future work will involve incorporating diverse sources, e.g. archaeological data, liturgical Latin from *Index Thomisticus* (Busa, 1974–1980), and other historical corpora like PROIEL (Haug and Jøhndal, 2008), focusing on a single large corpus to start allows us to rely on consistent digitization. Perseus contains over 6,000,000 (mostly) consistently digitized Latin words with proper nouns (mostly) capitalized (Smith et al., 2000). This capitalization scheme did not exist in the original manuscripts but is nonetheless crucial for identifying NE's. That being said, within Perseus, the subject matter is quite diverse, certainly containing a broad spectrum of NE's of interest to Classicists. Not only does the corpus include several domains as identified by the creators – epic, elegiac, iambic and lyric poetry, tragedy, comedy, historiography, oration, mythology, philosophy, inscriptions/papyri, in addition to letters and other works (Marchionini, 2000) – but it also includes a wide breadth of diachronic variation ranging from the entire canon of Classical Latin to many early Christian authors.

2.2   Annotation

We annotated Caesar's *De Bello Gallico* (*BG*) for all the GRP's, PRS's, and GEO's appearing therein. *BG* is a fitting source text to train an NER model because it both contains many NE's and is "a model of Latin style" (Cicero, *Brutus* 262), meaning that we should be able to adapt to target texts with greater ease than if we had annotated a more peripheral, less influential source text, e.g. a work of poetry or liturgical Latin. However, because we intend to use our NER model to tag many texts which may differ considerably from *BG* in terms of content, style, and density and distribution of NE's, we chose two other texts representative of target domains widely represented in Perseus (letters and elegiac poetry) and additionally annotated portions of them as well. In total, we annotated all 58,891 words of *BG*, 18,676 of Pliny the Younger's *Epistulae* (*Ep*) and 17,562 of Ovid's *Ars Amatoria* (*AA*). *Ep* shares many more qualities with *BG* than *AA* does. Proportionally, the former share more word forms and both are

---

[1]Busa's (1974–1980) *Index Thomisticus* is annotated for proper nouns, but does not distinguish groups from places from persons as we do. Furthermore, this corpus of liturgical Latin represents a vastly different variety of the language as compared to the Classical texts we have annotated in terms of era, style, and content, so we are indeed building a novel resource. Future work will leverage *Index Thomisticus* among other resources to facilitate adapting our NER model to cover liturgical Latin.

prose and relatively concrete, whereas *AA* is poetic, allusive, and abstract as evidenced by the fact that a given form is far more likely to have multiple meanings in *AA* as determined by the NE labels it receives. This suggests that our target texts will allow us to define a gradient scale to measure how well we adapt to target domains based on their similarity to our source.

To insure cohesive annotation among our three annotators (an undergraduate, a graduate, and a professor of Classics, each with at least 4 years of experience studying Latin), each individually annotated the same 5,000 words for NE's, over which an agreement score of 95.9% Fleiss' Kappa was achieved. Afterward, all 3 collaborated in correcting each error and the annotation guidelines were updated. Finally, another 5,000 words were individually annotated and the new agreement score of 99.3% demonstrated the consistency with which the new guidelines could be followed.

3 Fully Supervised NER Models

We built a fully supervised NER model equipped with a minimalistic, language-specific feature set and compared it to two baseline models: the only other NER technology for Latin, an unevaluated tagger from Johnson et al.'s (2014) Classical Languages Toolkit (CLTK), and a quality off-the-shelf NER model, the Stanford NER system (Finkel et al., 2005), trained on our data without language-specific features.

3.1 The Baseline Models

The CLTK NER baseline is rule based, performing a dictionary look-up and making a binary classification of entity/non-entity for each token using a gazetteer of NE's constructed by harvesting all capitalized, non-sentence-initial tokens from the Packard Humanities Institute Latin Libraries corpus (Packard Humanities Institute, 1992). Because no gold data was annotated to train or evaluate this system, our small annotated corpus presents the first opportunity to gauge its performance. Stanford's NER system is a more sophisticated conditional random field (CRF) model, although, being fully supervised in its off-the-shelf implementation, it lacks the extensive vocabulary that the CLTK system has access to. CRF's are undirected graphical models trained to maximize the conditional probability of a sequence of labels given the corresponding input sequence (Liao and Veeramachaneni, 2009), and are especially effective in NER due to their ability to rapidly learn from potentially large vectors of features belonging to each sequential token. Stanford NER leverages the widely used types of features discussed by McCallum and Li (2003), lexical, orthographic, semantic, conjoined sequences of features, and features of neighbors (we use the default feature set and parameters specified at `nlp.stanford.edu/nlp/javadoc/javanlp-3.6.0/edu/stanford/nlp/ie/NERFeatureFactory.html`), but additionally employs a Gibbs Sampling-based penalty system motivating consistency in labels for multiple occurrences of the same word type (Finkel et al., 2005).

3.2 Our Model

Our model, like Stanford's, is a CRF using similar features, though we alter ours to suit our language and corpus. We employ a POS tagger (Schmid, 1999) to leverage the highly informative morphological complexity of Latin. Finkel et al. (2005) claim only a negligible boost from using POS features in English NER and thus do not include them in the off-the-shelf version, yet we find that when implemented with creativity, the output of even a low accuracy POS tagger can be beneficial for Latin NER. For each token, we deconstruct the fine-grained POS tag into component parts ranging from case and mood distinctions to coarser distinctions between syntactic categories like nouns and verbs. We then run each token through a rule-based morphological analyzer (Whitaker, 1993), filtering out any components that the analyzer considers impossible. Furthermore, we combine the output of the tagger and analyzer with our own set of rules, thereby deducing a lemma (if one failed to be identified by the tagger or analyzer), component morphemes, and number (singular/plural), all to be used as features. Like Farber et al. (2008), which uses a similar process to leverage morpho-syntactic information in morphologically rich, low-resource Arabic, we too find that filtering POS tag output cuts down on noise, boosting accuracy. By additionally leveraging the newly enhanced LEMLAT (Budassi and Passarotti, 2016) morphological analyzer, or even substituting it for Whitaker's (1993), which has a smaller lexical base and struggles with graphical

Train/Test Splits

	Test Set	In or Out-of-Domain
Fold 1	PINY	OUT
Fold 2	OVID	OUT
Fold 3	CAESAR	IN

Table 1: Fold 1 tests on *Ep*, trains on the remaining annotated data. 2 tests on *AA*, and 3 on books 2 and 7 of *BG* which, when concatenated, resemble the lengths of the other 2 test sets. 3 tests "in-domain" as the training set is mostly from the same domain, i.e. the other 6 books of *BG*, the historiography domain.

Binary NE/non-NE Classification

	F	Prec	Rec	UNKF
FOLD 1 – TEST = PLINY				
CLTK	0.72	0.66	0.78	N/A
HDT-GAZ	0.96	**0.98**	0.95	0.96
HDT+GAZ	**0.97**	0.96	**0.97**	**0.96**
FOLD 2 – TEST = OVID				
CLTK	0.59	0.46	0.81	N/A
HDT-GAZ	0.89	**0.94**	0.85	0.89
HDT+GAZ	**0.91**	0.94	**0.88**	**0.91**
FOLD 3 – In-Domain TEST = GW				
CLTK	0.75	0.77	0.73	N/A
HDT-GAZ	0.99	0.99	0.98	0.97
HDT+GAZ	**0.99**	**1.00**	**0.99**	**0.98**

Full NER Classification Task

	F	Prec	Rec	UNKF
FOLD 1 – TEST = PLINY				
Stanford	0.55	0.63	0.49	0.47
HDT-GAZ	0.62	0.73	0.53	0.55
HDT+GAZ	**0.71**	**0.75**	**0.68**	**0.67**
FOLD 2 – TEST = OVID				
Stanford	0.41	0.57	0.32	0.40
HDT-GAZ	0.44	0.55	0.36	0.42
HDT+GAZ	**0.54**	**0.62**	**0.47**	**0.52**
FOLD 3 – In-Domain TEST = GW				
Stanford	0.89	0.90	0.88	0.75
HDT-GAZ	**0.91**	**0.91**	**0.91**	**0.77**
HDT+GAZ	0.91	0.91	0.91	0.76

Table 2: UNK's are words unseen in training, F, F-score, Prec, precision, Rec, recall, and GAZ, gazetteer.

variants, we expect even further gains in coverage and accuracy with this POS tagging strategy in the future.

Further tailoring of our feature set involved tweaking parameters meant to optimize NER in data-rich environments to suit our small corpus, like limiting the size of N-grams. Lastly, we implement one feature leveraging unlabeled data which identifies any sentence-initial token which appears elsewhere in the corpus without its first letter capitalized, suggesting that it is not an NE. We find higher order semantic features like those used in Rani et al. (2014) unhelpful. We attempted to generate such features using the unevaluated Word2Vec model released with CLTK, but it could not cluster words well enough to be useful given the huge disparity between the amount of training data available in Latin and English (Mikolov et al., 2013; Michel et al., 2010).

3.3 Results

Because of the stylistic, synchronic and diachronic breadth of the Perseus corpus relative to the limited coverage of annotated data, we present both in-domain and out-of-domain results by performing 3-fold, cross-domain evaluation as described in Table 1 to assess how accuracy declines as the test domain diverges from the source. Additionally, when calculating results, we do not consider non-NE's correctly labelled in our F-score metric. This avoids artificially inflating results in low NE-dense domains (*BG* is more NE-dense than *AA* and *Ep*). Table 2 compares both the performance of CLTK NER with our model in a binary NE/non-NE classification task, and Stanford NER's performance with our model's in classifying GRP's, PRS's, and GEO's. Additionally, it displays how our model's performance is affected when aided by 3 pre-existing Latin gazetteers (Perseus' markup of Smith (1854; 1870; 1890)).

Table 2 demonstrates that the CLTK detects too many named entities, often detecting NEs for words which can occur as both names and regular nouns or adjectives, like *Clarus*, "famous" or *Maximus*, "greatest", leading to low precision. Additionally, it cannot recognize NE's not previously stored in its dictionary, thus leading to recall errors. Both versions of our model, with and without gazetteers, outperform the Stanford baseline, proving that our language-specific POS features are helpful in coping with data sparsity. The benefit of using gazetteers, interestingly, wanes as baseline accuracy increases from Fold 2 to 1 to 3, providing no benefit in the latter. This stems from a mismatch between the gazetteers and the classification task: no gazetteer exists for GRP's and many GRP's share forms with members of the GEO gazetteer (the distinction determined by context), increasing the likelihood that these will be incorrectly tagged as GEO's. Yet as the style, topicality, and genre of the test set diverge

Accuracy vs. Density of Unknown NE's

	F	UNK's/NE's	Fold
In Domain	0.91	0.32	3
Similar Domain	0.71	0.8	1
Different Domain	0.54	0.96	2

Table 3: Decrease in accuracy as proportion of NE's in the test set not seen in training increases.

Determining the Difficulty of an UNK

	Subsets of UNK's	Accuracy
1	All UNK's (NE or non-NE)	0.96
2	Capitalized UNK's	0.77
3a	Capped UNK's appearing elsewhere uncapped	0.83
3b	Capped UNK's not appearing elsewhere uncapped	0.56

Table 4: The UNK's in row 2 are a subset of those in 1, as the UNK's in 3a and 3b are mutually exclusive, completely exhaustive subsets of those in 2. An UNK is "capitalized" if its first letter is capitalized. An UNK appears "elsewhere uncapped" if it exists somewhere in the Perseus corpus, differing only in that the first letter is not capitalized. Accuracy is reported over all 3 test sets combined.

from the training set, this problem becomes increasingly outweighed by the usefulness of having at least some gazetteer to refer to when confronted with an increased density of UNK's.

Despite our model's success in obtaining significant improvements over both baselines in all three folds, the ability to adapt to new domains is a weakness of fully supervised models. Performance drops from 91% within domain to 71% testing on a relatively similar domain (Fold 1), to 54% testing on a relatively obscure domain (Fold 2). The decline in accuracy in Table 3 suggests that the model frequently fails to leverage non-lexical features to correctly identify a label in the absence of lexical ones.

Table 4 demonstrates that forms like *Marius* (a PRS), which do not appear in the training set or possess a minimally different uncapitalized variant appearing elsewhere in Perseus, are very difficult to tag. We refer to such words as Priority 1 words. Forms like *Video*, "I see", which also do not appear in training but do show uncapitalized variants, are still challenging but much less so as most are non-NE's, only capitalized when sentence initial. We refer to these as Priority 2 words; however, these tend to be more frequent than priority 1's. We consider this tradeoff between difficulty and frequency as we tailor our pipeline to better handle capitalized UNK's.

4 Semi-Supervised Model

Semi-supervised learning involves supplementing with unannotated data during training. Liao and Veeramachaneni (2009), Rani et al. (2014), and Collins and Singer (1999) show that self-training, where unannotated data is used for training without querying the user, can overcome data sparsity or gaps between training and testing domains. However, the first two identify high precision unannotated sentences by relying on seed rules which are difficult to develop for Latin. While Liao and Veeramachaneni (2009) can rely on any capitalized word following a PRS to be part of the same NE, Latin's free word order frequently allows NE's from entirely different syntactic constituents to appear adjacent to one another, as in *Caesar [PRS] Haeduos [GRP] frumentum ... flagitare* "Caesar demands grain from the Aedui" (*BG* 1.16.1). Collins and Singer's (1999) implementation of Blum and Mitchell's (1998) co-training (the output of one tagger is used to train another) could be implemented without seed rules, yet, Pierce and Cardie's (2001) assessment of the limitations of co-training shows that when "all the classes are [not] represented according to their prior probabilities in every region in the feature space", as when we adapt to new domains in Perseus, we get Charniak's (1997) result where mistakes are magnified, not smoothed.

Active-learning, as opposed to self-training, allows the learner to query the user for additional annotation. Lynn et al. (2012) and Ambati et al. (2011) suggest that this is an effective solution for low-resource languages when self-training fails. Following Cohn et al. (1994), we modify the Query by Uncertainty tactic, where the tagger selects informative sentences based on how uncertain it is of the correct tag sequence and sends these to be annotated. Our modifications ensure that the most useful sentences are

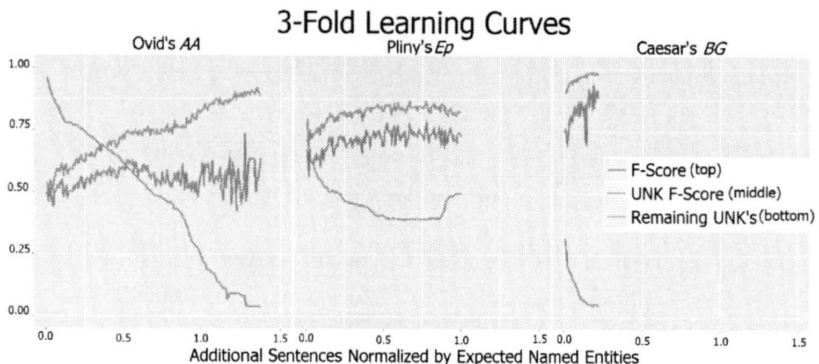

Figure 1: Learning Curves for our 3 folds demonstrate a strong negative relationship between Remaining UNK's and Accuracy. Remaining UNK's is the number of unknown words in what is left of the test set normalized by the total number of NE's therein. The increase in UNK accuracy as sentences are selected, though noisy when only few remain, demonstrates that the model learns to leverage non-lexical features as data is added to the training set.

annotated first by leveraging the data-mining discussed earlier (3.3) and Sokolovska's (2011) insight that a distribution over degrees of uncertainty is more beneficial.

The sentence selection algorithm begins by identifying all Priority 1 and 2 unknown words from the test set and lists all the unannotated sentences containing at least one. Primarily, the list is ranked by frequency of the relevant UNK weighted by priority level, reflecting that we are more likely to mis-tag Priority 1's than Priority 2's and that fixing high frequency mistakes is more important than low-frequency ones (sentences with multiple unknown words can be entered into the list multiple times but only extracted once). Secondarily, we rank sentences in the list by the sum of (a) the marginal probability with which the fully supervised tagger predicts the relevant UNK's tag, and (b) the median of these marginal probabilities over every occurence of that word form in the test set. A low sum of these two outranks higher sums, *ceteris paribus*, as this implies that the given sentence is highly informative and that the UNK it features is not likely to be tagged correctly a priori. The selection algorithm then progresses through this ranked list taking sentences out for annotation only if the relevant UNK therein has not already been added to the training set by a higher-ranking sentence. In order to ensure that, during training, the tagger optimally learns from sentences which were selected by the algorithm, we weight these sentences in the training data according to the fraction of all Priority 1 and 2 types from the test set which are represented therein. Intuitively, the algorithm addresses the sources of errors discussed previously, though one flaw (4.2) is still being addressed.

4.1 Experiment

We set out to determine if (a) our sentence selection algorithm is efficient and (b) we can reliably predict tagging accuracy based on how many sentences we have already selected and annotated. Such are the practical concerns of e.g. Classicists studying the portrayal of GRP's in the liturgical *Index Thomisticus* (Busa, 1974–1980). Accuracy on a held-out set does not concern them, only how many and which sentences must be annotated within *Index Thomisticus* to ensure that the remainder can be tagged with sufficient accuracy to meet their projects' needs. Thus, we return to our 3 domain-disjoint folds over which we tested the fully supervised model, pretending that the test sets represent never-before-seen documents of varying tagging difficulties. For each fold, we run our sentence selection algorithm on the test set, incrementally updating the training set with selected sentences and testing on those remaining. Figure 1 depicts the results from running the tagger on each fold until the learning curve levels off.

The accuracy on *BG* levels off at the top of the probability space once all capitalized UNK's have been seen. *AA* leveling off in the low 90's is an effect of the inherent challenge of tagging a text in which the same NE is frequently used to refer to different classes, merely reflecting the lower inter-annotator agreement in this test set. The flaw with the sentence selection algorithm is that Remaining UNK's never

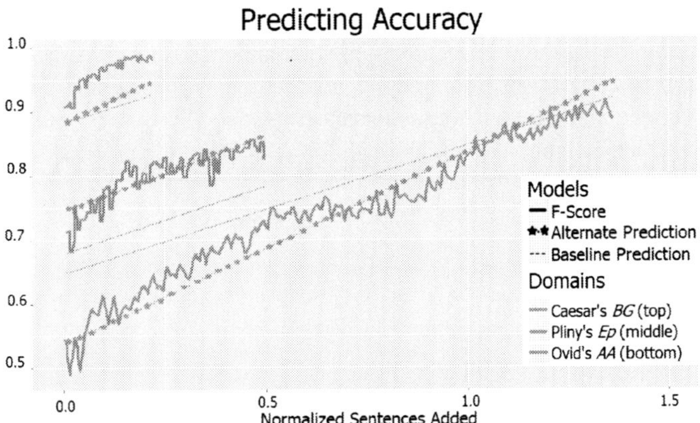

Figure 2: Leveraging distributional statistics of UNK's distinguishes the alternative model.

approach 0 in *Ep*. The algorithm fails to select sentences for some unknown PRS's because several (*Maximus, Clarus*, etc.) are homonymous with non-NE's, representing a third priority to be incorporated in the updated algorithm. However, for now, we can ignore the effect of homonymy by only considering results in *Ep* from 0 to 0.5 additional normalized sentences, the other texts being free of such effects.

4.2 Predicting Accuracy *Ex Ante*

We can use linear regression[2] to predict how accurately a text can be tagged based on how many sentences have been selected, enabling our Classicists to deduce how many sentences they must annotate to ensure sufficient tagging accuracy to support their work. We compare two potential regression models:

$$Y_b = \beta_0 + \beta_1 X_1 + \epsilon \tag{1}$$

$$Y_a = \beta_0' + \beta_1' X_1 + \epsilon' \tag{2}$$

The baseline Equation 1 predicts accuracy such that β_0, the accuracy before sentences are selected, is a function of the number of capitalized UNK's normalized by the expected number of NE's in the test set.[3] The rate at which accuracy changes, β_1, as sentences (normalized by the number of expected NE's) are added, X_1, is assumed to be constant across all train/test splits. The alternative Equation 2 predicts β_0' to be a function of the density of capitalized UNK's *weighted* by the proportions of priority levels represented therein, just as the sentence selection algorithm weights priority 1 words over priority 2's. β_1' is uniquely determined for every test set based on the type-to-token ratio of capitalized UNK's (also weighted by priorities), such that a higher type-to-token ratio predicts greater accuracy gains per sentence annotated. Figure 2 demonstrates that priority levels and type-to-token frequency ratios enhance our ability to predict accuracy gains via active learning and that accuracy can be well modeled through the upper-middle regions of the probability space. Ongoing work is addressing the effect of homonymy as well as the effect of similarity in distributions over NE labels between training and test sets – this is contributing to the greater-than-predicted accuracy in *BG*.

5 Conclusion

We present an active-learning NER pipeline for low-resource Latin that expedites accuracy gains at low annotation cost. Our pipeline enables researchers to gauge the reliability of NER output and upgrade that

---

[2] As we are in probability space, logistic regression would seem more fitting, but there are many complex non-linear effects due to e.g. the improvement of UNK accuracy as the density of UNK's decreases, such that we are still working on developing an adequately complex regression model; however, linear regression provides very suitable predictions of accuracy as texts improve through the upper-middle ranges of the probability space with which we are chiefly concerned.

[3] The number of NE's expected in the test set is the number of non-sentence-initial capitalized words plus the number of sentences which should start with an NE given equal distributions of NE's within sentences; however, this assumption is not entirely valid and we slightly over-predict NE's, though the minor effect should not bias our results.

reliability until it meets their standards for a given application. While still in development, our product makes novel contributions to the field including the first annotated corpus for evaluating NER in Latin and a formula for predicting tagging accuracy throughout the active learning process. This will all be made publicly available in the future: our annotated corpus and the supervised NER model trained on it as well as an interface for guiding users through the active learning process described here, enabling them to tailor our product to their own needs.

Acknowledgements

The authors of this paper are indebted to Nizar Habash and two anonymous reviewers for their advice.

References

Vamshi Ambati, Stephan Vogel, and Jaime G. Carbonell. 2011. Multi-Strategy Approaches to Active Learning for Statistical Machine Translation. *Proceedings of the 13th Machine Translation Summit.*

David Bamman and Gregory Crane. 2009. Structured Knowledge for Low-Resource Languages: The Latin and Ancient Greek Dependency Treebanks. Tufts University.

Avrim Blum and Tom Mitchell. 1998. Combining Labeled and Unlabeled Data with Co-Training. *COLT 98: Proceedings of the Eleventh Annual Conference on Computational Learning Theory*, pages 92–100.

Marco Budassi and Marco Passarotti. 2016. *Nomen Omen*: Enhancing the Latin Morphological Analyser Lemlat with an Onomasticon. *Proceedings of the 10th SIGHUM Workshop on Language Technology for Cultural Heritage, Social Sciences, and Humanities (LaTeCH)*, Berlin, Germany, 2016, pages 90–94.

Roberto Busa. 1974–1980. *Index Thomisticus.* Stuttgart-Bad Canstatt: Frommann-Holzboog. `www.corpusthomisticum.org/it/index.age`.

Eugene Charniak. 1997. Statistical Parsing with a Context-Free Grammar and Word Statistics. *Proceedings of the Fourteenth National Conference on Artificial Intelligence*, pages 598–603. Cambridge, MA; MIT Press.

Dag T. T. Haug and Marius L. Jøhndal. 2008. Creating a Parallel Treebank of the Old Indo-European Bible Translations. In Caroline Sporleder and Kiril Ribarov (eds.), *Proceedings of the Second Workshop on Language Technology for Cultural Heritage Data (LaTeCH 2008)*, pages 27–34.

David Cohn, Les Atlas, and Richard Ladner. 1994. Improving Generalization with Active Learning. *Machine Learning*, 15.2: 201–222.

Michael Collins and Yoram Singer. 1999. Unsupervised Models for Named Entity Classification. *Proceedings of the Joint SIGDAT Conference on Empirical Methods in Natural Language Processing and Very Large Corpora.*

Jenny R. Finkel, Trond Grenager, and Christopher Manning. 2005. Incorporating Non-local Information into Information Extraction Systems by Gibbs Sampling. *Proceedings of the 43nd Annual Meeting of the Association for Computational Linguistics (ACL 2005)*, pages 363–370.

Benjamin Farber, Dayne Freitag, Nizar Habash, and Owen Ranbow. 2008. Improving NER in Arabic Using a Morphological Tagger. In: N. Calzolari et al. (eds.), *Proceedings of the Language Resources and Evaluation Conference (LREC'08)*, pages 2509–2514.

Joseph L. Fleiss and Jacob Cohen. 1973. The equivalence of weighted kappa and the intraclass correlation coefficient as measures of reliability. *Educational and Psychological Measurement*, 33: 613–619.

Kyle P. Johnson et al. 2014-2016. CLTK: The Classical Language Toolkit. DOI 10.5281/zenodo.60021.

Wenhui Liao and Sriharsha Veeramachaneni. 2009. A Simple Semi-supervised Algorithm for Named Entity Recognition. *Proceedings of the NAACL HLT Workshop on Semi-Supervised Learning for Natural Language Processing*, pages 58–65. Boulder, CO: Association for Computational Linguistics.

Teresa Lynn, Jennifer Foster, Mark Dras, and Elaine Ul'Dhonnchandha. 2012. Active Learning and the Irish Treebank. *Proceedings of ALTA.*

Gary Marchionini. 2000. Evaluating Digital Libraries: A Longitudinal and Multifaceted View. University of North Carolina at Chapel Hill.

Andrew McCallum and Wei Li. 2003. Early Results for Named Entity Recognition with Conditional Random Fields, Feature Induction and Web-Enhanced Lexicons. *Proceedings of the Seventh Conference on Natural Language Learning (CONLL) at HLT-NAACL*, pages 188–191. NAACL Press.

Barbara McGillivray. 2014. *Methods in Computational Linguistics*. Leiden: E.J. Brill.

Barbara McGillivray, Marco Passarotti and Paolo Ruffolo. 2009. The *Index Thomisticus* Treebank Project: Annotation, Parsing and Valency Lexicon. *TAL*, 50.2: 103–127.

Jean-Baptiste Michel, Yuan Kui Shen, Aviva Presser Aiden, Adrian Veres, Matthew K. Gray, William Brockman, Google Books Team, Joseph P. Pickett, Dale Hoiberg, Dan Clancy, Peter Norvig, Jon Orwant, Steven Pinker, Martin A. Nowak, and Erez Lieberman Aiden. 2010. Quantitative Analysis of Culture Using Millions of Digitized Books. *Science*, 311.6014: 176–182.

Thomas Mikolov, Kai Chen, Greg Corrado, and Jeffrey Dean. 2013. Efficient Estimation of Word Representations in Vector Space. *Proceedings of Workshop at ICLR*.

Packard Humanities Institute. 1992. *PHI CD ROM Format Description*. Los Altos, CA.

David Pierce and Claire Cardie. 2001. Limitations of Co-Training for Natural Language Learning from Large Datasets *Proceedings of the 2001 Conference on Empirical Methods in Natural Language Processing*.

Edoardo Martia Ponti and Marco Passarotti. 2016. *Differentia Compositionem Facit*: A Slower-Paced and Reliable Parser for Latin. *Tenth International Conference on Language Resources and Evaluation (LREC 2016)*, 683–688.

Pratibha Rani, Vikram Pudi, and Dipti Sharma Misra. 2014. TagMiner: A Semisupervised Associative POS Tagger Effective for Resource Poor Languages. In: P. Cellier et al. (eds.): *Proceedings of DMNLP, Workshop at ECML/PKDD*, Nancy, France, 2014, pages 113–128.

Helmut Schmid. 1999. Improvements in Part-of-Speech Tagging with an Application to German. In: Susan Armstrong et al. (eds.): *Text, Speech and Language Technology Natural Language Processing Using Very Large Corpora*, pages 13–25. Dordrecht: Kluwer Academic Publishers.

David A. Smith, Jeffrey A. Rydberg-Cox, and Gregory R. Crane. 2000. The Perseus Project: a Digital Library for the Humanities. *Literary and Linguistic Computing*, 15: 15–25.

William Smith. 1854. *Dictionary of Greek and Roman Geography*. Perseus Project.

William Smith. 1870. *Dictionary of Greek and Roman Antiquities*. Perseus Project.

William Smith. 1890. *Dictionary of Greek and Roman Biography and Mythology*. Perseus Project.

Nataliya Sokolovska. 2011. Aspects of Semi-Supervised and Active Learning in Conditional Random Fields. *Proceedings of the European Conference on Machine Learning (ECML PKDD)*, pages 273–288. Berlin: Springer.

William Whitaker. 1993. William Whitaker's Words: `http://archives.nd.edu/words.html`.

Geographical Visualization of Search Results in Historical Corpora

Florian Petran

Ruhr-Universität Bochum

`petran@linguistics.rub.de`

Abstract

We present ANNISVis, a webapp for comparative visualization of geographical distribution of linguistic data, as well as a sample deployment for a corpus of Middle High German texts. Unlike existing geographical visualization solutions, which work with pre-existing data sets, or are bound to specific corpora, ANNISVis allows the user to formulate multiple ad-hoc queries and visualizes them on a map, and it can be configured for any corpus that can be imported into ANNIS. This enables explorative queries of the quantitative aspects of a corpus with geographical features. The tool will be made available to download in open source.

1 Introduction

Work on visualizing language corpora usually focuses more or less on specific phenomena, such as term relations or semantic structure of a text (such as (Cao et al., 2010) or (Fortuna et al., 2005)). Quantitative relations are represented with techniques from the data sciences, and the corpus is largely treated as an atomic entity — it is visualized as a whole, and not in parts. This is a necessity, first due to the broad and varied nature of linguistic phenomena present in annotated corpora, and due to the irrelevance of geographical distribution in most synchronic corpora. So in relation to corpora, visualization often means picturing complex annotations such as trees, or dependency relations. This type of visualization focuses on qualitative work.

Conversely, geographic visualization is usually done for the social sciences, or in historical studies. In those disciplines, queries are usually not formulated ad-hoc, but carefully prepared, since the data is harder to come by. So data is specifically gathered for a certain research question, and it is gathered to answer that question explicitly and only. Data sets are therefore less rich than linguistic corpora typically are. The tools reflect that in that they usually require the user to import query results generated elsewhere.

However, in corpora of dialects, or diachronic corpora, the geographical distribution can be a central, or at least very important feature. We present a solution for geographical visualization of arbitrarily complex, ad-hoc searches. The visualization itself is fairly simple — circles on a map, scaled for match count. However, the ability to combine it with very different type of corpora, and with user queries makes it a powerful tool for historical and dialectal research.

Section 2 below will discuss two tools that are partially similar in functionality. Section 3 explains the implementation of the application in technical detail (3.1), and the user interface (3.2). Section 4 shows our sample deployment. In Subsection 4.1 we give some brief details on the corpus used for the sample deployment, and Subsection 4.2 demonstrates the functionality on a short example. Finally, section 5 will discuss plans for further development.

2 Related Work

ANNIS (Krause and Zeldes, 2014) is a search architecture as well as an approach to the visualization of different annotation levels in corpora that is applicable for a vast array of linguistic corpora. It is realized as a web application with a browser interface as well as a webservice. Queries can be formulated in a

Proceedings of the Workshop on Language Technology Resources and Tools for Digital Humanities (LT4DH),
pages 94–100, Osaka, Japan, December 11-17 2016.

specialized language (ANNIS Query Language), that allows specification of annotations from sub-token to sentence levels, and simple or complex interactions between them. The ANNIS web interface present matches for the query in a KWIC-like format, where each match is shown with a context window to the left and right. This facilitates qualitative research by browsing the results, but for quantitative approaches, the results have to be exported for use in third party tools.

GeoBrowser[1] is a data sheet editor and geographical visualization tool that was developed for historical, or social sciences use. Data points are represented with scaled markers on a map overlay. The tool offers a range of historical maps to choose from by default. Data has to be imported in a spread sheet format, or entered in an online tool. The tool will then automatically retrieve the geolocations, place the markers accordingly, and, if applicable, cluster them according to the zoom level. If a timeline can be construed from the data, the tool will also allow to limit the visualization to a sub period, or run an animation of the timeline.

While GeoBrowser offers comprehensive options for geographical visualization, it has two main drawbacks for our purposes. First, the process of generating results and then importing them is too slow and cumbersome to allow for explorative visualization of ad-hoc queries. The process of exporting and importing implicitly assumes that the user has an exact plan of the phenomena he wants to visualize. And second, GeoBrowser is closed source with a centralized server architecture, while our tool will be made available to download as well.

Geographical visualization has a long tradition in dialectology that goes back to the late 19th century founding of the *Deutscher Sprachatlas* by Georg Wenker (1888). He had compiled a list of example sentences that were translated into local dialects by volunteers. The *Atlas* then mapped the geographic boundaries between the various pronunciation features (isoglosses) drawn from the example sentences. The mapping of isoglosses remained the dominant approach in dialect mapping for most of the 20th century. From 2001 on, the publishers of the *Atlas* have started to digitize the maps making them available online[2], but the material remains more or less static.

There is ongoing discussion on effective use of computer generated maps (Schmidt and Auer, 2011). Early work on this area focuses on combining digitized maps of isoglosses in semi-transparent overlays, allowing comparative view of various different maps. In the later 20th century, the approach of dialectometry used quantitative approaches and similarity calculations to visualize dialectal differences. Traditional means of quantitative mapping in cartography are choropleth maps, and isarithmic, or contour maps. Coropleth maps show variation in aggregated data by different color shades over predefined regions. Contour maps show regions with the same value as line-bounded areas on a map. Both approaches have been used for mapping of aggregated dialect data.

Similarities between pronunciations can be further visualized with beam maps, which show similarities with lines between sites – the darker the line, the more similar the data (Goebl, 1984). This relies on relatively simple similarity calculations, if the aggregate data is clustered, those clusters can also be visualized. For example, the composite cluster map approach (Kleiweg et al., 2004) tiles the map into polygons around collection sites, and then shades the polygon borders according to their distance in the cluster dendrogram.

Compared to these approaches, our visualization is fairly simplistic, and it is certainly not suitable for every research question. Its main advantage, however, is its flexibility, the ability to apply it to any corpus that can be imported into ANNIS and is annotated with some geographic features.

3 Application

3.1 Implementation

ANNISVis builds on an existing installation of the search tool ANNIS. ANNIS works as a client-server app itself, with a Java applet frontend and a Java server backend. It is highly configurable and able to import a large number of formats for linguistic corpora (Krause and Zeldes, 2014). A server application

---

[1] http://geobrowser.de.dariah.eu/
[2] https://regionalsprache.de/

in Python over WSGI queries the ANNIS webservice for a complete list of documents from the corpus. A document is the smallest sub-division of a corpus in ANNIS.

The server then looks for specific keywords in the meta annotations of the corpus (i.e. annotations that relate to an entire document) that denote a place of origin. The keywords are obviously corpus dependent, so they can be configured at deployment time of the application. On first launch, the coordinates for each place name are looked up using the Google geocoding API via the GeoPy library[3]. A fallback meta key for the location specification can be provided as well.

Since looking up the places for a corpus with a lot of documents can take a long time, the server caches the geolocations it looked up in a JSON file. In addition to the API lookup, the administrator of the server has the opportunity to supply a file with predefined locations. This serves as an override for cases the Google API gets wrong, such as historical dialect areas, or places that do not exist any more. In cases where multiple documents have the same location, they are combined for the purposes of displaying search results on the map. In this paper, we will refer to these combinations of document set and geolocation as location.

The text list is returned by the server webapp upon page loading, the rest of the functionality is realized client side in JavaScript (using JQuery[4] and the Google Maps API[5]) over XML requests to the ANNIS service. Each datum presented in the UI is in its own container element, so that the presentation can easily be adapted with CSS.

3.2 User interface

The search box allows the user to formulate any query using ANNIS Query Language (see Sec. 4.2 for a brief explanation). The ANNIS web service is then queried for the counts for each document set at each location separately, and the results are displayed as circles at their geolocation on the map as a result marker with a scaled size relative to the number of search results. The map is automatically centered to show all locations that are present in the corpus that has been configured.

Two techniques for scaling are available: global and local. With global scaling, the location with the highest number of search results receives the largest circle, and the other locations are scaled accordingly. It will be most useful for a corpus of roughly evenly sized documents. Local scaling adjusts each result marker according to the number of tokens in the document. It can be a way of dealing with a corpus that is somewhat unevenly distributed (as historical corpora often are due to limited text availability). However, not all phenomena are suitable for local scaling with this method. Low frequency phenomena make up a very small percentage of their documents, so they will result in very small markers that are not easily visible on the map. Both methods of scaling can therefore be selected by the user before submitting a search request.

Result markers have info popups that can be configured to show different information on that specific results. Currently, it shows a basic description of the query results in general, and the result count. Each query gets assigned a color with uniformly random distribution over red, green, and blue values. While predefined colors would look better, they are not feasible in a system where a user can make an arbitrary number of queries. The random distribution ensures that it is fairly unlikely that two query colors are too close to be distinguishable.

Multiple queries may show results in the same places, and the result markers of close by places may overlap or obscure each other due to the scaling. ANNISVis offers several ways of dealing with this. When the user clicks on markers that overlap, they will move apart ("spiderfy") with lines indicating their original locations (see Fig. 1). Furthermore, the user has options to hide markers, or to fore- or background markers. Operations can be performed through the query context menu, in which case they apply for all markers, or on the marker list accessible through the text list, in which case they apply only to the selected marker.

---

[3]https://github.com/geopy/geopy/
[4]https://jquery.com/
[5]https://developers.google.com/maps/

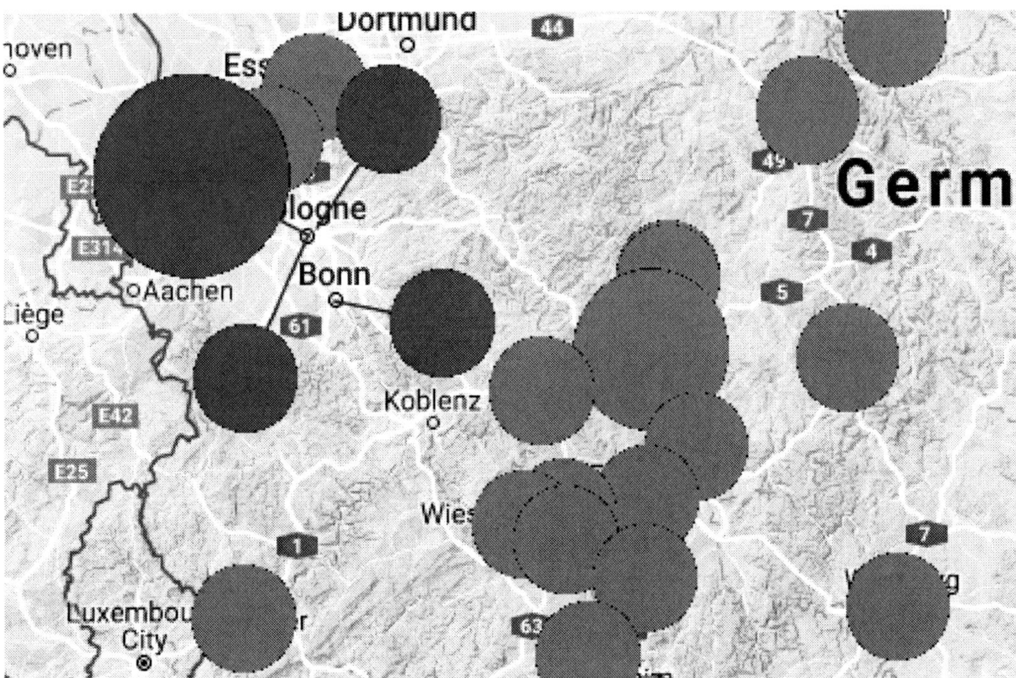

Figure 1: Part of a visualization with spiderfied markers. The spiderfied markers are in a slightly shaded version of the query color.

4 Sample Deployment

4.1 Language Data

The example below and our sample deployment uses the reference corpus Middle High German (REM), an annotated corpus of texts from about 1050 to 1350 AD (Petran et al., submitted). It combines and builds upon existing projects for historical corpora dating as far back as the 1980s. Some of the texts are fragments of only a few tokens, others are up to 100,000 tokens long. All texts are annotated with token level annotations (such as POS, morphology), and sub-token annotations for tokenization changes. The texts further have meta-annotation of the written dialect ("Schreibsprache") in different granularities, and some texts have their provenience annotated. The corpus aims to be largely balanced with regards to dialect, as far as the sources permit. This makes it very suitable to demonstrate the type of visualization our application can provide. However, especially the early part of the time period covered it was not possible to find enough texts for all dialects, which can lead to a skewed distribution of data, making it very suitable to

The meta key for the location lookup was configured to the place where the document was written. Unfortunately, this is not annotated for all documents. A number of factors come into play localizing a medieval document, including the place where a manuscript was written, where a scribe was born, where he was trained, and the adressee of a document. The obvious choice would be to use the dialect area annotation as fallback, however, those areas do not correspond to modern geographic entities, so no geocoding API recognizes them — they have to be manually geocoded. For the results shown in the screenshots below, we instead used the library where the manuscript is kept today as a placeholder. The library is not a valid localization by any of the standards outlined above, and the screenshots can therefore only serve as a proof of concept type demonstration. The real sample deployment will use manually geocoded dialect areas.

The geocoding worked well for the vast majority of the documents, but a few had to be manually corrected, such as St. Paul's abbey in Lavanttal (in Austria) which the API thought identical to St. Paul,

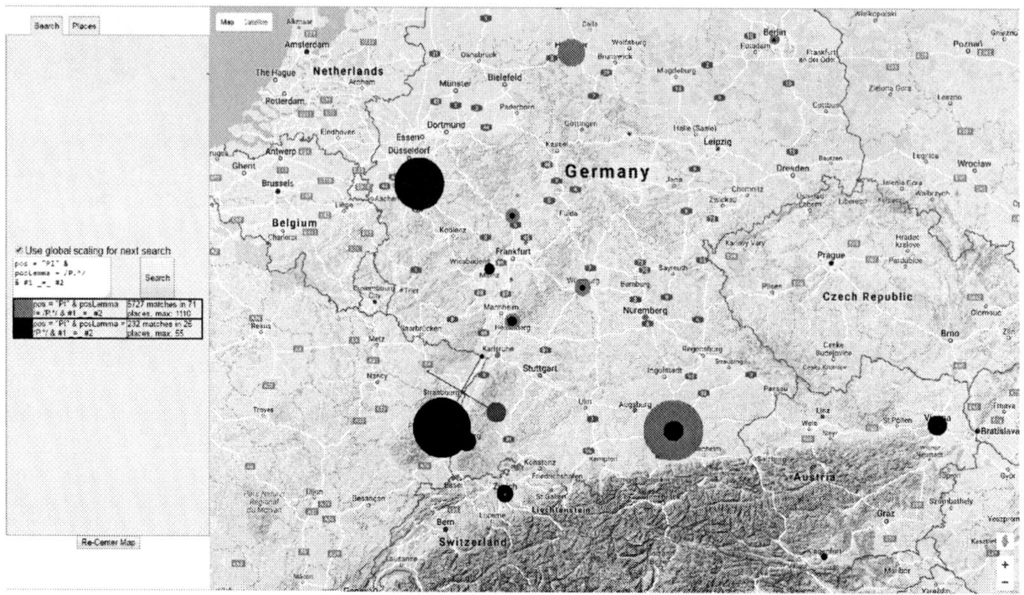

Figure 2: Visualization of two queries for pronouns

Minnesota.

A special feature of the corpus we used is its fine grained POS annotation (Dipper et al., 2013), which discerns the POS of the type (`posLemma`) and the POS of the token in its present usage (`pos`). For example, a prototypical adjective would be tagged ADJ as `posLemma`, and ADJA (attributive adjective) for `pos` if used in an attributive function (as opposed to an adverbial function for example). This enables a user to, among other things, study language change, as we will see below.

4.2 Example

An example user could be interested in studying pronouns in historical German dialects. Figure 2 shows such queries in our tool. The input box on the left shows the last user entered query in ANNIS Query Language (AQL). We will now briefly explain its syntax as far as it relates to this example[6].

Basic building blocks of AQL are search *nodes*, and interactions between the nodes. A search node is any query for annotations or annotation values. For example, a query for `pos` will return all elements with that annotation, while a query for `pos='PI'` will only return those that were annotated with PI (indefinite pronoun). `posLemma!=/P.*/` is a query using regular expressions that returns all elements where `posLemma` does not begin with P — that is, tokens that are not, according to their lemma, a pronoun.

As an example, consider (1). The token *man* — glossed as "one" here — is used as indefinite pronoun (PI), but the lemma originally means "man," a nomen appellativum (NA), and it can be used in this capacity in other places. This shows the language change from a single lemma *man* that can be used both as NA and PI to the modern situation where the PI is *man* and the NA is *Mann*.

(1)		*do*	*man*	*daz*	*kint*	*beſniden*	*ſcolte*
	pos	KOUS	PI	DDART	NA	VVINF	VMFIN
	posLemma	KO	NA	DD	NA	VV	VM
		when	one	the	child	circumcise	should

"when the child should be circumcised"

As a counterexample, consider (2). The token *niemen* is used as PI, and the type is also already a PI.

---

[6]for detailed documentation see `http://corpus-tools.org/annis/aql.html`

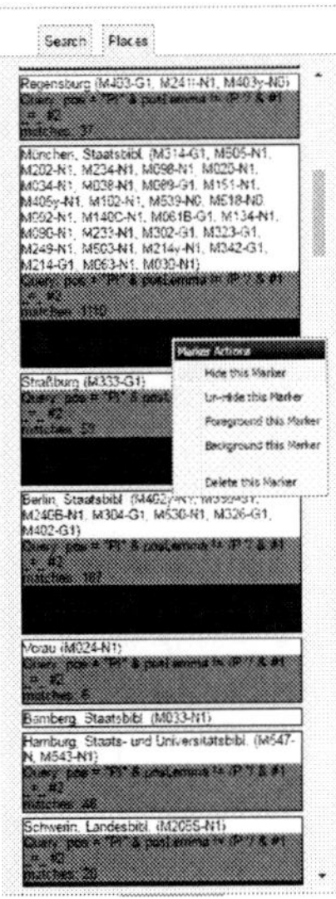

Figure 3: An entry in the text list

(2)

	ímo	*ſcol*	*niemen*	*gelôbe*
`pos`	PPER	VMINF	PI	VVINF
`posLemma`	PPER	VMINF	PI	VV
	him	should	nobody	believe

"no one should believe him"

The search statement can refer to nodes by index in order of specification, so the `posLemma!=/P.*/` in Figure 2 is referred to as `#2`. A number of operators can specify how the annotations have to interact. In this example, `#1_=_#2` specify that both search conditions must apply to the same position.

In simpler words, we search for tokens that are used as indefinite pronouns, but are not originally pronouns in the first (light grey) query, and indefinite pronouns that are originally (according to their lemma) pronouns in the second (dark grey) query.

On the map (Figure 3), we can clearly see a distribution where western regions seem to favor original pronouns, while texts located in Bavaria and further north have a lot of pronouns that are not originally pronouns. It also shows how we spiderfied the markers around Strasbourg so we can tell apart the individual, overlapping results. The exact number of matches is displayed in the info popup for each location, which is not shown in the example, but also in the entry for each individual result in the location list tab (see Figure 3). The location list also offers marker actions (discussed in Section 3.2) as a context menu. The text list entries also give the match counts, to enable comparative evaluation of the query results on a location basis.

5 Future Work

In its current form, the system does not consider the diachronicity of the data at all. For future iterations, tieing the markers to a slider for the temporal axis, similar to what GeoBrowser offers, will be implemented.

Both local and global scaling are not always optimal, due to the reasons explained in Sec. 3 above. For future development we will look into alternative ways of scaling marker size, and possibilities of combining scaling for text size and scaling for global maxima.

Finally, we would like to explore the possibilities of searches based on annotation values, where the system can rank their relevance for each document with a measure like tf-idf, and display the most relevant values on their map locations.

Resources

The following resources are provided with this paper.

1. The source code of the application described in this paper. It can be found at `https://github.com/fpetran/annisvis`

2. A sample deployment using the reference corpus Middle High German (REM). It can be found at `http://www.linguistics.rub.de/annisvis`

Acknowledgements

My work has been funded by the Deutsche Forschungsgemeinschaft (DFG) grant DI 1558/1. I thank the anonymous reviewers for their helpful comments and suggestions.

References

Nan Cao, Jimeng Sun, Yu-Ru Lin, David Gotz, Shixia Liu, and Huamin Qu. 2010. Facetatlas: Multifaceted visualization for rich text corpora. *IEEE Transactions on Visualization and Computer Graphics*, 16(6):1172–1181.

Stefanie Dipper, Karin Donhauser, Thomas Klein, Sonja Linde, Stefan Müller, and Klaus-Peter Wegera. 2013. HiTS: ein Tagset für historische Sprachstufen des Deutschen. *Journal for Language Technology and Computational Linguistics, Special Issue*, 28(1):85–137.

Blaz Fortuna, Marko Grobelnik, and Dunja Mladenic. 2005. Visualization of text document corpus. *Informatica*, 29(4).

Hans Goebl. 1984. *Dialektometrische Studien: Anhand italoromanischer, rätoromanischer und galloromanischer Sprachmaterialien aus AIS und ALF*. Niemeyer, Tübingen.

Peter Kleiweg, John Nerbonne, and Leonie Bosveld. 2004. Geographic projection of cluster composites. In Alan Blackwell, Kim Marriott, and Atsushi Shimojima, editors, *Diagrammatic Representation and Inference*, pages 392–394. Springer, Berlin.

Thomas Krause and Amir Zeldes. 2014. ANNIS3: A new architecture for generic corpus query and visualization. *Digital Scholarship in the Humanities*.

Florian Petran, Thomas Klein, Stefanie Dipper, and Marcel Bollmann. submitted. REM: A reference corpus of Middle High German — corpus compilation, annotation, and access. *Journal for Language Technology and Computational Linguistics*.

Jürgen Erich Schmidt and Peter Auer, editors. 2011. *Language and Space: an international handbook of linguistic variation*. de Gruyter, Berlin, Boston.

Implementation of a Workflow Management System for Non-Expert Users

Bart Jongejan
NFI-University of Copenhagen
Njalsgade 136, building 27
DK-2300 Copenhagen S
`bartj@hum.ku.dk`

Abstract

In the Danish CLARIN-DK infrastructure, chaining language technology (LT) tools into a workflow is easy even for a non-expert user, because she only needs to specify the input and the desired output of the workflow. With this information and the registered input and output profiles of the available tools, the CLARIN-DK workflow management system (WMS) computes combinations of tools that will give the desired result. This advanced functionality was originally not envisaged, but came within reach by writing the WMS partly in Java and partly in a programming language for symbolic computation, Bracmat. Handling LT tool profiles, including the computation of workflows, is easier with Bracmat's language constructs for tree pattern matching and tree construction than with the language constructs offered by mainstream programming languages.

1   Introduction

The CLARIN-DK infrastructure[1] has a workflow management system (WMS) that transforms, annotates and analyses the user's input. The WMS combines tools, deployed as web services, in just such a way that output is produced of the type that the user asked for, or it tells the user that such output cannot be made given the input and the available tools. The user is not required to be acquainted with the tools. In principle, neither do providers of new tools need to know which tools are registered. The currently registered tools are language technology (LT) tools (e.g., OCR, lemmatisation, syntactic analysis), but the WMS welcomes any tool that can run without direct user interaction, and new file types can be added if needed. For a description of the architecture and user interface of the WMS, see (Jongejan, 2013).

In this paper we lift the veil for the way the WMS is implemented, because we think that the symbolic computation programming language that was used for most of the implementation, Bracmat, can be used in other corners of digital humanities concerned with querying and transforming (semi-)structured data.

Symbolic computation software is primarily for solving mathematical equations, but has nevertheless a wide field of application. The WMS is one of the examples illustrating this. Tool registration, computation of workflows, simplification of the presentation of workflows before being presented to the user: each of these tasks calls for the operations that are the rationale for symbolic computation software.

Before designing the WMS, we discussed scenarios for how a user could interact with our WMS. In one scenario a user would have to assemble a workflow manually. A 'wizard' would made that task easier by for example not allowing a user to insert a tool that was not compatible with the output from already selected tools earlier in the workflow. In a more advanced scenario, the 'hairdresser' scenario, the WMS would combine the tools autonomously, while a user only had to specify the required result.

The hairdresser scenario was a logical next step, since there were already workflow systems that assisted users with assembling workflows of LT tools, for example our institute's simple but successful web-based toolbox. From the implementation point of view the hairdresser scenario had the advantage that the user interface would be simpler than in the wizard scenario. All that was needed was an input form to get the specification of the user's goal and a form where the user could choose one of the proposed

[1] https://clarin.dk/

Proceedings of the Workshop on Language Technology Resources and Tools for Digital Humanities (LT4DH),
pages 101–108, Osaka, Japan, December 11-17 2016.

workflows, if the WMS found more than one solution. There would be relatively little need for feedback to the user, since the user would not be able to make errors.

Both scenarios would require input and output profile information for each integrated tool, but in the hairdresser scenario this information was required to be complete, so that no workflows could be computed that, when executed, would fail to work because of an undocumented mismatch between tools. In the wizard scenario the user's expertise could supplement incomplete registered tool information.

We chose to implement the hairdresser scenario. Java was used for all interactions with other CLARIN-DK modules and Bracmat for the computation and management of the workflows. Eight person months were allotted to the implementation of the first version, which was ready in 2011.

This paper proceeds as follows. In section 2 we present Bracmat. In section 3 we discuss why symbolic computation software and especially Bracmat makes it easy to implement an automatic WMS. In section 4 we explain why an essential feature of symbolic computation, pattern matching (PM), is best done in a programming language that has PM as a language construct. In section 5 we refer to related work. In section 6 we tell how to obtain the WMS and Bracmat. In section 7 we present the conclusions.

2 Bracmat

Bracmat is a programming language for symbolic computation created[2] by the author. Bracmat was used to perform long chains of algebraic manipulations without human supervision or interaction with intermediary results. Very soon, after minor additions, Bracmat was also used for analysis and manipulation of a much wider class of complex data, such as (semi-)structured text, thereby maximally utilizing the high level programming language constructs that already were in place to handle algebraic expressions.

PM in tree structures is an important operation in rule-based systems for symbolic computation, term rewriting and theorem proving (Ramesh and Ramakrishnan, 1992). Bracmat is no exception and has an expressive PM syntax that, in a few words, is characterised by these three PM capabilities:

- Tree PM for analysing tree structured data,
- Evaluation during PM of expressions that are embedded inside patterns, and
- Associative PM to capture zero or more subtrees with a single pattern variable.

We refer to section 6 for pointers to the full documentation of the Bracmat language and to code examples. Let it be said here that there are no restrictions on what types of expressions can be evaluated while a pattern is matched against data. It is for example possible to formulate deeply nested, even recursive, embedded PM operations, or to accumulate partial results of a PM operation, or to print messages during PM to find errors in a pattern. Associative PM, a feature that we take for granted when applying *regexp* patterns to strings, allows a pattern component to capture not just one, but a stretch of zero or more elements from a list, for example a sublist of seven subtrees somewhere in a much longer list.

Bracmat has been used in several LT related projects. Here are a few examples.

Format transformation of data. Bracmat has built-in functions for reading and writing XML, HTML, SGML and JSON data, making it easy to inspect and transform such data as native Bracmat expressions. For some tools that are registered in the WMS, Bracmat transforms data from the CLARIN-DK TEI P5 format to tool specific formats (e.g., CONLL, Penn Treebank bracketed format) and back again.

Anonymisation of court orders. In software developed for a commercial publisher of juridical text, Bracmat is used for named-entity normalisation and anonymisation of digital editions of court orders. In contrast to LT tools that only accept pre-processed plain text, this software reads the source document, which is in a proprietary XML format, and transfers all lay-out to the output (Povlsen et al., 2016).

Validation of the Dutch text corpora MWE, D-COI, DPC, Lassi, and SoNaR (van Noord et al., 2013). Bracmat was used for sampling, for checking XML well-formedness, PoS-tag usage and agreement between documentation and annotation practice, and for preparation of the tables in the validation reports.

Multimodal communication in a virtual world. In the virtual world implemented in the Staging project (Paggio and Jongejan, 2005) the functionality and data structures that let the farmer agent keep track of the dialogue and that caused appropriate agent actions and speech acts were written in Bracmat.

---

[2]Bracmat (then: Bacmat) made its first public appearance during a colloquium at Vakgroep Informatica, (then) Rijksuniversiteit Utrecht, 12 December 1989.

3 Workflow Computation is Symbolic Computation

From the outset, we had an intuition that symbolic computation software, and especially Bracmat, could help us tremendously to implement a WMS according to the hairdresser model. Many techniques that are required in the automatic WMS are ingrained in symbolic computation: building and destroying tree structures, testing equality of tree structures, finding common factors, sorting, factorization, normalization, and backtracking.

At the core of the WMS is the automatic computation of workflows. The algorithm we chose for computing workflows is called 'dynamic programming' (Bellman, 1957). We start from the goal, finding the tool or tools that can produce the output. The input specifications of those tools constitute subgoals that are solved recursively. We reduce the computation time by storing solutions to already solved (sub)goals, so they can be re-used. This is called 'memoizing'. Dynamic programming is also used in LT, for example in the Earley algorithm (Earley, 1983) for parsing strings using a context free grammar.

The dynamic programming algorithm itself can be implemented in any programming language, but there are many related processes where the WMS benefits of symbolic computation. We only mention two: normalization of tool registration data and simplification of the presentation of candidate workflows.

3.1 Normalization of tool registration data

The registered information about a tool consists of boiler plate information and input/output specification. The boiler plate information consists of the name of the tool, the service URL of the tool, and metadata that are not needed for running a tool, such as the name of its creator. The input/output specifications are in three levels of detail: incarnations, features and value subspecifications. We briefly explain these.

```
 ────────────────── Registered I/O specification for the Brill-tagger ──────────────
 1│   ... other tools ...
 2│ + ( Brill-tagger
 3│   .   (facet,(segments*tokens^PennTree.PoS^PennTree))
 4│       (format,(flat.flat)+(TEIP5annotation.TEIP5annotation))
 5│       (language,(en.en))
 6│   )
 7│ + ( Brill-tagger
 8│   .   (facet,(segments*tokens NER.PoS^(Moses+Parole)))
 9│       (format,(flat.flat)+(TEIP5annotation.TEIP5annotation))
10│       (language,(da.da))
11│   )
12│ + ... other tools ...
```

$$(1)$$

> Two incarnations of the Brill tagger. The first incarnation is for English and requires as input segments and tokens. The tokens must obey the rules set for the Penn Treebank: $isn't \rightarrow is\_n't$, etc. It outputs Part of Speech tags from the Penn Treebank tag set. The second incarnation is for Danish. It also requires segments and tokens, but optionally it can also read named entity annotations (NER). The produced tags belong to the Moses tag set or the Parole tag set. Both incarnations handle either flat or TEI P5 input and output files.

At the top level are incarnations, illustrated in code example (1) as the two sets of I/O specifications for a Part of Speech tagger. The incarnations cannot be merged into one, because they differ in more than one feature: facet and language. Mixing the incarnations would suggest that the tagger could output Parole tags for English text, for example, which is not the case. For best performance and a compact visual representation, the WMS organizes a tool's I/O specifications in as few incarnations as possible.

At the second level are the already mentioned features. Features are (ideally) mutually independent: the value of a feature has no influence on the value another feature can have. The most important features are facet (or 'type of content'), file format and language. Not all features need to be specified. If, for example, a tool is not language sensitive, then the language feature does not need to be specified.

At the third level are optional subclasses of values at the second level. For example, an image-to-text tool may produce output in the file format 'RTF', with the precaution 'OCR' as subclass. If another tool's input format is 'RTF', subclass 'OCR', or just plain 'RTF', then there is a format match.

An incarnation is computed by an algorithm that is similar to partial factorization of a sum. Factorization not only creates organization that pleases the eye, but also speeds up the calculation of workflows: it takes only two comparisons to realize that the Brill tagger in example (1) does not support German, whereas a completely unfolded representation would require checking ten different incarnations[3].

How symbolic computation and PM can help to keep the tool metadata normalized is illustrated in code examples (2) and (3). The `tools` variable is a sum, where each term is an incarnation. In a sum all terms are automatically sorted and equal terms are automatically reduced to a single term.

Both examples are PM operations. A pattern is the right hand side operand of the match operator ':'. The pattern in (2) continues over several lines and exhibits all three PM capabilities mentioned in Section 2: It operates on **tree structured data** (the tool incarnations), is **associative** (the variables A, M and Z are bound to varying numbers of intervening tool incarnations), and contains an **embedded expression**. The embedded expression, itself a match operation, is the right hand side of the '&' operator. The pattern is also non-linear, since the pattern variable `ToolName` occurs more than once.

```
                          ──── Spot two incarnations that can be merged ────
 1    !tools
 2 :        ?A
 3      +  (?ToolName.?Features1)
 4      +  ?M
 5      +  ( !ToolName
 6        .    ?AA
 7             ( (?FeatureName,?Values2) ?ZZ
 8             &    !Features1
 9             : !AA (!FeatureName,?Values1) !ZZ
10           )
11        )
12      +  ?Z
```
(2)

"Find two incarnations of a tool that are equal except for one feature. Bind all other tool incarnations to A, M and Z, the values of the equal features to AA and ZZ, the name of the exception to `FeatureName`, and the differing values to the variables `Values1` and `Values2`."

Code example (3) illustrates the ease with which a rewritten `tools` list is built from smaller chunks.

```
                          ──── Merge two mergeable incarnations ────
 1        !A
 2      + !M
 3      + ( !ToolName
 4        .    !AA
 5             (!FeatureName, !Values1+!Values2)
 6             !ZZ
 7        )
 8      + !Z
 9 : ?tools
```
(3)

"Rewrite the list of tools by reducing the number of incarnations."

3.2 Simplification of the presentation of candidate workflows

If there is more than one viable workflow, the user must choose. One of the applied strategies to make this easier for the user is to minimise the amount of information that is shown to her. This is done by not showing details that are not needed to see the differences between any two workflows in the list. A maximally simplified list of workflows displays the names of the involved tools in each workflow and those feature values and feature value subclassifications that are needed to see the differences. To bring the differences to light, the similarities have to be found and eliminated in a process that dynamically constructs and gradually improves a pattern that describes those similarities. The mathematical analogue is finding and then eliminating the polynomial greatest common divisor in a number of polynomials.

---

[3]The first incarnation explodes to two incarnations, one for flat text and one for TEI P5 annotations. The second incarnation doubles three times: (a) with or without NER, (b) Moses or Parole tags and (c) flat or TEI P5 format.

4 Limitations to symbolic computation with general purpose programming languages

The data types that are needed for symbolic computation can be implemented in a general purpose programming language, but the PM facilities for querying such data require specialized languages.

There are several formal query languages that are designed for querying tree structured data. These query languages can be used in scripts and programs written in mainstream languages like Java.

At first sight, writing an application using both a programming language and a query language seems to combine all the advantages of the query language with all the advantages of the programming language, but there are some disadvantages that manifest themselves when queries need to be created dynamically or when they become so complex that they no longer can be expressed in the query language.

In our understanding, a query expression, or more generally a pattern, is a declarative (as opposed to procedural) depiction of constraints on data content and data structure. That depiction can, but need not, have some similitude to data that the pattern matches. Patterns are expressed in some 'pattern language' $\mathcal{P}$. If a programming language $\mathcal{L}$ is not a $\mathcal{P}$ at the same time, then the programmer must delegate PM to a library that implements a $\mathcal{P}$. While the use of libraries in many situations results in solutions with a good separation of functionality over distinct modules, this is not the case with PM. Given only input data, a PM library still lacks the instructions from the $\mathcal{L}$ program that tell the library what to do with the data, and those instructions have to be expressed in the $\mathcal{P}$ language. A $\mathcal{P}$ expression can have a very complex grammatical structure. That structure must somehow be constructed by the $\mathcal{L}$ program, but since $\mathcal{L}$ and $\mathcal{P}$ are different languages, the $\mathcal{L}$ program is blind for the full structure of $\mathcal{P}$ expressions and not able to understand their parts. The $\mathcal{L}$ program can only handle $\mathcal{P}$ expressions at a (much) lower level than the $\mathcal{P}$ library, for example at the character string level as in code example (4).

The Java code in (4) creates an object that strings characters together to form the XPath expression `/tei:TEI/tei:text/tei:spanGrp[@ana='#tokens']`. The structure observed in Java, consisting of three simple Java String objects that are concatenated, has no relation to the structure of the query. The full structure and semantics of the query is not understood before the constructed string is handed down to the XPath library and interpreted as a $\mathcal{P}$ expression.

```
————— Java code that dynamically creates and executes an XPath expression —————
1 Document xml = streamToXml(xmlFile);
2 String id = "tokens";
3 Node span = execXPath("/tei:TEI/tei:text/tei:spanGrp[@ana='#"+id+"']",xml);
```

$$(4)$$

The split between $\mathcal{L}$ and $\mathcal{P}$ creates a need for interpretation and consequently overhead that materializes as extra programming code and an extra load on the CPU, but there are more problems with separate $\mathcal{L}$ and $\mathcal{P}$ languages. Often, as in example (4), $\mathcal{P}$ expressions appear as string values in a program that is written in $\mathcal{L}$, so $\mathcal{L}$ plays the role of host language for an embedded language $\mathcal{P}$. While $\mathcal{L}$ expressions and statements are analysed and evaluated for correct syntax during compilation of the program, syntactic and other formal errors in $\mathcal{P}$ expressions are discovered at run time, if ever. This is very unfavourable, because in rule based applications the patterns are usually the real workhorses, the most difficult to get right and most in need of debug facilities. Last but not least, a critical consequence of the asymmetry between host and embedded language is that it is impossible to evaluate $\mathcal{L}$ expressions inside $\mathcal{P}$ expressions.

In section 3 we have given an example of the usefulness of expressions that are embedded in a pattern. This embedding is only possible if $\mathcal{P}$ and $\mathcal{L}$ are one and the same language, which is the case in Bracmat.

5 Related work

5.1 workflow management systems

WMS'es are made for different purposes. For technical minded researchers, there are WMS'es that are compared to the 'make' tool by their authors. Such systems are characterised by Spartan simplicity and they make it easy to run tasks repeatedly. Examples are LuigiNLP[4] and zymake (Breck, 2008). These systems run from the command line and do not have web-based components. The information about the involved tools is minimal, and can be as little as a file extension.

---

[4] https://github.com/LanguageMachines/LuigiNLP

The systems GATE (Cunningham et al., 2002), UIMA (Ferrucci and Lally, 2004), TextGrid (Neuroth et al., 2011), WebLicht (Hinrichs et al., 2010), Galaxy (Giardine et al., 2005), Taverna (Wolstencroft et al., 2013), Kathaa (Mohanty et al., 2016) and Kepler (Goyal et al., 2016) all have advanced graphical interfaces that make it easy for users to combine tools in viable workflows that do useful things, but they do not tell the user whether it is possible to create a workflow that has an output that fulfils the user's requirements. It is therefore a clear advantage to have knowledge of the available tools and of how they interconnect when constructing a workflow for a specific purpose with the help of these systems.

The ALPE (Pistol, 2011) model is a framework under implementation that has similarities with our approach, the aim being to automatically construct tool chains that connect input and output. ALPE is intended as an extension to systems like GATE and UIMA.

5.2 PM languages

One of the earliest attempts at devising a programming language addressing PM was COMIT (Yngve, 1958). Descendants of COMIT were the members of the SNOBOL family (Farber et al., 1964). SNOBOL had powerful string PM facilities, but a flow of control based on labels and conditional jumps that did not mix with the pattern syntax (Griswold and Hanson, 1980).

While COMIT patterns operated on data with a simple structure (tokens and their annotations in a vector representation), later implementations of PM against text either operated on character strings using *regexp* patterns, or on tree structured data using query languages such as XPath, XQuery, XSLT, Cypher and syntax description languages like TGrep2 (Rohde, 2005), Tregex (Levy and Andrew, 2006), TIGER (König et al., 2003) and TPEMatcher (Choi, 2011).

Some mainstream programming languages have PM facilities 'built in'. Perl, for example, has powerful string PM functionality and newer versions of C# have LINQ for querying structured data in an SQL-like way. Although LINQ is a great step forward, it does not deal with associative PM.

Many functional languages, such as Haskell, ML, and Scala, have a PM mechanism against tree structured data that inspects the root of the tree and adjacent tree nodes. The matching algorithm iterates over a set of patterns until a matching pattern is found. Each pattern is part of a 'case' that defines the action to take place after a match has occurred. Functional languages overcome the split between $\mathcal{L}$ and $\mathcal{P}$, but they do generally not support associative PM.

Term rewriting systems such as XQuery, XSLT, Trafola (Heckmann, 1988), Elan (Borovansky et al., 1996), Stratego (Visser, 2001), and Tregex+Tsurgeon (Levy and Andrew, 2006) scan a tree structure, searching for terms that match a given rule pattern. When a matching term is found, the transformation part of the rule is applied to that term. In most of these systems the PM mechanism itself is not fundamentally different from that in functional languages and does not support associative PM.

Associative and associative commutative PM languages (Slagle, 1974) look for multiple matches of the same pattern with the same subject by iterating over different partitions of the subject structure in sublists and subsets, respectively. Examples are tools for computer program analysis such as Maude (Clavel et al., 1998), Tom (Moreau et al., 2003), and Rascal (Klint et al., 2009). However, these languages do not overcome the split between $\mathcal{L}$ and $\mathcal{P}$.

There are not many associative PM languages for tree structured data that overcome the split between $\mathcal{L}$ and $\mathcal{P}$. The only such languages that the author is aware of are Bracmat and the functional language Egison[5]. Egison appeared in 2011, when the first version of the WMS already was implemented.

6 Availability

Bracmat and the CLARIN-DK WMS are available under the GPL 2 license and can be downloaded from GitHub[6]. Bracmat can be compiled and executed on any platform for which a standard C compiler is available, and it can be linked to Java and Python programs. For inspirational input, hundreds of tasks on the programming chrestomathy site rosettacode.org are solved with Bracmat. Included in the GitHub distribution is documentation and a technical paper that introduces those interested in LT to Bracmat.

---

[5]https://www.egison.org

[6]https://github.com/BartJongejan/Bracmat and https://github.com/kuhumcst/DK-ClarinTools

7 Conclusion

Construction of a workflow between an input and a goal specification is in many ways similar to solving a set of equations with a computer algebra system performing symbolic computation. Both processes consist of several steps, both processes can finally arrive at producing a tree or directed acyclic graph structure, both processes can run into dead ends and be forced to backtrack, both processes have to handle ambiguous or unspecified parts, both processes deal with PM and unification, both processes can be implemented recursively, both processes can be sped up by simplification and normalization of all expressions and by memoizing solutions for already reached subgoals, and both processes can give a multitude of results, one result, or no result at all. It is therefore logical to implement a workflow management system not directly in a low level programming language, but in a high level language that is dedicated to building tree structures and performing PM operations on such structures.

We have spelled out three desirable capabilities of a programming language with PM as language construct: PM against tree structured data, full programmatic control during PM, and associative PM. Of the currently existing programming languages very few combine all three of these advanced features.

We presented Bracmat, a programming language for symbolic computation that does combine these three capabilities. To demonstrate the usefulness of the pattern matching capabilities of Bracmat, we have given examples of practical language technology solutions that can find application in digital humanities. One of these examples is the easy to use CLARIN-DK workflow management system.

References

Richard Bellman. 1957. *Dynamic Programming*. Princeton University Press, Princeton, NJ, USA, 1 edition.

Peter Borovansky, Claude Kirchner, Hélène Kirchner, Pierre-Etienne Moreau, and Marian Vittek. 1996. Elan: A logical framework based on computational systems. In *Proceedings of the first international workshop on rewriting logic*, volume 4 of *Electronic Notes in Theoretical Computer Science*. Elsevier, sep.

Eric Breck. 2008. zymake: A computational workflow system for machine learning and natural language processing. In *Software Engineering, Testing, and Quality Assurance for Natural Language Processing*, pages 5–13, Columbus, Ohio, June. Association for Computational Linguistics.

Yong Suk Choi. 2011. TPEMatcher: A tool for searching in parsed text corpora. *Knowledge-Based Systems*, 24(8):1139 – 1150.

M. Clavel, F. Durán, S. Eker, P. Lincoln, N. Martí-Oliet, J. Meseguer, and J. Quesada. 1998. Maude as a meta-language. In *In 2nd International Workshop on Rewriting Logic and its Applications (WRLA'98)*, volume 15 of *Electronic Notes in Theoretical Computer Science*. Elsevier.

H Cunningham, D Maynard, K Bontcheva, and V Tablan. 2002. Gate: A framework and graphical development environment for robust nlp tools and applications. In *Proc. 40th Anniversary Meeting of the Association for Computational Linguistics (ACL)*.

Jay Earley. 1983. An efficient context-free parsing algorithm. *Commun. ACM*, 26(1):57–61, jan.

D. J. Farber, R. E. Griswold, and I. P. Polonsky. 1964. Snobol , a string manipulation language. *J. ACM*, 11(1):21–30, January.

D. Ferrucci and A. Lally. 2004. Building an Example Application with the Unstructured Information Management Architecture. *IBM Syst. J.*, 43(3):455–475, July.

Belinda Giardine, Cathy Riemer, Ross C. Hardison, Richard Burhans, Prachi Shah, Yi Zhang, Daniel Blankenberg, Istvan Albert, Webb Miller, W. James Kent, and Anton Nekrutenko. 2005. Galaxy: A platform for interactive large-scale genome analysis. *Genome Res*, 15:1451–1455.

Ankit Goyal, Alok Singh, Shitij Bhargava, Daniel Crawl, Ilkay Altintas, and Chun-Nan Hsu. 2016. Natural language processing using kepler workflow system: First steps. *Procedia Computer Science*, 80:712 – 721. International Conference on Computational Science 2016, {ICCS} 2016, 6-8 June 2016, San Diego, California, {USA}.

Ralph E. Griswold and David R. Hanson. 1980. An alternative to the use of patterns in string processing. In *Coalgebraic Methods in Computer Science, Electronic Notes in Theoretical Computer Science*, pages 153–172.

Reinhold Heckmann. 1988. A functional language for the specification of complex tree transformations. In H. Ganzinger, editor, *ESOP '88*, volume 300 of *Lecture Notes in Computer Science*, pages 175–190. Springer Berlin Heidelberg.

Erhard W. Hinrichs, Marie Hinrichs, and Thomas Zastrow. 2010. Weblicht: Web-based LRT services for German. In *ACL 2010, Proceedings of the 48th Annual Meeting of the Association for Computational Linguistics, July 11-16, 2010, Uppsala, Sweden, System Demonstrations*, pages 25–29. The Association for Computer Linguistics.

Bart Jongejan. 2013. Workflow management in CLARIN-DK. In *Proceedings of the workshop on Nordic language research infrastructure at NODALIDA 2013*, volume 089 of *NEALT Proceedings Series*, pages 11–20. Northern European Association for Language Technology (NEALT), May.

Paul Klint, Tijs van der Storm, and Jurgen J. Vinju. 2009. RASCAL: A domain specific language for source code analysis and manipulation. In *Ninth IEEE International Working Conference on Source Code Analysis and Manipulation, SCAM 2009, Edmonton, Alberta, Canada, September 20-21, 2009*, pages 168–177. IEEE Computer Society.

Esther König, Wolfgang Lezius, and Holger Voormann, 2003. *TIGERSearch 2.1 User's Manual*. IMS, Universität Stuttgart, September.

Roger Levy and Galen Andrew. 2006. Tregex and Tsurgeon: tools for querying and manipulating tree data structures. In *In 5th International Conference on Language Resources and Evaluation*.

Sharada Prasanna Mohanty, Nehal J Wani, Manish Srivastava, and Dipti Misra Sharma. 2016. Kathaa: A visual programming framework for nlp applications. In *Proceedings of the 2016 Conference of the North American Chapter of the Association for Computational Linguistics: Demonstrations*, pages 92–96, San Diego, California, June. Association for Computational Linguistics.

Pierre-Etienne Moreau, Christophe Ringeissen, and Marian Vittek. 2003. A pattern matching compiler for multiple target languages. In *12th Conference on Compiler Construction, Warsaw (Poland), volume 2622 of LNCS*, pages 61–76. Springer.

Heike Neuroth, Felix Lohmeier, and Kathleen Marie Smith. 2011. Textgrid - virtual research environment for the humanities. *IJDC*, 6(2):222–231.

Patrizia Paggio and Bart Jongejan. 2005. Multimodal communication in virtual environments. In Oliviero Stock and Massimo Zancanaro, editors, *Multimodal Intelligent Information Presentation*, volume 27 of *Text, Speech and Language Technology*, pages 27–45. Springer Netherlands.

I Pistol. 2011. *The Automated Processing of Natural Language*. Ph.D. thesis, Ph. D. thesis,"Alexandru Ioan Cuza" University, Faculty of Computer Science, Iasi.

Claus Povlsen, Bart Jongejan, Dorte Haltrup Hansen, and Bo Krantz Simonsen. 2016. Anonymization of court orders. In *11th Iberian Conference on Information Systems and Technologies (CISTI)*. AISTI, 6.

R. Ramesh and I. V. Ramakrishnan. 1992. Nonlinear pattern matching in trees. *J. ACM*, 39(2):295–316, April.

Douglas L. T. Rohde. 2005. Tgrep2 user manual.

James R. Slagle. 1974. Automated theorem-proving for theories with simplifiers, commutativity, and associativity. *J. ACM*, 21(4):622–642, October.

Gertjan van Noord, Gosse Bouma, Frank Van Eynde, Daniël de Kok, Jelmer van der Linde, Ineke Schuurman, Erik Tjong Kim Sang, and Vincent Vandeghinste. 2013. Large scale syntactic annotation of written dutch: Lassy. In Peter Spyns and Jan Odijk, editors, *Essential Speech and Language Technology for Dutch Results by the STEVIN-programme*. Springer.

Eelco Visser. 2001. Stratego: A language for program transformation based on rewriting strategies. System description of Stratego 0.5. In A. Middeldorp, editor, *Rewriting Techniques and Applications (RTA'01)*, volume 2051 of *Lecture Notes in Computer Science*, pages 357–361. Springer-Verlag, May.

Katherine Wolstencroft, Robert Haines, Donal Fellows, Alan Williams, David Withers, Stuart Owen, Stian Soiland-Reyes, Ian Dunlop, Aleksandra Nenadic, Paul Fisher, Jiten Bhagat, Khalid Belhajjame, Finn Bacall, Alex Hardisty, Abraham Nieva de la Hidalga, Maria P. Balcazar Vargas, Shoaib Sufi, and Carole Goble. 2013. The Taverna workflow suite: designing and executing workflows of web services on the desktop, web or in the cloud. *Nucleic Acids Research*, 41:W557–W561.

Victor H. Yngve. 1958. A programming language for mechanical translation. *Mechanical Translation*, 5(1):24–41, July.

Integrating Optical Character Recognition and Machine Translation of Historical Documents

Haithem Afli and Andy Way
ADAPT Centre
School of Computing
Dublin City University
Dublin, Ireland
{haithem.afli, andy.way}@adaptcentre.ie

Abstract

Machine Translation (MT) plays a critical role in expanding capacity in the translation industry. However, many valuable documents, including digital documents, are encoded in non-accessible formats for machine processing (*e.g.*, Historical or Legal documents). Such documents must be passed through a process of Optical Character Recognition (OCR) to render the text suitable for MT. No matter how good the OCR is, this process introduces recognition errors, which often renders MT ineffective. In this paper, we propose a new OCR to MT framework based on adding a new OCR error correction module to enhance the overall quality of translation. Experimentation shows that our new system correction based on the combination of Language Modeling and Translation methods outperforms the baseline system by nearly 30% relative improvement.

1 Introduction

While research on improving Optical Character Recognition (OCR) algorithms is ongoing, our assessment is that Machine Translation (MT) will continue to produce unacceptable translation errors (or non-translations) based solely on the automatic output of OCR systems. The problem comes from the fact that current OCR and Machine Translation systems are commercially distinct and separate technologies. There are often mistakes in the scanned texts as the OCR system occasionally misrecognizes letters and falsely identifies scanned text, leading to misspellings and linguistic errors in the output text (Niklas, 2010). Works involved in improving translation services purchase off-the-shelf OCR technology but have limited capability to adapt the OCR processing to improve overall machine translation performance. In this context, it is appropriate to investigate the integration of OCR and MT for improved translation accuracy. A novel integration of OCR, error correction and MT technology that results in overall improvements in translation output quality to the point of acceptance by professional translators for post-editing, would have a profound effect on the economics of translation in high-value (expensive) domains such as Historical documents translation. This paper explores the effectiveness of OCR output error correction and its impact on automatic translation. The correction uses a combination of language modelling and statistical machine translation (SMT) methods to correct OCR errors. Our goal is to address the question of whether a shared and novel integration of language processing encompassing OCR, error correction and MT could significantly improve the final translation quality of the text which has initially been OCRed. The remainder of the paper is organized as follows: Section 2 presents related work on OCR error correction; Sections 3 and 4 describe the proposed OCR to MT framework and the feasibility experiments conducted. Section 5 reports and discusses about the results and the directions for further work are provided in Section 6.

Proceedings of the Workshop on Language Technology Resources and Tools for Digital Humanities (LT4DH),
pages 109–116, Osaka, Japan, December 11-17 2016.

2 OCR error correction

2.1 Related work

The current state of the OCR output translation includes expensive manual intervention in order to correct the errors introduced in processing texts through OCR, or simply takes the approach of undertaking manual re-creation of the document in a machine-processable form. Alternatively, the document is retained in its original format and is provided as an 'image' to a professional translator to translate into the target language, though this means that the original 'source' language is not available for inclusion in Translation Memory for future use. In the worst case, the text is manually processed in its source text and then professionally translated into the target text without any automated processing at all.

A lot of research has been carried out on OCR error correction, with different strategies including the improvement of visual and linguistic techniques as well as combining several OCR system outputs (Hong, 1995; Schäfer and Weitz, 2012; Springmann and Ldeling, 2016). Such post-OCR correction, which represents the focus of this paper, is one of the main directions in this domain. In this way, we can consider the OCR system as a black-box, since this technique does not rely on any parameters specific to the OCR system. The goal of post-processing is to detect and correct errors in the OCR output after the input image has been scanned and completely processed.

The obvious way to correct the OCR misspellings is to edit the output text manually using translators or linguists. This method requires continuous manual human intervention which is a costly and time-consuming practice. There are two main existing approaches to automatically correct the OCR outputs.

The first approach is based on lexical error correction (Niwa et al., 1992; Hong, 1995; Bassil and Alwani, 2012). In this method, a lexicon is used to spell-check OCR-recognized words and correct them if they are not present in the dictionary. Although this technique is easy to implement, it still has various limitations that prevent it from being the perfect solution for OCR error correction (Hong, 1995). It requires a wide-ranging dictionary that covers every word in the language. Existing linguistic resources can usually target a single specific language in a given period, but cannot therefore support historical documents.

The second type of approach in OCR post-processing is context-based error correction. These techniques are founded on statistical language modelling and word n-grams, and aims to calculate the likelihood that a particular word sequence appears (Tillenius, 1996; Magdy and Darwish, 2006). Applying this technique on historical documents is challenging because the works on building corpora for this kind of task has been very limited. Furthermore, when many consecutive corrupted words are encountered in a sentence, it is difficult to choose the good candidate words. In this paper we conducted our experiments using a corpus of old-style French OCR-ed data from the 17th, 18th and 19th centuries in order to verify the applicability of our new OCR-to-MT framework.

2.2 Translation method

This technique centres on using an SMT system trained on the OCR output texts which have been post-edited and manually corrected. SMT systems handle the translation process as the transformation of a sequence of symbols in a source language into another sequence of symbols in a target language. Generally the symbols dealt with are the words in the two languages. We consider that our SMT system will translate OCR output to corrected text in the same language following the work of (Fancellu et al., 2014; Afli et al., 2016).

In fact, using the standard approach of SMT we are given a sentence (a sequence of OCR output words) $s^M = s_1...s_M$ of size M which is to be translated into a corrected sentence $t^N = t_1...t_N$ of size N in the same language (French in our case). The statistical approach aims at determining the translation t^* which maximizes the posterior probability given the source sentence. Formally, by using Bayes' rule, the fundamental equation is (1):

$$t^* = \arg\max_t Pr(t|s) = \arg\max_t Pr(s|t)Pr(t) \tag{1}$$

It can be decomposed, as in the original work of (Brown et al., 1993), into a language model probability $Pr(t)$, and a translation model probability $Pr(s|t)$. The language model is trained on a large quantity of French texts and the translation model is trained using a bilingual text aligned at sentence (segment) level, *i.e.* an OCR output for a segment and its ground-truth obtained manually. As in most current state-of-the-art systems, the translation probability is modelled using the log-linear model in (2):

$$P(t|s) = \sum_{i=0}^{N} \lambda_i h_i(s, t) \qquad (2)$$

where $h_i(s, t)$ is the $i^t h$ feature function and λ_i its weight (determined by an optimization process). We call this method *"SMT_cor "* in the rest of this paper. As (Nakov and Tiedemann, 2012; Tiedemann and Nakov, 2013) demonstrated, closely related languages largely overlap in vocabulary and have a strong syntactic and lexical similarities. We assume that we do not need to use the reordering model in the task of error correction in the same language.

2.3 Language Modelling

Language Modelling is the field of creating models for writing text so that we can assign a probability to a sequence of n consecutive words. Using this technique, the candidate correction of an error might be successfully found using the Noisy Channel Model (Mays et al., 1991).

Considering the sentence '*I drink a baer*‘, the error correction system would identify '*bear*‘ or '*beer*‘ as possible replacements for the non-word '*baer*‘, and then a language model would most likely indicate that the word trigram '*drink a beer*‘ is much more likely than '*drink a bear*‘. Accordingly, for each OCR-ed word w we are looking for the word c that is the most likely spelling correction for that word (which may indeed be the original word itself).

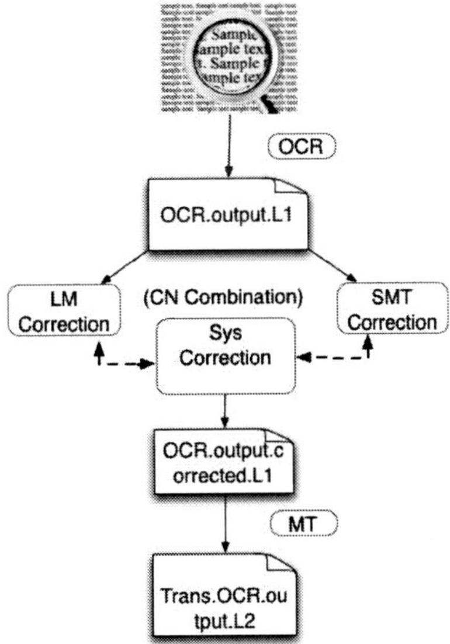

Figure 1: The proposed OCR-to-MT framework.

3 OCR-to-MT framework

The basic system architecture is depicted in Figure 1. We can distinguish three steps: automatic character recognition (OCR), error correction (Sys Correction) and machine translation (MT). The OCR system accepts original documents in language L1 (French in our case) and generates an automatic transcription. This text is then corrected by two different correction systems based on language modelling and SMT methods described in the previous section. Different correction systems can generate multiple input hypotheses with varying confidence for the combination system based on confusion networks. The final corrected text in L1 forms the input to the MT system. We anticipate that the automatic correction will improve the quality of the final translation to the language L2 (English in our case). Accordingly, this framework sets out to address the question of whether a shared and novel integration of language processing components from both OCR and MT can significantly improve the final translation quality of text which has initially been OCR-ed.

4 Impact of Error Correction on Automatic Translation

The proposed OCR-to-MT framework raises several issues. Each step can introduce a certain number of errors. It is important to highlight the feasibility of the approach and the impact of each module on the final automatic translation. Thus, we conducted three different types of experiments, described in Figure 2.

In the first experiment (*Exp. 1*) we use the OCR reference (*Ref.OCR.fr*) as input to the MT system. This is the most favourable condition, as it simulates the case where the OCR and the Error Correction systems do not commit any error. Accordingly, we consider this as the reference during the automatic evaluation process. In the second experiment (*Exp. 2*) – the baseline experiment – we use the OCR output (*OCR.output.fr*) directly as input to the MT system without any correction. Finally, the third experiment represents the complete proposed framework, described in Section 3.

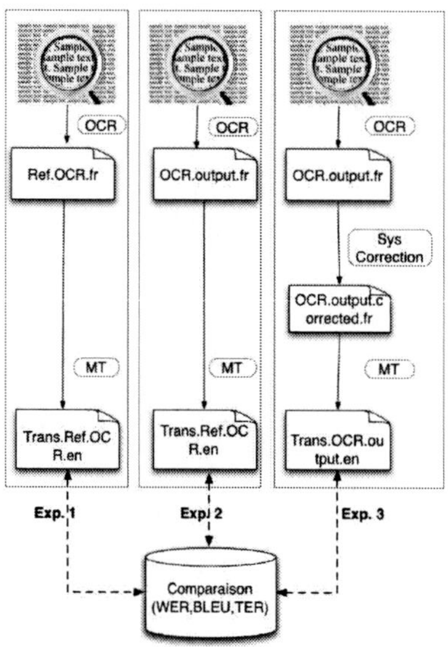

Figure 2: Different experiments to analyze the impact of the Error Correction module.

5 Experimental Results

5.1 Data and systems description

For the training of our models, we used a corpus of nearly 58 million OCR output words obtained from scanned documents, developed by (Afli et al., 2015). We used the corrected part of this corpus for the Language Model. Next, the OCR output sentences and the manually corrected version were aligned at word level and this bitext was used for our SMT error correction method. For testing, we used OCR-ed French data (dev17) from the 17th century, manually corrected. The statistics of all corpora used in our experiments can be seen in Table 1.

bitexts	# OCR tokens	# ref tokens
smt_17	1.98 M	1.96 M
smt_18	33.49 M	33.40 M
smt_19	23.08 M	22.9 M
dev17	9013	8946

Table 1: Statistics of MT training, development and test data available to build our systems.

For all of the different techniques used in this paper, the language model was built using the KenLM toolkit with Kneser-Ney smoothing and default backoff. For the SMT_cor method, an SMT system is trained on all available parallel data. Our SMT system is a phrase-based system (Koehn et al., 2003) based on the Moses SMT toolkit (Koehn et al., 2007). Word alignments in both directions are calculated, using a multi-threaded version of the GIZA++ tool (Gao and Vogel, 2008).

The parameters of our system were tuned on a development corpus, using Minimum Error Rate Training (Och, 2003). We combined our two systems using a Confusion Network (CN) combination system based on the work of (Wu et al., 2012). We call this combination $LM\_cor + SMT\_cor$.

5.2 Results

In order to evaluate the effectiveness of error correction, we used Word Error Rate (WER) which is derived from Levenshtein distance (Levenshtein, 1966). We compare results on the test data of the two different methods used in our experiments and their combination, against the baseline results which represent scores between OCR output and the corrected reference (called *OCR-Baseline*).

Table 2 reports on the percentage of Correctness, Accuracy and WER of different system outputs. The best model, using the *CN Comb.* system was able to decrease 5.39% of the OCR word errors (29.42% relative improvement). It can also be observed that the SMT_cor system improves the results more than LM_cor. Nonetheless, both underperform compared to the *CN Comb.* system. This is due to the fact that the two methods are not always correcting the same errors, so the CN combination can be beneficial in this case.

Systems	Correctness	Accuracy	WER
Baseline	83.92	81.68	18.32
LM_cor	84.82	82.57	17.43
SMT_cor	87.64	86.06	13.94
CN Comb.			
LM_cor + SMT_cor	**89.10**	**87.07**	**12.93**

Table 2: Word Error Rate (WER), Accuracy and Correctness results on on dev17 OCR-corrected data.

For the translation evaluation we used BLEU-4 score (Papineni et al., 2002), Smoothed BLEU (Lin and Och, 2004) and TER (Snover et al., 2006) calculated between the output of *Exp. 1* (our reference) and *Exp. 2* output (the baseline) or *Exp. 3* output (our proposed framework).

Table 3 lists the results of the two translation outputs from *Exp. 1* and *Exp. 2*. It shows that our proposed framework is very capable of correcting the final translation of the OCR-ed documents.

5.3 Analysis and Discussion

In order to better understand the impact of the error correction process and the problems of OCR'ed historical document translation, we prepared a manual human translation of our test set based on the

---

https://kheafield.com/code/kenlm
The source is available at `http://www.cs.cmu.edu/~qing/`

Systems	BLEU-4	Smooth BLEU	TER
Exp. 2	24.53	38.29	57.32
Exp. 3	**69.43**	**70.15**	**21.62**

Table 3: BLEU-4, Smooth BLEU and TER results on dev17 OCR-translated data.

transformation of the old French language to the current one and its translation to current English language without any modification on the original format. We find that comparing to the manual translation, the system can not get the correct context of the documents lines because of their short length. As we can see in the figure 3, the sentence starts with the word '*Quel*' and finish with the word '*Roi?*' is segmented on five lines which can cause a translation context problem for the MT system.

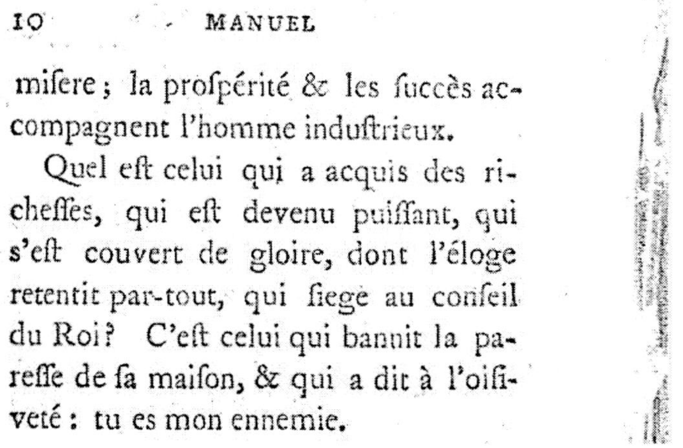
10 MANUEL

miſere ; la proſpérité & les ſuccès ac-
compagnent l'homme induſtrieux.
Quel eſt celui qui a acquis des ri-
cheſſes, qui eſt devenu puiſſant, qui
s'eſt couvert de gloire, dont l'éloge
retentit par-tout, qui ſiege au conſeil
du Roi? C'eſt celui qui bannit la pa-
reſſe de ſa maiſon, & qui a dit à l'oiſi-
veté : tu es mon ennemie.

Figure 3: Exemple of Historical French document with short length of its lines.

As almost all current MT systems are translating document line by line, we can say that the context of the translations is line-based even when we try to adapt the system to the domain of the document. The particularity of historical documents can cause a problem of context translation without a pre-processing of the corrected OCR output. Our results presented in table 4 show that the transformation of the OCR'ed data to one sentence per line as a pre-processing can improve the automatic translation results from 12.59 to 18.92 BLEU points which is a very important improvement.

Manual translation	without pre-processing	sentence per line
BLEU-4	12.59	18.92

Table 4: BLEU-4 results on dev17 OCR-translated data with- and without pre-processing compared to manual translation.

This experiment can open the way of thinking about improving our current MT methods and systems by getting the document-level context of translation.

6 Conclusion

In this paper, we presented a new framework of OCR-ed document translation. The proposed method consists of the integration of a new error correction system prior to the translation phase *per se*. We validate the feasibility of our approach using a set of experiments to analyze the impact of our OCR error correction module on the final translation. Experiments conducted on old-style French data showed that our methodology improves the quality of the translation of OCR documents. Accordingly, we believe that our method can be a good way to resolve the problem of correcting OCR errors for historical texts. We plan to test it on other different languages and types of data and try to integrate the correction system inside the OCR system architecture itself.

Acknowledgements

This research is supported by Science Foundation Ireland in the ADAPT Centre (Grant 13/RC/2106) (www.adaptcentre.ie) at Dublin City University. We would like to thank Wided Baazaoui for her useful and knowledgeable help on preparing the development- and test-set of this work.

References

Haithem Afli, Loïc Barrault, and Holger Schwenk. 2015. OCR Error Correction Using Statistical Machine Translation. *16th International Conference on Intelligent Text Processing and Computational Linguistics*, Cairo, Egypt.

Haithem Afli, Zhengwei Qiu, Andy Way, and Páraic Sheridan. 2016. Using SMT for OCR error correction of historical texts. In *Proceedings of LREC-2016*, pages 962–965, Portorož, Slovenia.

Youssef Bassil and Mohammad Alwani. 2012. OCR Post-Processing Error Correction Algorithm Using Google's Online Spelling Suggestion. *Journal of Emerging Trends in Computing and Information Sciences*, 3:90–99.

Peter F. Brown, Vincent J. Della Pietra, Stephen A. Della Pietra, and Robert L. Mercer. 1993. The mathematics of statistical machine translation: parameter estimation. *Comput. Linguist.*, 19:263–311.

Federico Fancellu, Andy Way, and Morgan O'Brien. 2014. Standard language variety conversion for content localisation via SMT. *17th Annual Conference of the European Association for Machine Translation*, pages 143–149, Dubrovnik, Croatia.

Q. Gao and S. Vogel. 2008. Parallel implementations of word alignment tool. In *Software Engineering, Testing, and Quality Assurance for Natural Language Processing*, SETQA-NLP '08, pages 49–57, in Columbus, Ohio, USA.

Tao Hong. 1995. *Degraded Text Recognition Using Visual and Linguistic Context*. Ph.D. thesis, University of New York, NY, USA.

P. Koehn, Franz J. Och, and D. Marcu. 2003. Statistical phrase-based translation. In *Proceedings of the 2003 Conference of the North American Chapter of the Association for Computational Linguistics on Human Language Technology*, volume 1, pages 48–54, Edmonton, Canada.

P. Koehn, H. Hoang, A. Birch, C. Callison-Burch, M. Federico, N. Bertoldi, B. Cowan, W. Shen, C. Moran, R. Zens, C. Dyer, O. Bojar, A. Constantin, and E. Herbst. 2007. Moses: open source toolkit for statistical machine translation. In *Proceedings of the 45th Annual Meeting of the ACL on Interactive Poster and Demonstration Sessions*, pages 177–180, Prague, Czech Republic.

V. I. Levenshtein. 1966. Binary codes capable of correcting deletions, insertions, and reversals. *Soviet Physics Doklady*, 10:707–710.

Chin-Yew Lin and Franz Josef Och. 2004. Automatic evaluation of machine translation quality using longest common subsequence and skip-bigram statistics. In *42nd Meeting of the Association for Computational Linguistics (ACL'04), Main Volume*, pages 605–612, Barcelona, Spain.

Walid Magdy and Kareem Darwish. 2006. Arabic OCR Error Correction Using Character Segment Correction, Language Modeling, and Shallow Morphology. In *Proceedings of the 2006 Conference on Empirical Methods in Natural Language Processing*, pages 408–414, Sydney, Australia.

Eric Mays, Fred J. Damerau, and Robert L. Mercer. 1991. Context based spelling correction. *Information Processing and Management*, 27(5):517–522.

Preslav Nakov and Jörg Tiedemann. 2012. Combining word-level and character-level models for machine translation between closely-related languages. In *Proceedings of the 50th Annual Meeting of the Association for Computational Linguistics: Short Papers - Volume 2*, ACL '12, pages 301–305.

Kai Niklas. 2010. *Unsupervised Post-Correction of OCR Errors.* Ph.D. thesis, Leibniz University Hannover, in Germany.

Hisao Niwa, Kazuhiro Kayashima, and Yasuham Shimeki. 1992. Postprocessing for character recognition using keyword information. In *IAPR Workshop on Machine Vision Applications*, volume MVA'92, pages 519–522, Tokyo, Japan.

Franz J. Och. 2003. Minimum error rate training in statistical machine translation. In *Proceedings of the 41st Annual Meeting on Association for Computational Linguistics*, volume 1, pages 160–167, Sapporo, Japan.

Kishore Papineni, Salim Roukos, Todd Ward, and Wei-Jing Zhu. 2002. Bleu: a method for automatic evaluation of machine translation. In *Proceedings of the 40th Annual Meeting on Association for Computational Linguistics*, pages 311–318, Philadelphia, Pennsylvania.

Ulrich Schäfer and Benjamin Weitz. 2012. Combining OCR outputs for logical document structure markup: Technical background to the ACL 2012 contributed task. In *Proceedings of the ACL-2012 Special Workshop on Rediscovering 50 Years of Discoveries*, pages 104–109, Jeju Island, Korea.

S. Snover, B. Dorr, R. Schwartz, M. Micciulla, and J. Makhoul. 2006. A study of translation edit rate with targeted human annotation. *Proceedings of Association for Machine Translation in the Americas*, pages 223–231, Cambridge, Massachusetts, USA.

Uwe Springmann and Anke Ldeling. 2016. OCR of historical printings with an application to building diachronic corpora: A case study using the RIDGES herbal corpus. *ArXiv e-prints*.

Jörg Tiedemann and Preslav Nakov. 2013. Analyzing the use of character-level translation with sparse and noisy datasets. *Proceedings of Recent Advences in Natural Language Processing*, pages 676–684.

Mikael Tillenius. 1996. Efficient generation and ranking of spelling error corrections. Technical report, Royal Institute of Technology, Stockholm, Sweden.

Xiaofeng Wu, Tsyoshi Okita, Josef van Genabith, and Qun Liu. 2012. System combination with extra alignment information. In *Second ML4HMT Workshop (COLING 2012)*, pages 37–44, Mumbai, India.

Language technology tools and resources for the analysis of multimodal communication

László Hunyadi
University of Debrecen
H-4032, Egyetem tér 1
Debrecen, Hungary
hunyadi@unideb.hu

Tamás Váradi
Research Institute for Linguistics,
Hungarian Academy of Sciences
Budapest, Hungary
varadi.tamas@nytud.mta.hu

István Szekrényes
University of Debrecen
H-4032, Egyetem tér 1
Debrecen, Hungary
szekrenyes@unideb.hu

Abstract

In this paper we describe how the complexity of human communication can be analysed with the help of language technology. We present the HuComTech corpus, a multimodal corpus containing 50 hours of videotaped interviews containing a rich annotation of about 2 million items annotated on 33 levels. The corpus serves as a general resource for a wide range of research addressing natural conversation between humans in their full complexity. It can benefit particularly digital humanities researchers working in the field of pragmatics, conversational analysis and discourse analysis. We will present a number of tools and automated methods that can help such enquiries. In particular, we will highlight the tool Theme, which is designed to uncover hidden temporal patterns (called T-patterns) in human interaction, and will show how it can applied to the study of multimodal communication.

1   Introduction

Following the origins of digital humanities ("literary and linguistic computing"), the text has always been central to it. However, when one gives a closer look at the words these texts are made of, a whole world opens before our eyes: words are just the expression of what can hardly be expressed by words: *human behavior*. The question then arises: can one truly understand and interpret *thoughts, reflections, intensions* based on words alone? And also: how much of all this can be traced back by following nonverbal events? Do gestures contribute to disambiguating words, or do they rather mask the unspoken context? And in any case: how objectively can we judge and react to a social interaction of competing verbal and nonverbal events?

The objective of the present paper is to show how language technology can help the investigation of such research questions, extending the horizons of Digital Humanities research. The rest of the paper is structured as follows. In section 2, we describe the HuComText Corpus, an extensively annotated corpus of 50 hours of video-recorded interviews, containing 450 000 running words and altogether 2 million annotation items. Section 3 describes automated methods used to facilitate corpus annotation. The corpus was basically annotated manually by trained annotators. There were three aspects of the annotation of the corpus that was automated by language technology tools. Section 3.1 describes how the prosodic annotation describing *pitch, intensity* and *speech rate* was prepared automatically using a language independent tool, *ProsoTool* (Szekrényes 2015). Section 3.2 introduces a web-service for the morphological annotation of the corpus. EmMorph is part of a newly developed open language technology processing chain for Hungarian available at https://e-magyar.hu/parser. Section 3.3 describes our experiences in using the WebMAUS service (Kisler et al. 2016) to prepare the time-alignment of the corpus at the word level.

Proceedings of the Workshop on Language Technology Resources and Tools for Digital Humanities (LT4DH),
pages 117–124, Osaka, Japan, December 11-17 2016.

2   About the HuComTech corpus

2.1   General description

The multimodal HuComTech corpus is a set of approximately 50 hours of video recorded dialogues comprising of 111 formal conversations (simulated job interviews) and 111 informal ones (guided by a standard scheme). The participants were 111 university students (aged 18-29), and the language of the dialogues in both settings was Hungarian. Each interview consisted of 15 sentences read aloud, a 10 minute guided conversation and 15 minutes of free conversation. The whole corpus contains about 450 000 word tokens. The initial aim of building the corpus was to acquire a wide range of data characteristic of human-human interaction in order to make generalisations for their implementation in more advanced human-machine interaction systems (Hunyadi, 2011).

2.2   Annotation principles

The annotation system of the HuComTech corpus involves 33 different levels of annotation including video (labelling both physical attributes such as gaze, head, eyebrows, hand, posture, and their interpretations for emotions, communicative, discourse and pragmatic functions), audio (labelling for the physical attributes of F0, intensity, speech rate, and their interpretations for emotions and communicative and discourse functions), and functional labelling of combined video+audio, following a partly manual, partly automatic scheme of labelling (Abuczki and Esfandiari-Baiat, 2013).

Annotations include video annotations for gaze, head movement, hand movement, posture, facial expressions, audio annotations for transcription, fluency of speech, turn management, emotions, as well as prosody (done automatically) for pitch movement, intensity and pause. The manual annotations are uniquely extended to spoken syntax and, to our knowledge also as first of its kind, to unimodal (video only) pragmatics complementing multimodal pragmatic annotation. All these different layers of annotation are meant to be studied simultaneously, allowing for the study of the eventual temporal and structural alignments of all available multimodal markers.

In addition to its automatic parsing, for syntactic labelling a special manual scheme is designed to code incompleteness of structure, highly specific to spoken language but difficult for machine recognition. Morphological parsing is complemented with the automatic time alignment of each running word in the text. This extensive annotation of 50 hours of dialogues results in about 2 million distinct pieces of data.

As a special feature of the corpus, annotation was done, when applicable, both multimodally (using the video and audio signals at the same time) and unimodally (relying only on the video cues without the sound channel). The rationale behind it was that whereas it is generally accepted that both the production and the perception/interpretation of a communicative event is essentially multimodal due to the participation of a number of (verbal and non-verbal) channels (modalities), both the analysis and generation of such an event by the machine agent needs to follow a complex of individual modalities, i.e. by the setting of the parameters of each of the modalities separately. Due to the highly structured and detailed nature of our material, in what follows we are going to restrict our presentation to data from prosody and morphology only. Even with these restrictions, the presentation will be an example of the multimodal nature of communication: the several levels of prosody and morphology annotation also yield a rich set of data which combine into complex multimodal patterns of elements (events) which contribute to the expression of various communicative functions in the usual multimodal way of optionality.

3   Automated methods of multimodal corpus annotation

3.1   Automatic annotation of prosody

Among manually annotated non-verbal modalities of the interactions, the annotation of prosody was implemented by a computer algorithm in the HuComTech corpus. Therefore not only the resulting prosodic labels, but the methodology itself can be used as a speech processing resource for the prosodic analysis of any spoken language corpora. The algorithm of *Prosotool* was implemented as a Praat script (Boersma and Weenik 2016) for transcribing the temporal modulation of three important prosodic phenomena: *pitch, intensity* and *speech rate*. Unlike other existing tools such as ToBI, *Prosotool* is language independent and does not require any training material. Only a pre-created, acoustic representation of speaker change is needed, marking utterance units in different annotation tiers per different speakers (see Figure 1.) in Praat TextGrid format.

During automatic pre-processing of recordings, the utterances of different speakers are separated from each other (excluding overlapping segments of speech) in order to make possible the isolated, preliminary analysis of the individual prosodic behavior of every participant, distinguishing four ordinal levels for every prosodic feature based on the individual distribution of the measured, physical

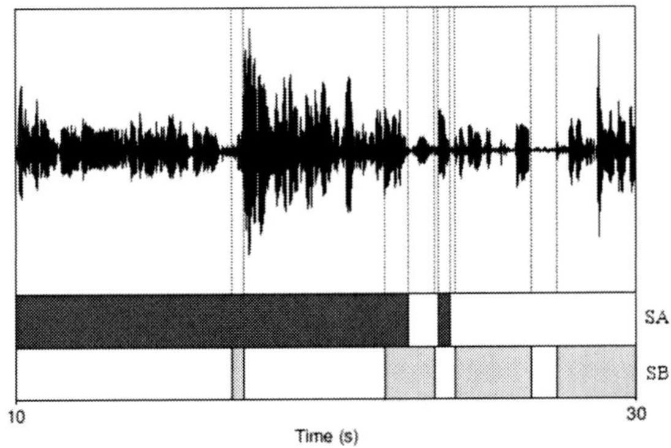

Figure 1. Acoustic representation of speaker change

values (F0, intensity and the actual syllable rates). In Figure 2, these consecutive levels (L1 < T1 < L1 < T2 < M < T3 < H1 T4 < H2) are defined using certain thresholds of F0 distribution.

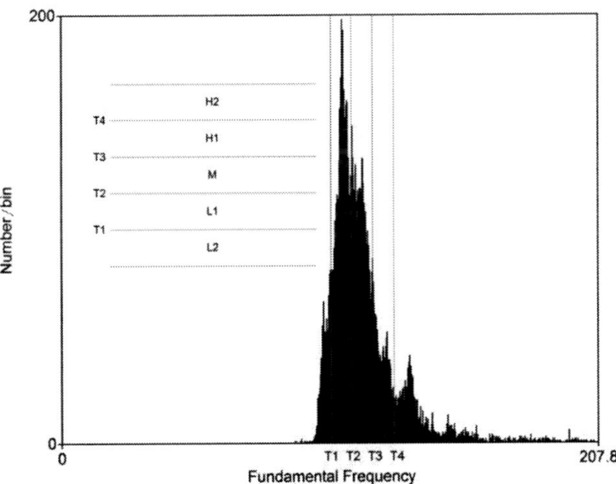

Figure 2. Individual vocal levels of the speaker

In the final output, the resulting annotation labels (in Praat TextGrid format) are not aligned with segmental units of speech (syllables, sentences etc.) but instead they follow the prosodic segmentation of interactions, the stylized segments of F0 and the intensity or syllable rate contour (see Figure 3.). This kind of prosodic segmentation aims at indicating those modulations of prosodic features which are (1) possibly independent from segmental units of speech (for instance, a tonal contour can integrate more syllables or words etc.) and (2) perceptually relevant, significant movements rather than momentary excursions of the measured physical values.

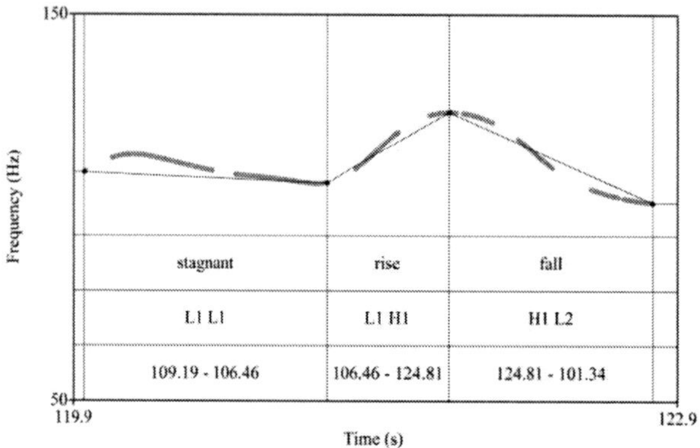

Figure 3. The result of prosodic annotation

As displayed in Figure 3, the resulting annotation consists of a three-level analysis of prosodic features. On the first level, the shape of every prosodic segment is classified using five categories of *rise*, *fall*, *descending*, *ascending* and *stagnant* accents. The classification is based on two main parameters, the duration and the amplitude of the movements. On the third level, the modulations are described as point-to-point vectors of the measured physical values (in Hertz, decibel or Syllable/second), while on the second level, the same vectors are associated with the four-level categories of the relative, individual scale as shown above.

It is intended that the *ProsoTool*'s algorithm will be freely available for research purposes within the framework of *E-magyar* digital language processing system[1]. The concept of stylization was inspired by Merten's *Prosogram* (Alessandro & Mertens 2004) and the psychoacoustic model of tonal perception (Hart 1976). The parameters of the pitch accents classification can also be found in the *Tilt* intonation model (Taylor 2000).

Figure 4. The emMorph web-service output

3.2 Morphological annotation

Morphological annotation of the corpus will be prepared with the emMorph morphological analyser, that is integrated in the recently developed e-magyar.hu language technology infrastructure. The e-magyar toolchain (https://e-magyar.hu) is a comprehensive Hungarian digital processing set prepared

---

[1] http://e-magyar.hu/

as a collaborative effort of the Hungarian NLP community. It integrates and enhances most of the tools developed in various labs from tokenizer to dependency parser. The flagship product of this new open infrastructure is the morphological analyser, which builds on the state-of-the art morphological analyser HUMOR (Prószéky and Tihanyi 1993) but is using a new annotation set (developed in consensus with theoretical linguists) and is implemented in finite state technology (using the HSFT engine). The infrastructure is open not just in the sense that most of its modules are available in open source to language technology specialists but also it makes its services available to non-developers, eminently targeting digital humanities researchers or even the general public. This is achieved through the web-service that allows the users to copy and paste an input text in a textbox on the website, select the kind of processing required and retrieve the results of the analysis. Figure 4 shows the morphological analysis in vertical form output of text copied into the input text box.

3.3 Automatic word alignment

The forced alignment of the HuComTech transcript with the speech signal is prepared using the WebMAUS tool developed and operated as a web service by the Institute of Phonetics and Speech processing of the Ludwig Maximilan University, München (http://clarin.phonetik.uni-muenchen-.de/BASWebServices/#/services.) The web service accepts a speech file and its transcript in a number of languages, including, fortunately, Hungarian. The size of the speech input file is limited to 200 Mb but the system also operates in batch mode i.e. it can accept a number of speech and text file pairs. There is extensive help and even a couple of YouTube videos to help the non-specialist digital humanities researches.

Even a carefully compiled and checked transcript such as the HuComTech corpus requires preprocessing before WebMAUS can be applied without a hitch. Some of the preprocessing steps are amenable to routine automation like filtering the transcript from any characters that do not correspond to sounds such as any codes, metainformation contained in brackets. Some of the phenomena that may cause misalignment are more subtle and have to do with the mismatch between the raw acoustic signal and its perception by the annotators. Apart from the length of stop consonents, items involved are often voiced hesitation phenomena orthographically put down as a single "ö" in Hungarian whereas its length may far exceed the maximum length of a segment the WebMAUS system is trained to accept. Another typical phenomenon (illustrated in Figure 5) concerns lenition or complete disappearance of sounds in words that are transcribed in full orthographic form.

Figure 5 records the case where the final "t" sound in the word "mint" is dropped between the word final and word initial nasals.

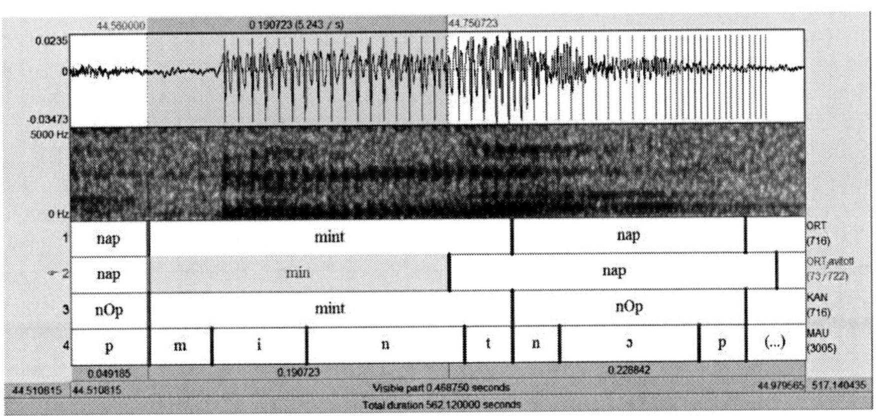

Figure 5. Adjustment of lenition phenomena in WebMAUS output

4 T-Pattern analysis

Multimodal communication involves a myriad of interlocking signals that are quite difficult to tease out and establish their interplay on each other. The HuComTech corpus with its annotation system involving as many as twelve tiers offers such a rich dataset of widely differing modalities (gaze, gesture, posture, prosody, emotions etc.) that it pauses a challenge for analysis and interpretation. In this section we present a radically new approach, the T-pattern analysis (Magnusson 1996) that promises to uncover hidden patterns in behaviour including human communication. The approach uses sophisticated multivariate analysis that establishes a hierarchical system of recurrent sequence of phenomena forming patterns (T-Patterns) based on the time length between their regular occurrences within a critical interval. Figure 6 shows a schematic way how a sequence of characters with no apparent structure to it reveals an increasingly complex pattern, as T-pattern analysis removes extraneous data and reveals the hidden patterns established on the basis of the temporal relationship between elements of patterns in a given time window. For more information on T-Pattern analysis and Theme, the software tool specially developed to detect T-patterns see Magnusson 2000 and Magnusson et al. 2016.

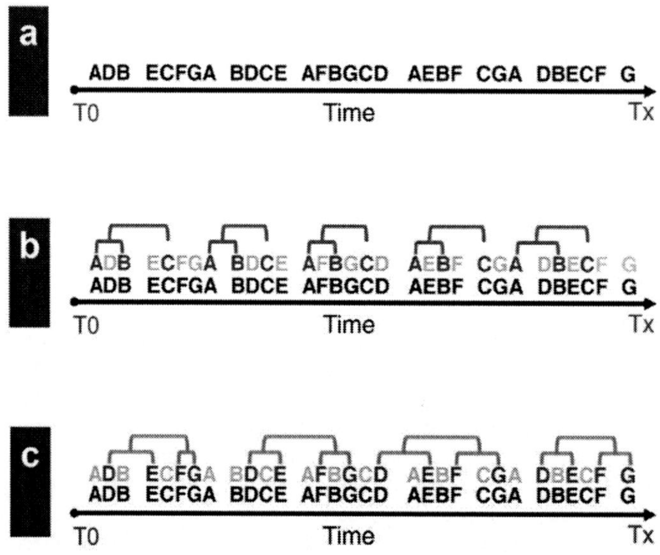

Figure 6. Emerging T-patterns through successive levels of analysis

T-pattern analysis has been applied to a wide range of phenomena and a software tool called Theme is available from PatternVision (http:// http://patternvision.com/) to carry out the research. It is suggested that it provides an exciting new perspective from which the hidden temporal structure of such complex phenomena as multimodal communication can be captured. The T-pattern analysis of the HuComTech corpus poses a challenge not only due to data size, but also the complexity of the nature of multimodal communication: the capturing of a given communicative function cannot usually be done by describing the temporal alignment of a number of predefined modalities and their exact linear sequences, since for the expression of most of the functions a given list of participating modalities includes optionalities for individual variation, and sequences are not necessarily based on strict adjacency relations. As a result, traditional statistical methods (including time series analysis) are practically not capable of capturing the behavioural patterns leading to functional interpretation.

Hunyadi et al. 2016 contains a tentative first analysis and as a follow-up we present Figure 7 showing T-patterns in multimodal topic management in the HuComTech corpus.

The T-Pattern analysis offers a framework to meet these serious challenges by simulating the cognitive process of human pattern recognition. The result is a set of patterns as possible expressions of a given function with their exact statistical significance. Moreover, it also suggests which of the constituting elements (events) of a given pattern can predict or retrodict the given function as a whole.

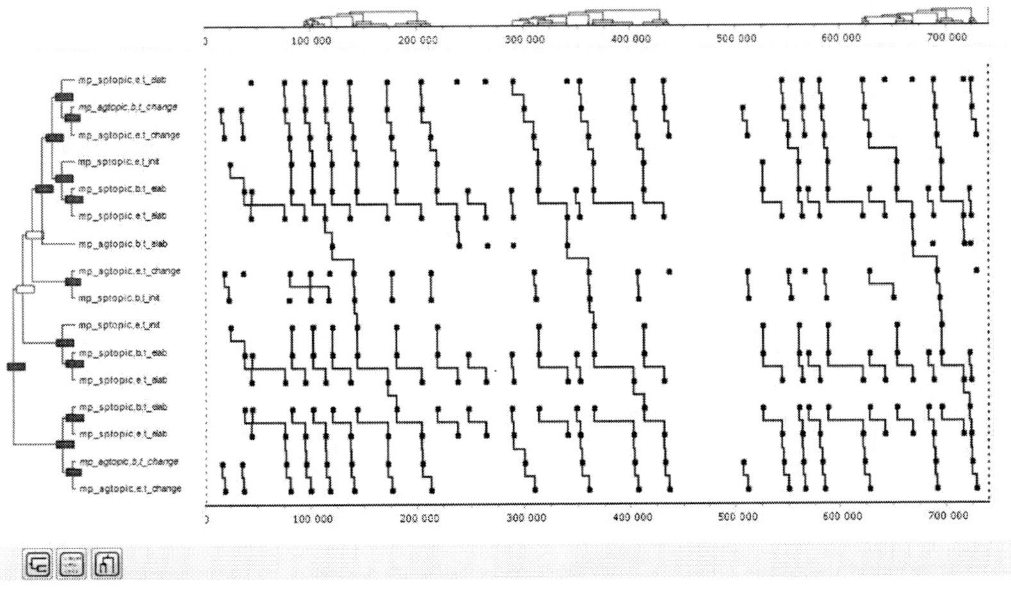

Figure 7 T-patterns in multimodal topic management in the HuComTech corpus

5   Conclusions

In this short paper, we showed how language technology can facilitate the analysis of complex research questions that arise from the study of multimodal human communication. To this end, we introduced a multimodal corpus containing 50 hours of dialogues annotated in rich detail in both unimodal and multimodal manner. We described three tools that were deployed to automate the annotation work, such as recording the prosodic phenomena of pitch, intensity and speech rate, the forced alignment of transcripts and speech signal and the morphological analysis of the text levels of annotation. We showed how T-pattern analysis can present an intriguing perspective to uncover hidden patterns in the temporal structure of multimodal communication.

Acknowledgement

The research reported in the paper was conducted with the support of the Hungarian Scientific Research Fund (OTKA) grants # K116938 and K116 402.

References

Ágnes Abuczki and Ghazaleh Esfandiari-Baiat, 2013 An overview of multimodal corpora, annotation tools and schemes. *Argumentum*, 9:86–98.

Christolihe d'Alessandro and Piet Mertens. 2004. Prosogram: semiautomatic transcription of prosody based on a tonal perception model. In *Proceedings of the 2nd International Conference of Speech Prosody*, pp. 23-26.

Luigi Anolli, Starkey Duncan Jr., Magnus S. Magnusson and Guiseppe Riva (eds.) 2000. *The Hidden Structure of InteractionFrom Neurons to Culture Patterns* http://www.emergingcommunication.com/volume7.html

Paul Boersma and David Weenik (2016). *Praat: doing phonetics by computer* [Computer program] version 6.0.13 http://www.praat.org

J. t'Hart(1976) Psychoacoustic backgrounds of pitch contour stylization. In *IPO- Annual Progress Report 11*, Eindhoven, The Netherlands, pp. 11–19.

László Hunyadi. 2011. Multimodal human-computer interaction technologies. Theoretical modeling and application inspeech processing. *Argumentum* 7:313–329 http://argumentum.unideb.hu/magyar/archivum.html-#7 (2011)

László Hunyadi, Tamás Váradi and István Szekrényes. (2016) The Multimodal HuComTech Corpus: Principles of Annotation and Discovery of Hidden Patterns of Behaviour in *Proceedings of LREC Workshop Multimodal Corpora: Computer Vision and Language Processing* available from https://db.tt/QWI9lLmA

Thomas Kisler, Uwe D. Reichel, Florian Schiel, Christoph Draxler, Bernard Jackl, and Nina Pörner. 2016. BAS Speech Science Web Services - an Update of Current Developments, *Proceedings of the 10th International Conference on Language Resources and Evaluation (LREC 2016)*, Portorož, Slovenia, paper id 668

Thomas Kisler, Florian Schiel and Han Sloetjes. 2012. Signal processing via web services: the use case Web-MAUS *Proceedings of Digital Humanities Conference 2012* available from https://www.-researchgate.net/publication/248390251_Signal_processing_via_web_services_the_use_case_WebMAUS

Magnus S. Magnusson, M. 1996. Hidden real-time patterns in intra- and interindividual behavior: Description and detection. *European Journal of Psychological Assessment*, 12, 112-123.

Magnus S. Magnusson. 2000. Discovering hidden time patterns in behavior: T-patterns and their detection. *Behavior Research Methods, Instruments, & Computers* 2000, 32 (I), 93-110.

Magnus S. Magnusson, Judee Burgoon and Maurizio Casarrubea (eds.) 2016. *Discovering Hidden Temporal Patterns in Behavior and Interaction. T-Pattern Detection and Analysis with THEME™*. Springer, New York.

Gábor Prószéky and László Tihanyi. 1993. Humor: High-Speed Unification Morphology and Its Applications for Agglutinative Languages. *La tribune des industries de la langue*, No. 10. 28–29., OFIL, Paris, France

István Szekrényes. 2015. ProsoTool, a method for automatic annotation of fundamental frequency In Baranyi Peter (ed.) *2015 6th IEEE International Conference on Cognitive Infocommunications (CogInfoCom)*. New York: IEEE, 2015. pp. 291-296.

Paul Taylor. 2000. Analysis and synthesis of intonation using the tilt model. *Journal of the Acoustical Society of America*, 107(3):1697-1714.

Large-scale Analysis of Spoken Free-verse Poetry

Timo Baumann
Department of Informatics
Universität Hamburg
baumann@informatik.uni-hamburg.de

Burkhard Meyer-Sickendiek
Department of Literary Studies
Freie Universität Berlin
bumesi@zedat.fu-berlin.de

Abstract

Most modern and post-modern poems have developed a post-metrical idea of lyrical prosody that employs rhythmical features of everyday language and prose instead of a strict adherence to rhyme and metrical schemes. This development is subsumed under the term *free verse prosody*. We present our methodology for the large-scale analysis of modern and post-modern poetry in both their written form and as spoken aloud by the author. We employ language processing tools to align text and speech, to generate a null-model of how the poem would be spoken by a naïve reader, and to extract contrastive prosodic features used by the poet. On these, we intend to build our model of free verse prosody, which will help to understand, differentiate and relate the different styles of free verse poetry. We plan to use our processing scheme on large amounts of data to iteratively build models of styles, to validate and guide manual style annotation, to identify further rhythmical categories, and ultimately to broaden our understanding of free verse poetry. In this paper, we report on a proof-of-concept of our methodology using smaller amounts of poems and a limited set of features. We find that our methodology helps to extract differentiating features in the authors' speech that can be explained by philological insight. Thus, our automatic method helps to guide the literary analysis and this in turn helps to improve our computational models.

1   Introduction

Lyrical analyses of poetry rely mainly on the poems' textual form, focusing on the analyst's philological insight of how to properly read a poem. Classic poetry has been analyzed extensively in this way, leading to a deep understanding of its prosodic structure which comprises rhyme and metrical schemes such as iambic or trochaic meter. The large amounts of manually analyzed works of such poetry have lead to tools like Metricalizer (Bobenhausen, 2011) which proposes metrical patterns given a poem's text and Sparsar (Delmonte and Prati, 2014) which uses such patterns for speech synthesis of metric poetry. These tools, however, do not work for *free verse poetry* which was started by modern and post-modern poets like Whitman, the Imagists, the Beat poets, and contemporary Slam poets. Regarding this kind of poetry, Finch (2000), Berry (1997), Silkin (1997), Meyer-Sickendiek (2012), Lüdtke et al. (2014) and many others manually analyze the prosodic forms and styles of some poems in great detail, providing a narrow but detailed view into free verse prosody. It will, however, not be possible to achieve a large phenomenal and analytical coverage by manual work alone.

At the same time, original recordings of modern and post-modern poets reciting their poetry are available, but neglected in philological research so far. We set out to change this. Through a collaboration with *Lyrikline*[1], we are able to use their speech and text database of modern and contemporary poetry, giving us access to hundreds of hours of author-spoken poetry. We aim to collaborate with further sources such as *PennSound* and *Poetry Foundation*. For the spoken and written poems, we create a text-speech alignment and using this alignment, we can extract a wide range of prosodic features as well as textual features using various tools. We then plan to use machine learning to learn styles and rhythmical/prosodic

---

[1]Lyrikline, http://www.lyrikline.org is an international website devoted to spoken contemporary poetry, established by *Literaturwerkstatt Berlin*, Germany.

Proceedings of the Workshop on Language Technology Resources and Tools for Digital Humanities (LT4DH),
pages 125–130, Osaka, Japan, December 11-17 2016.

figures (such as syncopation or cadence) based on annotations, to cluster similar poems (and poets) and their styles, or to identify 'outlier poems' which deserve further analysis.

In an iterative fashion, the results of automatic analyses are to be presented to a human philological analyst in a visual and understandable form and the interface to be developed will allow the annotation of particularities, including the addition of markables to annotate newly found types of noteworthy information. These will then be fed back to the machine-learning back-end and be used in the next cycle of automatic analyses. This *human-in-the-loop* approach to poetry analysis combines the strengths of human and machine analyses, namely deep understanding and broad coverage.

In the remainder of this paper we will first describe what sets apart free verse from the more traditional metric poetry in Section 2. This will highlight why traditional meter analysis tools cannot be used for free verse and why standard speech processing tools are more suitable for the task. In Section 3 we describe our methodology, in particular the contrasting of a null model to amplify the particularities of poetic speech. We describe our implementation in Section 4 and describe our preliminary experiments and results in Section 5. We close with a dicussion in Section 6 and outline future work.

2 Free Verse Poetry and Free Verse Prosody

The most important development in modern and postmodern poetry is the replacement of traditional meter by new rhythmical features: A structure of lyrical language was developed that renounced traditional forms like rhyme and meter, developing novel forms of prosody, accent, rhythm, and intonation to replace the traditional, and to forge a poetry instead based on the rhythms of contemporary American Speech (Gates, 1985; Gates, 1987). Music was another important influence, especially jazz, as well as efforts to visually register distinct free verse prosodies in print (Perloff, 1983). Prosody, as a specifically literary rhythm, was thus crucially redefined in modern American and European poetry.

This new kind of free verse prosody is marked by a new interplay of line and stanza, which may vary in different ways – line length, line integrity, line grouping, the dismemberment of the line, or systematic enjambement. William Carlos Williams developed the *isocolic* 'step-down line', a triadic alignment of tercets in which every line has its own arc of accentuation, while the gap between the lines is always the same size, resulting in a flowing rhythm. This mode of structuring a poem into cola (the rhethorical figure consisting of a clause which is grammatically, but not logically, complete) relates well to the idea of shallow parsing, or 'parsing by chunks' developed in linguistics (Abney, 1991). Under this influence, American Beat poet Allen Ginsberg develops an *isoperiodic* rhythm, in which lines are structured by "breath units", making them even closer to natural and fluent speech. Being influenced by Williams and Ginsberg, the famous Black Mountain poet Charles Olson based his idea of the "projective verse" on a similar relationship between the line and the poet's breathing (Olson, 1966), now combining isochronic and isoperiodic lines in order to create a more heterochronic rhythm (Golding, 1981). Even below the syllable, *sound poets* like Ernst Jandl used a prosody based on individual rhythmic phonemes.

As a result, the prosodic hierarchy to be considered for free verse is considerably more complex than for metric poetry and our working hypothesis of this hierarchy is depicted in Figure 1 (a). As can be seen, all levels of the linguistic hierarchy can carry poetic prosodic meaning, from the segment up to the periodic sentence. Based on this prosodic hierarchy, Figure 1 (b) depicts a categorization of some poets' works along two axes, the governing prosodic unit (x-axis) and the degree of iso/heterochronicity, or regularity of temporal arrangement (y-axis), according to philological analysis (Lüdtke et al., 2014). The green lines are meant as an estimate that outlines the limits of free verse poetry to prose.

To summarize, modern and post-modern free verse poetry has developed a broad range of prosodic styles stemming from a diverse set of structuring principles. Its prosody is often guided more by everyday speech than the prosodic principles of traditional poetry.

3 Methodology

Our methodology is to employ automatic analyses based on computational speech and language processing in combination with manual hermeneutical analyses. We will use machine learning techniques in a *human-in-the-loop* approach, in which we cycle between building (or extending) computational models and

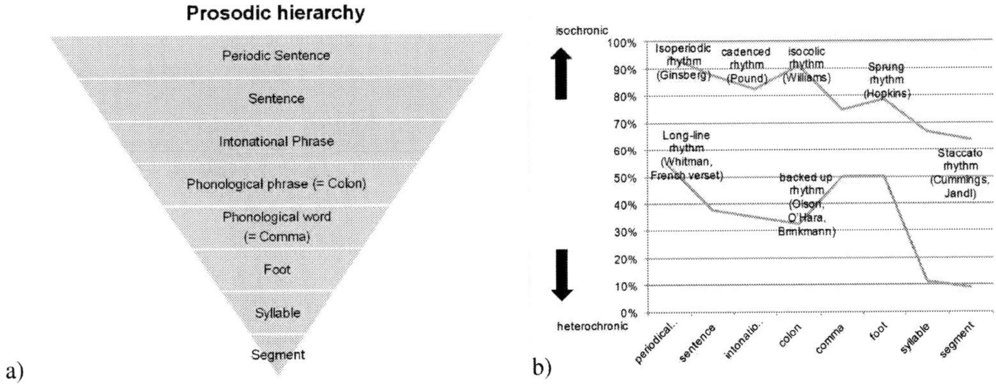

Figure 1: (a) Working hypothesis for a prosodic hierarchy for free verse poetry, as well as (b) a placement of poetic styles along the two axes governing unit and regularity of temporal arrangement.

manual philological analysis of phenomena (and the annotation of these phenomena).

The automatic analysis will, of course, be based on automatically extracted features that are potentially useful to describe and differentiate free verse prosody. Our goal is to find exactly those features and combinations that constitute free verse prosody. A prerequisite for computing such features is to create a text-speech alignment for the written poems and spoken recordings. In a next step, we extract phonological prosodic features such as ToBI labels (Silverman et al., 1992), which form the basis for phonetic prosodic features such as TILT (Taylor, 1998) or PaIntE (Möhler, 2001) parameters that describe individual tones, duration and loudness features, as well as silences as a basis for rhythmical structure and the level of isochronicity.

In order to build a *poetic prosody model* rather than just a prosody model for poetry, we contrast the features that we extract from the authentically spoken poems against a poetically naïve automatic reading. This *null model* of read-out poetry helps us to accentuate the peculiarities of the specific poetic styles and reduces the negative impact of data sparsity by focusing our analysis on the outstanding aspects of a poem.

Regarding higher-level prosodic analysis and feature extraction, poems will be split into prosodic segments and the combination of these prosodic segments will be assigned to types of rhythm. The patterns remain to be developed, since the existing research only discusses certain "figures of sound" or "figures of rhythm", both of which involve the repetition of some key linguistic component (Cooper, 1998). This processing step may yield similar results as depicted in Figure 1 (b) above. In addition, we use unsupervised learning, such as clustering techniques and outlier detection in order to steer the manual philological analysis towards potentially interesting parts and phenomena in the large corpora. We use existing meta-information (e.g. about poetic type) to train classifiers.

In our procedure, we will analyze classifier models with the aim of generating explanations for poetic categorization (e. g. RIPPER (Cohen, 1995) induces rule-based models that are easy to analyze), and these explanations can be valued (and in the strongest case rejected) by the human analyst. In this way, the human expert is able to steer the prosody modeling process away from computationally optimal but philologically ungrounded decision-making towards those aspects of poetic prosody that are deemed philologically relevant.

4   Implementation

We use text-speech alignment software as presented by Köhn et al. (2016) using a variation of the SailAlign algorithm (Katsamanis et al., 2011) based on the Sphinx-4 speech recognizer (Walker et al., 2004). Our prosodic analyses so far are limited to ToBI and we use AuToBI (Rosenberg, 2010) to generate an automatic intonation annotation.

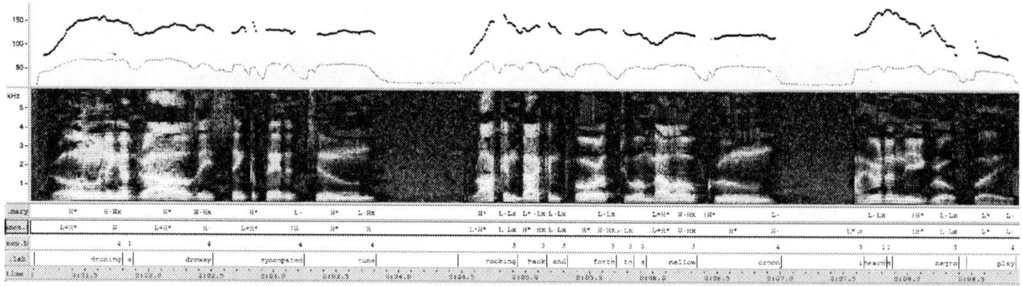

Figure 2: Example analysis of the first lines of Langston Hughes: "The Weary Blues." Shown from bottom to top: time, word alignment, ToBI breaks and tones, null-model estimate of ToBI tones, spectrogram, signal power (dB) and pitch (in Hz).

To generate our null-model version of a naïve, non-poetic reading of the poem's text, we use MaryTTS (Schröder and Trouvain, 2003) to synthesize speech audio which we then feed into the same alignment and analysis pipeline as we use for the author's speech. In this way, we limit the effect of MaryTTS and AuToBI internally using different interpretations of the ToBI standard.

In our preliminary experiments, we perform simple comparisons of the relative and contrastive occurrence of ToBI labels in read-out poems of different styles. Once annotations of notable structures become available, machine-learning tools such as WEKA (Witten and Frank, 2000) will be used as outlined above.

Our system is planned to be developed into a web-based client and server architecture. In this way, the human-in-the-loop hermeneutical analysis and interaction can be performed via any computer (and annotations can be parallelized). Furthermore, there is no need to install and update any software on the client-side, minimizing the risk of inconsistent data-handling or versioning issues.

5 Preliminary Experiments

We have performed preliminary experiments based on 10 poems from different modern and postmodern poets that cover the full range of free verse poetry and using only a limited set of prosodic features.

Regarding automatic text-speech alignment, we find positive results. For half of the poems, 90-98 % of the words after tokenization are successfully forced-aligned, which we deem a sufficient quantity to perform further analyses. Particular outliers in our sample with only 15 % of words aligned are W.C. Williams (very old recordings and a softly mumbling voice) as well as A. Stewart, who's experimental permutative poetry is overlaid with music and heavy echos, and C. Bök, who's segmental sound poetry already defies the trained grapheme-to-phoneme conversion models. Alignment of the (synthesized) null-model data is near perfect, as expected. Alignment quality seems reasonable but we have not yet formally evaluated it (e.g. in terms of root-mean-squared-error – RMSE – of boundary placement).

Regarding prosodic modelling, we have focused on ToBI labels so far, as these are less prone to pick up speaker characteristics than phonetically motivated features such as TILT parameters. AuToBI successfully produces tone alignments for aligned poetry (including the null-model audio), and again, although we have not formally evaluated the quality, annotations appear reasonable. However, the particularities of poetic speech are not covered in AuToBI's standard models and one future goal is to improve or extend these models over the course of our project. An example analysis is presented in Figure 2.

By contrasting the ToBI labels found in the author's speech with those for the null model, we can amplify what makes the prosodic style of a poem special. We find that in the first line, all L+H$\ast$ accents correspond to H$\ast$ accents in the null model, the passage *back and forth* receives two H$\ast$s instead of just one L$\ast$. Such an accumulation of differences struck the first author (a relatively theory-agnostic speech scientist) to be somewhat notable, and the second author (the philological expert on the team) explained that precisely this could be one manifestation of the poetic *syncopation* appearing in the poem.[2] Our

---

[2]Notice that rhythmical aspects such as low syllable rate in the first line contrasted by high syllable rate in the second are further indicators, for which, however, we still build our feature extraction; the example merely shows our guiding principle.

human-in-the-loop approach works exactly like this: the system finds candidate peculiarities in poems based on a measure of surprisal, which can then be named, described and explained by the human expert. In this case, we decided to next annotate several syncopations in multiple poems to build a model of the syncopation phenomenon. This model will then be used to (a) find further syncopation candidates which can be assessed by a human annotator in order to actively learn better models, and (b) as additional input into the style models to be developed.

The manual observations from the first line of the poem can be generalized by contrasting the occurrence of ToBI tones in the author's speech relative to the null model in the full poem. Using such statistics, we find that Hughes uses more than 3 times as many $L+H*$ as the null model would. Looking at the confusion matrix (i.e., what Hughes uses instead of the tones expected by the null model), we find that these accents generally occur in places where the null model would use $H*$ or no accent at all. We can compare different poems (and their prosodic styles) by comparing the respective differences to their null models.

We have performed a preliminary comparison based on tone differences of the aligned poems. We find that different deviations from the null model (as described above) occur in poems of different style. At least some of these differences do not appear to be based on speaker characteristics but on poetic style – like the $L+H*$ which may be an artifact of the slow and connected speaking style interleaved with faster syncopations as in Hughes' example. We plan to next train classifying models for different poetic styles. However, the amount of data and features exploited so far is clearly insufficient to report even preliminary results of machine-learned models.

6 Discussion and Future Work

We have presented our procedure for the large-scale analysis of spoken free verse poetry. The prosody of free verse poetry in many cases uses the rhythms of everyday speech (with some exceptions and extensions), which is why we base our procedures on conventional speech processing tools. Our methodology aims to single out what makes a poem special and to build a model of prosodic styles based on these specialities. We use a *human-in-the-loop* approach which allows us to analyze large amounts of spoken poetry and to focus manual analysis on the most important aspects found in the corpus.

In our preliminary experiments, we found that robust forced alignment works reasonably well for spoken poetry, yet still poses some interesting research problems, such as emphatic speech, onomatopoeic expressions, consonant or vowel clusters, prosodic disfluencies caused by line-breaks, etc. Likewise, we believe that current tools for intonation analysis (such as AuToBI) can fruitfully be used to analyze free verse, but that adaptations are necessary to leverage the full potential.

Our initial experiments are limited in data but will be scaled up to cover hundreds of hours of poems, enabling the reasonable use of machine-learning techniques over a multitude of features, finally also including text processing methods. Poetry is a particularly interesting form of language as, being art, it does not focus on function but uses creativity and surprisal to create something *new* and in a very dense form: What is an irrelevant *outlier* in standard machine learning tasks may be *outstanding* and important in our case. As such, poetry is intrinsically hard to model for machine learning approaches which rely on the repetition with small deviation of training data.

Our immediate next steps will be to import the full corpus from Lyrikline (and more), to set up a management database for existing meta-data and to build our web-based interface. Based on this, we will start to analyze the stability of potentially significant features of prosodic style across different poems (and recordings) of one poet and next within pre-established and annotated literary styles. This step will result in the development of further higher-level features that we will annotate and use to enhance our models.

Acknowledgements The authors would like to thank Manfred Stede, Claudia Müller-Birn, Arthur Jacobs, Wolfgang Menzel and Robert Tolksdorf for fruitful discussions of the topic.

References

Steve Abney. 1991. Parsing by chunks. In R. Berwick, S. Abney, and C. Tenny, editors, *Principle-based Parsing*, pages 257–278. Kluwer.

Eleanor Berry. 1997. The free verse spectrum. *College English*, 59(8):873–897.

Klemens Bobenhausen. 2011. The Metricalizer^2–automated metrical markup of German poetry. *Current Trends in Metrical Analysis, Bern: Peter Lang*, pages 119–131.

William Cohen. 1995. Fast effective rule induction. In *Proceedings of the 12th International Conference on Machine Learning*, pages 115–123. Morgan Kaufmann.

Gordon Burns Cooper. 1998. *Mysterious music: Rhythm and free verse*. Stanford University Press.

Rodolfo Delmonte and Anton Maria Prati. 2014. Sparsar: An expressive poetry reader. In *Proceedings of the Demonstrations at the 14th Conference of the European Chapter of the Association for Computational Linguistics*, pages 73–76, Gothenburg, Sweden, April. ACL.

Annie Finch. 2000. *The ghost of meter: Culture and Prosody in American Free Verse*. University of Michigan Press, Ann Arbor.

Rosemary L. Gates. 1985. The identity of American free verse: The prosodic study of Whitman's 'Lilacs'. *Language and Style*, 18(Summer):248–276.

Rosemary L. Gates. 1987. Forging an American poetry from speech rhythms: Williams after Whitman. *Poetics Today*, 8(3):503–527.

Alan Golding. 1981. Charles Olson's metrical thicket: Toward a theory of free-verse prosody. *Language and Style*, 14:64–78.

Athanasios Katsamanis, Matthew Black, Panayiotis G Georgiou, Louis Goldstein, and S Narayanan. 2011. Sailalign: Robust long speech-text alignment. In *Proc. of Workshop on New Tools and Methods for Very-Large Scale Phonetics Research*.

Arne Köhn, Florian Stegen, and Timo Baumann. 2016. Mining the Spoken Wikipedia for speech data and beyond. In *Proceedings of LREC 2016*.

Jana Lüdtke, Burkhard Meyer-Sickendieck, and Arthur M Jacobs. 2014. Immersing in the stillness of an early morning: Testing the mood empathy hypothesis of poetry reception. *Psychology of Aesthetics, Creativity, and the Arts*, 8(3):363.

Burkhard Meyer-Sickendiek. 2012. *Lyrisches Gespür. Vom geheimen Sensorium moderner Poesie*. Fink, Munich.

Gregor Möhler. 2001. Improvements of the PaIntE model for f0 parametrization. Technical report, Institut für Maschinelle Sprachverarbeitung (IMS), Stuttgart, September.

Charles Olson. 1966. *Selected Writings of Charles Olson*. New Directions, New York.

Marjorie Perloff. 1983. To give a design: Williams and the visualization of poetry. In Carroll F. Terrell, editor, *William Carlos Williams: Man and Poet*, page 159–186. The National Poetry Foundation, Orono, USA.

Andrew Rosenberg. 2010. AutoBI – a tool for automatic ToBI annotation. In *Proceedings of Interspeech*, pages 146–149.

Marc Schröder and Jürgen Trouvain. 2003. The German text-to-speech synthesis system MARY: A tool for research, development and teaching. *International Journal of Speech Technology*, 6(3):365–377, October.

Jon Silkin. 1997. *The life of metrical and free verse in twentieth-century poetry*. Macmillan, Basingstoke.

Kim Silverman, M. Beckman, J. Pitrelli, M. Ostendorf, C. Wightman, P. Price, J. Pierrehumbert, and J. Hirschberg. 1992. ToBI: A standard for labeling english prosody. In *Second International Conference on Spoken Language Processing*, Alberta, Canada, October.

Paul Taylor. 1998. The TILT Intonation Model. In *Proceedings of the ICSLP 1998*, pages 1383–1386.

Willie Walker, Paul Lamere, Philip Kwok, Bhiksha Raj, Rita Singh, Evandro Gouvea, Peter Wolf, and Joe Woelfel. 2004. Sphinx-4: A flexible open source framework for speech recognition. Technical report, Sun Microsystems, Inc., Mountain View, USA.

Ian. H. Witten and Eibe Frank. 2000. *Data Mining. Practical Machine Learning Tools and Techniques with Java Implementations*. Morgan Kaufmann, Rhodes, Greece.

PAT Workbench: Annotation and Evaluation of Text and Pictures in Multimodal Instructions

Ielka van der Sluis
Center for Language
and Cognition
University of Groningen
`i.f.van.der.sluis`
`@rug.nl`

Lennart Kloppenburg
Center for Language
and Cognition
University of Groningen
`l.kloppenburg`
`@rug.nl`

Gisela Redeker
Center for Language and
Cognition
University of Groningen
`g.redeker`
`@rug.nl`

Abstract

This paper presents a tool to investigate the design of multimodal instructions (MIs), i.e., instructions that contain both text and pictures. The benefit of including pictures in information presentation has been established, but the characteristics of those pictures and of their textual counterparts and the relation(s) between them have not been researched in a systematic manner. We present the PAT Workbench, a tool to store, annotate and retrieve MIs based on a validated coding scheme with currently 42 categories that describe instructions in terms of textual features, pictorial elements, and relations between text and pictures. We describe how the PAT Workbench facilitates collaborative annotation and inter-annotator agreement calculation. Future work on the tool includes expanding its functionality and usability by (i) making the MI annotation scheme dynamic for adding relevant features based on empirical evaluations of the MIs, (ii) implementing algorithms for automatic tagging of MI features, and (iii) implementing automatic MI evaluation algorithms based on results obtained via e.g. crowdsourced assessments of MIs.

1 Introduction

This paper presents a tool to facilitate a rigorous empirically oriented study on the design and use of multimodal instructions (MIs), i.e., instructions that contain both text and pictures. MIs are ubiquitous in all walks of modern life (medicine, electronics, flatpack furniture, recipes, etc.). In general, it has been established that including pictures in information presentation is beneficial for readers and users (e.g., Glenberg and Roberts, 1999; Kjelldahl, 1992; Mayer, 2009; Schriver, 1997). But what are the characteristics of the pictures, texts and the relation(s) between them in these presentations? To illustrate the abundant variety of presentational aspects in MIs and the apparent lack of authoring guidelines, Figures 1 and 2 present two MIs for operating an automated external defibrillator (AED). Already at first sight the two instructions differ in numerous ways, e.g. the number of steps, the number of actions to carry out per step, the type of pictures, layout in terms of columns and rows, the amount of text (per step), the occurrence and type of arrows used in pictures, the use of indices, labels and references.

Our main goal is to systematically investigate how text and pictures are best combined in MIs in terms of effectiveness in their context of use. For now, we consider primarily MIs in health communication. Our corpus-based studies will allow investigation of the breadth of instructional design, while existing studies on MIs (Houts et al., 2006; Katz et al., 2006) generally focus on human processing of particular instructions. Outcomes of our work will aid (semi-)automatic annotation, evaluation and generation of MIs as well as the formulation of authoring guidelines on how to combine text and pictures effectively according to judgments and performance of readers and users and dependent on, for instance, the function of the MI (e.g., to learn a task or to perform a task only once).

Proceedings of the Workshop on Language Technology Resources and Tools for Digital Humanities (LT4DH),
pages 131–139, Osaka, Japan, December 11-17 2016.

Various tools exist for picture annotation (e.g., Cusano et al., 2003, Russel et al., 2008), text annotation (e.g., Erdman et al., 2000; Ogren, 2006; Stenetorp et al., 2012) and video annotation (e.g., Brugman & Russel, 2004; Do et al., 2016; Kipp, 2001). However, to our knowledge only the UAM tool (O'Donnell 2008) supports the annotation of both text and pictures. UAM supports semi-automatic tagging of text and allows parts of pictures to be selected and labelled, but not to our knowledge relational annotations.

In this paper we present the PAT Workbench for annotation, storage and retrieval of MIs. The workbench supports manual annotation based on a coding scheme that describes MIs in terms of the factors that potentially influence the effectiveness of MIs. The 42 categories of the coding scheme were inspired by studies on human processing of multimodal presentations (e.g., Arts et al., 2011; Dupont & Bestgen, 2006; Florax & Ploetzner, 2010; Heiser & Tversky 2006; Van Hooijdonk & Krahmer, 2008; Maes & Noordman, 2004; Morrow et al., 2005). Like UAM (O'Donnell, 2008) and Anvil (Kipp, 2001), the workbench includes inter-annotator agreement calculation and a method to resolve any differences between annotations and obtain a gold standard annotation.

In Section 2 we present the PAT Workbench, In Section 3, we present an overview of our current MI corpus with 194 annotated first-aid instructions. In Section 4, we conclude with a discussion of future work on the PAT Workbench.

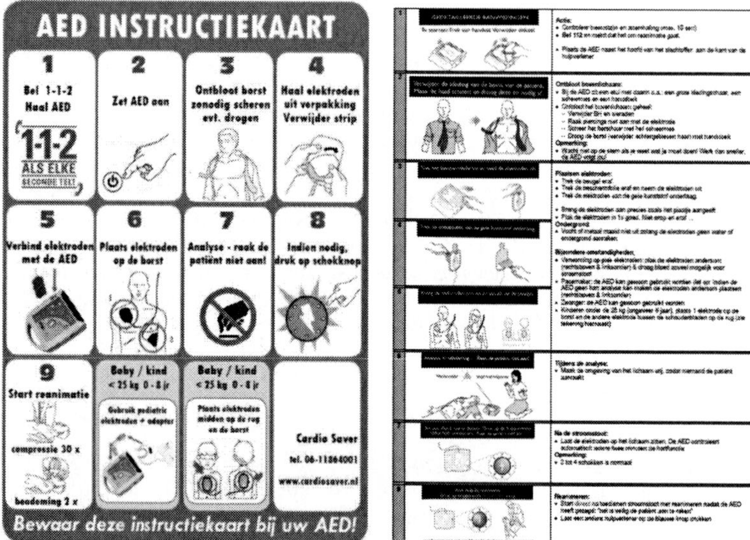

<table><tr><td>Figure 1: AED MIT by cardiosaver.nl.</td><td>Figure 2: AED MIT by ProCardio.nl.</td></tr></table>

2   The PAT Workbench

2.1   System description

The PAT Workbench is an online tool that was built to facilitate the annotation, storage and retrieval of MIs collected by master students in Communication and Information Sciences at the University of Groningen. Each year, about 200 new annotated MIs are added to the corpus. These MIs concern first-aid tasks like applying a band-aid, removing ticks, or reanimating a person. The PAT Workbench is a web application written in PHP using the CodeIgniter Framework[1]. The design of the website features a Bootstrap[2] template called Dark Admin[3]. Data creation and manipulation is facilitated through a MySQL database. This relational database structure allows an efficient design of connections between concepts such as users, user groups, group assignments, documents and annotations. Documents are

---

[1] https://www.codeigniter.com/

[2] http://getbootstrap.com/

[3] http://www.prepbootstrap.com/bootstrap-theme/dark-admin

not stored in this database, but in a separate directory structure where each document is linked by its identification code to its entry in the database (which contains the metadata).

The current version of the PAT Workbench has a menu structure with five main topics: Search, Add, Assignment, Manual, Collection and Manual, and includes the following functionalities:

- Detailed MI search system with filtering options
- Viewing panel to inspect MIs
- Function to upload MIs to the workbench
- Annotation panel to annotate MIs according to the PAT coding scheme
- Assignment panel to create and manage collaborations with other annotators
- Revision history for annotators
- Function to add annotated MIs to the MI corpus
- MI browser to select MIs for viewing
- Web-friendly manual for annotating MIs
- Documentation at the levels of installation/use, code, and database.

The interface of the current version of PAT is in Dutch; an English version is in preparation.

2.2 Adding MIs

Users of the PAT Workbench can add (sets of) MIs in PDF format to their own corpus via the menu item 'Add'. A user becomes the owner of MIs that he/she adds from the collection of free MIs in the MI corpus and of the new MIs that he/she uploads to the workbench. When uploading MIs, the user is prompted to select a set of documents. For each document the user needs to specify some metadata about the MI it contains (e.g., title, description, target audience, background information, source), aided by a simultaneously offered view of the MI (see Figure 3). Based on the metadata, the system checks if the MI is not uploaded already. To make sure that no duplicates exist, the user can also manually check the uploaded MIs based on a keyword search that retrieves MIs using the metadata; the retrieved MIs can be browsed and inspected with a simple document viewer. In addition, uploaded PDF documents are converted to plain text using OCR (ABBYY[4]).

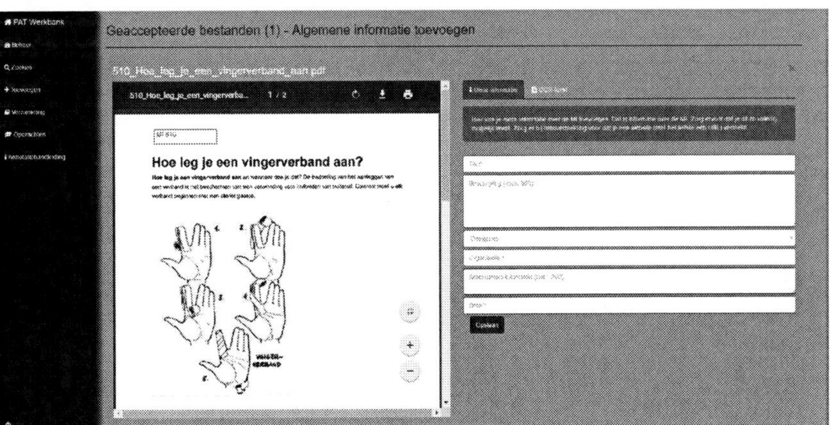

Figure 3: Panel for uploading MIs and adding metadata.

2.3 Annotation panel

Figure 4 presents the annotation panel. The grey part of the screen offers a two-column view of an uploaded MI. The left side offers either a view of the document as it was uploaded to the PAT Workbench, a view of OCR output, the annotation manual, or the annotation history of the document.

---

[4] https://www.abbyy.com/en-eu/en/cloud-ocr-sdk/

The right side presents a tabulated view of the main annotation categories: (1) function, (2) text, (3) pictures and (4) text-picture relations.

The annotation scheme used in the PAT Workbench is the improved version of a scheme that was used by 13 annotators who annotated a corpus of 227 health care instructions (Van Dijk et al. 2016). The corpus described in Section 3 was annotated with the improved scheme. In Tables 1 to 4 below the scheme is presented in terms of the four main categories, including their subcategories with values. Note that the illocutionary properties of text and pictures are defined so that they can be aligned in terms of actions and control information. Correspondences between text and pictures are defined in terms of number of steps, indices and layout. Future work will also consider relations in terms of implements, agents and actions. Other extensions will include annotations of MIs per picture and per textual unit. Currently all annotations concern the MI as a whole.

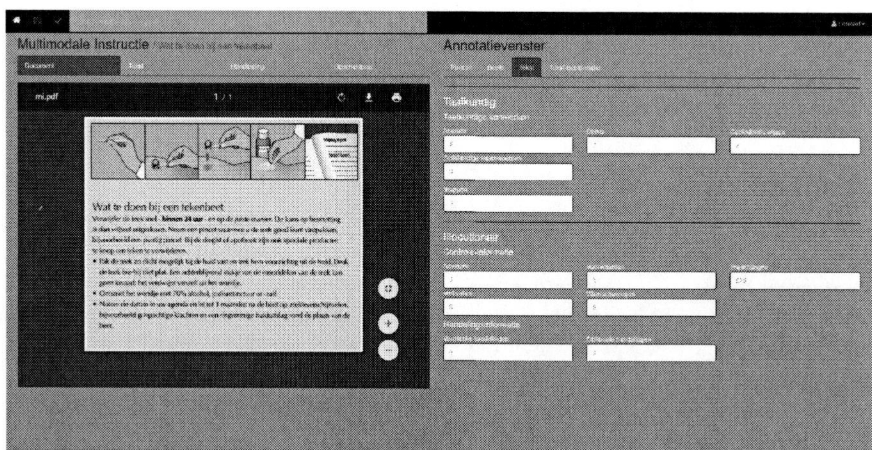

Figure 4: Panel for annotating MIs.

Main category	Subcategory	Value
1. Identification MI		
	A) Title	Text
	B) Description	Text
	C) Target group	*Adults, children, medics*
	D) Organisation	Text
	E) Background Knowledge	Text
	F) Source	Text
2. Function MI		
	A) Reading-to-do	0 or 1
	B) Reading-to-learn	0 or 1
	C) Reading-to-decide during instruction	0 or 1
	D) Reading-to-decide after instruction	0 or 1

Table 1: Functional aspects of MIs.

Main category	Subcategory	Value
3. Text: Length		
	A) Number of steps	*Count*
	B) Number of sentences	Count
	C) Word count	Count
4. Text: Linguistic properties		
	A) Nouns	Count

	B) Anaphora	*Count*
	C) Deixis	*Count*
	D) Imperatives	*Count*
	E) Form of address	Formal, informal, avoiding
5. Text: Illocutionary properties		
	A) Compulsory actions	*Count*
	B) Optional actions	*Count*
	C) Control information, warnings, conditionals, motivations, advisements, explanations, other	*Count*
	D) Extra information	
	Notes	Text

Table 2: Textual aspects of MIs.

Main category	**Subcategory**	**Value**
6. Picture: Visual properties		
	A) Number of pictures	*Count*
	B) Picture type	*Drawing, photo, other*
	C) Human appearance	*Count*
	D) Text in picture	*Count*
	E) Pictograms	*Count*
	F) Arrows	Count
	G) Indication	*Numbers, letters, none*
	H) Clock-time indications	*Count*
7. Picture: Illocutionary properties		
	A) Compulsory actions	*Count*
	B) Optional actions	*Count*
	C) Result of action	*Final, partial result*
	D) Function	*Localisation, identification*
	E) Control information, warning, explanation, other	*Count*
	F) Extra information	0 or 1
	Notes	

Table 3: Pictorial aspects of MIs.

Main category	**Subcategory**	**Value**
9. Text-picture relation		
	A) Correspondence in steps	*0 or 1*
	B) Text-picture layout	*Numbers, lines, blocks, titles, other*
	C) Textual reference to pictures	*Count*
	Notes	Text

Table 4: Text-picture relations in MIs.

2.4 Collaborative annotation

The PAT Workbench administrator can formulate a collaboration assignment for a particular group of users, and the members of the group can then invite other members to annotate a subset of the MIs they own using the collaboration panel. The collaboration panel includes a progress indicator for the annotations. Agreement between two annotations of each MI is calculated per subcategory to help the 'owner' of the MI to double-check and improve the annotation, which the administrator then adds to the MI corpus as the gold standard annotation of the MI.

2.5 MI Retrieval

MIs of which the annotation is agreed on by at least two annotators and which have thus been added to the gold standard annotated corpus, can be retrieved via the main menu item 'Search'. The link points to a panel with two tabs (Figure 5), one to perform an extensive search and one to browse the database. The latter option offers a tiled view of all MIs in the corpus that includes a picture of the MIs and the metadata (i.e. title, description, uploader, owner, target audience, source, web address and date). The extensive search offers a keyword search, which can be augmented with the values of the subcategories presented in italics in Tables 1 to 4. The output of the PhP-based search engine is displayed with the simple MI browser that is also used to browse the corpus, which allows selection and display of individual MIs.

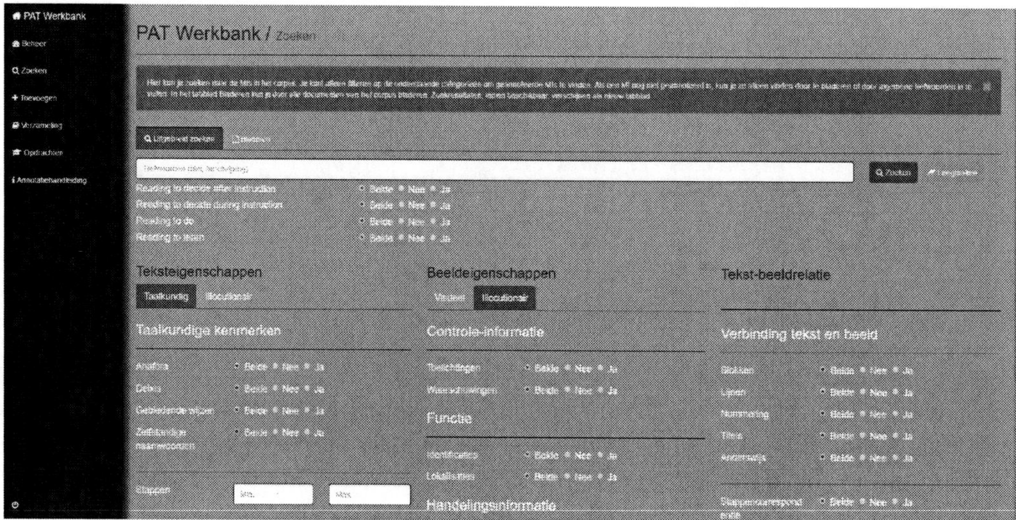

Figure 5: Search panel of the PAT Workbench.

2.6 Manuals and documentation

The PAT Workbench includes an illustrated annotation manual (Van Dijk et al. 2016) which is available in PDF format via the main menu as well as via the annotation panel. In addition, the system itself is documented at the installation/use level, code level, and database level.

2.7 Administrator Interface to manage MIs and Users

The administrator interface includes three different administration panels:
- On the User panel, the administrator may add or remove users of three types (student, researcher, administrator) or edit details of users (i.e. name, student number, email address and type).
- On the Group panel, the administrator can create a user group for a particular time span. For each group the administrator can add and remove users and formulate collaboration assignments.
- On the Corpus panel, the administrator can edit and remove MIs. The administrator may also unlock MIs from their owners to allow other users to change or extend the annotations. In all cases 'remove' means 'flag as inactive or invisible', as no user or MI is actually removed from the database to allow restore and repair.

2.8 Evaluation and Usability

Currently, an extensive evaluation of the system is in progress. A preliminary task-based user study on the administrator interface included an observation of the administrator (the first author of this paper) performing tasks while thinking aloud. She had not seen the administrator interface before, but was closely involved in the design and implementation of the underlying functionality. After she had performed the tasks assigned to her, she filled out two standard usability questionnaires, SUS (Brook, 1986) and CSUQ (Lewis, 1995), and was interviewed by the experimenter who asked her to reflect on her task performance and the way she filled out the questionnaires.

Observations of the task-based performance brought to light various flaws that are currently being remedied. Most prominent were issues with system feedback (e.g., system confirmations, visual cues, mouse-over information) and uniformity (e.g., potential user actions are indicated with buttons as well as icons). Overall this (admittedly biased) evaluation was very positive, but also identified a number of minor points where the interface could be improved.

After the implementation of those improvements, an analysis of the PAT Workbench is currently being conducted by an independent expert who will perform a functional analysis, a heuristic inspection of the whole application, identification of the main tasks and a cognitive walkthrough of these main tasks. A more extensive user study with potential users of the PAT Workbench will be conducted inspecting the usability of the PAT Workbench in terms of its main tasks using a think-aloud protocol, usability questionnaires and interviews.

3   MI corpus

The annotated MI corpus currently contains 192 MIs, 166 of which are designed for adult users, 9 for children and 17 for medics. The MI functions are distributed as follows: reading-to-do (120), reading-to-learn (85), reading-to-decide-during-instruction (17), and reading-to-decide-after-instruction (6); some MIs have multiple functions. Thirteen annotators familiar with the annotation scheme annotated, double-checked and agreed on the annotations of 106 MIs, subsequently the annotators coded 86 new MIs.

The annotation of linguistic properties shows that the mean number of steps in the MIs is 5.78, varying from 1 to 14. The mean number of sentences in the MIs is 10.37, varying from 1 to 41. The mean number of imperatives in the MIs is 6.93, ranging from 0 (24 MIs) to 25. The mean number of anaphora used is 1.01, where 90 MIs do not include any anaphora and the maximum number of anaphora used in an MI is 11.

Table 5 presents counts of illocutionary properties of text and pictures in the 192 MIs. By far the most text segments and pictures refer to compulsory actions. Conditionals, motivations, and advisements cannot be reliably identified in pictures and were thus only annotated for the texts.

	Text	**Picture**
Compulsory actions	1266	767
Optional actions	190	45
Control information	110	26
Warnings	171	4
Conditionals	113	NA
Motivations	98	NA
Advisements	244	NA
Explanations	141	166

Table 5: Total number of illocutionary properties of text and pictures (NA = 'Not annotated').

The annotation of visual properties shows that the mean number of pictures included in the MIs is 4.25 ranging from 1 to 23. In 66 MIs these pictures are photographs, 125 MIs use drawings and one MI uses a combination of photographs and drawings. The total of 816 pictures include 95 instances of text in picture and 8 instances of pictograms, 258 arrows and 12 time indications. Human body parts are included in 764 pictures. Pictures are used for identification purposes in 535 cases and for localisation purposes in 28 cases. While actions are usually referred to by action verbs in the text, pictures often present not the process, but the results (439 pictures) or partial results of actions (302 pictures).

Annotation of text-picture relations reveals a correspondence in 71 MIs in terms of the number of steps in the text and the number of pictures. In 27 MIs text and pictures are connected through numbering, 28 MIs use lines, 32 MIs use blocks and 13 MIs use titles. In 21 MIs textual references to pictures are included ranging from 1 (8 MIs) to 14 (1 MI).

4   Future Work

The current version of the PAT Workbench will be improved based on results from the planned expert and user evaluations. Additional functionalities we envisage include:

- Recognition of the document structure where OCR fails due to e.g., columns and pictures in the MIs. Fully parsed MIs will allow for automatic tagging of lexical and grammatical features and will considerably reduce the need for manual annotation of linguistic text features as presented in Table 2. Currently, the Alpino parser (Van Noord, 2006) is used for simple NLP tasks like counting words and sentences.
- Development and implementation of an algorithm to annotate illocutionary aspects of text and pictures in MIs.
- Annotation of individual pictures and textual units, which allow description of individual picture-text relations. These relations will include actions or illocutionary aspects that are described and visualised. As implemented in the UAM tool for pictures (O'Donnell, 2008), identification and annotation of features of pictures is envisioned.
- Development and implementation of an evaluation algorithm that scores features of MIs in terms of predicting readers' and users' ratings of the quality of MIs. These ratings will be based on crowdsourcing experiments in which readers are asked to rate MIs as well as on empirical studies in which users perform the actions instructed in MIs.
- A more extensive administrator panel will be implemented that allows a dynamic annotation scheme, i.e. to add new and disable existing annotation categories and their values. Obviously, these changes need to be made in tandem with the search options and the method used to calculate inter-annotator agreement.
- An English interface will be provided to improve the system's accessibility.

Implementation of automatic methods for annotation and evaluation will allow us to annotate larger amounts of MIs and thus to extend and generalise the workbench to process other types of MIs (e.g., indoor navigation, cooking recipes, construction manuals) and possibly instruction videos in the future.

References

Arts, A., Maes, A., Noordman, L. & Jansen C. (2011). Overspecification in written instruction. *Linguistics, 49* (3), 555-574.

Brooke, J. (1996). SUS: A quick and dirty usability scale. In Jordan P. W., Thomas B., Weerdmeester B. A., McClelland I. L. (Eds.), *Usability Evaluation in Industry* (pp. 189-194). London: Taylor & Francis. (Also see http://www.cee.hw.ac.uk/~ph/sus.html).

Brugman, H. & Russel, A. (2004): Annotating multi-media / multi-modal resources with ELAN. In *Proceedings of the fourth International Conference on Language Resources and Evaluation (LREC)*. Lisbon: Portugal, 2065–2068.

Cavicchio, F., & Poesio, M. (2009). Multimodal corpora annotation: Validation methods to assess coding scheme reliability. In M. Kipp, J.-C. Martin, P. Paggio, and D. Heylen (Eds.), *Multimodal Corpora* LNAI 5509, Berlin: Springer, 109-121.

Cusano, C., Ciocca, G., & Schettini, R. (2003). Image annotation using SVM. In *Electronic Imaging 2004* (pp. 330-338). International Society for Optics and Photonics.

Van Dijk, J., Van der Sluis, I. and Redeker, G. (2016). Annotation of Text and Pictures in Health Care Instructions. Presented at TABU'2016, 3 June, 2016.

Tuan Do, Nikhil Krishnaswamy, and James Pustejovsky. (2016). "ECAT: Event Capture Annotation Tool." Interoperability for Semantic Annotation (ISA) 2016, at the 10th Edition of the Language Resources and Evaluation Conference, Portoroz, Slovenia, May 28, 2016.

Dupont, V., & Bestgen, Y. (2006). Learning from technical documents: The role of intermodal referring expressions. *Human Factors, 48* (2), 257-264.

Florax, M., & Ploetzner, R. (2010). What contributes to the split-attention effect? The role of text segmentation, picture labelling, and spatial proximity. *Learning and Instruction, 20* (3), 216-224.

Glenberg, A., & Robertson, D. (1999). Indexical understanding of instructions. *Discourse Processes, 28* (1), 1-26.

Heiser, J., & Tversky, B. (2006). Arrows in comprehending and producing mechanical diagrams. *Cognitive Science, 30* (3), 581-592.

Van Hooijdonk, C. & Krahmer, E. (2008). Information modalities for procedural instructions: The influence of text, static and dynamic visuals on learning and executing RSI exercises. *IEEE Transactions on Professional Communication, 51* (1), 50-62.

Houts, P., Doak, C., Doak, L., & Loscalzo, M. (2006). The role of pictures in improving health communication: A review of research on attention, comprehension, recall, and adherence. *Patient Education and Counseling, 61* (2),173-190.

Katz, M., Kripalani, S., & Weiss, B. (2006). Use of pictorial aids in medication instructions: a review of the literature. *American Journal of Health-System Pharmacy, 63* (23), 2391-2398.

Kipp, M. (2001) Anvil - A Generic Annotation Tool for Multimodal Dialogue. *Proceedings of the 7th European Conference on Speech Communication and Technology (Eurospeech)*, pp. 1367-1370.

Kjelldahl, L. (1992) *Multimedia: Systems, Interaction and Applications.* Berlin: Springer.

Lewis, J. R. (1995) IBM Computer Usability Satisfaction Questionnaires: Psychometric Evaluation and Instructions for Use. *International Journal of Human-Computer Interaction, 7* (1), 57-78.

Maes, A., Arts, A. & Noordman, L. (2004). Reference management in instructive discourse. *Discourse Processes, 37*(2), 117-144.

Mayer, R. (2009). *Multimedia learning.* Cambridge University Press.

Morrow, D., Weiner, M., Young, J., Steinley, D., Deer, M., & Murray, M. (2005). Improving medication knowledge among older adults with heart failure: a patient-centered approach to instruction design. *The Gerontologist, 45* (4), 545-552.

Van Noord, G. (2006, April). At last parsing is now operational. In *TALN06. Verbum Ex Machina. Actes de la 13e conference sur le traitement automatique des langues naturelles* (pp. 20-42).

Ogren, P. V. (2006, June). Knowtator: a protégé plug-in for annotated corpus construction. In *Proceedings of the 2006 Conference of the North American Chapter of the Association for Computational Linguistics on Human Language Technology: Companion volume: Demonstrations* (pp. 273-275).

O'Donnell, M. (2008). Demonstration of the UAM CorpusTool for text and image annotation. In *Proceedings of the 46th Annual Meeting of the Association for Computational Linguistics on Human Language Technologies: Demo session* (pp. 13-16).

Russell, B. C., Torralba, A., Murphy, K. P., & Freeman, W. T. (2008). LabelMe: a database and web-based tool for image annotation. *International Journal of Computer Vision, 77*(1-3), 157-173.

Schriver K. (1997). *Dynamics in Document Design: Creating Texts for Readers.* John Wiley & Sons: New York, NY.

Stenetorp, P., Pyysalo, S., Topić, G., Ohta, T., Ananiadou, S., & Tsujii, J. I. (2012). BRAT: a web-based tool for NLP-assisted text annotation. In *Proceedings of the Demonstrations at the 13th Conference of the European Chapter of the Association for Computational Linguistics* (pp. 102-107).

Semantic Indexing of Multilingual Corpora
and its Application on the History Domain

Alessandro Raganato[1]**, Jose Camacho-Collados**[1]**, Antonio Raganato**[2] **and** **Yunseo Joung**
Department of Computer Science[1], Department of Political Sciences[2]
Sapienza University of Rome
{raganato,collados}@di.uniroma1.it
{raganatoantonio,louisejoung}@gmail.com

Abstract

The increasing amount of multilingual text collections available in different domains makes its automatic processing essential for the development of a given field. However, standard processing techniques based on statistical clues and keyword searches have clear limitations. Instead, we propose a knowledge-based processing pipeline which overcomes most of the limitations of these techniques. This, in turn, enables direct comparison across texts in different languages without the need of translation. In this paper we show the potential of this approach for semantically indexing multilingual text collections in the history domain. In our experiments we used a version of the Bible translated in four different languages, evaluating the precision of our semantic indexing pipeline and showing its reliability on the cross-lingual text retrieval task.

1 Introduction

In recent years there has been a growing interest in automatically processing historical corpora due to the increasing number of available text collections in the field (Dekkers et al., 2009). However, few software applications for non-expert users have been developed for processing and indexing historical texts, and these applications are in the main based on statistical processing techniques only (Piotrowski, 2012). Even though these techniques have been and are currently widely used, they have clear limitations. First, standard statistical processing techniques based on keywords do not handle the inherent ambiguity within language. Second, occurrences of the same concept/event/entity are often referred to via different lexicalizations (e.g. *Louis XIV*, *Louis the Great* and *Sun King*), which are not captured by keyword-based text retrieval techniques. Finally, these approaches are bound to remain monolingual by nature, limiting their applicability to multilingual corpora, which is growing in interest over the years (Johansson, 2007). There have been recent approaches to automatically link cultural heritage items from text corpora to knowledge bases (Brugman et al., 2008; Fernando and Stevenson, 2012; Hall et al., 2012; Efremova et al., 2014; Poelitz and Bartz, 2014) but without going beyond the monolingual level. In fact, to date most approaches towards the accessibility of cultural heritage content in multiple languages have focused on the generation of natural language content through knowledge bases or via the Semantic Web (Davies, 2009; Dannélls et al., 2013).

Instead, we propose a knowledge-based pipeline for automatically processing multilingual corpora which overcomes all previously mentioned limitations by going beyond standard statistical techniques and keyword-based queries. Our approach is based on the disambiguation of text corpora through a knowledge base. Disambiguation is then exploited for semantically indexing multilingual text collections by associating each concept/entity with a unique identifier independent on the language and the surface form. This in turn enables direct applications across languages such as cross-lingual text retrieval, and opens up new lines of research to study cross-cultural differences from multilingual text corpora (Gutiérrez et al., 2016).

Proceedings of the Workshop on Language Technology Resources and Tools for Digital Humanities (LT4DH),
pages 140–147, Osaka, Japan, December 11-17 2016.

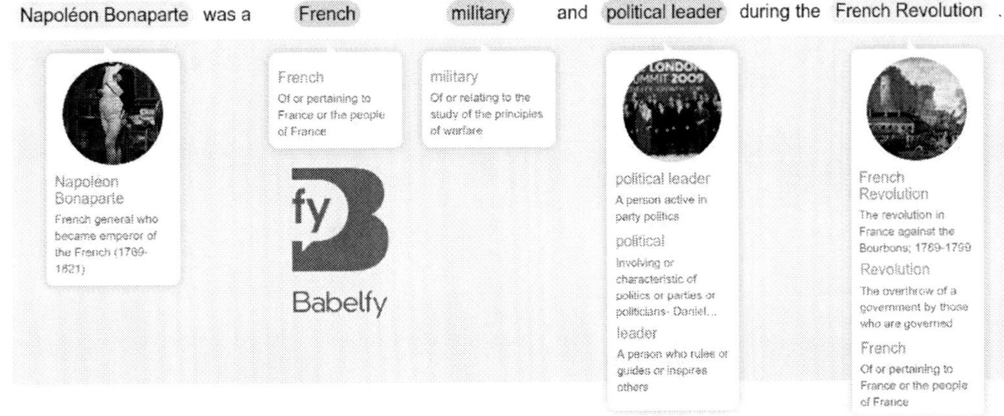

Figure 1: Sample output disambiguation.

2 Methodology

In this section we explain our pipeline for the semantic processing of multilingual corpora. For the semantic processing we rely on BabelNet (Navigli and Ponzetto, 2012), a large multilingual encyclopedic dictionary and semantic network. BabelNet[1] integrates various resources such as WordNet (Miller, 1995), Open Multilingual WordNet (Bond and Foster, 2013), Wikipedia, OmegaWiki, Wiktionary and Wikidata, among others. All the aforementioned resources are merged into a very large lexical resource in which equivalent concepts and entities are aggregated from the different resources in a unique instance, called BabelNet synset. Each synset contains all the synonyms and definitions harvested from the respective resources in a range of different languages. In fact, BabelNet includes 271 languages and has already shown its potential in various multilingual and cross-lingual Natural Language Processing applications (Moro et al., 2014; Camacho-Collados et al., 2015; Camacho-Collados et al., 2016b). We propose to use this knowledge base to semantically index large collections of multilingual texts. Our methodology is divided in two main steps: (1) corpus preprocessing including disambiguation and entity linking (Section 2.1) and (2) semantic indexing (Section 2.2).

2.1 Disambiguation and Entity Linking

The goal of this step is to associate each content word[2] with a unique unambiguous identifier (i.e., a BabelNet synset). First, texts are preprocessed (tokenized, Part-Of-Speech tagged and lemmatized) using Stanford CoreNLP (Manning et al., 2014) and TreeTagger (Schmid, 1994) on the languages for which these tools are available. For the remaining languages we rely on the multilingual preprocessing tools integrated in Babelfy. Since the disambiguation is targeted to historical texts, we include a list of stopwords belonging to the archaic form of a given language for the languages for which this list is available. For example, for English we used a list[3] including archaic expressions such as *thou* or *ye*. These stopwords are therefore not taken into account in the disambiguation process.

Then, preprocessed texts[4] are disambiguated using Babelfy (Moro et al., 2014), a state-of-the-art knowledge-based Word Sense Disambiguation and Entity Linking system based on BabelNet. Babelfy[5] exploits a densest subgraph heuristic for selecting high-coherence semantic interpretations of the input text and has been shown to perform on par with supervised systems on both Word Sense Disambiguation

---

[1]http://babelnet.org

[2]Multiwords are also considered on the disambiguation.

[3]http://bryanbumgardner.com/elizabethan-stop-words-for-nlp/

[4]As mentioned earlier, for the languages not covered by Stanford CoreNLP and TreeTagger we directly rely on the Babelfy pipeline.

[5]http://babelfy.org

Figure 2: Semantic indexing of multilingual corpora: sample retrieved texts given *Edward IV* as input.

and Entity Linking tasks. Figure 1 shows a sample output disambiguation of a sentence as given by Babelfy.

2.2 Semantic indexing

Finally, for indexing a given text collection we directly use the output provided on the disambiguation step. Given a certain BabelNet synset or an instance from Wikipedia (recall from Section 2 that BabelNet is a multilingual resource containing Wikipedia among other resources), our system provides all the texts in a given corpus containing that instance. This is particularly interesting when the corpus is composed by texts in different languages as it directly benefits from the multilingual disambiguation performed in the previous section. Instead of translating a given concept or entity in different languages, our model is able to retrieve all the texts in which the given concept or entity occurs, irrespective of the text language. For instance, given a corpus of texts in different languages about the Late Middle Ages, our system would automatically retrieve all the texts in which the king of England *Edward IV* occurs (see Figure 2). This may be especially useful for carrying out a research on a specific person/event, as it differs from usual searches based on keywords which are focused on a single language and do not deal with ambiguity and synonymy.

3 Cross-lingual text retrieval

One of the most straightforward applications from the semantic indexing of corpora is cross-lingual text retrieval. The task of cross-lingual text retrieval consists of, given an input query, retrieving the texts which are more relevant to the input query. In this case, the user introduces a text as input (included in the corpus or not) and as an output our system retrieves the n most similar texts within the corpus, which may be written in a different language from the language of the input text. This application may be particularly useful to retrieve texts referring to the same period of history in large collections of corpora in different languages. Unlike usual monolingual retrieval systems based on word overlapping, our semantic pipeline can seamlessly retrieve texts in any given language thank to the disambiguation step (see Section 2.1).

Our approach to the cross-lingual retrieval of texts fully relies on the disambiguation performed for semantically indexing text collections. Each text is associated with the set of its disambiguated instances. Then, we simply use the Jaccard similarity coefficient for sets (Jaccard, 1901) to measure the similarity between different texts. Since disambiguated instances (i.e., multilingual BabelNet synsets) are comparable across languages, no translation is needed to measure the similarity. In Section 4.2 we show the effectiveness of this approach for the task, performing on par or better than models requiring a pre-translation step.

4   Evaluation

We perform an evaluation to test the disambiguation quality of our multilingual semantic processing pipeline (Section 4.1) and the cross-lingual text retrieval application (Section 4.2). For both evaluations we use the same reference corpus, which is the Bible[6] translated into four different languages: English, Spanish, French, and Russian. Each language version consists of 1189 chapters of different sizes, ranging from 21 to 2423 words (588 words on average).

4.1   Disambiguation

In order to measure the disambiguation quality of Babelfy in the history domain, we manually annotated two chapters of the Bible for English and Spanish[7]. Table 1 shows the precision of our system and the Most Common Sense[8] (MCS) baseline in the evaluation set. Babelfy outperforms the MCS baseline in both languages, obtaining an overall precision of 68.8% for English and 58.8% for Spanish. Not surprisingly, the history domain is hard for a standard disambiguation system, which has been shown to perform above 70% in news corpora (Navigli et al., 2013). However, for nouns, which are the items our pipeline is especially targeted for, our system achieves considerably better results (63.4% for Spanish and 74.2% for English). The results of an open-domain disambiguation system clearly improving over the MCS baseline are indeed encouraging towards the development of a domain-specific disambiguation system. As future work we plan to adapt the disambiguation pipeline to the history domain by both refining the sense inventory and training on domain-specific corpora.

		English	Spanish
All	Our	68.8	58.8
	MCS	51.1	44.0
Nouns	Our	74.2	63.4
	MCS	58.7	47.8

Table 1: Precision (%) of Babelfy after preprocessing and the MCS baseline in the Bible.

4.2   Cross-lingual text retrieval

In this section we evaluate the effectiveness of our cross-lingual text retrieval pipeline (Section 3). The experimental setup is described in Section 4.2.1 and the results are presented in Section 4.2.2.

4.2.1   Experimental setup

Task description.   Given a chapter of the Bible in one language (i.e., input language), the task consists of retrieving the same chapter in another language (i.e., output language) among the 1189 possible chapters[9]. Formally, given a chapter of the Bible in the input language, the system calculates the similarity between the given chapter and all the chapters in the output language. The chapter of the output language obtaining the highest similarity score is selected as retrieved chapter for the system. This task is intended to test the cross-lingual text retrieval application proposed in Section 3, which is based in the semantic indexing presented in Section 2.2.

---

[6]`homepages.inf.ed.ac.uk/s0787820/bible/`

[7]We release this sense-annotated evaluation corpus of 594 annotations for the research community at our website.

[8]MCS has traditionally been a hard baseline to beat for automatic disambiguation systems (Navigli, 2009).

[9]Although the chapters in the Bible have not been translated literally from sentence to sentence (some chapters were rewritten differently for certain languages), the Bible may be viewed as a reliable chapter-aligned comparable corpus for the evaluation.

Input Language	System	English	Spanish	French	Russian
English	Our	-	99.4	98.7	96.9
	MT+Jacc.	-	99.8	99.8	99.7
	MT+W2V	-	88.4	81.4	82.3
Spanish	Our	99.2	-	99.8	96.6
	MT+Jacc.	99.8	-	99.8	99.8
	MT+W2V	88.8	-	99.0	97.5
French	Our	98.6	99.7	-	95.2
	MT+Jacc.	99.7	99.9	-	99.9
	MT+W2V	83.0	99.2	-	96.0
Russian	Our	97.6	98.1	96.7	-
	MT+Jacc.	99.9	99.7	99.7	-
	MT+W2V	91.1	98.2	97.0	-

Table 2: Accuracy (%) of all comparison systems for the cross-lingual text retrieval task in the Bible.

Comparison systems. We include two baselines relying on monolingual text similarity measures after translation, using English as pivot language. This monolingual similarity measurement after translation is the most common approach in cross-lingual text similarity tasks (Agirre et al., 2016). For these baselines all the Bible chapters in languages other than English were automatically translated to English using the *Bing Translator* Machine Translation system[10], which covers the four languages considered in the evaluation. The first baseline system (**MT+Jacc.**) calculates the similarity between the content words of the output texts after translation by using the Jaccard index. The second baseline (**MT+W2V**) leverages word embeddings to calculate the similarity between the translated texts. The similarity measure consists of the cosine similarity between the average vector of the content word embeddings of both respective translated texts. This approach based on the centroid vector is often used in the literature to obtain representations of sentences and documents (Chen et al., 2014; Yu et al., 2014). As word embeddings we use the pre-trained Word2Vec (Mikolov et al., 2013) vectors trained on the Google News corpus[11].

4.2.2 Results and Discussion

Table 2 shows the accuracy[12] results of all comparison systems in the cross-lingual text retrieval task using the Bible as gold standard comparable corpus for four different languages: English, Spanish, French, and Russian. Given the current state of MT systems, the high results obtained by the translation-based system are not surprising. However, our simple system based on inherently imperfect disambiguation achieves comparable results to the baseline based on the lexical similarity measure after translation (MT+Jacc.) and improves considerably the results of the system based on word embeddings after translation (MT+W2V). This improvement over the system based on word embeddings may be due to two main factors. First, since the translation is carried out automatically, it may be prompt to errors. Second, even though word embeddings have already shown its potential in obtaining accurate semantic representations of lexical items, they may not be so accurate to model larger semantic units such as documents. In fact, word embeddings are in the main used in tasks which make use of the local context of words, e.g., dependency syntactic parsing (Weiss et al., 2015; Bansal et al., 2014), rather than in tasks requiring the global semantic representations of documents or paragraphs.

The results are especially meaningful considering that our system does not require a prior translation step between languages. In fact, obtaining and integrating reliable translation models for all pairs of languages is generally a heavily impractical task (Jones and Irvine, 2013). This is definitely an encouraging

---

[10] https://www.bing.com/translator

[11] https://code.google.com/archive/p/word2vec/

[12] Accuracy is computed as the number of times a system retrieves the same chapter in the output language divided by the total number of chapters (i.e., 1189).

```
<dataset language="EN" title="GEN">
<paragraph id="p.1">
    <text>
        In the beginning God created the heaven and the earth.
        And the earth was without form, and void; and darkness was upon the face of the deep.
        And the Spirit of God moved upon the face of the waters.
        ...
    </text>
    <annotations>
        <annotation source="MCS" anchor="beginning" bfScore="--" coherenceScore="--">bn:00009632n</annotation>
        <annotation source="BABELFY" anchor="God" bfScore="0.7620" coherenceScore="0.7913">bn:00040878n</annotation>
        <annotation source="MCS" anchor="created" bfScore="--" coherenceScore="--">bn:00086008v</annotation>
        <annotation source="BABELFY" anchor="earth" bfScore="0.8485" coherenceScore="0.8079">bn:00029424n</annotation>
        ...
    </annotations>
</paragraph>
...
```

Figure 3: XML snippet from the Book of Genesis.

result towards the use of multilingual lexical resources as a bridge to connect corpora from different languages.

5 Release

As a result of this work, we provide a tool for semantically indexing any given corpus[13] and release it at `http://wwwusers.di.uniroma1.it/~raganato/semantic-indexing`. The tool is intended for non-expert users, i.e., users that do not require any prior programming knowledge.

First, the input corpus is disambiguated (see Section 2.1) and is automatically stored in standard XML-formatted files, following the annotation format used in Camacho-Collados et al. (2016a). In our case an XML file is produced for each document and documents are disambiguated paragraph by paragraph by default. Figure 3 shows a sample XML output file for a portion of the Bible. Each file contains a list of `paragraph` tags. Each paragraph tag is composed by the original plain text and its sense annotations. The `annotation` tag refers to the sense annotations provided as a result of the disambiguation process. Each annotation includes its disambiguated BabelNet id, containing four attributes:

- `source`: this attribute indicates whether the disambiguation has been performed by Babelfy or if the system has back-off to the Most Common Sense (MCS) heuristic.

- `anchor`: this attribute corresponds to the surface form of the concept or entity as found within the paragraph.

- `bfScore`: this attribute corresponds to the Babelfy confidence score.

- `coherenceScore`: this attribute corresponds to the coherence score[14].

Finally, we provide a simple interface where users may introduce unambiguous BabelNet ids or Wikipedia pages to retrieve their occurrences in the whole corpus. A user may also introduce a word (or a multiword expression) as input. In this case the interface would ask the user to provide the desired sense among all the options. For instance, if the user introduces *Alexander* as input, the user will be required to select between *Alexander the Great* or *Czar Alexander III* among others.

The cross-lingual text retrieval application is additionally included in the provided interface. For this application the user gives a document/paragraph as input and the system will retrieve the closest documents/paragraphs as given by our pipeline (see Section 3).

---

[13]The input corpus may be given as a collection of simple raw text files. More details on the required input format are provided in the website.

[14]See Camacho-Collados et al. (2016a) or Babelfy API guide (`http://babelfy.org/guide`) for more information about these two scores.

6 Conclusion and Future Work

In this paper we presented a pipeline for processing historical corpora and showed its potential for semantically indexing multilingual corpora and for the cross-lingual text retrieval task. We provide an interface for non-expert users for semantically indexing any given multilingual corpus, including a demo based on the Bible already processed for the four languages included in the evaluation: English, Spanish, French and Russian. Note that even though in this paper we have only discussed the potential of using our pipeline for historical texts, our pipeline may be used for multilingual corpora coming from different domains as well.

As future work we aim at improving the disambiguation pipeline on historical corpora by refining the semantic network of BabelNet to the history domain. Additionally, we plan to apply our pipeline to study the role of various historical characters according to texts from different cultures written in different languages.

Acknowledgments

The authors gratefully acknowledge the support of the Sapienza Research Grant Avvio alla Ricerca 2015 No. 56. 

We would also like to thank the anonymous reviewers for their helpful comments and Claudio Delli Bovi for helping us with the annotations and for his comments on the manuscript.

References

Eneko Agirre, Carmen Baneab, Daniel Cerd, Mona Diabe, Aitor Gonzalez-Agirrea, Rada Mihalceab, German Rigaua, Janyce Wiebef, and Basque Country Donostia. 2016. Semeval-2016 task 1: Semantic textual similarity, monolingual and cross-lingual evaluation. *Proceedings of SemEval*, pages 497–511.

Mohit Bansal, Kevin Gimpel, and Karen Livescu. 2014. Tailoring continuous word representations for dependency parsing. In *ACL (2)*, pages 809–815.

Francis Bond and Ryan Foster. 2013. Linking and Extending an Open Multilingual Wordnet. In *ACL (1)*, pages 1352–1362.

Hennie Brugman, Véronique Malaisé, and Laura Hollink. 2008. A common multimedia annotation framework for cross linking cultural heritage digital collections. In *Proceedings of LREC*.

José Camacho-Collados, Mohammad Taher Pilehvar, and Roberto Navigli. 2015. A Unified Multilingual Semantic Representation of Concepts. In *Proceedings of ACL*, pages 741–751, Beijing, China.

José Camacho-Collados, Claudio Delli Bovi, Alessandro Raganato, and Roberto Navigli. 2016a. A Large-Scale Multilingual Disambiguation of Glosses. In *Proceedings of LREC*, pages 1701–1708, Portoroz, Slovenia.

José Camacho-Collados, Mohammad Taher Pilehvar, and Roberto Navigli. 2016b. Nasari: Integrating explicit knowledge and corpus statistics for a multilingual representation of concepts and entities. *Artificial Intelligence*, 240:36–64.

Xinxiong Chen, Zhiyuan Liu, and Maosong Sun. 2014. A unified model for word sense representation and disambiguation. In *Proceedings of EMNLP*, pages 1025–1035, Doha, Qatar.

Dana Dannélls, Aarne Ranta, Ramona Enache, Mariana Damova, and Maria Mateva. 2013. Multilingual access to cultural heritage content on the semantic web. *LaTeCH 2013*, page 107.

Rob Davies. 2009. EuropeanaLocal–its role in improving access to Europes cultural heritage through the European digital library. In *Proceedings of IACH workshop at ECDL2009 (European Conference on Digital Libraries)*, Aarhus, Denmark.

Makx Dekkers, Stefan Gradmann, and Carlo Meghini. 2009. Europeana outline functional specification for development of an operational european digital library. *Europeana Thematic Network Deliverable*, 2.

Julia Efremova, Bijan Ranjbar-Sahraei, and Toon Calders. 2014. A hybrid disambiguation measure for inaccurate cultural heritage data. In *The 8th workshop on LaTeCH*, pages 47–55. Citeseer.

Samuel Fernando and Mark Stevenson. 2012. Adapting wikification to cultural heritage. In *Proceedings of the 6th Workshop on Language Technology for Cultural Heritage, Social Sciences, and Humanities*, pages 101–106. Association for Computational Linguistics.

E. D. Gutiérrez, Ekaterina Shutova, Patricia Lichtenstein, Gerard de Melo, and Luca Gilardi. 2016. Detecting cross-cultural differences using a multilingual topic model. *Transactions of the Association for Computational Linguistics*, 4:47–60.

Mark M Hall, Paul D Clough, Oier Lopez de Lacalle, Aitor Soroa, and Eneko Agirre. 2012. Enabling the discovery of digital cultural heritage objects through wikipedia. In *Proceedings of the 6th Workshop on Language Technology for Cultural Heritage, Social Sciences, and Humanities*, pages 94–100. Association for Computational Linguistics.

Paul Jaccard. 1901. *Distribution de la Flore Alpine: dans le Bassin des dranses et dans quelques régions voisines*. Rouge.

Stig Johansson. 2007. Seeing through multilingual corpora. *Language and Computers*, 62(1):51–71.

Ruth Jones and Ann Irvine. 2013. The (un) faithful machine translator. *LaTeCH 2013*, page 96.

Christopher D. Manning, Mihai Surdeanu, John Bauer, Jenny Finkel, Steven J. Bethard, and David McClosky. 2014. The Stanford CoreNLP natural language processing toolkit. In *Association for Computational Linguistics (ACL) System Demonstrations*, pages 55–60.

Tomas Mikolov, Kai Chen, Greg Corrado, and Jeffrey Dean. 2013. Efficient estimation of word representations in vector space. *CoRR*, abs/1301.3781.

George A Miller. 1995. Wordnet: a lexical database for english. *Communications of the ACM*, 38(11):39–41.

Andrea Moro, Alessandro Raganato, and Roberto Navigli. 2014. Entity Linking meets Word Sense Disambiguation: a Unified Approach. *Transactions of the Association for Computational Linguistics (TACL)*, 2:231–244.

Roberto Navigli and Simone Paolo Ponzetto. 2012. BabelNet: The automatic construction, evaluation and application of a wide-coverage multilingual semantic network. *Artificial Intelligence*, 193:217–250.

Roberto Navigli, David Jurgens, and Daniele Vannella. 2013. SemEval-2013 Task 12: Multilingual Word Sense Disambiguation. In *Proceedings of SemEval 2013*, pages 222–231.

Roberto Navigli. 2009. Word Sense Disambiguation: A survey. *ACM Computing Surveys*, 41(2):1–69.

Michael Piotrowski. 2012. Natural language processing for historical texts. *Synthesis Lectures on Human Language Technologies*, 5(2):1–157.

Christian Poelitz and Thomas Bartz. 2014. Enhancing the possibilities of corpus-based investigations: Word sense disambiguation on query results of large text corpora. *EACL 2014*, page 42.

Helmut Schmid. 1994. Probabilistic part-of-speech tagging using decision trees. In *Proceedings of the international conference on new methods in language processing*, volume 12, pages 44–49.

David Weiss, Chris Alberti, Michael Collins, and Slav Petrov. 2015. Structured training for neural network transition-based parsing. In *Proceedings of ACL*, page 323333.

Lei Yu, Karl Moritz Hermann, Phil Blunsom, and Stephen Pulman. 2014. Deep learning for answer sentence selection. In *NIPS Deep Learning Workshop*.

Tagging Ingush – Language Technology For Low-Resource Languages Using Resources From Linguistic Field Work

Jörg Tiedemann
Department of Modern Languages
University of Helsinki, Finland
`firstname.lastname@helsinki.fi`

Johanna Nichols and **Ronald Sprouse**
Department of Linguistics
University of California, Berkeley
`firstname@berkeley.edu`

Abstract

This paper presents on-going work on creating NLP tools for under-resourced languages from very sparse training data coming from linguistic field work. In this work, we focus on Ingush, a Nakh-Daghestanian language spoken by about 300,000 people in the Russian republics Ingushetia and Chechnya. We present work on morphosyntactic taggers trained on transcribed and linguistically analyzed recordings and dependency parsers using English glosses to project annotation for creating synthetic treebanks. Our preliminary results are promising, supporting the goal of bootstrapping efficient NLP tools with limited or no task-specific annotated data resources available.

1 Introduction

Linguistic diversity is not only a fascinating research area for general linguists but also represents one of the main challenges for language technology. Natural language processing (NLP) becomes essential for people in the digital age and support of low-resource languages is a natural task that needs to be emphasised in the development of tools and applications. Modern language technology relies to a large extent on data-driven techniques that focus on machine learning techniques based on annotated linguistic data and large quantities of raw text. However, such techniques are usually not applicable for low-resource languages where sufficient training data is not available. On the other hand, a lot of effort is spent in field linguistics to record, transcribe and analyse minority languages – a resource that is under-explored in language technology.

In this paper, we take the example of Ingush, a Nakh-Daghestanian language, which has been thoroughly described by general linguists with data sets collected over several years. We use those manually created and curated collections of transcribed recording to bootstrap tools that can be used to process the language and to annotate utterances with interlinear glosses and syntactic dependencies. The paper is the first step in developing technology that could be used to support linguistic field work but also to develop NLP applications that can work with the Ingush language.

In the following, we first introduce Ingush and the linguistic resources developed for that language. Thereafter, we present our work on developing an interlinear gloss tagger and outline an approach for bootstrapping part-of-speech taggers and dependency parser by means of alignment and cross-lingual transfer models.

2 The Ingush Language

Ingush (glottolog code ingu1240) is a Nakh-Daghestanian language with some 300,000 speakers, traditionally spoken in the central Caucasus highlands in the Republic of Ingushetia and Chechen Republic of Russia. The language has extensive systems of both consonants and vowels, largely suffixing morphology, mostly dependent-marking morphosyntax, ergative alignment, and German-like AOV/V2 word order complete with detachable prefixes and proclitics in final position of V2 clauses, though with some

Proceedings of the Workshop on Language Technology Resources and Tools for Digital Humanities (LT4DH),
pages 148–155, Osaka, Japan, December 11-17 2016.

flexibility to use AOV order even in main clauses. Nouns belong to gender classes marked by root-initial agreement on about one-third of the verbs and one-fourth of the adjectives; there are four gender markers. Clause combining mostly uses converbs, some of which require S/O sharing and all of which use much null anaphora. Null arguments result from sharing (in some converb clauses and all infinitive and relative clauses) and unspecified reference; though not a pro-drop language there are many null arguments. The language is further described in Nichols (2011).

An active program to record the speech of the oldest generations of Ingush began in the mid 1990s and reached speed in 2002, with 50-100 hours of recorded speech added annually. Recordings are mostly made in the homes of speakers. There are also some legacy recordings made in the late 1980s and early 1990s. A number of the recorded speakers were born in the very early 20th century and at least one in the very late 19th century. Quality varies: legacy materials were made on inexpensive household cassette recorders; more recent recordings are often made on mobile telephones. There are also about 100 hours of video recordings.

The corpus for this project is the transcribed portion of those recordings, plus a number of transcribed published folklore and literature works which have no audio or have a recorded reading of the published text. The transcription is an all-lower-ASCII Latin system, slightly more abstract than phonemic. It is not ismorphic to the Cyrillic orthography, which is mostly phonemic for consonants but greatly underdifferentiates the vowels. Annotation is standard single-line interlinears with lexical gloss and morpheme/category identifications, plus a smooth translation.

Most of the annotated data was created with dedicated tools developed for the Berkeley Interlinear Text Corpus, BITC. They are designed for group collaborations and support semi-automatic interlinearization by building a lexicon of interlinears on the fly, which enables systematic annotations of large quantities of data. The system also provides powerful search capacities making it very useful as a dictionary. These tools and data sets have contributed greatly to the efficiency of grammatical analysis and grammar writing and in this work, we investigate their use in automatic language processing.

3 Data Preparation

As described above, the Berkeley Ingush Corpus includes a well organised collection of transcribed utterances together with interlinear glosses and translations into fluent English. Figure 1 shows an example taken from the corpus.

Ingush:	Cwaqqa hama dwajihwaajaacar, jihwaajarii?
Tokenized:	cwaqqa hama dwajihwaajaacar jihwaajarii
Interlinear glosses:	any thing DX-J.take away.PNW.NEG J.take away.PNW=Q
English:	Nothing had been taken away, right?

Figure 1: An example record from the Berkeley Ingush Corpus.

In this way, the data forms a manually curated parallel corpus with three dimensions that are all useful for our purposes. The interlinear glosses are the actual annotation that we try to produce from transcribed Ingush input and the English translations become interesting for transfer models we will discuss towards the end of the paper.

One of the main problems is that manually annotated data sets from many years of linguistic field work contain inconsistencies, which is unavoidable even with extensive efforts on normalizing their contents. The records include incomplete annotations and analyses, which we have to take care of when preparing data sets for training models that rely on the correctness of the examples. Therefore, we implemented a tool that extracts and converts data sets into a format that we can feed into our training procedures.

The first step is to convert the character encoding from mainly MacRoman to Unicode UTF8. The second step includes various heuristics to normalize the data and to exclude unreliable records. The following list summarizes the processing steps we have taken:

- Remove comments and separate alternative translations: Some records include alternatives for the translations into English. They are sometimes included in square brackets but most of the time

149

they are separated by multiple space characters. Square brackets otherwise contain comments and explanations, which we cannot safely use, and, therefore, we remove them. Possible translation alternatives that we extract by splitting on multiple space characters are then tested by comparing the lengths (in terms of tokens) to the lengths of the Ingush original string. If the length-ratio between the smallest potential translation alternative is smaller than the ratio between the raw input string and the concatenated English translation then we will discard splitting the translation string and consider it as one single translation. Otherwise, we keep multiple translation alternatives and duplicate the record with different translations in each of them.

- We replace spaces (that usually indicate multi-word-units) with underscores to make it easier to handle the data by subsequent processes. An example can be seen in Figure 1 (*take away*). Some morphosyntactic descriptions also include spaces and we replace them by dots.

- Some interlinears are incomplete and do not cover all tokens in the input. In many cases, this may only exclude some unimportant final tokens and we use the heuristics that we accept interlinears that are at most two items too short.

- We save all records that have non-empty entries for all three records, tokenized Ingush, interlinear glosses and English translations and convert the interlinear glosses into a factorized representation. Here, we separate lexical information from morphosyntactic descriptions to create a generalized tagset that we can use to train automatic annotation tools by means of standard sequence labeling models.

Figure 2 shows the result of our pre-processing on the previous example. Lexical information in the interlinear annotation is replaced by a placeholder 'xx' and the lexical information is included as a separate factor (before the slash). The *delexicalized* gloss terms are then also added to the original Ingush tokens to form the essential training data that we will use in our tagging experiments below. The task is, hence, to tag each Ingush token from arbitrary input with the complex but delexicalised tags given by our training data (line one in Figure 2).

<pre>
Tagged Ingush: cwaqqa/xx hama/xx dwajihwaajaacar/DX-J.xx.PNW.NEG jihwaajarii/J.xx.PNW=Q
Tagged Glosses: any/xx thing/xx take_away/DX-J.xx.PNW.NEG take_away/J.xx.PNW=Q
      English: nothing had been taken away , right ?
</pre>

Figure 2: Preprocessed data: Tagged source language, split glosses and tokenized English.

Note that we had to perform various additional pre-processing steps to increase consistency of the data. We had to normalize the use of dots (older versions used mid-dots for marking morpheme boundaries), we removed question marks, normalized the use of brackets, spaces, multiple dots, the use of conjunctive markers, normalized the specification of alternatives, foreign languages and multi-word units. We also made the inflectional markup for person and number more consistent and added a special tag for foreign words.

	Ingush		Tags		English	
	tokens	types	tokens	types	tokens	types
training	102,043	19,964	101,826	8,190	130,186	7,257
test	6,222	2,375	6,165	1,261	7,099	1,268

Table 1: Statistics of the data sets. *Tags* refers to the delexicalised interlinears. The test data contains 888 sentences and the training data includes 9,209 sentences.

The final data may still contain additional noise and inconsistencies but our main interest is now to see whether it is sufficient to train annotation tools that can produce interlinear-like tags from unrestricted Ingush input. For this we divided the corpus into training and test sets. Table 1 summarizes the statistics of the data sets. We can clearly see the inflectional complexity of Ingush which is striking in the type/token ratio in comparison to English. The statistics also show the complexity of the tagset we are looking at even after delexicalization. Note that the glosses are certainly not a fixed tagset but a productive annotation scheme. Nevertheless, we will treat the task as a standard classification-based sequence-labeling process as we will explain below.

4 Tagging with Interlinear Glosses

One of the goals of our experiments is to automatically create glosses and interlinears. The first step to approach this goal is to be able to produce delexicalized interlinears for arbitrary utterances in transcribed Ingush. We model the task as a sequence labeling task in which we search for the optimal tag sequence given a sequence of input tokens and a model that is trained on annotated data. We use the tagged corpus described in the previous section and train a model based on conditional random fields (CRFs) (Lafferty et al., 2001), which is optimized for large tag sets that contain morphological features rather than single part-of-speech labels. We apply *marmot* (Mueller et al., 2013),[1] a popular tool for morphologically-rich languages and treat morpheme descriptions separated by dots as our inflectional features to be produced by the tagger. The model describes a structural prediction task and a standard CRF defines a globally normalized log-linear model of the conditional probability of a tag sequence $\vec{y} = y_1, y_2, .., y_n$ given a sentence $\vec{x} = x_1, x_2, ..., x_n$ of n tokens that can be used to guide the predictions:

$$p(\vec{y}|\vec{x}) = \frac{exp \sum_{t,i} \lambda_i \cdot \phi_i(\vec{y}, \vec{x}, t)}{Z(\vec{\lambda}, \vec{x})}$$

In this formulation, ϕ_i is a feature function and λ_i its associated weight, t is the token index and $Z(\vec{\lambda}, \vec{x})$ is a normalising constant. Marmot provides an efficient implementation of that model using pruned training and tag decomposition. The latter is especially important for tasks like ours where the tag set becomes extremely large. In training, we then learn the parameters of the model that maximise the prediction accuracy with respect to the training data and at test time we apply common inference procedures to search for the best tag sequence given some input data and the model we have created.

The main challenge is certainly the complexity of the interlinears we wish to produce. We simplify the task by ignoring the compositional way of interlinear glosses and assume that we can treat their components as individual morphological features. We, hence, train the tagger with standard settings using the morpheme-delimiter to split the interlinears into sub-tags and hope that the model can cope well enough with predicting even complex annotations. Let us first look at the overall outcome of this model before diving into a deeper analyses of the results and some simple ways of improving the performance. Table 2 summarizes the performance of the tagger when applied to our unseen test set.

(scores in %)	including xx	without xx
average precision	82.68	71.43
average recall	81.51	67.76
accuracy	65.50	54.72

Table 2: Tagging transcribed Ingush with delexicalized interlinears.

We present three metrics that demonstrate the performance of the model: Precision, recall and accuracy. The latter refers to the standard metric of comparing gold standard labels with the proposed ones. This means that the metric only accepts exact matches of the entire interlinear string per token. However, the interlinear glosses are typically composed of various elements and, therefore, we are interested in measuring the closeness of the tags created.[2] Hence, we divide the tags into parts again (separated by morpheme-boundary markers) and compare gold standard interlinears with proposed tags by means of string similarity measures. In particular, we compute the longest common subsequence (LCS) between

---

[1] Available from `http://cistern.cis.lmu.de/marmot/`.

[2] Note that dot-separated elements sometimes refer to categories that are fused into a single morpheme but in general the sequential order matters referring to the sequence of morphological elements of the corresponding word.

reference	predicted	including xx		without xx		token
		P	R	P	R	
xx.NW.D.NEG	xx.NW.D.NEG	100	100	100	100	xeattaadaac
DEM.PL.OBL	DEM.OBL	100	67	100	67	cy
xx.PL.DAT	xx.PL.DAT	100	100	100	100	bierazhta
D.PST=PTC	D.xx.PST=CUM	50	67	67	67	dar=q
DX-xx-J.xx.NW.J.NEG	DX-xx.AUX.NEG.PRS	25	20	25	25	dwachyjeannajaac
xx:NEG.PRS	xx.PRS.NEG	33	50	50	50	xaac
xx-J.xx.CVtemp	xx-D.xx.CVtemp	67	67	50	50	chyjiecha
J.xx.NEG.WP	J.AUX.NEG.WP	75	75	75	100	jaxandzar

Table 3: Examples of predicted interlinear glosses (precision (P) and recall (R) scores in %).

the two strings of morpheme descriptions (not characters) and use that subsequence to estimate precision and recall. Recall is then the ratio of correctly tagged morpheme descriptions (the sum of the lengths of each LCS) and the total number of morpheme descriptions included in the reference set. Precision is the ratio of the same number of correctly tagged morpheme descriptions divided by the number of proposed morpheme descriptions in the automatically tagged data. To illustrate this on an example, in the second row of Table 3, the longest common subsequence ('DEM.OBL') has length 2, which is the same as the length of the predicted tag (giving precision = 100%) whereas the reference annotation has length 3 which gives recall=67% in that example.

As we can see in the Table 2, the tagger reaches quite reasonable performances in terms of precision and recall. The scores go down for more complex tags as we can see when leaving out the placeholder tags for lexical information (xx). Table 3 shows some examples of predicted interlinears and their references from the test set. The examples show that the model is capable of predicting quite complex descriptions. In many cases, the errors are rather minor and in many cases acceptable or just an artifact of the manual annotation as manual inspections reveal.

(scores in %)	unambiguous	ambiguous		unknown
		(train)	(test+train)	
precision	95.06	83.64	49.19	72.13
recall	95.44	83.50	49.72	66.27
accuracy	90.38	70.74	4.24	34.39

Table 4: Tagger performance for ambiguous and unknown words. 1207 unambiguous cases, 1209 unknown words, 3457 ambiguous cases (train) and 165 tokens that are unambiguous in training but have a different tag in the test data (test+train).

An important question is how well the system handles ambiguous and unknown words. The latter is important, in particular, to show the ability of classifying unseen items that may appear in new material that is collected. Table 4 lists the scores for different categories with respect to tagging ambiguity and overlap with the training data. Not surprisingly, words that are unambiguous obtain high scores in all metrics (above 90%). Still, some of the words are mistagged, which is due to the contextual dependencies in the CRF model. Even though glosses are very much standardized, more than half of the test tokens refer to ambiguously analyzed words. There are two categories of ambiguous words, the ones that have multiple interlinears in the training data and the ones that are unambiguous (but probably very infrequent) in training but have a different interlinear in the test set compared to the one in training. Naturally, the latter case is particularly difficult for the tagger to handle correctly as the only information available in training is without variation whereas the model is expected to produce a different result at test time. The problem can especially be seen in the accuracy score (=4.24%). Fortunately, this is a very infrequent case. Finally, we have unknown words and we can say that the model is well capable of analyzing those words with reasonable precision. Considering the data size and the complexity of the task this is a very encouraging result.

Looking at the result above, one also wonders if the performance can still be improved. Especially the errors among unambiguous words are unsatisfactory and a simple solution would be to force the labels to follow the markup from the training data. In our final tagging experiments we therefore study the impact of these entries on the overall results. Table 5 summarizes the outcome of those tests.

(scores in %)	precision	recall	accuracy
unambiguous only	21.32 (9.69)	21.30 (13.35)	19.81 (12.49)
tag all with 'xx'	73.26 (n/a)	51.66 (n/a)	36.32 (n/a)
most frequent tag	69.63 (55.34)	70.01 (60.34)	61.80 (53.25)
tagger	82.68 (71.43)	81.51 (67.76)	65.50 (54.72)
tagger + unambiguous	83.65 (73.15)	82.38 (69.38)	67.29 (56.99)
tagger + most frequent	84.07 (73.07)	83.39 (71.74)	68.77 (59.60)

Table 5: Tagging unambiguous words and known words (in brackets without considering xx).

First of all, we can see that only tagging words for which we have unambiguous tags from training does not work well, which is to be expected with the large number of ambiguous items in the data. Using a baseline of attaching the most frequent interlinear (including xx) to each known word performs much better but is still not very satisfactory (especially when looking at precision and recall). Surprisingly, even precision drops quite significantly compared to the sequence labeling approach of the statistical tagger. However, enforcing tags of known words according to the training data on top of the statistical tagger leads to visible improvements. Not only fixing unambiguous words to the analyses from the training data but also the baseline approach of using the most frequent interlinears to replace the predictions of the tagger improve the overall results (especially in recall and accuracy). The final precision and recall values of above 84% and 83% are quite satisfactory.

5   Alignment and Annotation Transfer

The next step we would like to explore is annotation transfer through the English glosses to bootstrap a syntactic dependency parser. Cross-lingual parsing has become increasingly popular (Hwa et al., 2005; Tiedemann, 2014; Xiao and Guo, 2014) and has been suggested for handling low-resource languages for which no explicit training data is available. Annotation projection typically requires parallel data sets and word alignment to transfer information from one language to another. As discussed earlier, the glossed data sets nicely form a parallel corpus with English translations of the collected and transcribed Ingush utterances. Furthermore, we also have the interlinears that give additional information that will be useful in the alignment of running texts. Below, we outline our approach of combining links between interlinear glosses and English with statistical word alignment between Ingush and running English, which will be the basis of our initial annotation projection experiments.

5.1   Alignment Through Interlinear Glosses

Interlinear glosses provide rich information about the recorded data sets. First of all, they are nicely aligned with the tokens in the original input. Furthermore, they include lexical information in English that can be used to find corresponding parts in the smooth English translations that we will use to transfer syntactic annotation from.

The first step in our process consist of parsing the English translations to obtain lemmatized and syntactically analyzed sentences with annotation that we would like to project in the end. Here, we apply UDPipe (Straka et al., 2016) with its pre-trained model for processing English trained on the universal dependency treebanks version 1.2.[3] UDPipe includes all necessary steps from part-of-speech tagging to morphological analyses and dependency parsing, which makes it a convenient tool to apply in our pilot study.

---

[3] http://universaldependencies.org

In our preprocessing steps, we already separated lexical information from morphosyntactic information in the interlinears. We now use the lexical information to match lemmas in the parsed English translations. We use several heuristics to increase the number of words that can be matched:

- We split multi-word units (for which we joined components using underscores) to match individual parts with existing lemmas and wordforms in the parsed data. We also check alternatives that are given in some of the interlinears.

- We expand placeholder tokens (1sg, 2sg, etc) with English pronouns they usually refer to.

- We implement a prefix match to test whether the lexical information from the interlinear is completely contained in a lemma or wordform of the parsed English glosses or vice versa.

- We always use the link closest to the relative token position in the sentence in cases where there are alternative matches.

Via the position of the interlinears, we can now align English words with corresponding Ingush words. All non-matching words remain unaligned and we will treat them using automatic word alignment as explained below. In total, we obtain 38,665 links in the way described above out of the 110,167 tokens in the parallel training data (which is around 35.1% of the data).

5.2 Adding Statistical Word Alignment

A large portion of the data cannot be aligned using the string matching techniques described above. Therefore, we also run automatic word alignment using techniques that have been proposed in the field of statistical machine translation (SMT). In particular, we apply fast_align, an efficient implementation and reformulation of the IBM model 2 (Dyer et al., 2013). We run the alignment in both directions and apply symmetrisation heuristics (grow-diag-final-and) as commonly used in the SMT community. Finally, we merge automatic word alignments with the links obtained by matching interlinear glosses.

The symmetrized word alignment provides 83,863 links and, therefore, a much larger coverage of the data set. However, we expect that statistical alignment is of lower quality than matching manually created interlinears especially with the small data sets we have available. Therefore, we give preference to the interlinear links and only add alignments for words that have not been aligned otherwise. Using this strategy, we obtain a total of 80,974 linked words, about 73.5% of the complete data. Note that the statistical word alignment emphasizes coverage and, therefore, includes a lot of many-to-many links whereas the merged alignment focuses more on precision and, hence, contains a slightly smaller number of links.

5.3 Dependency Parsing of Aligned Translations

Finally, we can now use the aligned training data to transfer annotations from the parsed English glosses to the tokenized Ingush input. We use simple heuristics mapping universal part-of-speech labels and dependency relations based on a direct correspondence assumption. Figure 3 shows two examples of projected dependency structure using the annotation projection approach. We ignore all unaligned words and create a synthetic treebank that we can use to train a statistical parser. Several options are possible for training such a parser model and we opt for the *mate-tools* (Bohnet and Kuhn, 2012) that have been shown to produce highly accurate parsing models for a variety of languages.

Unfortunately, at this point we cannot say much about the quality of this initial parser as we do not have any gold standard available. In future work, we will manually check transfered annotation and parsing results and iteratively bootstrap a usable parser based on some kind of active learning schema.

6 Conclusions

This paper presents on-going work on creating NLP tools for a low-resource language, Ingush, using data from extensive linguistic fieldwork. We discuss the challenges of converting data sets to useful training resources in data-driven language technology and outline the benefits of the rich annotation

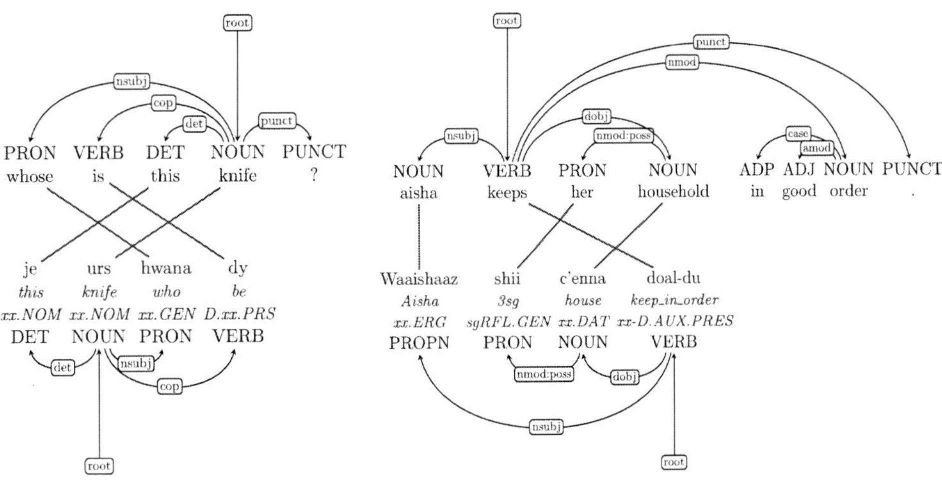

Figure 3: Aligned and projected dependency trees.

given by typological work. Interlinear glosses are very informative and capture important linguistic knowledge that can be facilitated in training automatic analyzers and syntactic parsers based on cross-lingual transfer models. We present an efficient tagger that can produce delexicalized interlinear glosses from raw transcriptions and we hope that these methods can develop into tools for linguistic field work and other applications for our selected target language or similar cases.

References

Bernd Bohnet and Jonas Kuhn. 2012. The Best of Both Worlds – A Graph-based Completion Model for Transition-based Parsers. In *Proceedings of EACL*, pages 77–87.

Chris Dyer, Victor Chahuneau, and Noah A. Smith. 2013. A simple, fast, and effective reparameterization of IBM Model 2. In *Proceedings of NAACL*, pages 644–648.

Rebecca Hwa, Philip Resnik, Amy Weinberg, Clara Cabezas, and Okan Kolak. 2005. Bootstrapping Parsers via Syntactic Projection across Parallel Texts. *Natural Language Engineering*, 11(3):311–325.

John Lafferty, Andrew McCallum, and Fernando Pereira. 2001. Conditional random fields: Probabilistic mod- els for segmenting and labeling sequence data. In *Proceedings of ICML*.

Thomas Mueller, Helmut Schmid, and Hinrich Schütze. 2013. Efficient higher-order CRFs for morphological tagging. In *Proceedings of the 2013 Conference on Empirical Methods in Natural Language Processing*, pages 322–332, Seattle, Washington, USA, October. Association for Computational Linguistics.

Johanna Nichols. 2011. *Ingush Grammar*, volume 143 of *UC Publications in Linguistics*. Berkeley-Los Angeles: University of California Press.

Milan Straka, Jan Hajič, and Straková. 2016. UDPipe: trainable pipeline for processing CoNLL-U files performing tokenization, morphological analysis, POS tagging and parsing. In *Proceedings of LREC*.

Jörg Tiedemann. 2014. Rediscovering Annotation Projection for Cross-Lingual Parser Induction. In *Proceedings of COLING*, pages 1854–1864.

Min Xiao and Yuhong Guo. 2014. Distributed Word Representation Learning for Cross-Lingual Dependency Parsing. In *Proceedings of CoNLL*, pages 119–129.

The MultiTal NLP tool infrastructure

Driss Sadoun, Satenik Mkhitaryan, Damien Nouvel, Mathieu Valette
ERTIM, INALCO, Paris, France
`firstname.lastname@inalco.fr`

Abstract

This paper gives an overview of the *MultiTal* project, which aims to create a research infrastructure that ensures long-term distribution of NLP tools descriptions. The goal is to make NLP tools more accessible and usable to end-users of different disciplines. The infrastructure is built on a meta-data scheme modelling and standardising multilingual NLP tools documentation. The model is conceptualised using an OWL ontology. The formal representation of the ontology allows us to automatically generate organised and structured documentation in different languages for each represented tool.

1 Introduction

The work reported in this paper is initiated by INALCO (*National Institute for Oriental Languages and Civilisations*, also called *Langues'O*), a Paris-based institution for teaching and researching. It spans about 95 languages from Central Europe, Africa, Asia, America and Oceania. Historically devoted to the teaching of languages and cultures, INALCO also conducts theoretical and applied research on languages. In the context of globalisation, some new language communities indeed require to access the information-based society and the Internet. Due to the lack of responsive services, these communities have difficulties accessing language resources for their respective languages and are forced to use one of the *lingua franca* already well established on the Internet. As a side-effect, this also raises the risk of language impoverishment. Yet, making those languages exist on the Internet is now a necessary step for the sustainability of language diversity. Language localisation on the Internet is not only an economic issue but also a social and cultural one. Faced with the rapid growth of demand for NLP technologies, we have started the project *MultiTAL* (`http://multital.inalco.fr:2230`) of systemic description of tools processing different languages in order (i) to promote and ease the accessibility of NLP tools, (ii) to document them, (iii) finally, to plan technology transfer from one language to another.

The stakes of such a challenge are many. First, humanities and social sciences have to deal with a deep change given the increasing disaffection of students and young researchers for their disciplines. The digitisation of patrimonial funds and the emergence of new forms of communication, culture and entertainment (gaming, social networks, etc.) help in opening up new research issues. Digital humanities (DH) is the credible response to those changes. INALCO, as one of the main stakeholders in language and culture studies in Europe, faces the gap between, on one hand, the fast evolution of new technology for a few number of cultures, and, the other hand, the richness and diversity of cultures left behind the technological progress. Moreover, economic demand for localisation of products leads us to offer linguistic solutions to solve it (eg. automatic translation).

Thus, complementing the already rich offerings by looking at existing NLP tools, our aim is to offer an easy-access expert service to an accurate and *critical* documentation for a selected set of NLP tools and languages in our scope, rather than providing a long list of tools for well-resourced languages -but not always verified, except by the author.

Proceedings of the Workshop on Language Technology Resources and Tools for Digital Humanities (LT4DH),
pages 156–163, Osaka, Japan, December 11-17 2016.

What we mean by critical documentation is building a general framework and a standard for documentation, and testing its implementation on various NLP tools. In practice, the framework has been designed using an ontology. By formalising and standardising the documentation, we aim first at designing a kind of best practice guideline for tool developers; second, at making it easier for such documentation to be read and set up for new potential beneficiaries i.e. non-expert users, for instance, linguists, students and scholars in DH, but also opinion analysts, companies that aim to enter new foreign markets, etc. - in brief, all the people who have to process foreign languages with weakly documented NLP tools. Thus, we require descriptions to be as concise, understandable and uniform as possible.

We focused first on a set of the so-called Eastern languages: here, Arabic, Chinese, Hindi, Hungarian, Japanese, Russian, Tibetan, etc. These languages present major interests for our purpose: they use different writing systems (logographic, alphabetic, etc.) which are also typographic challenges; they come from various linguistic families (Indo-European, Japonic, Semitic, Sino-Tibetan) and, even if for some they are not, strictly speaking, under-resourced languages, the tools for processing them are not always easy to handle.

Another benefit is that properly storing structured information related to NLP tools will greatly facilitate automatic generation of their descriptions. As such, our project is constrained on both aspects: relevant existing information about tools has to be saved into our inventory in order to generate concise and informative documentation.

2 Related work

Over the last few years, the number of digitized materials has considerably grown. The willingness to take into account this new digital content has led to the popularization of the use of Language Resources (*LR*) and NLP technologies. However, *LR* are still difficult to find because they are drowned in the mass of web content. Moreover, their documentation is often monolingual and written either in the developers' language (such as Arabic, Chinese, Japanese or Russian) or in a *lingua franca* (such as English or French) (cf. section 3.1). This situation makes it difficult for scholars to use or re-use *LR* that could be useful for their work or research. Hence, storing and distributing LR has become an issue in itself. This has been addressed by many initiatives all around the world as the CLARIN projet (Váradi et al., 2008), the *Central and South-East European Resources* (CESAR) (VÁRADI and TADIĆ, 2012) which is a part of *META-SHARE* (Piperidis, 2012), the *INESS Norwegian* infrastructure for the construction and exploration of treebanks (Rosén et al., 2012), the large scale database *SHACHI* for collecting *LR* in Asian and Western countries (Tohyama et al., 2008), the *Digital Research Infrastructure for the Arts and Humanities* (Tonne et al., 2013) or the LRE MAP (Calzolari et al., 2012). These initiatives are essential to promote the research and development of language technologies. They also may provide a real picture of tools and resources that are currently available for several languages (Skadina et al., 2013; TADIĆ, 2012; Del Gratta et al., 2014). Collecting and documenting *LR* makes them more accessible. However, regarding NLP tools it does not necessarily makes them more usable. Our approach focuses on detailing NLP tools usage from their installation to their execution.

In order to describe and share *LR*, different meta-data models have been proposed (Gavrilidou et al., 2011; Broeder et al., 2012; McCrae et al., 2015a). The models of each provider depend on their coverage and the kind of LRs they manage. Hence, there are as many meta-data models for describing *LRs* as *LR* infrastructures, which may represent a limit for resource sharing and lead to the re-creation of already existing *LR* resources (Cieri et al., 2010). To address this issue, different attempts have been made, such as an initiative for harmonising between *ELRA* and *LDC* catalogs (Cieri et al., 2010) and more recently ontologies were used to devise interconnections among resources (Chiarcos, 2012) or to make meta-data available from different sources under a common scheme (McCrae et al., 2015a; McCrae et al., 2015b). In the perspective of an interoperability between our meta-data model and the existing ones, and in order to ease a possible integration into large infrastructure as *CLARIN* or *META-NET* we chose to use an ontology for storing *MultiTal* infrastructure data. The resulting triple store is accessible and freely available at http://multital.inalco.fr:2230.

Most existing LR infrastructures focus on EU languages and invite developers of resources or tools to describe them themselves. Even if it eases access to LR technologies, when it concerns NLP tools it does not necessarily make their use any easier. Indeed, most of the time their usage instructions remain too poorly documented. In our project, we ambition to inventory NLP tools processing written non-*EU* languages or more precisely languages taught at the *INALCO*. In this framework, each NLP tool is identified, tested and fully documented by an intern speaking the language the tool processes. Then, if the tool appears to run correctly its information is stored within our meta data model (ontology) and its resulting documentation is made available. Our aim is to ensure that tools described on *MultiTal* infrastructure can be properly installed and executed by end-users. As *MultiTal*'s end-users may not be language technology experts and their mother tongue may vary, we use an ontology verbalisation method (Androutsopoulos et al., 2014; Cojocaru and Trăuşan Matu, 2015; Keet and Khumalo, 2016) detailed in (Sadoun et al., 2016) to automatically produce documentation in multiple languages. So that we provide end-users with simple, structured and organised documents containing NLP tool information and detailing instructions of how to install, configure and run tools fitting their needs.

3 MultiTal infrastructure

Nowadays, *language technologies* (*LT*) make it possible for scholars to analyze millions of documents in multiple languages with very limited manual intervention. However, retrieving and using appropriate *LT* is not always easy. The *MultiTal* infrastructure is designed to help scholars to integrate NLP technology into their activities. This by easing their access to, and their understanding of, NLP tools' usage. Tools described within the infrastructure are those that have been previously tested (cf. section 3.1). The reason is twofold: first, to promote tools that run satisfactorily, given that some of those found on the net are prototypes that may be obsolete or unfinished. Second, a major part of tools are designed by researchers or individuals who are not expert at tool packaging. Hence, even tools that run correctly may be poorly documented and so be difficult to install and execute even for an expert. Testing them allows us to dive into the difficulties that may arise and then formalize within our model (cf. section 3.2) the different steps of installation and execution procedures. Once a tool description is formalized within the ontology, we automatically generate a concise and structured description of the tool containing, among other things, the basic instructions that the user should execute to install and use it (cf. section 3.3).

Figure 1 gives an overall picture of the general data flow of *Multital* project. First, NLP interns speaking different languages capture information about NLP tools from existing web documentation and from what they learned by testing them. The gathered information is filled via a web platform and stored within an ontology. Ontology knowledge is then easily retrievable through a platform that provides fully documented NLP tools' descriptions. Moreover, the conceptualized information serves the automatic generation of multilingual documentations which are freely available for scholars via the *MultiTal* platform.

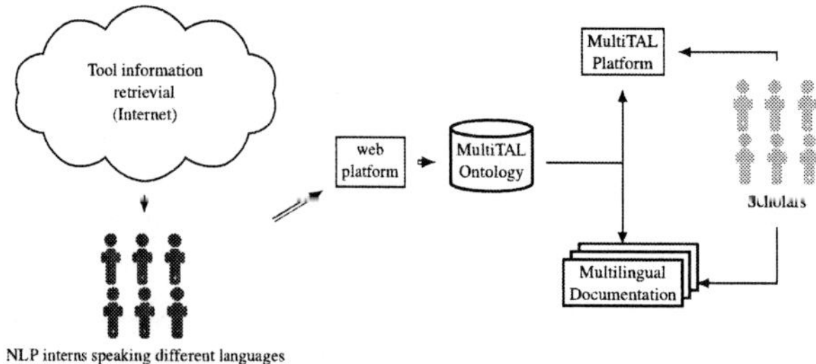

Figure 1: General data flow of MultiTAL project

3.1 Tool documentation protocol

Over the last years, the number of NLP tools has considerably grown. However, as NLP tools are often developed by lone researchers, in the framework of temporary projects (PhD theses, funded projects) they do not always follow guidelines and good practices for documenting their tools. Indeed, NLP tool developers are not expert at packaging and promoting their own tools. Thus, most of the produced tools are under-described (often for personal use) and often entirely or mostly described in a monolingual documentation either in developers' native language or in English. For example, among the selected NLP tools documented in our platform, 77% of them had a documentation available only in a single language (cf. Table 1). Hence, available documentation for NLP tool usage is not always comprehensive or well structured and may be quite complicated for a non-expert which makes it difficult for non native speakers of that language to use the tool. This leads to a limited use of such NLP tools. *MultiTal* project aims at overcoming these drawbacks.

MultiTal project is highly multilingual by nature as it is aimed at scholars working on various languages: our assumption is that NLP tools processing a (or various) language(s) should provide well formed documentation for multiple languages to facilitate and foster their use. Indeed, it often happens that scholars want to use NLP tools for processing documents written in a language they do not fluently speak.

Within our framework, NLP Tools are selected for a given language and according to the NLP tasks they perform. We consider any repositories from academic, institutional or personal websites. Before being added to our inventory, each NLP tool is tested in order to ensure that it can be installed and executed properly. Table 1 shows that more than a half of tested tools were not kept by our interns. NLP tools processing a language are systematically tested by an intern speaking that language. Testing is a very valuable step because it allows for instance the intern to check on which operating systems (OS) the tool can run and which are the requirements to make it run correctly. The intern may have the possibility to offer some simple patches if the tool has bugs that can be easily fixed, as for instance: adding encoding declaration, correcting typos in the execution command or in function names, pinpointing intermediate steps omitted in the original documentation, etc. Moreover, it can detail installation and execution procedures as atomic instructions that end-users must perform in order to run the documented tool. Then, all gathered information is entered via a web platform and stored in an ontology that formalises our meta-data model. For example, our Russian intern retrieved 13 tools processing Russian (cf. Table 1), 9 of them were documented only in Russian. For each of them, the intern has tested their installation and execution procedures and their ability to actually process Russian. Then she provided detailed and structured information which is formalised according to our meta-data model (cf. section 3.2) which enables us to automatically generate documentation from the model in multiple languages -such as English and French (cf. section 3.3).

Language	selected	rejected	Monolingual documentation	Multilingual documentation
Arabic	25	15	20	5
Chinese	16	34	15	1
Hindi	14	4	14	0
Hungarian	3	0	3	0
Japanese	14	19	6	8
Marathi	3	0	0	3
Russian	13	15	9	4
Tibetan	4	7	4	0
Total	92	94	71	21

Table 1: NLP tools documentation within the platform.

3.2 MultiTal meta-data model

To be effective, our meta-data model of NLP documentation should contain all the information needed by an NLP tool user. The kinds of information that should be included in tool documentation is typically those that should be include in a *ReadMe* file: a simple and short written document that is distributed along with a piece of software. It is written by the developer and is supposed to contain basic, crucial information that the user should know before running the software. Writing a clear *Readme* file is essential for effective software distribution and use: a confusing one could prevent the user from using the tool. To our knowledge there are no established best practices for writing a *ReadMe*. So, in order to determine what kinds of information should be included, we proceeded to a joint study of:

1. NLP tool documentation for various languages (Chinese, English, French, Japanese, Tibetan, Hindi, Russian, etc.) that we have already tested.

2. Structured *ReadMe* files (more than fifty thousands) crawled from GitHub repositories.

3. Other meta-data models as *META-SHARE* (Gavrilidou et al., 2011) or *CMDI* (Broeder et al., 2012).

This study allowed us to identify the most frequent and pertinent information used to document an NLP tool. We based the conceptualization of the ontology representing our meta-data model on these results. As done for the *META-SHARE* and *CMDI* meta-data models, we define bundles of properties (super properties). These properties define the characteristics of an NLP tool such as its name, its date of creation, its *affiliation* (author, institution, project), its *license*, the system *configuration* on which it could run, its *installation* procedures or the *tasks* it performs, etc. Figure 2 details the conceptualized bundles of properties, together with examples of some sub-properties for the bundles *Affiliation* and *Task*. Currently, the ontology contains 46 *concepts*, 52 *object properties* and 167 *data type properties*.

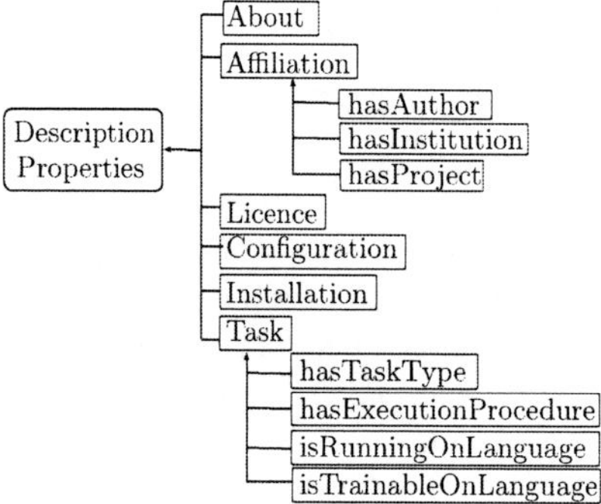

Figure 2: A piece of the ontology properties

We distinguish two levels of meta-data: a *mandatory level* which provides everything the user should know before using the tool, i.e. basic elements that will commonly form a *ReadMe* ; and a *non mandatory level* that contains descriptions which could be helpful to relate the tool to other tools, labs, methods or projects. Properties depicted in Figure 2 are all of the *mandatory level*.

The originality of the proposed model is that it focuses on NLP tools usage. The aim is to promote the use of language technologies within communities which are not familiar with their use. Hence, the model is task- and language-oriented as the choice of an NLP tool depends mostly on these two features. As a result, tools are characterized by the tasks they can perform on a given language. Indeed, tools may perform different NLP tasks and for the same tool processed languages may vary according to each task. Moreover, a task may have several execution procedures depending on the targeted language, the *OS*, the system configuration, the terminal or graphical mode and so on. In addition, a tool may have several installation procedures which depend also on the same factors. These procedures represent the core information for running a tool. As they can be long and tedious, it is important to describe them in a simple and comprehensive way. To do so, in our conceptual model, both installation and execution procedures are divided in their atomic instructions. Thus, when an intern enters a new procedure via the web platform, the procedure is split into atomic instructions. Each instruction is then conceptualised as triple <subject - **property** - object>. Figure 3 depicts an example of how an installation procedure (IP_i) of the *Morphological Analyzer & Stemmer Darwish* is conceptualised within the ontology. First, the procedure is split into its atomic instructions (on the left of the figure). Then each instruction is conceptualised as a semantic triplet (on the middle of the figure). In addition, instructions of a procedure are numbered in order to be ordered when translated from the ontology to a documentation in a targeted language. As for the French translation depicted on the right part of the figure. Indeed, the final aim is to provide end-users structured multilingual documentation detailing the different installation and execution procedures that an NLP tool may be charcterised by. The automatic generation of multilingual documentation is discussed in the next section.

The produced ontology is downloadable and queryable via *SPARQL* from the *MultiTal* infrastructure interface. From a medium-term perspective, we plan to provide automatically generated executable scripts for tools installation and execution for different OS. Moreover, *SPARQL* queries allows us to identify compatible NLP tools in terms of tasks, languages, OS, inputs, outputs, etc. -such that they can be associated in parallel or in pipeline to improve or compare their performance.

Figure 3: Conceptualisation of an installation procedure for the NLP tool *Darwish*.

3.3 Automatic generation of multilingual documentation

Before using any tool, it is generally recommended and sometimes unavoidable to read its documentation. To be understandable, this documentation should indeed be in a language that the user can read. When it comes to software products, this documentation is often called a *ReadMe* file (cf. Section 3.2).

In our framework, we focus on NLP tools processing languages that are taught at INALCO. These languages are for most of them not *lingua franca*. Till now, for the eight languages we investigated, 77% of the selected tools were documented only in the developer's mother tongue or in English (cf. Table 1). Otherwise, a version in English or French was also available. So, in order to ease and improve the experience of end-users, the *MultiTal* infrastructure aims at providing multilingual documentation for NLP tools processing different languages. To do so, we use an ontology verbalisation approach detailed in (Sadoun et al., 2016) that benefits from the formalization of NLP tools information to automatically generate multilingual *ReadMe* files that contain simplified and structured information about each tool such as its license, its installation, execution or training instructions or the language it processes etc.

3.4 MultiTal infrastructure in practice

The *MultiTal* project is conducted at the *INALCO* institution which is a crossroads for Languages and Civilizations. It hosts students, lecturers and researchers of several disciplines from all around the world practicing almost one hundred different languages. Many of these scholars are confronted to a constantly increasing number of digitized data, so that the use of NLP technologies becomes more and more valuable for their practice. *MultiTal* infrastructure is dedicated to making such technologies more accessible regardless of the expertise or spoken language of end-users.

Currently, the infrastructure contains documentation for 92 NLP tools. These documented tools perform 202 NLP tasks of 46 different types. They are distributed across more than eight languages as some of them process more than one language. Though, for each tool a distinction is made between the languages it manages that have been tested and those that have not been tested yet.

The *MultiTal* infrastructure website is currently available in seven languages (English, French, Spanish, Chinese, Russian, Arabic and Japanese.). Figure 4 shows a fragment of the research interface. Selection of tools can be made according to the NLP task they perform, the language they manage, their developer(s), their institution, the way they are accessible (downloadable, on-line or web-service), etc. In addition, NLP tools' documentation inventory gives us key information and statistics. For example,

Figure 4: List of task types (in French) performed by the documented NLP tools.

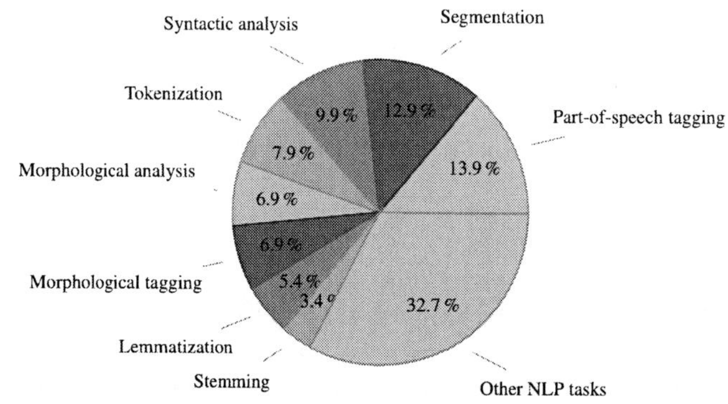

Figure 5: Distribution of NLP tasks performed by documented NLP tools.

the Pie chart depicted in Figure 5 details the distribution of NLP tasks performed by all the documented tools. On the chart, we can see the eight most performed tasks. We can also produce statistics regarding each language (or family) of languages to see, for example, how advanced those languages are in terms of NLP processing and whether they are under-resourced languages or not.

Finally, we count on *INALCO*'s scholars diversity to make the infrastructure grow. Our scholars will both have the benefit of the multilingual NLP documentation provided by the *MultiTal* infrastructure and the opportunity to help us to make it evolve.

4   Conclusion

For a typical scholar, finding NLP tools relevant to their need is not as easy as it should be. Even when relevant NLP tools are found it appears that they are not that simple to use. The *MultiTal* infrastructure is initiated to overcome this situation. In this paper, we described the *MultiTal* infrastructure meta-data model based on the use of an ontology. We motivated our choice which aims to ease and foster the use of NLP tools by scholars of different disciplines. In a short term perspective, we plan to evaluate the effectiveness of the produced documentation, to see whether it provides all the needed information and if it is easy to follow for non NLP experts.

In the future, by considering the produced expertise about NLP tools, we ought to be able to develop methods for adapting some of the tools to languages they have not been designed for, by training them. Indeed, alongside tool identification, we collect information about tagged corpora in order to use them as training ones. Finally, the formalisation of execution procedures into their atomic instructions already allows us to run execution scripts. We intend to use these scripts to combine the execution of different NLP tools either in pipelines or in parallel in order to compare and/or increase their performance.

References

Ion Androutsopoulos, Gerasimos Lampouras, and Dimitrios Galanis. 2014. Generating natural language descriptions from OWL ontologies: the naturalowl system. *CoRR*, abs/1405.6164.

Daan Broeder, Dieter Van Uytvanck, Maria Gavrilidou, Thorsten Trippel, and Menzo Windhouwer. 2012. Standardizing a component metadata infrastructure. In *the Eighth International Conference on Language Resources and Evaluation (LREC 2012)*, pages 1387–1390. European Language Resources Association (ELRA).

N. Calzolari, R. Del Gratta, G. Francopoulo, J. Mariani, F. Rubino, I. Russo, and C. Soria. 2012. The LRE map. Harmonising Community Descriptions of Resources. In *LREC*, pages 1084–1089.

Christian Chiarcos. 2012. Ontologies of linguistic annotation: Survey and perspectives. In *Proceedings of the Eight International Conference on Language Resources and Evaluation (LREC'12)*.

Christopher Cieri, Khalid Choukri, Nicoletta Calzolari, D Terence Langendoen, Johannes Leveling, Martha Palmer, Nancy Ide, and James Pustejovsky. 2010. A road map for interoperable language resource metadata.

Dragoş Alexandru Cojocaru and Ştefan Trăuşan Matu. 2015. Text generation starting from an ontology. In *Proceedings of the Romanian National Human-Computer Interaction Conference - RoCHI*, pages 55–60.

Riccardo Del Gratta, Francesca Frontini, Anas Fahad Khan, Joseph Mariani, and Claudia Soria. 2014. The lremap for under-resourced languages. *CCURL 2014: Collaboration and Computing for Under-Resourced Languages in the Linked Open Data Era*, page 78.

Maria Gavrilidou, Penny Labropoulou, Stelios Piperidis, G Francopoulo, M Monachini, F Frontini, Victoria Arranz, and Valérie Mapelli. 2011. A metadata schema for the description of language resources (lrs). *Language Resources, Technology and Services in the Sharing Paradigm*, page 84.

C. Maria Keet and Langa Khumalo. 2016. Toward a knowledge-to-text controlled natural language of isizulu. *Language Resources and Evaluation*, pages 1–27.

John P. McCrae, Penny Labropoulou, Jorge Gracia, Marta Villegas, Víctor Rodríguez-Doncel, and Philipp Cimiano, 2015a. *The Semantic Web: ESWC 2015 Satellite Events*, chapter One Ontology to Bind Them All: The META-SHARE OWL Ontology for the Interoperability of Linguistic Datasets on the Web, pages 271–282.

J.P. McCrae, P. Cimiano, V.R. Doncel, D. Vila-Suero, J. Gracia, L. Matteis, R. Navigli, A. Abele, G. Vulcu, and P. Buitelaar. 2015b. Reconciling Heterogeneous Descriptions of Language Resources. *ACL-IJCNLP*, page 39.

Stelios Piperidis. 2012. The meta-share language resources sharing infrastructure: Principles, challenges, solutions. In *Proceedings of the Eight International Conference on Language Resources and Evaluation (LREC'12)*.

Victoria Rosén, Koenraad De Smedt, Paul Meurer, and Helge Dyvik. 2012. An open infrastructure for advanced treebanking. In *META-RESEARCH Workshop on Advanced Treebanking at LREC*, pages 22–29.

Driss Sadoun, Satenik Mkhitaryan, Damien Nouvel, and Mathieu Valette. 2016. Readme generation from an owl ontology describing nlp tools. In *2nd International Workshop on Natural Language Generation and the Semantic Web at INLG*.

Inguna Skadina, Andrejs Vasiljevs, Lars Borin, Krister Lindén, Gyri Losnegaard, Bolette Sandford Pedersen, Roberts Rozis, and Koenraad De Smedt. 2013. Baltic and nordic parts of the european linguistic infrastructure. In *Proceedings of the 19th Nordic Conference of Computational Linguistics (NODALIDA 2013)*, pages 195–211.

Tamás VÁRADI1 Marko TADIĆ. 2012. Central and south-east european resources in meta-share. In *24th International Conference on Computational Linguistics*, page 431.

Hitomi Tohyama, Shunsuke Kozawa, Kiyotaka Uchimoto, Shigeki Matsubara, and Hitoshi Isahara. 2008. Construction of a metadata database for efficient development and use of language resources.

D. Tonne, J. Rybicki, S.E. Funk, and P. Gietz. 2013. Access to the dariah bit preservation service for humanities research data. In *Parallel, Distributed and Network-Based Processing (PDP), 21st Euromicro International Conference*, pages 9–15.

Tamás VÁRADI and Marko TADIĆ. 2012. Central and south-east european resources in meta-share. In *24th International Conference on Computational Linguistics*, pages 431–437.

Tamás Váradi, Peter Wittenburg, Steven Krauwer, Martin Wynne, and Kimmo Koskenniemi. 2008. Clarin: Common language resources and technology infrastructure. In *6th International Conference on Language Resources and Evaluation (LREC 2008)*.

Tools and Instruments for Building and Querying Diachronic Computational Lexica

Anas Fahad Khan[*†]
[*]Dipartimento di Studi Umanistici
Universita' di Ca' Foscari
Dorsoduro 3246, 30123 Venezia, Italy
fahad.khan@unive.it

Andrea Bellandi[†]**, Monica Monachini**[†]
[†]Istituto di Linguistica Computazionale
"Antonio Zampolli"
Via G. Moruzzi 1, 56121 Pisa, Italy
name.surname@ilc.cnr.it

Abstract

This article describes work on enabling the addition of temporal information to senses of words in linguistic linked open data lexica based on the *lemonDia* model. Our contribution in this article is twofold. On the one hand, we demonstrate how *lemonDia* enables the querying of diachronic lexical datasets using OWL-oriented Semantic Web based technologies. On the other hand, we present a preliminary version of an interactive interface intended to help users in creating lexical datasets that model meaning change over time.

1 Introduction

The necessity for a flexible and accurate way of representing diachronic lexical information computationally is particularly evident when dealing with "classical" languages such as Ancient Greek, Latin or Sanskrit where we have access to a corpus of texts covering a long period in the language's evolution. It is also the case for modern languages like French, Italian or English where we can count on an existing legacy of texts that attest to various different periods in those languages' development. An important requirement for representation formats for diachronic lexico-semantic resources is that they should facilitate cross-linguistic, typological research of the kind that takes into account different language features both across diverse languages as well as different time periods. One way of working towards meeting such requisites is through the adoption of the linked open data (LOD) paradigm as a means of modelling and publishing such lexical datasets. This not only ensures a minimum level of inter-operability between different datasets through the shared use of the Resource Data Framework (RDF) and common vocabularies/data categories, but it also allows us to exploit various RDF based technologies such as the Web Ontology Language (OWL) when working with such data. We discuss this in more detail below.

In this article we will focus on a model/vocabulary for representing diachronic semantic information as RDF triples called *lemonDia*, which we have introduced in previous work (see (Khan et al., 2014) and (Khan et al., 2016)). In the present work we will look at the more practical aspects of using *lemonDia* and show how *lemonDia* enables the querying of diachronic lexical datasets, using two OWL oriented Semantic Web based technologies, the Semantic Web Rule Language (SWRL) and the Semantic Query-Enhanced Web Rule Language (SQWRL). We will also introduce an interactive tool which we are developing and which is intended to assist users in creating lexical linked open datasets that include information about meaning change over time. One of the main difficulties with incorporating temporal information within RDF datasets is that the rigid subject-predicate-object triple structure of RDF prevents the addition of an extra time argument; this can be resolved in several ways, none of which are entirely satisfactory. *lemonDia* uses the modelling 'trick' of explicitly representing senses as processes in time, or perdurants, but this can be difficult to grasp for non-expert users. Making the whole process of working of assigning temporal periods to lexical entries easier and therefore making the *lemonDia* model more accessible, was one of the main motivations behind the creation of our interactive tool.

Proceedings of the Workshop on Language Technology Resources and Tools for Digital Humanities (LT4DH),
pages 164–171, Osaka, Japan, December 11-17 2016.

The article is organized as follows: Section 2 presents the diachronic dataset that we worked with and that provided the main case study for our tool; Section 3 briefly describes *lemonDia* and Section 4 shows how it is possible to make temporal queries over the dataset from Section 2; Section 5 describes the preliminary version of our interactive tool. Finally, Section 6 draws the conclusions and outlines future work.

2 The Old English Shame/Guilt Dataset

The examples which we will present in this article are taken from a lexical dataset of Old English (OE) emotion terms produced by Díaz-Vera (E Díaz-Vera, 2014) as part of a wider study into the cognitive implications of meaning change. The lexical entries in the dataset have been categorized into those relating to shame/embarrassment and those relating to guilt. The dataset contains both emotion terms which are classified as "literal" – that is emotion terms that aren't the result of a semantic shift from another domain – and non-literal terms, where there is a clear shift from another domain into the domain of shame or guilt. These latter are classified further on the basis of the semantic shifts in question. The time period in which Old English was spoken is divided into 3 consecutive intervals in the OE dataset. These are:

- OE1 (before 950)

- OE2 (950-1050)

- OE3 (1050-1150) .

For simplicity the literal word senses in the dataset are assumed to be valid throughout the whole period in which Old English was spoken. Other senses have an associated period which corresponds to one or more of the three individual periods. These periods can be encoded in RDF-OWL as proper intervals using ProperInterval from the time vocabulary[1]. We have encoded the second interval, OE2, as follows:

```
:OE2 rdf:type owl:NamedIndividual ,
    <http://www.w3.org/2006/time#ProperInterval> ;
    <http://www.w3.org/2006/time#hasBeginning> :year_950
    <http://www.w3.org/2006/time#hasEnd> :year_1050 .
```

3 Using *lemon* and *lemonDIA*

lemon was originally intended as a model for enriching ontologies with linguistic information (McCrae et al., 2010). However it quickly came to take on the status of a de facto standard for representing lexicons as linked open data. Indeed *lemon* has so far been used to convert the Princeton WordNet and Wiktionary (McCrae et al., 2012), as well as FrameNet and VerbNet (Eckle-Kohler et al., 2015), among other well known resources. The design of *lemon* was heavily influenced by the Lexical Markup Framework (LMF) (Francopoulo et al., 2006), but with numerous simplifications to the original LMF specifications. In addition unlike LMF the *lemon* model focuses specifically on creating lexico-semantic resources with an ontological component where the ontology represents the extensions of the word senses in the lexicon. So that in the *lemon* model every lexical sense necessarily connects a lexical entry with a specific ontology vocabulary item. *lemonDia* (Khan et al., 2014) was designed as an extension for *lemon* with the specific purpose of enabling the addition of temporal information to senses. We felt this was necessary even though the original *lemon* model did have a usedSince property (a subproperty of lemon:context) which allowed users to specify the date from which a word was used with a given sense. However this property by itself was clearly not flexible enough to represent the evolution of word senses over time.

The main idea with *lemonDia* is to add a temporal parameter to the sense relation linking together a Lexical Entry and a Lexical Sense. As mentioned above RDF has the restriction that all statements must conform to a subject-predicate-object structure. We therefore chose to treat lexical senses as *perdurants*

---

[1] http://www.w3.org/2006/time

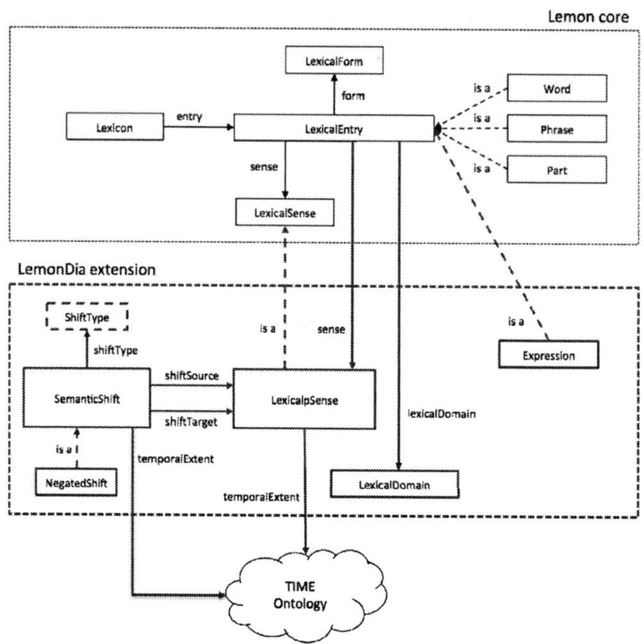

Figure 1: The lemonDia model (LexicalSense and LexicalpSense refer to ontology elements).

with an inherent temporal extent and defined a special subclass of LexicalSense in *lemonDia* called Lex-icalpSense. Every member of LexicalpSense has an associated time period, a time:ProperInterval which it is linked to via the *lemonDia* temporalExtent property. A graphical representation of the *lemonDia* extension is depicted in Figure 1, and more details are given in (Khan et al., 2016). So for instance the lexical entry for the verb *areodian* from the OE dataset, meaning both 'to turn red' as well as the more specific 'to redden with shame' can be linked to two different instances of LexicalpSense corresponding to each of these two senses:

```
:AREODIAN_VB a lemon:LexicalEntry ;
    lemon:language "ang" ;
    lemon:sense :sense_Red_AREODIAN_VB,
    :sense_Shame_AREODIAN_VB ;
    lexinfo:partOfSpeech lexinfo:Verb .
```

Since these two senses are perdurants they have an associated temporal extent. In the next section we will look at how to use *lemonDia* and other semantic web technologies to encode and then query, information about these senses and their associated temporal intervals.

4   Entering and Querying Temporal Information

When it comes to working with temporal intervals representing the time periods in which a given language (or language variety) was spoken, or in which a given word had a specific sense, we have to reckon with the fact that in many cases we don't have a specific start date – either in terms of a year or maybe even a century – or, when appropriate, an end date. This is of course presents a major obstacle in querying such datasets using a language such as SPARQL. Fortunately, we can overcome this lack of data through the use of Allen's basic relations to define time periods in terms of their relations to each other (Allen, 1983), that is qualitatively instead of quantitatively (see (Batsakis et al., 2009)). For instance we can define the time period in which proto-European was spoken in terms of the fact that it came before the period in which proto-Germanic was spoken, which in its own turn gave birth to the Germanic languages for which we have written evidence.

An extremely useful resource for working with such time periods in OWL was developed by Batsakis and consists of a set of rules in the Semantic Web Rule Language (SWRL) encoding the Allen relations[2]. SWRL is, as the name suggests, a rule language specifically designed for the semantic web; it is a subset of Datalog[3] and is strictly more expressive than OWL. Although SWRL as a whole is undecidable there is a subset of the language, the set of DL-safe rules, in which all variables appearing in the consequent of the rule must also appearin the antecedent, that is decidable. The rules and the examples that we are working with belong to this subset. Another Semantic Web technology that is relevant here is the Semantic Query-Enhanced Web Rule Language (SQWRL), a query language that allows the querying of OWL datasets using a query syntax based on SWRL. SQWRL is specifically tailored to querying datasets in OWL a task for which SPARQL is arguably less well adapted (O'Connor and Das, 2009).

SWRL rules, such as those developed by Batsakis, enable us to combine the basic intervals defined above, i.e., OE1, OE2, OE3, to define new intervals. For instance the temporal extent associated with the sense *sense_Shame_AREODIAN_VB*, OE23, is the sum of the two periods OE2 and OE3.

```
:sense_Shame_AREODIAN_VB a lemond:LexicalpSense ;
    lemon:reference dbpedia:Shame ;
    lemond:temporalExtent anglo:OE23 .
```

This period OE23 can be defined as follows, using the intervalStarts and intervalFinishes Allen relations and the two intervals OE2 and OE3 previously defined.

```
:OE23  rdf:type owl:NamedIndividual ,
            <http://www.w3.org/2006/time#ProperInterval> ;
            <http://www.w3.org/2006/time#intervalStarts> :OE2 ;
            <http://www.w3.org/2006/time#intervalFinishes> :OE3.
```

Using SQWRL we can write queries that exploit the logical axioms and rules in our dataset and that, using an OWL reasoner, are able to take into consideration knowledge, and in our case temporal knowledge, that is only implicit in the dataset itself. We now give three examples of queries typifying useful kinds of query that one can make on such a dataset. To start off with the following query will produce a list of all the lexical entries in the dataset and the number of senses which they have:

```
lemon:sense(?x, ?y) -> sqwrl:select(?x) ^ sqwrl:count(?y)
```

We can also produce a list of all the senses that have a temporal extent of OE1:

```
lemond:LexicalpSense(?x) ^ lemond:temporalExtent(?x,anglo: OE1)
-> sqwrl:select(?x)
```

The following query finds all the senses that contain the sense OE1:

```
lemond:LexicalpSense(?x) ^ lemond:temporalExtent(?x,?y)
^intervalContains(?y, anglo:OE2)-> sqwrl:select(?x)
```

The use of SWRL and SQWRL seems to be gathering traction. The latest version of *Protégé* (*Protégé* 5.0.0), probably the most popular free tool available for constructing and editing ontologies, comes pre-packaged with a tab for carrying out SQWRL queries on OWL datasets.

5   Our Interactive System for Creating *lemonDIA* lexicons

In the previous section we looked at some of the queries that can be performed on a dataset like the Old English one which we introduced earlier in the article. One of the motivations for this was to show the potential benefits of creating datasets using the *lemonDia* model. In order to overcome the initial hurdles to creating *lemonDia* datasets in the first place however, we have developed an interface which assists the user in doing this. Before we go on to describe this interface we will look in the following section at some related work.

---

[2]https://github.com/sbatsakis/TemporalRepresentations
[3]https://www.w3.org/Submission/SWRL/

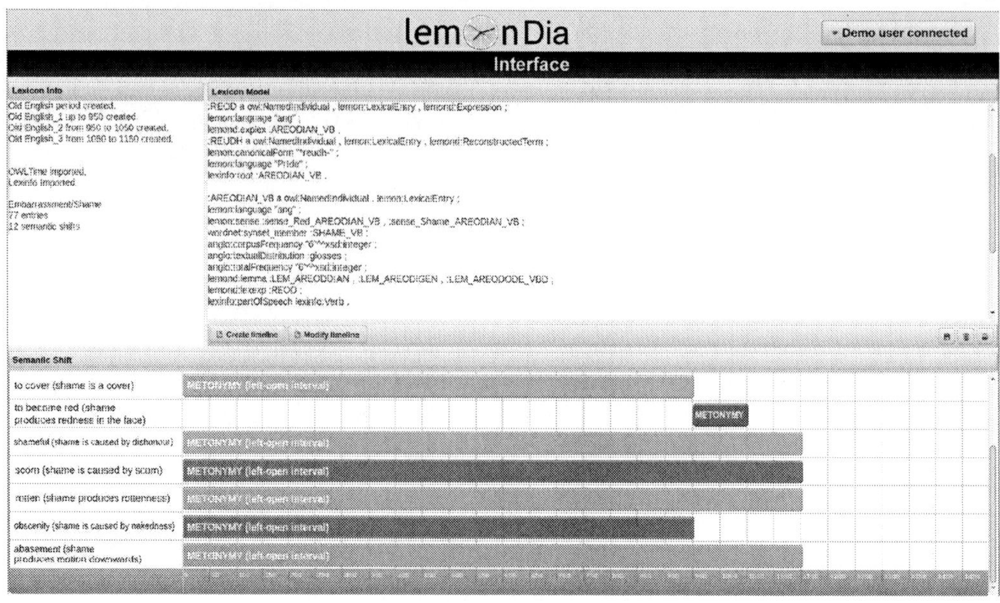

Figure 2: Main interface for creating and visualizing *lemonDia* lexica.

5.1 Related Work

A number of tools have been developed in order to work with standards and vocabularies such as LEX-INFO (Cimiano et al., 2011), LMF, and *lemon*. For example, in (Johnson et al., 2005) the authors discuss LexGrid, a tool enabling the integration of terminologies and ontologies through a common model. They present an overview of the editor's functional capabilities in relation to technologies offered by the Lex-Grid platform.(Ringersma and Kemps-Snijders, 2007) describes the development of a flexible web based lexicon tool, LEXUS which allows the creation of lexica within the structure of the ISO LMF standard and uses the proposed concept naming conventions from the ISO data categories, thus enabling interoperability, search and merging. Another generic platform for working with computational lexica, is presented in (Bel et al., 2008): the COLDIC system has been specially designed to allow the user to concentrate on the lexicographical task at hand while being autonomous in the management of the tools. Montiel et. al. (Montiel-Ponsoda et al., 2008) propose a tool, developed as a plug-in of NeOn[4] to support a model called the Linguistic Information Repository (LIR). LIR is a holistic linguistic information repository, that provides a complete set of linguistic elements in each language for localizing ontology elements. It also allows access to linguistic information distributed in heterogeneous resources of varying granularities, and makes it possible to establish relations between linguistic elements. Another plug-in for the NeOn toolkit has been developed in (Buitelaar et al., 2009). (Touhami et al., 2011) proposes a new model whose use is illustrated within a supervised annotation environment in which the user can manually enrich an Ontological and Terminological Resource (OTR) by associating each new found term to the appropriate domain concepts. They have developed their OTR editor called TextViz as a plug-in in the *Protégé*-OWL framework. It also helps the user to visualize the textual manifestations of concepts in the corpus used to construct the OTR. Finally, in (Kenter et al., 2012), an editor for constructing corpus-based lexica and correcting word-level annotations and transcription errors in corpora, is presented. The editor has been extensively tested in a project in which a historical corpus was manually annotated and used to produce a lexicon, with the lexicon being further extended on the basis of a much larger corpus.

As regards *lemon*, in (McCrae and Unger, 2014) the authors use ontology design patterns (Gangemi, 2005) for defining how certain lexico-semantic phenomena should be modelled. Their goal in creating such a catalogue of ontology-lexicon design patterns is to facilitate the process of developing ontology-

---

[4]NeOn toolkit is available at http://neon-toolkit.org

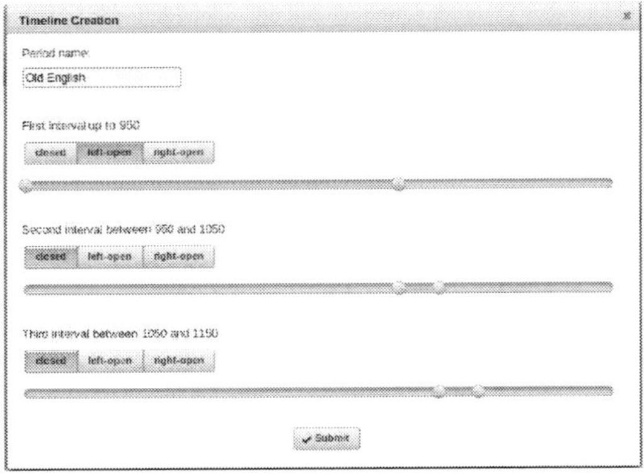

Figure 3: Interface for creating time intervals.

lexica, by replacing complex combinations of frame semantics and first-order logic axioms with simple patterns with only a few parameters. Finally, in (Montiel-Ponsoda et al., 2012), a platform called *lemon source* is presented. It supports the creation of linked lexical data and it builds on the concept of a semantic wiki to enable collaborative editing of the resources by many users concurrently.

5.2 The Interface

Our intent in this work has been to create a user-friendly interface that would facilitate users in the building of diachronic lexica using the *lemonDia model* without that is involving them too deeply in the details of the formal model underlying the representation. Our interface is web-based and supports the creation both of linked data lexica and related temporal timelines. It accepts as input files in CSV or Excel formats. The rows in these files should include information on (but without being necessarily limited to) written forms, lemmas, roots, etymologies, collocations, meanings, semantic shifts, and the time intervals in which each sense was used. Before importing this input file, it is necessary to enter information about the different time periods listed in the CSV, e.g., OE1. The interface allows users to specify how many time intervals to create, and each interval can be specified by means of the pop-up panel shown in Figure 3.

A lexicon is then generated using the data contained in the input file. Afterwards it is possible to export this lexicon in various formats, such as RDF/XML and TURTLE, or JSON, in order to use it, for example, as input to one of the stages in a Natural Language Processing pipeline. Once the lexicon has been created, the user can visualize all semantic shifts using a graphical mode that uses a timeline graph. Figure 2 shows an example. The interface is composed of three panels. The "lexicon info" panel shows the time intervals that make up the period covered by the evolution of the language; the "model" area contains the lexicon; and the "semantic shift" area shows the temporal evolution of the senses in the lexicon. Figure 2 gives the timelines of seven senses belonging to the lexical field of the word "shame": so that we can see, for example, the usage of the sense "to become red" is attested between 950 and 1050 in the old english corpus, and the semantic shift type is a metonomy.

From the technical point of view, the tool is based on a software design pattern known as "three-tier architecture", and exploits Apache Tomcat v7.0 as a web server. The system was implemented using the Java 2 Standard Edition (J2SE) framework which allows the easy manipulation of unicode characters and can be extended to other languages using different writing systems. The OWLAPI has been used for the management of the *lemonDia* model. The presentation tier has been implemented by means of Java Server Faces (JSF) and Primefaces v5.1. This technology allows concurrent access to the imported lexicon and in subsequent versions, we are planning to add functionality that will allow more than one user to carry out management and query tasks on the lexicon at the same time.

6 Future Work

In this article we have shown how the *lemonDia* model can facilitate the creation and subsequent querying of temporal information in diachronic lexical linked open datasets. Furthermore, we have described a preliminary version of a user-friendly interface that assists non expert users in the creation of diachronic lexica. Our tool allows users to import a CSV or Excel file containing lexical data and to subsequently encode the lexicon in RDF using the *lemonDia* model, as well as browsing the temporal information associated with word senses in the lexicon.

We are planning on developing a first release of this tool as an open source application in the near future. In subsequent work we would like to concentrate on the following four aspects: i) extending our tool in order to support the management and editing of the imported lexicon; ii) enhancing the tool with query capabilities by means of a controlled natural language query interface; iii) enabling the importation of ontologies and the association of ontological concepts with individual word senses; iv) extending the *lemonDia* model with the attestations of the word in the corpus.

Acknowledgements

We would like to thank Javier Díaz-Vera for making the Old English emotion dataset available to us.

References

James F Allen. 1983. Maintaining knowledge about temporal intervals. *Communications of the ACM*, 26(11):832–843.

Sotiris Batsakis, Euripides Petrakisb, Ilias Tachmazidisa, and Grigoris Antonioua. 2009. Temporal representation and reasoning in owl 2.0. *Semantic Web Journal*.

Nuria Bel, Sergio Espeja, Montserrat Marimon, and Marta Villegas. 2008. Coldic, a lexicographic platform for lmf compliant lexica. In Bente Maegaard Joseph Mariani Jan Odijk Stelios Piperidis Daniel Tapias Nicoletta Calzolari (Conference Chair), Khalid Choukri, editor, *Proceedings of the Sixth International Conference on Language Resources and Evaluation (LREC'08)*, Marrakech, Morocco, may. European Language Resources Association (ELRA). http://www.lrec-conf.org/proceedings/lrec2008/.

Paul Buitelaar, Philipp Cimiano, Peter Haase, and Michael Sintek. 2009. Towards linguistically grounded ontologies. In *Proceedings of the 6th European Semantic Web Conference on The Semantic Web: Research and Applications*, ESWC 2009 Heraklion, pages 111–125, Berlin, Heidelberg. Springer-Verlag.

Philipp Cimiano, Paul Buitelaar, John McCrae, and Michael Sintek. 2011. Lexinfo: A declarative model for the lexicon-ontology interface. *Web Semantics: Science, Services and Agents on the World Wide Web*, 9(1).

Javier E Díaz-Vera. 2014. From cognitive linguistics to historical sociolinguistics: The evolution of old english expressions of shame and guilt. *Cognitive Linguistic Studies*, 1(1):55–83.

Judith Eckle-Kohler, John McCrae, and Christian Chiarcos. 2015. lemonUby - A large, interlinked, syntactically-rich lexical resource for ontologies. *SEMANTIC WEB*, 6(4):371–378.

Gil Francopoulo, Monte George, Nicoletta Calzolari, Monica Monachini, Nuria Bel, Y Pet, and Claudia Soria. 2006. Lexical markup framework (lmf. In *In Proceedings of LREC2006*.

Aldo Gangemi. 2005. Ontology design patterns for semantic web content. In *Proceedings of the 4th International Conference on The Semantic Web*, ISWC'05, pages 262–276, Berlin, Heidelberg. Springer-Verlag.

Thomas M. Johnson, Harold R. Solbrig, Daniel C. Armbrust, and Christopher G. Chute. 2005. Lexgrid editor: Terminology authoring for the lexical grid. In *AMIA 2005, American Medical Informatics Association Annual Symposium, Washington, DC, USA, October 22-26, 2005.*

Tom Kenter, Tomaž Erjavec, Maja žorga Dulmin, and Darja Fišer. 2012. Lexicon construction and corpus annotation of historical language with the cobalt editor. In *Proceedings of the 6th Workshop on Language Technology for Cultural Heritage, Social Sciences, and Humanities*, LaTeCH '12, pages 1–6, Stroudsburg, PA, USA. Association for Computational Linguistics.

Fahad Khan, Federico Boschetti, and Francesca Frontini. 2014. Using lemon to Model Lexical Semantic Shift in Diachronic Lexical Resources. Proceedings of the Workshop on Linked Data in Linguistics 2014 (LDL-2014).

Fahad Khan, Javier E. Díaz-Vera, and Monica Monachini. 2016. Representing polysemy and diachronic lexico-semantic data on the semantic web ? In Isabelle Draelants, Catherine Faron-Zucker, Alexandre Monnin, and Arnaud Zucker, editors, *Proceedings of the Second International Workshop on Semantic Web for Scientific Heritage co-located with 13th Extended Semantic Web Conference (ESWC 2016), Heraklion, Greece, May 30th, 2016.*, volume 1595 of *CEUR Workshop Proceedings*, pages 37–46. CEUR-WS.org.

John P. McCrae and Christina Unger. 2014. Design patterns for engineering the ontology-lexicon interface. In Paul Buitelaar and Philipp Cimiano, editors, *Towards the Multilingual Semantic Web*, pages 15–30. Springer.

John McCrae, Guadalupe Aguado-de Cea, Paul Buitelaar, Philipp Cimiano, Thierry Declerck, Asunción Gómez Pérez, Jorge Gracia, Laura Hollink, Elena Montiel-Ponsoda, Dennis Spohr, et al. 2010. The lemon cookbook.

John McCrae, Elena Montiel-Ponsoda, and Philipp Cimiano, 2012. *Integrating WordNet and Wiktionary with lemon*, pages 25–34. Springer.

Elena Montiel-Ponsoda, Guadalupe Aguado-de Cea, Asuncin Gmez-Prez, and Wim Peters. 2008. Modelling multilinguality in ontologies. Poster, CoLing 2008.

Elena Montiel-Ponsoda, J. McCrae, and Philipp Cimiano. 2012. Collaborative semantic editing of linked data lexica. In *Proceedings of the Eight International Conference on Language Resources and Evaluation (LREC'12)*, pages 2619–2625. European Language Resources Association (ELRA).

Martin O'Connor and Amar Das. 2009. Sqwrl: A query language for owl. In *Proceedings of the 6th International Conference on OWL: Experiences and Directions - Volume 529*, OWLED'09, pages 208–215, Aachen, Germany, Germany. CEUR-WS.org.

Jacquelijn Ringersma and Marc Kemps-Snijders. 2007. Creating multimedia dictionaries of endangered languages using LEXUS. In *INTERSPEECH 2007, 8th Annual Conference of the International Speech Communication Association, Antwerp, Belgium, August 27-31, 2007*, pages 1529–1532.

Rim Touhami, Patrice Buche, Juliette Dibie-Barthélemy, and Liliana Ibănescu, 2011. *An Ontological and Terminological Resource for n-ary Relation Annotation in Web Data Tables*, pages 662–679. Springer Berlin Heidelberg, Berlin, Heidelberg.

Tracking Words in Chinese Poetry of Tang and Song Dynasties with the China Biographical Database

Chao-Lin Liu[†] and Kuo-Feng Luo[‡]
[†]Department of East Asian Languages and Civilizations, Harvard University, USA
[†]Institute for Quantitative Social Science, Harvard University, USA
[†‡]Department of Computer Science, National Chengchi University, Taiwan
chaolinliu@fas.harvard.edu

Abstract

Large-scale comparisons between the poetry of Tang and Song dynasties shed light on how words and expressions were used and shared among the poets. That some words were used only in the Tang poetry and some only in the Song poetry could lead to interesting research in linguistics. That the most frequent colors are different in the Tang and Song poetry provides a trace of the changing social circumstances in the dynasties. Results of the current work link to research topics of lexicography, semantics, and social transitions. We discuss our findings and present our algorithms for efficient comparisons among the poems, which are crucial for completing billion times of comparisons within acceptable time.

1   Introduction

Words are basic units for sentences, with which we convey ideas. Understanding the meanings carried by words, both explicitly and implicitly, is essential for correct and successful communication. The ability to "read between the lines" is important for thorough understanding. In addition to considering collocations, for Chinese, the ways a word that was commonly used and the stories that associated with certain phrases often influence an expression's connotation sensed by readers of appropriate background knowledge. For instance, "梧桐" /wu2 tong2/ [1] literally means Chinese parasol trees, but was often used in poetry about separations. Hence, "梧桐" has become a symbol of separation in literary works, similar to that "olive twigs" symbolizes peace in the Western world.

With the availability of the text files of the poetry, we can search, analyze, and compare their contents to learn about the history of word usage in the literature algorithmically. Software tools allow us to conduct research about poetry in a larger scale and from various perspectives that were practically hard for human experts to achieve before.

Studying Chinese poetry with computing technologies started at least two decades ago, so we do not mean to provide a comprehensive review of the literature. Lo and her colleagues implemented a computer assisted environment (Lo et al. 1997). Hu and Yu (2001) reported some analyses of unigrams and bigrams in Tang poems, and looked for Chinese synonyms in Tang and Song poems (Hu & Yu 2002). Lee attempted to do dependency parsing of Tang poems (Lee & Kong 2012), and explored the roles of named entities, e.g., seasons and directions, in Tang poems (Lee & Wong 2012).

We present some experiences in analyzing and comparing the contents of the Complete Tang Poem (全唐詩 /quan2 tang2 shi1/, CTP henceforth) and the Complete Song Lyrics (全宋詞 /quan2 song4 ci2/, CSL henceforth) with software tools. We choose CTP and CSL because Tang (618-907AD) and Song (960-1279AD) are arguably the most influential stages in the history of Chinese literature and because poem (詩, /shi1/) and lyrics (詞, /ci2/) are, respectively, the most representative forms of poetry in these dynasties. The influences of the poetry in these dynasties last until today. In addition, we access the China Biographical Database (Fuller 2015, CBDB henceforth) for information about the poets to enhance the overall results of our investigation. We can expand our work to cover literature of earlier and later dynasties whenever the text files and biographical data become available.

---

[1] Chinese words will be followed by their Hanyu Pinyin and tones.

Proceedings of the Workshop on Language Technology Resources and Tools for Digital Humanities (LT4DH),
pages 172–180, Osaka, Japan, December 11-17 2016.

We implement tools for efficient comparisons and analyses of poems and apply some freeware in our work. There are, respectively, 42,863 and 19,394 items in our CTP and CSL files. Comparing each item with others needs more than 1.9 billion comparisons. The number of comparisons will increase exponentially when we expand our study into Complete Song Poem, which has more than 185 thousand items. Hence, an efficient strategy for comparing poems is very important.

In Section 2, we provide more background information about analyzing poetry with software tools, and illustrate the benefits of considering biographical data in the analysis of literary works in Section 3. We turn our attention to algorithms for comparing the contents of poems in Section 4, and, in Section 5, we discuss some interesting findings that we noticed with the help of our tools. We briefly review some challenging issues and make concluding remarks in Section 6.

2   More Background Information

Software tools for textual analysis provide ample opportunities for us to study Chinese poetry from a variety of new positions. On comparing the poems of Li Bai (李白)[2] and Du Fu (杜甫), two very famous Tang poets, Jiang (2003) presented his observations from a close-reading viewpoint, and we showed the poets' differences from a distant-reading standpoint (Liu et al. 2015).

Researchers may focus their investigation on a special aspect of CTP, e.g., Pan (2015) introduced his observations about words about plants and flowers in Chinese poetry. We consider that colors portray the scenery that could be delivered by a poem; just like that audio effects drive the atmosphere in a movie. The most frequent color in CTP is white (白 /bai2/). Following this direction, we have reported some findings about poets' styles and cultural implications that are related to colors (Liu et al. 2015, Cheng et al. 2015). In addition, we found that red (紅 /hong2/) is the most frequent color in CSL (Liu 2016), and it is possible to link this observation to social and cultural circumstances of the Song dynasty. Poets, both male and female, may express themselves from female perspectives and may use females as metaphors for goals that were hard to achieve (Cheng et al. 2015, Sun 2016).

In addition to offering efficient search and comparison capabilities, software tools should facilitate the research by linking more relevant data about the poets. When studying the poems of a specific poet, a researcher should learn about the poet's life to better appreciate the meanings hidden in the poems.

We test this intuition by using the China Biographical Database (CBDB) in our work. CBDB provides information about approximately 360,000 individuals primarily from the 7th through 19th centuries in China. We demonstrate two applications of the information about the birth year, death year, and the alternative names of the poets in CBDB in the next section.

3   Linking Historical and Literary Analysis

3.1   Social Networks among Poets

Social network analysis (SNA) proves to be an effective instrument in social science studies. It is perhaps a bit surprising that researchers had attempted to study connections among poets without the assistance of modern computers (Wu 1993), although the results are not perfect.

In CTP, a poet may mention another poet's name in the title or in the content of a poem. It is not difficult to determine whom was mentioned if the complete names were used.

CBDB records the poets' alternative names, with which we can find more connections between poets. Often, the alternative names are short, containing just one or two characters, and it is not easy to pinpoint the alternative names in the contents of the poems.

We rely on some heuristics to increase the precision of our SNA analysis. For instance, we use the string of the alternative names as an evidence for the relationship between two poets only if one poet mentioned the other

Figure 1. Poet network for high Tang

---

[2] The first word is the surname in Chinese names.

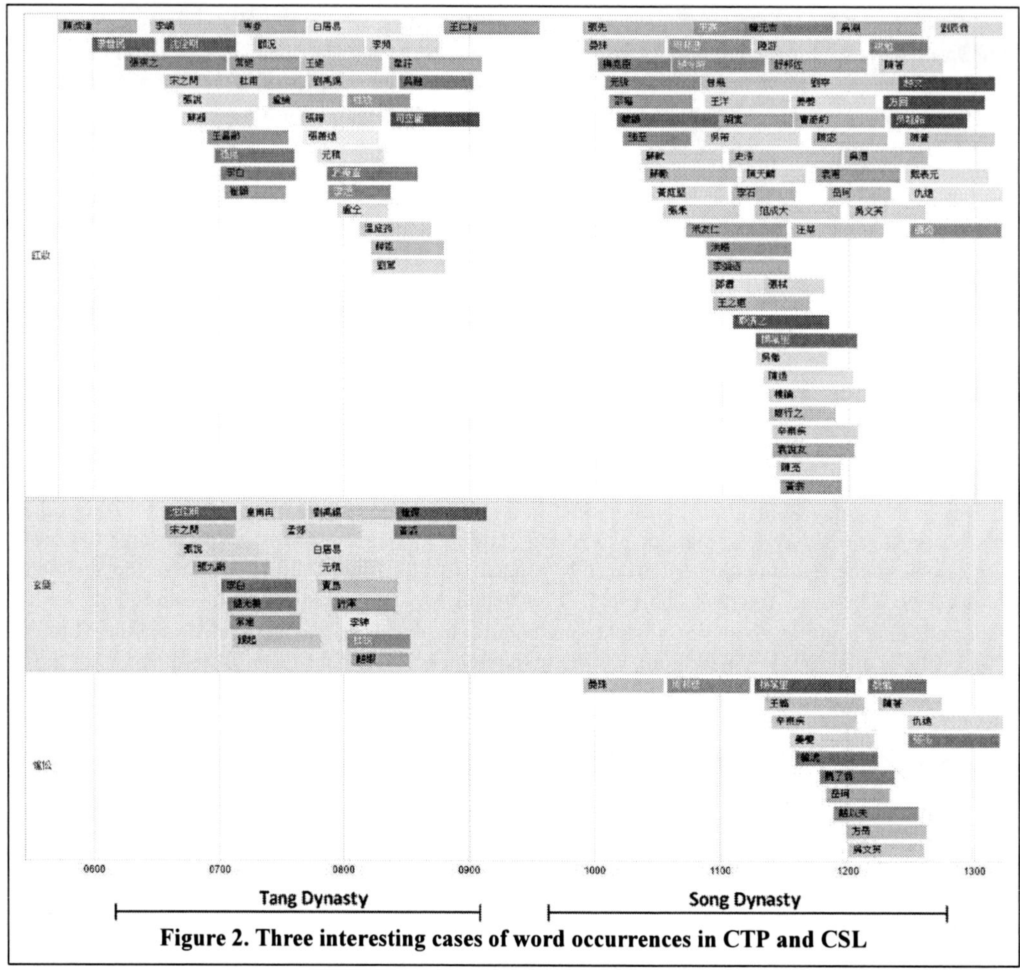

Tang Dynasty | **Song Dynasty**

Figure 2. Three interesting cases of word occurrences in CTP and CSL

with the latter's full name in other poems. This design choice may hurt the recall rate, and may be adjusted if necessary.

Figure 1 shows a social network that indicates the mentioning of poets' names for poets of the high-Tang period (713-765AD)[3]. The arrows point to the names that were mentioned in the poems (of the poets whose names are at the tails of the arrows), and thicker arrows suggest higher frequencies.

The social networks thus identified can be used for historical and literary studies. After experts verify the relationships, we can record the relationships in CBDB to enrich the contents of CBDB. One may also analyze and compare the styles and subjects of the poems of the poets who frequently mentioned each other to check, for example, whether friends had common interests in their poems.

3.2　A History of Word Occurrences

Compiling a comprehensive Chinese word dictionary is a huge, if not formidable, task. Luo (1986) led hundreds of scholars to achieve a contemporary version in 1986. We can enhance the lexicon with more examples from the Tang and Song poetry.

Specifically, we apply techniques of information retrieval (Manning et al. 2008) to track how words were used in Chinese literature over time. With the birth and death years of the poets that were recorded in CBDB, we can draw a chart like Figure 2 to show a history about the words[4]. The horizontal axis of Figure 2 shows the years of Tang and Song dynasties, and the widths of the

---

[3] Figure 1 was created with Gephi <https://gehpi.org>.

[4] Figure 2 was produced with the support of Google Charts <https://developers.google.com/chart/>.

```
Algorithm FindCommon
  Input: 1. sets of poems S={S₁, S₂, …, Sᵢ,…,S_N}, each Sᵢ is a
            collection of poems (either CTP or CSL or others),
            i.e., Sᵢ = {P_{i,1}, P_{i,2}, …, P_{i,qi}}, where a P_{j,k} is the k-th
            poem in Sⱼ
         2. basic filtering conditions, F
         3. output format requests, R
  Output: common parts of any two poems in S
Steps:
1  Compute an indexed list of characters, V, that are used in S
2  For any two poems, Pₓ and Pᵧ, do the following.
   2.1 Look up the characters of Pₓ in V, and save the indexes
       for the characters in Iₓ. Repeat this step for Pᵧ to create
       Iᵧ.
   2.2 Compare the indexes in Iₓ and Iᵧ to find the characters
       that appear in both Pₓ and Pᵧ. Record the locations of the
       common characters in Cₓ and Cᵧ, respectively.
   2.3 Emit the common words in format R, along with basic
       information about Pₓ and Pᵧ, if the common words satisfy F
```

Figure 3. Our algorithm for comparing poems

rectangles that contain the poets' names[5] indicate the poets' life span. We do not show poets whose life spans are not known in Figure 2. The figure is divided into three parts, from top to bottom, for "紅妝" /hong2 zhuang1/, "玄髮" /xuan2 fa3/, and "惺忪" /sing1 song1/, each showing the poets who used these three words.

An interface like Figure 2 can provide useful information that a traditional lexicon may not achieve easily. First, the chart offers a distant reading of the history of the word's occurrences. Although there were more poets in CTP than in CSL, more CSL poets used "紅妝" in their works than CTP poets did, which provides hints about social changes (cf. Sun 2016). We can easily see that "玄髮" was used only in CTP and that "惺忪" might have been an invented word in the Song dynasty.

Second, we can strengthen the charts for close reading, style analysis, and other applications. Researchers can click on the poets' names to read the poems that actually used the specific words, e.g., "紅妝", for further investigation. Given the time stamps on the horizontal axis, one may study how poets used "紅妝" in a specific time period, e.g., high Tang or Southern Song periods. Maybe more interesting is that we can automatically extract the poems that used a specific word to study whether the meanings carried by the word changed over time. Moreover, for language learners, our work can serve as a source of sample poems that used selected words.

4   Locating Shared Words of Poems

4.1   Comparing Individual Poems

We design the algorithm, `FindCommon` in Figure 3, to compare large sets of poems efficiently. To simplify our illustration, we assume that there are only two items in CTP and only one item in CSL, and we refer to an individual work as a poem, temporarily ignoring whether they are Tang poems or Song lyrics.

In CTP, we have the following two poems authored by Liu Yu-Xi (劉禹錫).

P_{11}: 山圍故國周遭在，潮打空城寂寞回。淮水東邊舊時月，夜深還過女牆來。[6]
P_{12}: 朱雀橋邊野草花，烏衣巷口夕陽斜。舊時王謝堂前燕，飛入尋常百姓家。

---

[5] All Chinese characters within the boxes are poets' names, and we do not provide their Hanyu Pinyin here.
[6] We could not show the Hangyu Pinyin for the poems due to page limits. The titles of P_{11}, P_{12}, and P_{13}, are, respectively, "石頭城" /shi2 tou2 cheng2/, "烏衣巷" /wu1 yi1 siang4/, and "大石金陵" /da4 shih2 jin1 ling2/.

In CSL, we have the following item authored by Zhou Ban-Yan (周邦彥)

P₂₁: 佳麗地，南朝盛事誰記？山圍故國繞清江，髻鬟對起。怒濤寂寞打孤城，風檣遙度天際。

斷崖樹、猶倒倚，莫愁艇子誰係？空餘舊跡鬱蒼蒼，霧沉半壘。夜深月過女牆來，傷心東望淮水。

酒旗戲鼓甚處市？想依稀，王謝鄰裏，燕子不知何世，向尋常巷陌人家。相對如說興亡，斜陽裏。

At the first step, we scan the contents of every poem in the datasets, and record each different character in a list. The characters are indexed for efficient lookup operations, and this list serves as a basis for comparing the contents of individual poems. With the three poems, we may have a V like {"山":0, "圍":1, "故":2, …, "月":20, "夜":21, "深":22, "還":23, "過":24, "女":25, "牆":26, "來":27, …}. We chose to index at the character level so that we can find all of the shared characters in poetry.

At step 2.1, we convert a poem into a list of indexes (from V) for characters that appeared in the poem. In this illustration, I_{11} will be "0, 1, 2, …, 27". P_{21} is long, so I_{21} will be a long list of indexes. The sentence "夜深月過女牆來" in P_{21} will contribute "20, 21, 22, 24, 25, 26, 27" to I_{21}.

At step 2.2, we compare the lists of indexes for P_x and P_y to find common characters. Comparing indexes of characters is computationally more efficient than directly comparing the characters. After computing the intersection of I_{11} and I_{21}, we can determine that "月", "夜深", "過女牆來" appeared in P_{11} and P_{21}. Note that P_{21} does not use "還", so C_{11} will read like { …, "月", "夜深", "過女牆來"}. C_{11} includes characters in P_{11} and P_{21}, when we compare them. Likewise, each character in "夜深月過女牆來" of P_{21} appeared in P_{11}, so C_{21} would read like {…, "夜深月過女牆來", …}.

At step 2.3, we can select the strings that would appear in the final report. If researchers are not interested in unigrams, like "月" in this illustration. We can remove strings that are shorter than a given threshold, and this can be done via F in the input.

This example also shows us that there are at least two ways to report the common characters of two poems. In the current case, we may report different common strings, i.e., C_{11} or C_{21}, depending on our standpoint as we just explained. This can be controled via R in the input. Notice that the choice of standpoint can have a variety of influences on the output, e.g., when we compare P_{12} and P_{21}, C_{12} and C_{21} will contain "陽斜" and "斜陽", respectively.

In summary, if we compare P_{11} and P_{21} and report all of the common strings (including unigrams) in terms of words in P_{21}, we will find {"山圍故國", "寂寞打", "城", "空", "舊", "夜深月過女牆來", "東", "淮水"}. If we compare P_{12} and P_{21} and report all of the common strings in terms of words in P_{21}, we will find {"舊", "王謝", "燕", "尋常巷", "家", "斜陽" }.

We produce the following record after we compare P_{11} and P_{21} and report all of the common strings (including unigrams) in terms of words in P_{21}. In addition to the common words, we add the poet names and the IDs of the poems that are compared for each record. A record contains three fields that are separated by "|||". We put P_{21} in the leftmost field because the common words, which are grouped in the rightmost field, are listed in the terms that appeared in P_{21}, i.e., from the standpoint of P_{21}.

Zhou-Ban-Yan_P₂₁||| Liu-Yu-Xi_P₁₁|||[山圍故國, 寂寞打, 城, 空, 舊, 夜深月過女牆來, 東, 淮水]

Zhou-Ban-Yan_P₂₁||| Liu-Yu-Xi_P₁₂|||[舊, 王謝, 燕, 家, 尋常巷, 斜陽]

We can offer different viewpoints for researchers to examine the words shared by the poems. Although we read "夜深月過女牆來" in P_{21}, this string actually came from three shorter strings in P_{11}. i.e., "月", "夜深", and "過女牆來". Hence, a researcher can choose to see the list of common words in the following manners, by appropriately setting R when s/he runs FindCommon.

Zhou-Ban-Yan_P₂₁||| Liu-Yu-Xi_P₁₁|||[山圍故國, 寂寞打, 城, 空, 舊, 月, 夜深, 過女牆來, 東, 淮水]

Liu-Yu-Xi_P₁₁ ||| Zhou-Ban-Yan_P₂₁|||[山圍故國, 打空城寂寞, 淮水東, 舊, 月, 夜深, 過女牆來]

4.2 Selecting Interesting Candidates

We have 42,863 items in CTP and 19,394 items in CSL. An exhaustive comparison procedure that considers two viewpoints of a poem pair would conduct more than 3.8 billion comparisons in FindCommon. On one personal desktop computer with an Intel i7-4790 3.6G CPU, the Microsoft

Windows 10 64-bit Operating System, 32G RAM, and an ordinary hard disk, it took about 35 hours to complete the comparisons with our Java programs.

The computation time will increase noticeably when we include the Complete Song Poems (全宋詩 /quan2 song4 shi1/, CSP henceforth) in the comparison procedure. Like CTP and CSL, different sources of CSP may contain slightly different numbers of poems. There are more than 185 thousand items in our CSP. Comparing just one viewpoint for all items in CTP, CSL, and CSP needs more than 30 billion comparisons and will consume about 10 days with one computer.

Of course, the results of comparing any pair of poems are mutually independent, so we could and should run the comparisons in parallel on multiple machines. Nevertheless, this is a resource-consuming step, and we do not want to repeat these basic comparisons again and again.

Therefore, we organize the search for poem pairs that may have interesting common words into two stages. At the first stage, we employ `FindCommon` to compare all pairs of poems and find all common strings, including unigrams. We record the common strings of any pair of poems, except those pairs that share no or only one character, assuming that these instances are not of interest.

This, as one may expect, will produce huge output files, and, indeed, comparing just CTP and CSL will generate an output file that is larger than 300G in size. The actual size of the output file varies with F and R that we set when we run `FindCommon`.

At the second stage, a researcher will set criteria for selecting records from what we have obtained at the first stage. This will help the researcher to focus on a much smaller set of pairs of poems than those records that we obtain at the first stage. We continue to employ the previous example to illustrate the main idea.

We will obtain the following two instances when we compare P_{11} and P_{12} at the first stage. At the second stage, a researcher can choose to ignore both instances by asking the filter to output instances in which the list of common words has at least two bigrams. Alternatively, the researcher may choose to check instances that have at least two substrings, and, in this case, the second instance will survive.

Liu-Yu-Xi_P_{11}|||Liu-Yu-Xi_P_{12}|||[邊舊時]
Liu-Yu-Xi_P_{12}|||Liu-Yu-Xi_P_{11}|||[舊時, 邊]

5 Shared Texts among Poetry of Tang and Song Dynasties

We discuss some interesting instances in which terms, sentences, or imageries were shared among Tang and Song poetry in this section (cf. Wang 2003). Although our findings can lead to several types of further investigations, we present samples that roughly fall into two categories. The shared words can nurture certain similar or related imagery in poems, and the shared words and expressions may suggest some authorship or version issues of the poetry.

The running example that we elaborated in previous section is a famous example of using several terms from multiple sources in a new poem (cf. Chen & Wang 2001). In a more complete account, Zhou Ban-Yan also used a poem of Xie Tiao (謝朓) and a Yuefu poem (樂府詩)[7] in P_{21}. We did not discuss these additional poems partially because they are not part of CTP or CSL.

We summarize the results of the comparisons in Section 4 in the following manner. We mark shared characters with tiny ripples under them. The shared characters are colored in green for items in CTP and in blue for items in CSL. The original poems are shown along with poets' names on the left.

Liu Yu-Xi: 山圍故國周遭在，潮打空城寂寞回。淮水東邊舊時月，夜深還過女牆來。(CTP)
Liu Yu-Xi: 朱雀橋邊野草花，烏衣巷口夕陽斜。舊時王謝堂前燕，飛入尋常百姓家。(CTP)
Zhou Ban-Yan: 佳麗地，南朝盛事誰記？山圍故國繞清江，髻鬟對起。怒濤寂寞打孤城，風檣遙度天際。斷崖樹、猶倒倚，莫愁艇子誰係？空餘舊跡鬱蒼蒼，霧沉半壘。夜深月過女牆來，傷心東望淮水。酒旗戲鼓甚處市？想依稀，王謝鄰裏，燕子不知何世，向尋常巷陌人家。相對如說興亡，斜陽裏。(CSL)

Sometimes, poets would directly reuse the same sentences that had been used in other poems. In CSL, He Zhu (賀鑄) reused two sentences in a poem of Du Mu (杜牧) in CTP.

---

[7] Xie Tiao: 江南佳麗地，金陵帝王州。逶迤帶綠水，迢遞起朱樓。飛甍夾馳道，垂楊蔭御溝。凝笳翼高蓋，疊鼓送華輈。獻納雲臺表，功名良可收。Yuefu: 莫愁在何處，莫愁石城西；艇子打兩槳，催送莫愁來。

Du Mu: 清時有味是無能，閑愛孤雲靜愛僧。欲把一麾江海去，樂游原上望昭陵。(CTP)
He Zhu: 閑愛孤雲靜愛僧，得良朋。清時有味是無能，矯聾丞。況復早年豪縱過，病嬰仍。如今痴鈍似寒蠅，醉懵騰。(CSL)

In another example, He Zhu reorganized a few terms of Li Shang-Yin (李商隱) in his own poem.

Li Shang-Yin: 為有雲屏無限嬌，鳳城寒盡怕春宵。無端嫁得金龜婿，辜負香衾事早朝。(CTP)
He Zhu: 章台遊冶金龜婿。歸來猶帶釅釅醉。花漏怯春宵。雲屏無限嬌。絳紗燈影背。玉枕釵聲碎。不待宿醒銷。馬嘶催早朝。(CSL)

The follow example shows that He Zhu shared words with three poets: Zhang Ji (張籍), Xu Hun (許渾), and Cui Tu (崔塗) in one poem.

Zhang Ji: 青山歷歷水悠悠，今日相逢明日秋。系馬城邊楊柳樹，為君沽酒暫淹留。(CTP)
Xu Hun: 紅花半落燕於飛，同客長安今獨歸。一紙鄉書報兄弟，還家羞著別時衣。(CTP)
Cui Tu: 海棠花底三年客，不見海棠花盛開。卻向江南看圖畫，始慚盧到蜀城來。(CTP)
He Zhu: 排辦張燈春事早。十二都門。物色宜新曉。金犢車輕玉驄小。拂頭楊柳穿馳道。蓴羹鱸鱠非吾好。去國謳吟，半落江南調。滿眼青山恨西照。長安不見令人老。(CSL)

`FindCommon` would also discover Xin Qi-Ji (辛棄疾) and Wun Bing (文丙) shared some words in their poems.

Wun Bing: 可憐同百草，況負霜霜姿。歌舞地不尚，歲寒人自移。階除添冷淡，毫末入思惟。盡道生雲洞，誰知路嶺巇。(CTP)
Xin Qi-Ji: 暗香橫路雪垂垂。晚風吹。晚風吹。花意爭春，先出歲寒枝。畢竟一年春事了，緣太早，卻成遲。未應全是雪霜姿。欲開時。未開時。粉面朱唇，一半點胭脂。醉裡謗花花莫恨，渾冷淡，有誰知。(CSL)

It is certainly possible for us to compare poems in CTP. We could find the following two items that were listed under the names of different authors, with very different titles, and in two different volumes. The names of the poets are Lu Lun (盧綸) and Lu Shang-Shu (盧尚書). Despite these differences, the poems are extremely similar, and differ only in one character, which we show in red and mark with an under ripple.

Lu Lun: 夕照臨窗起暗塵，青松繞殿不知春。君看白鬢誦經者，半是宮中歌舞人。(CTP)
Lu Shang-Shu: 夕照紗窗起暗塵，青松繞殿不知春。君看白首誦經者，半是宮中歌舞人。(CTP)

Is it possible that Lu Shang-Shu is Lu Lun and that Lu Lun revised his own work? According to the biographical information of Lu Lun, he once served as the head of "戶部" /hu4 bu4/, which was called Shang-Shu ("尚書"). From this perspective, it is possible that this Lu Shang-Shu is Lu Lun, but we will not elaborate on this issue here.

We show two more pairs of poems in CTP whose authors might be the same below. In the following pair, the poems are similar, but their titles ("別佳人" /bie2 jia1 ren2/ vs. "別妻" /bie2 ci1/) are related yet different. The names of their authors are different but could be pronounced similarly.

Cui Ying (崔膺): 攤上流泉攤下分，斷腸嗚咽不堪聞。嫦娥一入月中去，巫峽千秋空白雲。(CTP)
Cui Ya (崔涯): 攏上泉流攏下分，斷腸嗚咽不堪聞。嫦娥一入月中去，巫峽千秋空白雲。(CTP)

The following poems of Lu and Luo differ in just one character. They have the same title and the pronunciations of the names of their authors are very similar.

Lu Yin (盧殷): 累年無的信，每夜夢邊城。袖掩千行淚，書封一尺憤。(CTP)
Luo Yin (羅隱): 累年無的信，每夜望邊城。袖掩千行淚，書封一尺金。(CTP)

The following two poems in CTP also differ in only one character. The poets are Zhang Ba-Yuan (張八元) and Zhu Fang (朱放), two really different persons, and the titles of the poems are the same. We checked the pages of a hard copy of the CTP, and verified the different characters, i.e., "夫" /fu1/ and "天" /tian1/. Hence, we have identified another type of authorship problem.

Zhang Ba-Yuan: 昨辭夫子棹歸舟，家在桐廬憶舊丘。三月暖時花競發，兩溪分處水爭流。近聞江老傳鄉語，遙見家山減旅愁。或在醉中逢夜雪，懷賢應向剡川遊。(CTP)
Zhu Fang: 昨辭天子棹歸舟，家在桐廬憶舊丘。三月暖時花競發，兩溪分處水爭流。近聞江老傳鄉語，遙見家山減旅愁。或在醉中逢夜雪，懷賢應向剡川遊。(CTP)

The following poems in CTP show yet another type of challenge. The poets are Dai Shu-Lun (戴叔倫), Qing Jiang (清江), and Ke Zhi (可止). Dai was the eldest, and Ke was born at least 50 years after Qing deceased. The titles and contents of Qing's and Ke's poems were exactly the same. The title of Dai's poem is different. Moreover, both Qing's and Ke's poems differ from Dai's in just one character.

Dai Shu-Lun: 空門寂寂澹吾身，溪雨微微洗客塵。臥向白雲晴未盡，任他黃鳥醉芳春。(CTP)
Qing Jiang: 空門寂寂淡吾身，溪雨微微洗客塵。臥向白雲情未盡，任他黃鳥醉芳春。(CTP)
Ke Zhi: 空門寂寂淡吾身，溪雨微微洗客塵。臥向白雲情未盡，任他黃鳥醉芳春。(CTP)

6 Discussions and Concluding Remarks

Implied meanings of words and collocations could vary from poet to poet and from dynasty to dynasty. Connotation and imagery associated with words in poetry still show their influences in modern Chinese. We design FindCommon to identify and show the poetry that contained the shared words and collocations, and discuss possible applications of such findings. In addition to the Complete Song Poem, we certainly can and should extend the current work to include earlier Chinese poetry, i.e., Shijing (詩經), Verses of Chu (楚辭), and Hangfu (漢賦), and later ones, e.g., Complete Qing Poem (Zhu 1994) to accomplish a more complete history of words and collocations in Chinese poetry.

Results of the current work can be improved if we can achieve high-quality word segmentation in poetry. The quality of the corpora based on which we conduct the comparisons directly affects researchers' observations. As long as we can obtain more reliable and authoritative corpora, we can rerun the analysis and offer better services to humanities researchers.

Responses to Reviewers' Comments

1. Tang and Song are two major dynasties in China's history. The spans of Tang and Song are, respectively, 618-907AD and 960-1279AD, which are now marked in Figure 2.

2. We implemented the algorithm that is listed in Figure 3. It is currently designed to compare Chinese poetry, but we could revise it to handle poetry of other languages.

3. We provided the Hanyu Pinyin for the Chinese words in this paper, except those appeared in Figure 2 and Section 4. The majority of Chinese words in Figure 2 are poets' names. In this Section 4, we discussed words used in poems and listed the poems that we compared. Words and sentences in poems generally convey imagery that is beyond their literal meanings, and it would take many words and require significant background information to appropriately translate the words and poems. Translating poems is a huge task and requires a lifetime dedication, see for example (Owen 2016). Hence, we chose to list just the words, which might be acceptable, because we focused on literal comparisons between poems in this paper.

4. The algorithm FindCommon listed in Figure 3 can produce all co-occurrences, though the actual output depends on the settings of F ad R. The types of co-occurrences that can be identified and presented to a researcher for further inspection will then depend on the filtering procedure that we outlined in Section 4.2. It is the researcher's judgement as to what types of co-occurrences that will be examined in the research.

Acknowledgements

We thank Lik Hang Tsui, Hongsu Wang, and Shuhua Zhang of the CBDB project for the informative conversations with the first author. We also thank the anonymous reviewers for their helpful comments and suggestions. This research was supported in part by the grant MOST-104-2221-E-004-005-MY3 from the Ministry of Science and Technology of Taiwan, the grant USA-HAR-105-V02 of the Top University Strategic Alliance, and the Senior Fulbright Research Grants 2016-2017.

References

You-Bing Chen (陈友冰) and De-Shou Wang (王德寿). 2001. *Selected Appreciation of Song Lyrics: Northern Song* (宋詞清賞、北宋篇), 138–139, Chung Cheng Bookstore (中正書局). (in Chinese)

Wen-Huei Cheng (鄭文惠), Chao-Lin Liu, Wen-Yun Chiu, and Chu-Ting Hsu. 2015. Phenomenology of emotion politics of color: Digital humanities research on the lyrical genealogy of 'White' in the poetry of middle Tang dynasty, *Proc. of the 6th Int'l Conf. on Digital Humanities and Digital Archives*, 481–522.

Michael A. Fuller. 2015. *The China Biographical Database User's Guide*, Harvard University. <http://projects.iq.harvard.edu/cbdb/home>

Junfeng Hu (胡俊峰) and Shiwen Yu (俞士汶). 2001. The computer aided research work of Chinese ancient poems, *ACTA Scientiarum Naturalium Universitatis Pekinensis*, 37(5):725–733. (in Chinese)

Junfeng Hu and Shiwen Yu. 2002. Word meaning similarity analysis in Chinese ancient poetry and its applications, *J. of Chinese Information Processing* (中文信息学报), 16(4):39–44. (in Chinese)

Shao-Yu Jiang (蔣紹愚). 2003. "Moon" and "Wind" in Li Bai's and Du Fu's poems – Using computers for studying classical poems, *Proc. of the 1st Int'l Conf. on Literature and Information Technologies*. (in Chinese)

John Lee and Yin Hei Kong. 2012. A dependency treebank of classical Chinese poems, *Proc. of the 2012 Conf. of the North American Chapter of the Association for Computational Linguistics: Human Language Technologies*, 191–199.

John Lee and Tak-sum Wong. 2012. Glimpses of ancient China from classical Chinese poems, *Proc. of the 24th Int'l Conf. on Computational Linguistics*, posters, 621–632.

Chao-Lin Liu. 2016. Quantitative analyses of Chinese poetry of Tang and Song dynasties: Using changing colors and innovative terms as examples, *Proc. of the 2016 Int'l Conf. on Digital Humanities*, 260–262.

Chao-Lin Liu, Hongsu Wang, Chu-Ting Hsu, Wen-Huei Cheng, and Wei-Yun Chiu. 2015. Color aesthetics and social networks in complete Tang poems: Explorations and discoveries, *Proc. of the 29th Pacific Asia Conf. on Language, Information and Computation*, 132–141.

Fengju Lo (羅鳳珠), Yuanping Li, and Weizheng Cao. 1997. A realization of computer aided support environment for studying classical Chinese poetry, *J. of Chinese Information Processing*, 1:27–36. (in Chinese)

Zhufeng Luo (罗竹风, chief editor). 1986. *Comprehensive Chinese Word Dictionary* (汉语大辞典), Shanghai Cishu Publisher (上海辞书出版社). (in Chinese) <http://hd.cnki.net/kxhd/>

Christopher D. Manning, Prabhakar Raghavan, and Hinrich Schütze. 2008. *Introduction to Information Retrieval*, Cambridge University Press.

Stephen Owen. 2015. *The Poetry of Du Fu*, The Series of Library of Chinese Humanities, De Gruyter. open access: <https://www.degruyter.com/view/product/246946>

Fuh-Jiunn Pan (潘富俊). 2015. *Plants in Classic Chinese Literature* (草木緣情:中國古典文學中的植物世界), The Commercial Press (商務印書館). (in Chinese)

Yan-Hong Sun (孙艳红). 2016. Expressive styles of the Tang and Song Lyrics (唐宋词本体特征的表现形式), *Chinese Social Sciences Today* (中国社会科学网-中国社会科学报), 5 July 2016. (in Chinese)

Wei-Yung Wang (王偉勇). 2003. *A Study on the Comparisons of Tang and Song Poetry* (宋詞與唐詩之對應研究), Wen-Shi-Zhe Publisher (文史哲出版社). (in Chinese)

Ru-Yu Wu (吴汝煜). 1993. *Index for Communication Poems of Tang and Wu-Dai* (唐五代人交往詩索引), Shanghai Guji Publisher (上海古籍出版社). (in Chinese)

Ze-Jie Zhu (朱则杰). 1994. Establishing the editorial board for the Complete Qing Poem (全清诗边纂筹备委员会成立), Studies in Qing History (清史研究), 0(3):96.

Using TEI for textbook research

Lena-Luise Stahn
Georg Eckert Institute for
International Textbook Research
stahn@leibniz-gei.de

Steffen Hennicke
Georg Eckert Institute for
International Textbook Research
hennicke@leibniz-gei.de

Ernesto William De Luca
Georg Eckert Institute for
International Textbook Research
deluca@leibniz-gei.de

Abstract

The following paper describes the first steps in the development of an ontology for the textbook
research discipline. The aim of the project WorldViews is to establish a digital edition focussing
on views of the world depicted in textbooks. For this purpose an initial TEI profile has been
formalised and tested as a use case to enable the semantical encoding of the resource 'textbook'.
This profile shall provide a basic data model describing major facets of the textbook's structure
relevant to historians.

1 Introduction

1.1 Textbook research and Digital Humanities

Textbook research has resulted in many forms of output, especially with its inter- and multidisciplinary
approach as it is conducted at the GEI. The institute with its researchers from various different disciplines provides an excellent setting for cooperation and collaboration amongst these. As an increasing
amount of projects is being executed in an interdisciplinary way and also in cooperation with the research
infrastructure departments, the GEI evolves into a centre for the Digital Humanities, resulting in interdisciplinary and multimedial projects and digital plattforms. In recent years this development has proved as
rather cumbersome for information retrieval and data reuse. The research results, most of them in digital
form, end as legacy data in the sense of not being able to integrate them in the institute's information
portals[1] because of data heterogeneity, therefore not beeing discovered and eventually not being used.
This happens most often shortly after their production. The workflow usually consists of establishing a
model for the digital representation each time anew. Rules or best practices on how to model textbook
research data in a uniformal way in order to ensure their long term usability and stability do not exist.
This is what makes the knowledge organisation situation at the GEI complicated.

1.2 Lack of Data Models and its impact on knowledge organisation in textbook research

But whereas models of the disciplines' knowledge exist in other fields, as for instance thesauri[2] or ontologies[3] providing access to the discipline's knowledge and information, the multidisciplinary character of
textbook research aside its relatively short existence up to this day prohibit the development of a thorough data model, which would offer more powerful ways for knowledge organisation than controlled
vocabularies used by the library for indexing purposes.

A large amount of the GEI's resources are available as XML-based fulltext after processing them with

---

[1] http://www.edumeres.net/
[2] e.g.   AGROVOC Multilingual Agricultural Thesaurus, http://aims.fao.org/vest-registry/
vocabularies/agrovoc-multilingual-agricultural-thesaurus
[3] e.g. Gene Ontology Consortium, http://geneontology.org/

Proceedings of the Workshop on Language Technology Resources and Tools for Digital Humanities (LT4DH),
pages 181–186, Osaka, Japan, December 11-17 2016.

OCR (e.g. GEI-Digital[4], EurViews[5]). The Metadata Encoding and Transmission Standard[6] (METS) is used to describe them in a machine-readable way. Although METS is commonly used it does not offer adequate possibilities for the description of a textbook's content and characteristics, e.g. the specific school types and levels of education. By defining a model for structuring and encoding the data in a more thorough way, both data standardisation and integration on the one side and improved exploitation on the other side would be supported, improving the GEI data sources' retrieval, reuse and long term availability.

2 Project aims

2.1 Objective: Use Case WorldViews

A first attempt in this direction is the project WorldViews, funded by the BMBF and started in the beginning of 2015. A critical digital edition of textbook sources will be compiled, which is intended to serve historians with an entry point for discovering relevant, reliable and hard-to-find research materials on topics regarding textbooks. The materials may provide inspiration or even the corpus for medium scaled research endeavours or the foundation of more extensive research for additional sources. By establishing this digital collection comprising excerpts of textbooks and annotating them in regard to a particular research question (figure 1), a use case is being set up for developing and testing a first profile fit for the semantically contextualisation of the resources.

Annotation is interpretation, its purpose is to make a statement on the annotated element's appearance and/or meaning. By encoding elements in texts, aside from machine readability and long term availability, their detectability is ensured, in order to make them comparable and find relations. To support its semantic contextualisation the annotation language needs to be adapted to the specific text type, in the WorldViews context the textbook excerpts and editors' contributions. The use case WorldViews is the first project making an attempt to define such a specific annotation profile for the text type 'textbook'.

Since there existed no profile or standard for the description of textbooks, it was decided to use an adaptation of the TEI Guidelines[7] for encoding, mainly because of its common and well tested use for encoding text resources in the humanities, therefore ensuring compatibility and longterm usability in the context of Digital Humanities (DH) tools and methods. Furthermore it provided the flexibility and extension possibilities needed to adapt it to the project's research questions.

The Guidelines formulated by the TEI Consortium have become a quasi standard in the DH community for the encoding of historical text resources. Since their development in 1994 their XML-based structure has proved most useful for a broad range of text types, mainly based on its flexibility in adapting it to the respective discipline, resource types and research questions. In forming a TEI profile based on textbook research one of the project's expected results will be, whether TEI is able and an appropriate way to encode textbooks as well.

TEI commits to two essential axioms (TEI Simple Primer, 2016): First, a document is an "ordered hierarchy of content objects" (OHCO) (DeRose et al., 1990), and second, the presentation and the structure of a document can be cleanly separated. In the context of textual documents, both axioms are problematic. However, both axioms have proofed to be true often enough to be useful. Also the project team encountered these problems when trying to model each and every aspect of the text both on structural or presentation level at the same time. This most often resulted in a compromise between humanists and information scientists, receiving a model purposeful to both sides' present needs: as "an instance of the fundamental selectivity of any encoding. An encoding makes explicit only those textual features of importance to the encoder." (TEI Lite, 2012) Although deeply wished by the historians, most layout aspects were neglected.

[4] http://gei-digital.gei.de/viewer/
[5] http://www.eurviews.eu/nc/start.html
[6] http://www.loc.gov/standards/mets/
[7] http://www.tei-c.org/index.xml

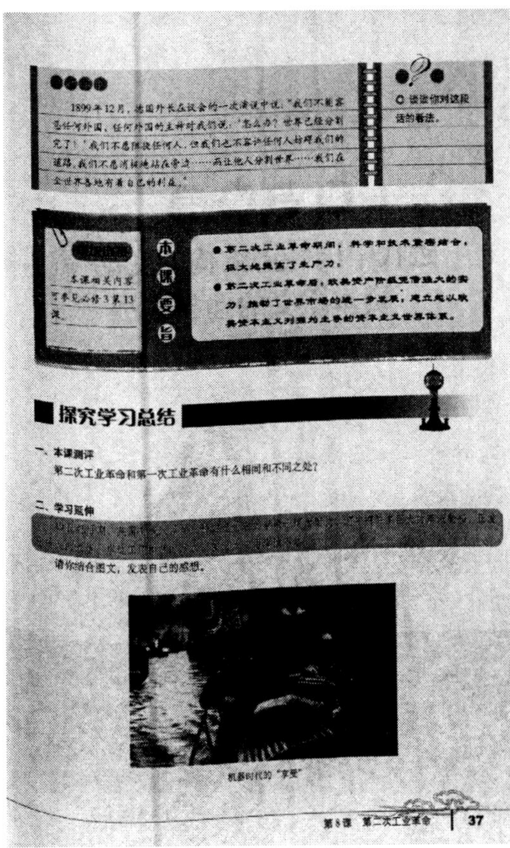

Figure 1: Example of a WorldViews source: chinese textbook excerpt

2.2 Approach: Using language technology in the humanities

First steps comprised of determining the characteristic elements of the used and established data within the project. This had to be done in close collaboration with the historians and cultural scientist involved in the project. Since they would eventually apply the data model, the usability of TEI during the research process could be tested as well when adopted by people not familiar with language technology tools.

Relevant questions had to be answered considering the kind of the arising research data. A necessity was to clearly formulate the annotations' purposes in order to avoid modeling data not relevant in the project context. This step showed the usual difficulties in asking the humanists of expressing their current - and possibly even future - research questions in an explicit way, fit for modeling them in a machine-readable form.

The wide variety of text types used in textbooks formed the problem of how to encode central characteristic text types, e.g. tasks ("pädagogische Anweisung") or clozes. It needed to be determinded how to treat visual elements like pictograms, infographics or timelines, often extended onto the next page, as well as image and text descriptions like image captions, texts in maps and marginalia, as they are increasingly used in modern educational resources. The humanists expressed their need especially for encoding these elements as they, as a major didactic method, play an important role in conveying the excerpt's world view.

A major issue applied to the corpus' multilingual character: the digital collection WorldViews, with its focus on world representations in textbooks from all around the world, would comprise of sources in various different languages, not necessarily written in latin alphabets or in a left-right direction (figure 2).

German label	English label	TEI element	TEI attributes / values
Quelle	source		
Logische Textgliederung	text division	<div>	@type="chapter|section|part" @sample="initial|final|medial| complete|unknown"
Textsegmente	Text segments	<seg>	@type="authorText|assignment| question|definition|explanation| pedagogicalGuideline| pedagogicalIntroducation| chapterSummary|multipleChoice| dossier"
Überschrift	heading	<head>	@type="[type of head]"
Absatz	paragraph	<p>	
Seitenumbruch	pagebreak	<pb>	@n="[next page number]"
Zeilenumbruch	linebreak	<lb/>	
Tabelle	table	<table>	
Tabellenbeschriftung	table caption	-<head>	
Tabellenzeile	table row	-<row>	
Tabellenzelle	table cell	−<cell>	@role="label" @cols="[spaltenumfang]" @rows="[zeilenumfang]"
Listen	lists	<list>	
Listenbeschriftung	list caption	-<head>	
Listenelement	list element	-<item>	
Zitate	quote	<q>	@type="direct,indirect" @source="[source of quote]"
Hervorhebung im Text	text highlighting	<hi>	@rend="spacedOut|bold|italic| underline|strikethrough| blockCapitals|smallCapitals"
Anmerkung des Bearbeiters	editorial note	<note>	@type="editorial"
Anmerkung des Schulbuchautors	note of author	<note>	@place="foot|end|left|right" @n="[Fussnotenzeichen]" @type="footnote|endnote|gloss"
Verweis	reference	<ref>	@target="[#xml:id]—[URI]" @type="[type of reference]"
Grafisches Element	figure	<figure>	@type="infographic|politicalMap| pictogram|photography|diagram| caricature|poster|painting|cartoon| speechBubble|arrows|drawing| mindmap|timeline" @place="[indication of location on page]"
Titel der Abbildung	figure caption	-<head>	
Text zur Abbildung	figure text		
Beschreibung des Bildinhalts	figure description	-<figDesc>	
URI der Bilddatei	graphic URI	-<graphic url= />	@url=[image file path]
Bibliographische Angabe	bibliographic description	<bibl>	@xml:lang=de | en
Titel	title	-<title>	
Autor	author	-<author>	

Table 1: Extract of the TEI profile established for textbook resources in WorldViews

```xml
<body>

    <!-- page 36 -->
    <pb n="36"/>

    <div type="section">

       <head>世界市场的发展</head>

       <p>第二次工业革命比第一次工业革命的发展更为迅猛，也更为广泛。它在多个国家和几乎所有的工业领域同时展开，促进了生产力的巨大增长，世界各地经济联系更加密切。</p>
       <p>第二次工业革命中出现的许多新型交通工具和通讯手段，大大加强了世界各地的联系。汽车越来越多，火车和轮船越来越先进，交通运输日益便利；电报，电话的出现进一步加强了世界各地之间商业信息的交流与转播。</p>

       <!-- Bild auf Seite 36 -->
       <figure place="inline">
         <!-- [Bildlegende unten] -->
         <figDesc>铺设电缆</figDesc>
         <!-- [Bildlegende seitlich] -->
         <p>19世纪三四十年代，出现了有线电报。19世纪中后期，电报和电话把世界各地更紧密地联系在一起。1869年，从英国伦敦到印度城市卡里卡特的电缆铺设完成，图为印度工人在铺设电缆。</p>
       </figure>

       <p>在第二次工业革命的推动下，世界市场进一步发展。1870年以后的三十多年间，世界贸易？增长了三倍左右。亚洲，非洲和拉丁美洲等地区的非工业国家生产的粮食和原料源源不断地运往工业化国家，工业化国家生产的工业品则销往全世界，国际分工日益明显。</p>
       <p>第二次工业革命期间，资本主义列强在全世界划分殖民地和努力范围，掀起了瓜分世界的狂潮。19世纪末20世纪初，世界基本被资本主义列强瓜分完毕，亚洲，非洲和拉丁美洲广大地区基本上都沦为殖民地或半殖民地。资本主义国家在输出商品，掠夺原材料的同时，直接向殖民地或半殖民地输出资本；殖民地和半殖民地的民族资本主义工业开始了艰难的发展历
```

Figure 2: Example of the above chinese textbook excerpt's fulltext in TEI

Some examples of the decisions for TEI elements to be used on the type 'textbook':

- <figDesc>is important because images on a textbook page may not be licenced yet and are therefore not displayed in the frontend. In such cases, <figDesc>allows to provide a meaningful textual description of the images and of those aspects of the image that are relevant to the narrative.

- @type:
  In order to retain flexibility regarding future extensions of the profile, text passages have been qualified by means of custom data values for type attributes. That allows for easy complementing of new relevant types of text passages.

- marginalia (defined as note of the textbook author):
  <note type="gloss" place="outer margin">Ausbildung des Ritterstandes</note>with possible types: @type="footnote—endnote—gloss"

3 Knowledge Organisation: From specific to general data modeling

3.1 Expected results

The project's major outcome is expected to be a profile for text resources meeting exactly the purpose of encoding elementary characteristics of textbooks. By the project's process of closely collaborating with the historians the profile's easy handling and managebility by people not used to working with language technology tools will be ensured. By referring to common standards also the compatibility with existing profiles and guidelines like TEI-Simple (TEI Simple Primer, 2016) and TEI-Lite (TEI Lite, 2012) is considered in order to retain its long term usability. These aspects will suppport the WorldViews profile to become the first version of a basic format for textbook sources.

The project will have impact on the GEI's research working processes as well: a workflow is formalised and tested which will support future interdisciplinary projects to determine their major elements based on the research output the projects are expected to generate. It will serve as an example of what major research questions could be, how difficult text types and layouts can be handled. Furthermore it will show how information and computer scientists and humanists can communicate on a mutual level in order to achieve the needed data model formulated in a way meeting both sides of researchers' needs as exactly as possible.

3.2 Future Work

Future work may address the question of how the use case WorldViews can serve as a first survey, forming the basis for a general data model, outlining the research done at the GEI. This data model, integrated in the institute's information retrieval tools and portals, would form a major part in supporting the knowledge organisation at the GEI. The WorldViews model's ability to support the long-term objective of formalising an ontology for the textbook research needs further research and use cases. This development could eventually support the GEI's intention of becoming an internationally acting centre in this research field.

References

DeRose, Steven, David Durand, Elli Mylonas, and Allen Renear. 1990. *What is text, really?* Journal of Computing in Higher Education, 1 (2): 3-26.

TEI Simple Primer, `https://github.com/TEIC/TEI-Simple`.

TEI Lite, `http://www.tei-c.org/release/doc/tei-p5-exemplars/html/tei_lite.doc.html`.

Web services and data mining: combining linguistic tools for Polish with an analytical platform

Maciej Ogrodniczuk

Institute of Computer Science, Polish Academy of Sciences
maciej.ogrodniczuk@ipipan.waw.pl

Abstract

In this paper we present a new combination of existing language tools for Polish with a popular data mining platform intended to help researchers from digital humanities perform computational analyses without any programming. The toolset includes RapidMiner Studio, a software solution offering graphical setup of integrated analytical processes and Multiservice, a Web service offering access to several state-of-the-art linguistic tools for Polish. The setting is verified in a simple task of counting frequencies of unknown words in a small corpus.

1 Introduction

Applying language technologies to data used by the humanities is not always easy for researchers with no technical background. Even though some are probably used to querying language corpora, using regular expressions or analysing tabular data, obstacles related to complex local installation and configuration of language tools are sometimes insurmountable. This is where Web services and Web applications come in handy but still, they offer fragmented solutions, often making result sets difficult to export or further analyse which in turn keeps most parts of the process manual.

In this paper we demonstrate how a robust linguistic Web service framework for Polish could be linked to a mature data science platform to offer both easy-to-start graphical user interface to test research hypotheses and a powerful analytical environment for data mining. Section 2 describes the tools being combined, Section 3 presents the motivation behind this step, Section 4 lists the configuration details and Section 5 offers a sample scenario illustrating the capabilities of the platform and showing how easily the setting can be used in daily tasks of a corpus linguist.

2 The toolset

2.1 RapidMiner

RapidMiner, formerly known as YALE (Yet Another Learning Environment), is a data mining platform developed at the Technical University of Dortmund (Mierswa et al., 2006) and successfully transformed into commercial application, currently one of the leaders in the Gartner Magic Quadrant for Advanced Analytics (Kart et al., 2016). Basic Edition of the platform (limited to 10,000 rows and 1 logical processor) is freely available as AGPL; cost-free licences can also be granted for educational purposes.

The main feature of the platform is its user-friendly interface (see Figure 1) which facilitates setting up complex processes by dragging-and-dropping configurable building blocks — *operators*, selected from the 1500 currently available. Operators offer procedures for data loading, text transformation, processing and visualisation, statistical analysis and many other sophisticated tasks. Data in RapidMiner are modelled as *examples* carrying certain *attributes* which corresponds to tabular representation with examples as rows and attributes as columns. Each processor requires certain data inputs and produces a number of outputs which makes chaining easy. New operators, free to use or available for a fee, can be integrated as extensions and are installed via RapidMiner Marketplace.

Proceedings of the Workshop on Language Technology Resources and Tools for Digital Humanities (LT4DH),
pages 187–195, Osaka, Japan, December 11-17 2016.

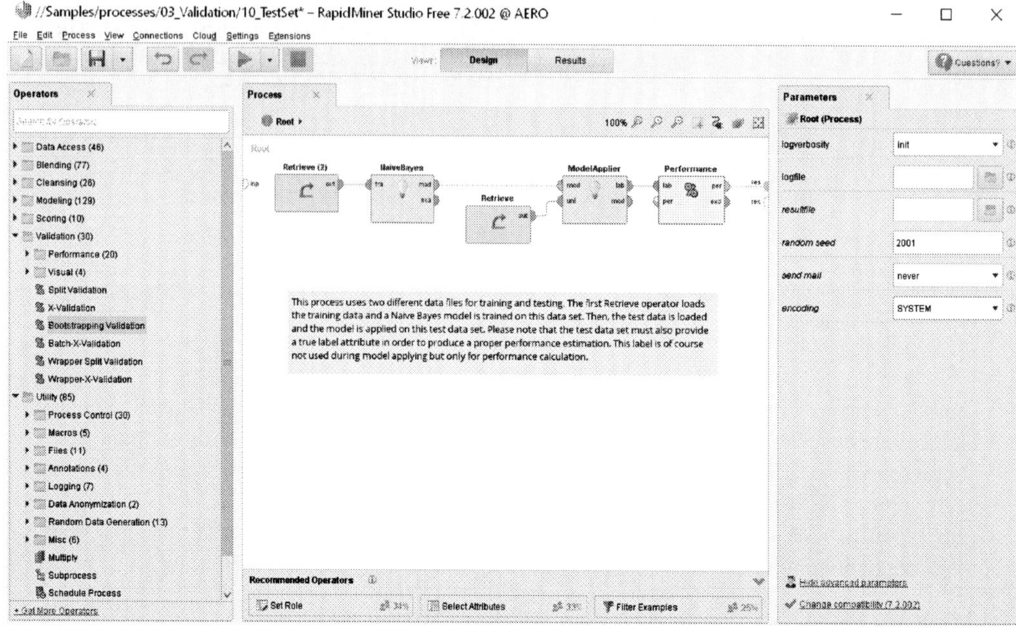

Figure 1: Graphical user interface of RapidMiner Studio

The usage of the environment is two-phased: in the first (design) phase the process is constructed graphically, with operators being ordered, configured with individual parameters and linked with input–output pipes. In the second phase the process is run and results displayed or saved to a file. Configuration of processes is saved in an XML file so it can be exported and moved between RapidMiner configurations. The workspace is intuitive and resembles programmer's desktop without the coding pane but keeping its capabilities such as setting breakpoints, browsing partial results etc.

2.2 Multiservice

Multiservice (Ogrodniczuk and Lenart, 2012) is a platform created in CLARIN to make offline language processing tools for Polish available as Web services and offer their chaining thanks to a common linguistic representation format and asynchronous execution architecture. As of 2016, the toolset comprises several disambiguating taggers (with paragraph-, sentence- and token-level segmentation and morphological analysis): Pantera (Acedański, 2010), WMBT (Radziszewski and Śniatowski, 2011), Concraft (Waszczuk, 2012), WCRFT (Radziszewski, 2013), ensemble tagger PoliTa (Kobyliński, 2014), sentiment analyser Sentipejd (Buczyński and Wawer, 2008), dependency parser (Wróblewska, 2014), shallow parser Spejd (Przepiórkowski and Buczyński, 2007), named entity recognizer Nerf (Waszczuk et al., 2013), two coreference resolvers Ruler (Ogrodniczuk and Kopeć, 2011) and Bartek (Ogrodniczuk et al., 2015, chapter 12), OpenTextSummarizer (Rotem, 2003) adjusted for Polish and two other summarization tools: Lakon (Dudczak, 2007), Świetlicka's summarizer (Świetlicka, 2010) and Nicolas (Kopeć, 2016).

Interaction with Multiservice is currently available via a dedicated API available in Java and Python or a Web demo of the service (`http://multiservice.nlp.ipipan.waw.pl/`). Both these methods have their drawbacks: programmatical access is in most cases too difficult to use by representatives of the humanities and the Web application offers only a brat-based (Stenetorp et al., 2012) interface showing layers of annotations in separate tabs plus a JSON output of results which requires separate retrieval and script-based processing.

All integrated tools use a common XML TEI P5-based representation and interchange format, a packaged adaptation of the de facto Polish standard for linguistic stand-off description used in the National Corpus of Polish (Przepiórkowski et al., 2012). The format allows for representing layers of annotation, various levels of ambiguity and disambiguation choices; below we present a fragment of morphosyntactic description of the word „dni" (En. *days*):

```
<seg xml:id="p4.s12.seg5" corresp="segmentation.xml#p4.seg221">
  <fs type="morph">
    <f name="orth">
      <string>dni</string>
    </f>
    <f name="disamb">
      <fs type="tool_report">
        <f fVal="#p4.s12.seg5.lex1.msd1" name="choice"></f>
        <f name="interpretation">
          <string>dzień:subst:pl:acc:m3</string>
        </f>
      </fs>
    </f>
  </fs>
</seg>
```

3 Motivation and initial experiments

Existing architectures such as the CLARIN Language Resource Switchboard (Zinn, 2016), WebLicht services (Hinrichs et al., 2010) or the Multiservice alone are not capable of carrying out complex processing combining linguistic analyses with text mining or advanced statistical calculations. Our solution to the problem would therefore be a combination of a general-purpose analytic tool and dedicated linguistic services. But before we begin it is worth veryfing whether RapidMiner out-of-the-box functionality would not be sufficient to complete this task. Since text analysis is one of the primary tasks for RapidMiner users, it may seem improbable that no existing configuration can be found to make it perform reliable linguistic analysis for Polish — definitely not an under-resourced language. Still, it occurs that Polish is much under-represented as far as integration of existing linguistic tools is concerned. The RapidMiner Studio offers various out-of-the-box linguistic analytic mechanisms but they are all incapable of processing Polish at a satisfactory level. Two type of tools are offered and were tested in this respect: integrated tools offered by the platform in the text processing extension and a proprietary text mining extension Rosette Text Toolkit.

The native processing provides standard filters for e.g. language-independent tokenization and stemming or stopword filtering for several languages available, but unfortunately not for Polish. For this reason it cannot be effectively used for any serious processing.

In turn, Rosette Text Toolkit is a multi-language solution offering processors for various linguistic tasks, including sentiment analysis, entity linking and many more. Even though Polish is one of the options in three basic components (Extract Sentences, Tokenization and Morphology), the toolkit seems to be unaware of specificities of Polish which makes it unacceptable in any application. To illustrate it in context of the task proposed later, Figure 2 presents results of the lemmatization and POS tagging of the first two lines of a linguistic poem „Słopiewnie" (Tuwim, 1971) famous for its neologisms. The results are highly unacceptable. Line 2 shows wrong lemma of a common noun present in contemporary dictionaries (should be lemmatized to *białodrzew*) while lines 4, 9 and 10 present various kind of problems for neologisms: the first and the last should be left as ignored words or analysed as verbs while the lemma assigned for the noun from line 9 is more than bizarre. In this case bad results are worse than none; it is not possible to distinguish new terms from wrong analyses of the dictionary terms neither turn off the lemma guessing mode.

These findings seem to prove that generic tools may not adapt to other languages easily since language specificities add to complexity of the task. At the same time linguistic analysis is successfully tackled with state-of-the-art linguistic tools available for individual languages — see Figure 3 for the same example analysed with Pantera tagger available both as offline application and as Web service.

Row No.	Token	Lemma	PartOfSpeech
1	W	w	ADP
2	białodrzewiu	białodrzewiu	NOUN
3	jaśnie	jasny	ADV
4	dźni	dźni	ADJ
5	słoneczko	słoneczko	NOUN
6	,	,	PUNCT
7	miodzie	miód	NOUN
8	złoci	złoć	NOUN
9	białopałem	białopałemo	NOUN
10	żyśnie	żyśna	NOUN

Figure 2: Results of POS tagging by Rosette Text Toolkit

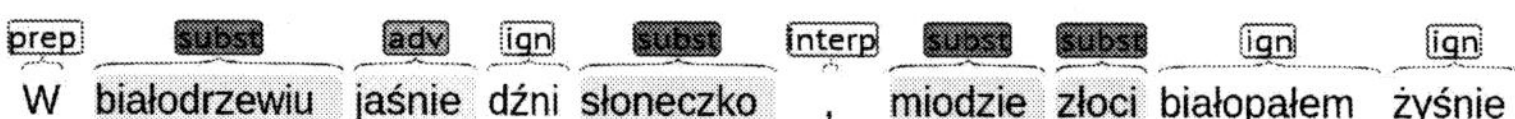

Figure 3: Results of POS tagging by the Multiservice

4   Interaction with the Multiservice

Interaction with Web services in RapidMiner can be achieved with ENRICH DATA BY WEBSERVICE operator[1] from the Web mining extension toolset. Request method (POST for Multiservice), request URL and the XML content of request body are set in processor parameters.

4.1   Web service request execution

The requests are being sent to `http://ws.multiservice.nlp.ipipan.waw.pl:80/WebService-1.0-SNAPSHOT/ClarinWS`. The listing below presents the structure of the initial `analyzeChain` request which commissions the work — in our case, processing the attribute *text* retrieved from an example with Pantera (lemmatizer and disambiguating tagger) and setting the output format of the result to be TEI P5:

```
<?xml version="1.0"?>
<s:Envelope xmlns:s="http://schemas.xmlsoap.org/soap/envelope/"
            xmlns:n="http://ws.multiservice.zil.ipipan.waw.pl/">
  <s:Body>
    <n:analyzeChain>
      <text><%text%></text>
      <parts>
        <part>
          <serviceName>Pantera</serviceName>
        </part>
      </parts>
      <inputFormat>TEXT</inputFormat>
      <outputFormat>TEI</outputFormat>
    </n:analyzeChain>
  </s:Body>
</s:Envelope>
```

---

[1]Operators can be renamed to better illustrate their specific function but we use original names to facilitate re-creation of the process by the reader.

Due to asynchronous mode of execution of the Multiservice, the first interaction is intended only to begin the work and results in sending back the identifier of the task, which is a textual token. The TEI response must be retrieved separately when processing stops. Verification of processing status is possible with separate calls quoting the token:

```
<s:Body>
  <n:getStatus>
    <token><%token%></token>
  </n:getStatus>
</s:Body>
```

Querying for status returns IN_PROGRESS when processing is still running and DONE when it ended successfully[2]. Results can be retrieved in a similar manner:

```
<s:Body>
 <n:getResult>
   <token><%token%></token>
 </n:getResult>
</s:Body>
```

4.2 Modelling the status checking loop

LOOP UNTIL operator is used to periodically query for appropriate status of the linguistic processing. Figure 4 shows the details of the process: since processing components have access to examples and attributes only, the best method of interacting with the process is by passing values in the result set as input and output to subsequent operators. Only one attribute with a given name can exist, so the process removes *status* from the set (which contains a single row of data), adds the value of the current status as a new *status* attribute and filters examples leaving only those with IN_PROGRESS status which results in an empty dataset when processing has finished vs. a single row when it is still in progress. Then PERFORMANCE operator is used to count the rows in the result set and pass the value to the parent processor to stop execution when the result set contains any rows. A delay of 100 ms is introduced to limit the number of requests (although it could be removed to increase performance).

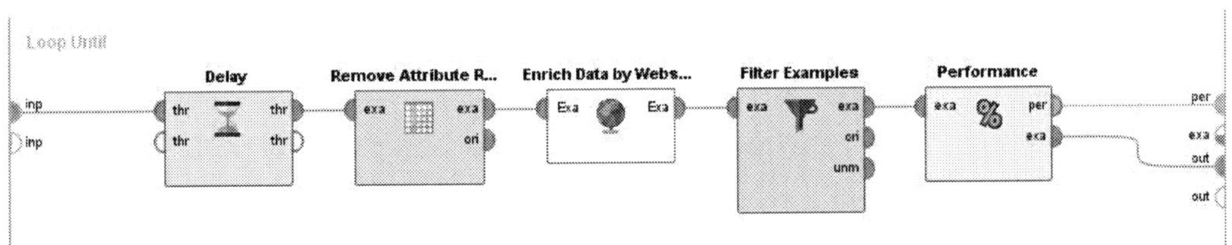

Figure 4: Using the LOOP UNTIL operator to wait for completion of the linguistic analysis

5 Sample analysis: frequency of unknown words in a text set

The process can be easily modelled within a LOOP FILES operator which, for each file retrieved from a folder, reads the document, converts it to internal representation of text and creates example set from text; then retrieves the results of the Web service execution and extracts parts of data relevant for further processing. After execution of the process the result sets from all partial results can be aggregated, selected attributes grouped and their frequencies counted.

The demonstration of such setting was used to prepare a list of unknown words in a set of texts corresponding to chapters from Solaris (Lem, 1970), a novel by Stanisław Lem, Polish science-fiction writer famous for his lexical creativity. This mini-corpus was composed of UTF-8-encoded plain text files with a total of 57K words.

The configuration of operators (with LOOP UNTIL detailed in Figure 4 and embedded process LOOP FILES integrated as sub-box to maintain single-picture view) is presented in Figure 5. Files in a folder

---

[2]There are also other statuses for different situations, please see the Multiservice description at http://zil.ipipan.waw.pl/Multiservice.

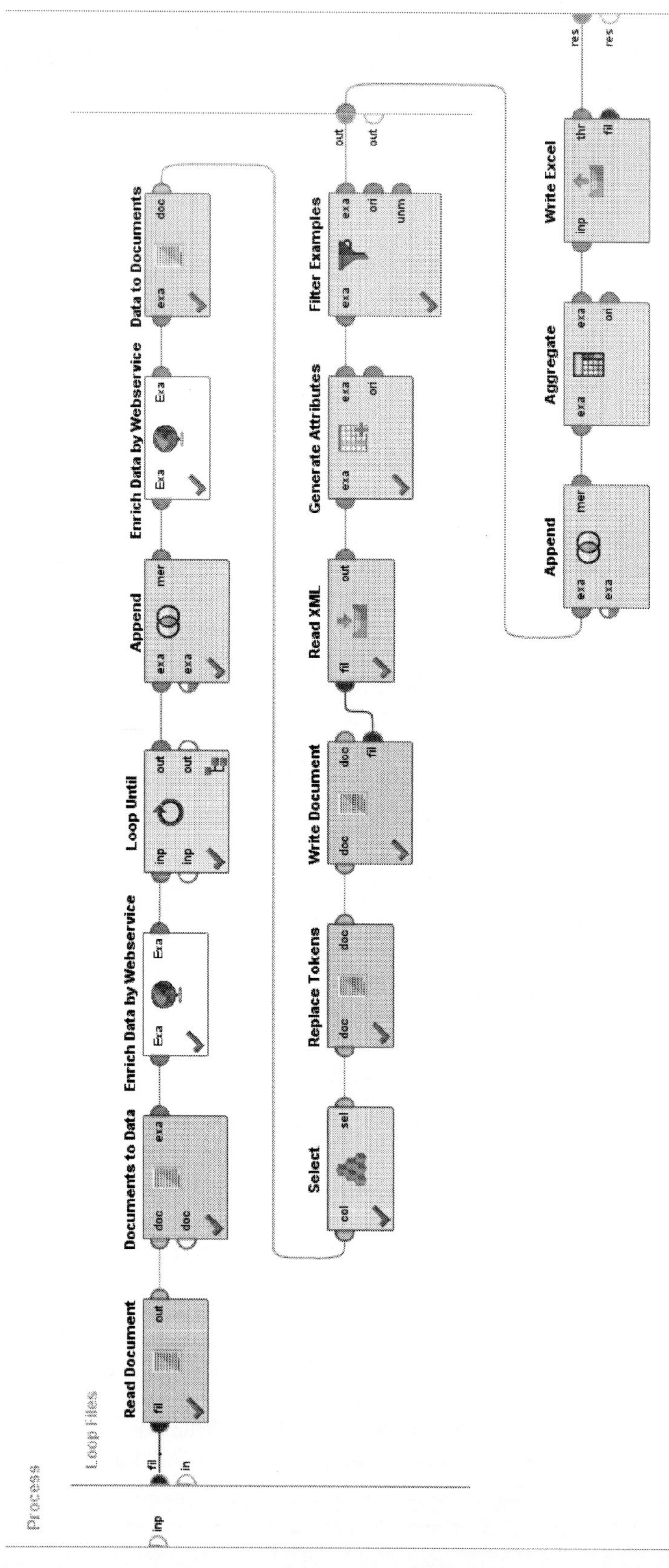

Figure 5: The multi-level setting of operators for calculating frequency of unknown words in a text set

are browsed and the Web service is called for the text content of each file. Pantera tagger processes the input and generates three layers of annotation: sentence segmentation, tokenization and disambiguated morphosyntax. Result sets are created from the XML TEI content with READ XML operator which extracts morphosyntactic interpretations selected by the tagger by evaluating an XPath expression `//f[@name='interpretation']/string` (cf. TEI excerpt in Section 2.2). The result string is then used as a source for two regular expressions which generate new attributes corresponding to lemma and POS tag of each token. Finally for each file, the example set is filtered to keep only rows with `tag` value equal to `ign` which corresponds to an unknown word[3]. Outside the loop the results are appended to form a single example set and then aggregated by counting frequencies of distinct lemmata. At the end, the result is exported to an Excel file.

The setting can look complex at first glance yet it can be easily reused: for researchers familiar with the NKJP format it would be sufficient to update path expressions to extract different parts of the linguistic analysis provided by the Web service. More advanced users can experiment with the platform, investigate capabilities of other available operators and create different data flows.

The result of processing of Solaris showed 278 unrecognized words (Figure 6 presenting the top of the list) which could be easily further categorized by the researcher.

Row No.	lemma	count(lemma) ↓
20	Harey	11
14	Gibarian	7
30	Sartorius	5
32	Snaut	4
15	Gibariana	3
18	Gravinsky	2
33	Snauta	2
54	mimoid	2
55	mimoidu	2
67	solariańskiej	2

Figure 6: Unrecognized orthographic forms with frequencies greater than one in Lem's Solaris — the result of the experimental setting

6 Conclusions

Availability of data mining tools and growing supply of linguistic Web services offered non-expert users new methods of combining resources and tools to perform their analytical tasks. In this respect our approach seems to go in line with requirements of the humanities, rarely interested in complex installation or configuration of software.

The experimental setting could be improved in many ways, e.g. by including process branches depending on Web service execution status (which can fail), adaptation of the setting to maximum request size allowed by the server or application of sophisticated analytical mechanisms offered by RapidMiner.

Since the motivation of the attempt was to illustrate how linguistic processing for Polish can be integrated into a larger environment rather than optimize it for performance, there are obviously more efficient methods for carrying out the same simple task, with components running locally and extraction

---

[3]Early filtering helps maintain the 10,000-row limit for the community version of Rapidminer.

scripts implemented in expressive programming languages. Still, the setting offers a valuable playground for non-technical researchers and might be used to raise their interest in further exploration of more advanced analytical tools.

Acknowledgements

The work reported here was financed as part of the investment in the CLARIN-PL research infrastructure funded by the Polish Ministry of Science and Higher Education.

References

Szymon Acedański. 2010. A Morphosyntactic Brill Tagger for Inflectional Languages. In Hrafn Loftsson, Eiríkur Rögnvaldsson, and Sigrún Helgadóttir, editors, *Advances in Natural Language Processing*, volume 6233 of *Lecture Notes in Computer Science*, pages 3–14. Springer.

Aleksander Buczyński and Aleksander Wawer. 2008. Shallow parsing in sentiment analysis of product reviews. In Sandra Kübler, Jakub Piskorski, and Adam Przepiórkowski, editors, *Proceedings of the LREC 2008 Workshop on Partial Parsing: Between Chunking and Deep Parsing*, pages 14–18, Marrakech. ELRA.

Adam Dudczak. 2007. Zastosowanie wybranych metod eksploracji danych do tworzenia streszczeń tekstów prasowych dla jezyka polskiego (En. Application of selected data exploration methods to summarization of Polish newspaper articles). MSc thesis.

Erhard W. Hinrichs, Marie Hinrichs, and Thomas Zastrow. 2010. Weblicht: Web-based LRT services for german. In *ACL 2010, Proceedings of the 48th Annual Meeting of the Association for Computational Linguistics, July 11-16, 2010, Uppsala, Sweden, System Demonstrations*, pages 25–29. The Association for Computer Linguistics.

Lisa Kart, Gareth Herschel, Alexander Linden, and Jim Hare. 2016. Magic Quadrant for Advanced Analytics Platforms. Technical report, Gartner.

Łukasz Kobyliński. 2014. PoliTa: A multitagger for Polish. In Nicoletta Calzolari, Khalid Choukri, Thierry Declerck, Hrafn Loftsson, Bente Maegaard, Joseph Mariani, Asuncion Moreno, Jan Odijk, and Stelios Piperidis, editors, *Proceedings of the Ninth International Conference on Language Resources and Evaluation, LREC 2014*, pages 2949–2954, Reykjavík, Iceland. ELRA.

Mateusz Kopeć. 2016. Nicolas Summarizer. [on-line] http://zil.ipipan.waw.pl/Nicolas.

Stanisław Lem. 1970. *Solaris*. A Harvest book. Harcourt.

Ingo Mierswa, Michael Wurst, Ralf Klinkenberg, Martin Scholz, and Timm Euler. 2006. YALE: rapid prototyping for complex data mining tasks. In Tina Eliassi-Rad, Lyle H. Ungar, Mark Craven, and Dimitrios Gunopulos, editors, *Proceedings of the Twelfth ACM SIGKDD International Conference on Knowledge Discovery and Data Mining, Philadelphia, PA, USA, August 20-23, 2006*, pages 935–940. ACM.

Maciej Ogrodniczuk and Mateusz Kopeć. 2011. Rule-based coreference resolution module for Polish. In *Proceedings of the 8th Discourse Anaphora and Anaphor Resolution Colloquium (DAARC 2011)*, pages 191–200, Faro, Portugal.

Maciej Ogrodniczuk and Michał Lenart. 2012. Web Service integration platform for Polish linguistic resources. In *Proceedings of the Eighth International Conference on Language Resources and Evaluation, LREC 2012*, pages 1164–1168, Istanbul, Turkey. ELRA.

Maciej Ogrodniczuk, Katarzyna Głowińska, Mateusz Kopeć, Agata Savary, and Magdalena Zawisławska. 2015. *Coreference in Polish: Annotation, Resolution and Evaluation*. Walter De Gruyter.

Adam Przepiórkowski and Aleksander Buczyński. 2007. Spejd: Shallow Parsing and Disambiguation Engine. In Zygmunt Vetulani, editor, *Proceedings of the 3rd Language & Technology Conference*, pages 340–344, Poznań, Poland.

Adam Przepiórkowski, Mirosław Bańko, Rafał L. Górski, and Barbara Lewandowska-Tomaszczyk, editors. 2012. *Narodowy Korpus Jezyka Polskiego (En. National Corpus of Polish; in Polish)*. Wydawnictwo Naukowe PWN, Warsaw.

Adam Radziszewski and Tomasz Śniatowski. 2011. A memory-based tagger for Polish. In Zygmunt Vetulani, editor, *Proceedings of the 5th Language & Technology Conference: Human Language Technologies as a Challenge for Computer Science and Linguistics*, pages 29–36, Poznań, Poland.

Adam Radziszewski. 2013. A tiered CRF tagger for Polish. In R. Bembenik, Ł. Skonieczny, H. Rybiński, M. Kryszkiewicz, and M. Niezgódka, editors, *Intelligent Tools for Building a Scientific Information Platform: Advanced Architectures and Solutions*. Springer Verlag.

Nadav Rotem. 2003. The Open Text Summarizer. [on-line] `http://libots.sourceforge.net/`.

Pontus Stenetorp, Sampo Pyysalo, Goran Topić, Tomoko Ohta, Sophia Ananiadou, and Jun'ichi Tsujii. 2012. BRAT: a web-based tool for NLP-assisted text annotation. In *Proceedings of the Demonstrations at the 13th Conference of the European Chapter of the Association for Computational Linguistics*, EACL'12, pages 102–107, Stroudsburg, PA, USA. Association for Computational Linguistics.

Joanna Świetlicka. 2010. Metody maszynowego uczenia w automatycznym streszczaniu tekstów (En. Machine learning methods in automatic text summarization; in Polish). Master's thesis, Warsaw University, Poland.

Julian Tuwim. 1971. *Wiersze zebrane*. Wiersze zebrane. Czytelnik.

Jakub Waszczuk, Katarzyna Głowińska, Agata Savary, Adam Przepiórkowski, and Michał Lenart. 2013. Annotation tools for syntax and named entities in the National Corpus of Polish. *International Journal of Data Mining, Modelling and Management*, 5(2):103–122.

Jakub Waszczuk. 2012. Harnessing the CRF complexity with domain-specific constraints. The case of morphosyntactic tagging of a highly inflected language. In *Proceedings of the 24th International Conference on Computational Linguistics (COLING 2012)*, pages 2789–2804, Mumbai, India.

Alina Wróblewska. 2014. *Polish Dependency Parser Trained on an Automatically Induced Dependency Bank*. Phd thesis, Institute of Computer Science, Polish Academy of Sciences, Warsaw.

Claus Zinn. 2016. The CLARIN Language Resource Switchboard. [on-line] `https://www.clarin.eu/sites/default/files/zinn-CLARIN2016_paper_26.pdf`.

Author Index